LIST OF CONTRIBUTORS

Dr MG Brook MD FRCP
Consultant Physician and Clinical Lead
Departments of HIV and Genitourinary
Medicine
Central Middlesex and Northwick Park
Hospitals
London

Dr KE Harman DM MA MB BChir FRCP
Consultant Dermatologist
Department of Dermatology
Leicester Royal Infirmary
Leicester

Dr P Klenerman DPhil MRCP(UK)
Wellcome Trust Research Fellow
Nuffield Department of Medicine
University of Oxford
Oxford

Dr DAJ Moore FRCP
Reader in Infectious Diseases and Tropical
Medicine
Department of Infectious Diseases and
Immunity
Imperial College London
London

Dr NJ Mortimer MRCP(UK) ACMS
Consultant Dermatolgist and Dermatologic
Surgeon
Skin Centre Specialist Medical Facility
Tauranga
New Zealand

Dr WA Newsholme DTM&H
MRCP(UK)
Consultant Physician
Dpartment of Clinical Infectious Diseases
and Infection Control
Imperial College Hospitals NHS Trust
London

Dr GS Ogg BM BCh DPhil FRCP
MRC Senior Clinical Fellow and Honorary
Consultant Dermatologist
Oxford Radcliffe Hospitals NHS Trust
Oxford

Dr NM Stone BA(Hons) FRCP
Consultant Dermatologist
Royal Gwent NHS Trust
Newport

Dr MJ Wiselka MD FRCP
Consultant Physician
Department of Infection and Tropical
Medicine
University Hospitals of Leicester NHS Trust
Leicester Royal Infirmary
Leicester

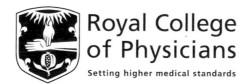

Royal College
of Physicians
Setting higher medical standards

© 2008 Royal College of Physicians of London

Published by:
Royal College of Physicians of London
11 St. Andrews Place
Regent's Park
London NW1 4LE
United Kingdom

Set and printed by Graphicraft Limited, Hong Kong

First edition published 2001
Reprinted 2004
Second edition published 2008

ISBN: 978-1-86016-268-8 (this book)
ISBN: 978-1-86016-260-2 (set)

Distribution Information:
Jerwood Medical Education Resource Centre
Royal College of Physicians of London
11 St. Andrews Place
Regent's Park
London NW1 4LE
United Kingdom
Tel: +44 (0)207 935 1174 ext 422/490
Fax: +44 (0)207 486 6653
Email: merc@rcplondon.ac.uk
Web: http://www.rcplondon.ac.uk/

MEDICAL MASTERCLASS

EDITOR-IN-CHIEF

JOHN D FIRTH DM FRCP

Consultant Physician and Nephrologist
Addenbrooke's Hospi
Cambridge

NHS ʳʳary. St James':

INFECTIOUS DISEASES AND DERMATOLOGY

EDITORS

KAREN E HARMAN DM MA MB BChir FRCP

Consultant Dermatologist
Department of Dermatology
Leicester Royal Infirmary
Leicester

MARTIN J WISELKA MD FRCP

Consultant Physician
Department of Infection and Tropical Medicine
Leicester Royal Infirmary
Leicester

Second Edition

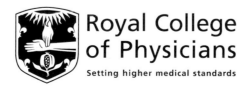

Royal College
of Physicians

Setting higher medical standards

Disclaimer

Although every effort has been made to ensure that drug doses
and other information are presented accurately in this publication, the
ultimate responsibility rests with the prescribing physician. Neither the
publishers nor the authors can be held responsible for any consequences
arising from the use of information contained herein. Any product
mentioned in this publication should be used in accordance with the
prescribing information prepared by the manufacturers.

The information presented in this publication reflects the opinions of its
contributors and should not be taken to represent the policy and views of the
Royal College of Physicians of London, unless this is specifically stated.

Every effort has been made by the contributors to contact holders of
copyright to obtain permission to reproduce copyrighted material. However,
if any have been inadvertently overlooked, the publisher will be pleased to
make the necessary arrangements at the first opportunity.

CONTENTS

CONTENTS

DERMATOLOGY

PACES Stations and Acute Scenarios 175

Diseases and Treatments 243

Investigations and Practical Procedures 281

Self-assessment 285

FOREWORD

Since its initial publication in 2001, *Medical Masterclass* has been regarded as a key learning and teaching resource for physicians around the world. The resource was produced in part to meet the vision of the Royal College of Physicians: *'Doctors of the highest quality, serving patients well'*. This vision continues and, along with advances in clinical practice and changes in the format of the MRCP(UK) exam, has justified the publication of this second edition.

The MRCP(UK) is an international examination that seeks to advance the learning of and enhance the training process for physicians worldwide. On passing the exam physicians are recognised as having attained the required knowledge, skills and manner appropriate for training at a specialist level. However, passing the exam is a challenge. The pass rate at each sitting of the written papers is about 40%. Even the most prominent consultants have had to sit each part of the exam more than once in order to pass. With this challenge in mind, the College has produced *Medical Masterclass*, a comprehensive learning resource to help candidates with the preparation that is key to making the grade.

Medical Masterclass has been produced by the Education Department of the College. A work of this size represents a formidable amount of effort by the Editor-in-Chief – Dr John Firth – and his team of editors and authors. I would like to thank our colleagues for this wonderful educational product and wholeheartedly recommend it as an invaluable learning resource for all physicians preparing for their MRCP(UK) examination.

Professor Ian Gilmore MD PRCP
President of the Royal College of Physicians

PREFACE

The second edition of *Medical Masterclass* is produced and published by the Education Department of the Royal College of Physicians of London. It comprises 12 textbooks, a companion interactive website and two CD-ROMs. Its aim is to help doctors in their first few years of training to improve their medical knowledge and skills; and in particular to (a) learn how to deal with patients who are acutely ill, and (b) pass postgraduate examinations, such as the MRCP(UK) or European Diploma in Internal Medicine.

The 12 textbooks are divided as follows: two cover the scientific background to medicine, one is devoted to general clinical skills [including specific guidance on exam technique for PACES, the practical assessment of clinical examination skills that is the final part of the MRCP(UK) exam], one deals with acute medicine and the other eight cover the range of medical specialties.

The core material of each of the medical specialties is dealt with in seven sections:

- Case histories – you are presented with letters of referral commonly received in each specialty and led through the ways in which the patients' histories should be explored, and what should then follow in the way of investigation and/or treatment.

- Physical examination scenarios – these emphasise the logical analysis of physical signs and sensible clinical reasoning: 'having found this, what would you do?'

- Communication and ethical scenarios – what are the difficult issues that commonly arise in each specialty? What do you actually say to the 'frequently asked (but still very difficult) questions?'

- Acute presentations – what are the priorities if you are the doctor seeing the patient in the Emergency Department or the Medical Admissions Unit?

- Diseases and treatments – structured concise notes.

- Investigations and practical procedures – more short and to-the-point notes.

- Self assessment questions – in the form used in the MRCP(UK) Part 1 and Part 2 exams.

The companion website – which is continually updated – enables you to take mock MRCP(UK) Part 1 or Part 2 exams, or to be selective in the questions you tackle (if you want to do ten questions on cardiology, or any other specialty, you can do). For every question you complete you can see how your score compares with that of others who have logged onto the site and attempted it. The two CD-ROMs each contain 30 interactive cases requiring diagnosis and treatment.

I hope that you enjoy using *Medical Masterclass* to learn more about medicine, which – whatever is happening politically to primary care, hospitals and medical career structures – remains a wonderful occupation. It is sometimes intellectually and/or emotionally very challenging, and also sometimes extremely rewarding, particularly when reduced to the essential of a doctor trying to provide best care for a patient.

John Firth DM FRCP
Editor-in-Chief

ACKNOWLEDGEMENTS

Medical Masterclass has been produced by a team. The names of those who have written or edited material are clearly indicated elsewhere, but without the support of many other people it would not exist. Naming names is risky, but those worthy of particular note include: Sir Richard Thompson (College Treasurer) and Mrs Winnie Wade (Director of Education), who steered the project through committees that are traditionally described as labyrinthine, and which certainly seem so to me; and also Arthur Wadsworth (Project Co-ordinator) and Don Liu in the College Education Department office. Don is a veteran of the first edition of *Medical Masterclass*, and it would be fair to say that without his great efforts a second edition might not have seen the light of day.

John Firth DM FRCP
Editor-in-Chief

We have created a range of icon boxes that sit among the text of the various *Medical Masterclass* modules. They are there to help you identify key information and to make learning easier and more enjoyable. Here is a brief explanation:

> Iron-deficiency anaemia with a change in bowel habit in a middle-aged or older patient means colonic malignancy until proved otherwise.

This icon is used to highlight points of particular importance.

> Dietary deficiency is very rarely, if ever, the sole cause of iron-deficiency anaemia.

This icon is used to indicate common or important drug interactions, pitfalls of practical procedures, or when to take symptoms or signs particularly seriously.

INFECTIOUS DISEASES

Authors:

MG Brook, P Klenerman, DAJ Moore, WA Newsholme and MJ Wiselka

Editor:

MJ Wiselka

Editor-in-Chief:

JD Firth

PACES STATIONS AND ACUTE SCENARIOS

1.1 History taking

1.1.1 A cavitating lung lesion

> ### Letter of referral to a general medical outpatient clinic
>
> Dear Doctor,
>
> **Re: Mrs Christina Leigh-Thompson, aged 48 years**
>
> Thank you for seeing this woman as an urgent case. She developed a cough and fever about 5 weeks ago, and was seen by one of my partners and given a course of amoxicillin. However, matters have not improved and last week she had two episodes of haemoptysis. I organised a CXR, which reveals a cavitating lesion in the left upper lobe. Is this an infection, or is there something else going on?
>
> Yours sincerely,

Introduction

The possible causes of cavitation on the CXR include both infectious and non-infectious conditions (Table 1). It is essential to consider pulmonary tuberculosis (TB) in all cases of pulmonary cavitation because of the obvious potential infectious risk to others. Patients should therefore be considered as potentially infectious and isolated until TB has been excluded.

History of the presenting problem

Length of illness

The duration of the history is critical in establishing a differential diagnosis. The common possibility with a short duration (less than 1 week) is lung abscess resulting from *Staphylococcus aureus* or *Klebsiella pneumoniae*, but consider cavitation after pulmonary infarction. If the duration is longer, as in this case, think of pulmonary TB, invasive fungal infection or non-infectious causes, such as primary or secondary carcinoma of the lung or Wegener's granulomatosis.

Infective cause

Ask about features suggesting an infective cause.

- Aspiration: epilepsy, blackouts, alcohol abuse and recent dental work can all lead to aspiration.

- Travel abroad: there is an increased risk of pulmonary TB if the patient has travelled to developing countries, and invasive fungi with travel to North or South America (see Section 2.9).

- Drug use: active intravenous drug use is a risk factor for right-sided endocarditis, with resultant infected pulmonary emboli and abscess formation.

Note that general symptoms, eg fever or night sweats, suggest an infectious aetiology but are non-specific, as is a history of weight loss.

Frequency	Condition	Notes
Common	Bacterial lung abscess	Usually has a short history (but not always), copious sputum, high fever and neutrophil leucocytosis. Common organisms include *Staphylococcus aureus* (particularly post influenza) and *Klebsiella pneumoniae*
	Lung neoplasm	The possibility of primary (particularly squamous cell carcinoma) or secondary lung cancer always needs to be considered, particularly in older patients with a history of smoking
	Tuberculosis	Consider especially in high-risk groups: patients from Indian subcontinent/South-east Asia; those who are socially deprived/malnourished; and alcoholics
Less common	Pulmonary embolus	Pulmonary infarction may occasionally cavitate. There is usually associated dyspnoea and pleuritic chest pain. Specific thrombophilic risk factors may be present
	Fungal lung abscess	Consider particularly in the immunosuppressed, or patients with a relevant travel history
	Wegener's granulomatosis	Typically history of many months of general ill-health. Nasal/upper airway symptoms. Renal involvement (proteinuria and haematuria)

TABLE 1 POSSIBLE CAUSES OF A CAVITATING LUNG LESION

Non-infective cause

The following features suggest a non-infective cause.

- Dyspnoea or pleurisy could clearly be features of pneumonia but are also consistent with pulmonary embolism (PE), and a history of a recent deep venous thrombosis would be much more compellingly in favour of this diagnosis.

- A history of ear (discharge, bleeding and deafness), nose (discharge and bleeding), eye (scleritis), skin (vasculitic rash) or neurological (particularly mononeuritis) problems would support the diagnosis of Wegener's granulomatosis. (See *Nephrology*, Sections 1.4.3 and 2.7.6; and *Rheumatology and Clinical Immunology*, Section 2.5.2.)

Other relevant history

Is there a previous history of TB? If yes, which anti-TB drugs were given and for how long? Consider relapse of TB or invasive fungal infection.

Is the patient at risk of TB? You will need to explore a full social history, including travel/immigration issues, alcohol intake/drug use and risk factors for HIV. See *Clinical Skills for PACES* for detailed discussion of history-taking technique, but the key issue here is to explain why you want the information before you ask for it: 'There is a cavity, a hole, in your lung. We need to know why this has developed. One of the things that can do this is TB. Have you had TB in the past? Or are you at risk of it? The things that can put people at risk include . . .'.

Risk factors for TB

- Contact with a person with TB, particularly a family member.
- Ethnic origin, foreign residence or recent immigration, particularly from a developing country.

- Heavy alcohol intake or intravenous drug use.
- Immunocompromise as a result of HIV, immunosuppressive drugs, renal failure, etc.
- Homelessness, poverty and overcrowding.

Is there chronic lung disease? Aspergilloma (fungus ball, see Section 2.9.2) occurs in pre-existing lung cavities.

Does the patient have a past history of PE or of vasculitis/Wegener's granulomatosis?

Plan for investigation and management

Urine and blood tests

- Dipstick urine for protein and blood: quantitate proteinuria by measurement of urinary albumin/creatinine ratio; if haematuria is present, perform microscopy to look for red blood cells and casts. An active urinary sediment would suggest Wegener's granulomatosis in this context.

- FBC: expect neutrophilia in bacterial lung abscess; monocytosis is sometimes seen in TB.

- Electrolytes and renal/liver/bone function tests: renal function may be impaired in anyone who is acutely ill, and also in those with Wegener's granulomatosis; it is important to check liver function before starting anti-TB treatment.

- Inflammatory markers: C-reactive protein and erythrocyte sedimentation rate are likely to be substantially elevated in most conditions causing lung cavitation, but it is useful to establish a baseline to judge treatment response.

Cultures

- Sputum specimens are required for microscopy, culture, and mycobacterial smear and culture. If the cough is non-productive, sputum production may be induced with nebulised saline. If sputum is unavailable or negative on acid-fast smears, gastric washings and/or bronchoscopy should be performed.

- Blood cultures may yield an organism if an abscess is the result of haematogenous infection.

Imaging

- CXR: upper zone shadowing with or without cavitation should always raise TB as an important differential diagnosis. In addition, pulmonary TB may also present with miliary shadowing or with a pleural effusion.

- CT scan: provides more detail of the extent of pulmonary involvement and can be particularly useful for the detection of mediastinal lymphadenopathy, assessment of empyema or diagnosis of aspergilloma.

The radiological appearances of pulmonary TB may be atypical in advanced HIV infection. Cavitation is much less common and the appearances may be of focal consolidation or disseminated bronchopneumonia.

Other tests

The following may be required.

- Mantoux or Heaf test: likely to be positive in active pulmonary TB (see Section 3.2), but is commonly negative in the setting of immunosuppression such as HIV.

- Interferon-γ tests, eg T spot-TB and QuantiFERON (see Section 3.2): helpful in the diagnosis of latent or active TB, and may be more sensitive than tuberculin skin testing in immunocompromised patients.

- HIV testing: may be needed after appropriate discussion with the patient.

- Antineutrophil cytoplasmic antibody: positive in Wegener's granulomatosis. However, note that a false-positive indirect immunofluorescence test can be seen in infectious conditions, and only make the diagnosis of vasculitis if one of the more specific tests (for antibodies to proteinase 3 or myeloperoxidase) is positive (see *Rheumatology and Clinical immunology*, Section 3.2.5).

- Tissue sampling: consider bronchoscopy; consider pleural biopsy if effusion is present.

Management

Pulmonary tuberculosis Quadruple therapy with oral rifampicin, isoniazid, pyrazinamide and ethambutol for 2 months, followed by 4 months of rifampicin and isoniazid, is recommended for all patients in the UK. If an organism is found to be resistant to one or more of these drugs, a combination of drugs based on the sensitivity profile must be commenced and a physician with experience in treating resistant TB should be involved in the case.

Baseline visual acuity and colour vision testing must be performed before commencing ethambutol. Patients must be warned of the small risk of visual deterioration when on ethambutol, and should stop ethambutol and seek medical advice immediately if they notice any visual problems. Be careful of drug-induced hepatitis, particularly in elderly people, people with alcohol problems and those with underlying liver disease.

Further discussion

Treatment of tuberculosis

Compliance with medication is the key to successful treatment; this should be emphasised to all patients. All cases of suspected or proven TB must be notified to the local Consultant in Communicable Disease Control (CCDC, based at the Health Protection Agency), and this initiates contact tracing. Each patient should have a named TB specialist nurse who will help to supervise treatment and coordinate contact tracing. In cases where adherence to treatment may be difficult, directly observed therapy should be initiated.

Multidrug-resistant TB and extensively drug-resistant TB

Multidrug-resistant TB (MDR-TB) is defined as resistance to two or more antituberculous drugs, including isoniazid and rifampicin. MDR-TB should be suspected in patients who may have acquired TB abroad, who have a past history of treated TB, who are drug or alcohol abusers and those who are co-infected with HIV.

Extensively drug-resistant TB is defined as MDR-TB plus resistance to (i) any fluoroquinolone and (ii) at least one of the three injectable second-line drugs: capreomycin, kanamycin sulfate and amikacin. Outbreaks of extensively drug-resistant TB among HIV-infected populations in Africa have proved almost universally fatal.

People with suspected drug-resistant TB should be isolated in an appropriate facility with negative-pressure ventilation. Therapy of this group of patients should be guided by a physician with expertise in the management of TB. Polymerase chain reaction-based probes can help to identify resistance genes and aid in the choice of antimicrobial therapy.

1.1.2 Fever and lymphadenopathy

> ### Letter of referral to a general medical outpatient clinic
>
> Dear Doctor,
>
> **Re: Mrs Linda Neil, aged 57 years**
>
> Thank you for seeing this librarian, who presents with a fever and a palpable lymph node in her neck that she has had for some weeks. She is new to the practice but has been previously well. If it was a straightforward infective thing I would expect it to have settled down, but it has not done so and I would be grateful if you could see her as a matter of urgency.
>
> Yours sincerely,

Introduction

The wide variety of causes of lymphadenopathy (Table 2) make a structured approach to diagnosis essential. Most cases are benign/reactive and secondary to a self-limiting infectious cause. The probability of malignancy increases with age: this is an important diagnosis not to miss, as are infectious causes that need specific treatment, eg mycobacterial infection.

History of the presenting problem

What and how long?

A detailed description is required.

- How long has she been unwell?

- What symptoms did she notice first?

TABLE 2 PRINCIPAL CAUSES OF LYMPHADENOPATHY

Category	Cause	Examples
Infectious	Viruses	Common: EBV, CMV, parvovirus, enteroviruses Less common: HIV, hepatitis B, rubella
	Bacteria	Common: *Staphylococcus aureus*, *Streptococcus pyogenes* Less common: cat scratch disease (*Bartonella* spp.), syphilis, Lyme disease, rickettsiae
	Mycobacteria	Common: *Mycobacterium tuberculosis* Less common: atypical mycobacteria
	Parasites	*Toxoplasma* spp., trypanosomiasis, leishmaniasis
	Fungi	Sporotrichosis, coccidioidomycosis
Non-infectious	Malignancy	Metastatic disease, lymphoma, chronic lymphatic leukaemia
	Collagen–vascular disorders	SLE, rheumatoid arthritis
	Miscellaneous	Sarcoidosis, Kawasaki's disease, Kikuchi's necrotising lymphadenitis, Castleman's disease, amyloidosis, histiocytosis X, hypersensitivity reactions

CMV, cytomegalovirus; EBV, Epstein–Barr virus; SLE, systemic lupus erythematosus.

Lymphadenopathy with a travel history

Differential diagnoses include the following.

- TB: not to be forgotten, and a possibility even without a travel history. Suspicion is greater in certain ethnic populations (those from the Indian subcontinent and South-east Asia).
- Rickettsial disease: ask about a history of tick bite, and in routine clinical practice (although clearly not possible in station 2 of PACES) look for an eschar at the site. Check for regional lymphadenopathy and rash. Patients often complain of headache.
- Trypanosomiasis, African or American: again ask about history of insect bite. The patient may have a lesion at the site of the original bite and regional lymphadenopathy.
- Leishmaniasis: patients can have locally enlarged nodes with the cutaneous form, or this can be more widespread with the visceral form.
- Endemic mycoses (coccidioidomycosis and histoplasmosis): is there a history of travel to parts of North and Central America?

- Has she noticed any other enlarged lymph nodes elsewhere?

- Has she measured her temperature? High fever (>39°C), particularly if associated with rigors, supports an infective diagnosis.

- Are there any other systemic features (weight loss or night sweats)?

- Are there any other symptoms, eg generalised rash, suggesting a viral infection or (very much less likely) syphilis, or localised symptoms that might indicate malignancy?

Is lymphadenopathy local or generalised?

Regional lymphadenopathy is usually secondary to a local problem draining to that set of nodes, eg pharyngitis with cervical lymphadenopathy; scalp infection with occipital nodes, lower leg cellulitis and inguinal nodes;

enlarged axillary nodes and breast carcinoma; supraclavicular nodes; and gastrointestinal malignancy. Inguinal lymphadenopathy raises a new set of possibilities with sexually transmitted disease (STD) and metastatic genital neoplasia. Generalised lymphadenopathy suggests a systemic problem.

Other relevant history

Take a full social, travel and sexual history. Do not forget the obvious, such as her country of origin. Be sure to clarify a travel history because time spent in the tropics widens the differential diagnosis. A 57-year-old woman is still at risk of sexually acquired infection and if no diagnosis is immediately apparent, a sexual history needs to be taken. This will clearly need to be approached with particular tact and care (see *Clinical Skills for PACES*).

In the past, has she had previous malignancy, tuberculosis (TB), STDs or connective tissue disease?

Plan for investigation and management

In routine clinical practice you would clearly perform a thorough physical examination of all systems and the findings would help guide your plan for investigation and management. You should state this to the patient, and to the examiner in discussion. Do not underestimate your first impressions. A 57-year-old woman with few constitutional symptoms and painless lymphadenopathy that has developed over many weeks has malignancy until proved otherwise. A 57-year-old woman with a short history of fevers and painful lymphadenopathy probably has group A streptococcal or *Staphylococcus aureus* infection.

Investigation of fever and lymphadenopathy

- FBC, film, monospot or Paul–Bunnell test for glandular fever.
- CXR.
- Blood cultures.
- Serum for appropriate serology.
- Fine-needle aspirate and/or lymph node biopsy (remember cytology and histology, but also routine bacterial and mycobacterial culture).

Blood tests

- FBC and ask for review of a blood film: atypical lymphocytes are commonly seen in viral infections such as EBV and CMV.

- Electrolytes, renal and liver function: is there an associated hepatitis?

- Inflammatory markers: erythrocyte sedimentation rate and/or C-reactive protein; useful as a baseline.

- Blood culture.

- Serum sample for storage, which can be used for serological testing (with consent if appropriate) for other infectious agents: EBV, CMV, *Toxoplasma* spp., *Bartonella* spp., syphilis, HIV, etc. Remember that the presence of a specific IgM antibody to a pathogen suggests recent infection, and presence of a specific IgG antibody suggests previous exposure.

Chest radiograph

Look closely at the mediastinum for hilar involvement, also at the lung fields. Other imaging may be needed, such as a CT scan of the thorax, abdomen and pelvis to ascertain the extent of lymphadenopathy.

Fine-needle aspirate/lymph node biopsy

If the diagnosis is not clear, it will almost certainly be necessary to obtain tissue. This should be sent for culture, including for mycobacteria, as well as for histology.

Management

Management will depend on the cause.

- Viral infections, eg EBV and CMV, are essentially self-limiting in the immunocompetent.

- Pyogenic lymphadenopathy: antibiotic therapy, aspiration or drainage if an abscess forms.

- Toxoplasmosis: usually self-limiting and rarely needs specific treatment (see Section 2.13.4). Be aware of circumstances where you should ask for specialist advice, eg pregnancy and immunosuppression.

- Cat scratch disease: generally self-limiting, but may need antimicrobial therapy if associated with systemic symptoms.

- Mycobacterial infections (see Section 2.6).

- Lymphoma and metastatic malignancy.

Further discussion

Sometimes this sort of presentation might take multiple rounds of tests, starting with the most likely and common, and then working through the list of differential diagnoses listed in Table 2. It is important to inform the patient of negative as well as positive test results. If the patient is clinically stable, it would be reasonable to institute the key blood and imaging tests and review them within a week. If there is clinical doubt, and especially if a

significant bacterial infection is possible, it would be prudent to admit this patient.

1.1.3 Still feverish after 6 weeks

Letter of referral to an infectious diseases outpatient clinic

Dear Doctor,

Re: Mr Jim Daniel, aged 49 years

Thank you for seeing this teacher who initially presented 6 weeks ago with fever and malaise. Despite investigation in the community I have been unable to establish a diagnosis, and he remains febrile. He has no significant past medical history that I am aware of.

Yours sincerely,

Introduction

This patient apparently has 'pyrexia of unknown origin' (PUO). This term can be applied to those with documented fever for which no cause has been found after a period of investigation, although there is discussion about the need for an updated definition. A systematic approach to the problem is required: details of the clinical scenario will alter the likely aetiology, eg infection is much the likeliest cause in the returning traveller, the immunocompromised host or when the fever has developed within the hospital. Endocarditis, extrapulmonary tuberculosis (TB) and occult abscesses (commonly intra-abdominal) need careful consideration, but non-infectious causes of fever must not be neglected (Table 3).

TABLE 3 SOME NON-INFECTIOUS CAUSES OF FEVER

Non-infectious cause	Common or important examples
Malignancies	Lymphoma Renal cell carcinoma Hepatoma Atrial myxoma
Autoimmune rheumatic disorders	Systemic lupus erythematosus (SLE), polyarteritis nodosa Adult Still's disease
Granulomatous diseases	Granulomatous hepatitis Sarcoidosis Crohn's disease Giant cell arteritis/polymyalgia rheumatica
Hyperthermia	Malignant neuroleptic syndrome
Drugs	Phenytoin, rifampicin, azathioprine, sulphonamides
Inherited disorders	Familial Mediterranean fever
Factitious	Münchausen's syndrome
Other	Thromboembolic disease

Pyrexia of unknown origin

- Confirm that the patient really has a fever.
- A thorough review of the history is essential: occupation, travel history, pets, contacts (eg TB), medication, recreational drug use, past history and family history.
- Detailed clinical examination.
- Careful analysis of the results of investigations.

History of the presenting problem

A detailed history is required.

- Has pyrexia been documented?

- For how long have the symptoms been present? In general, the longer the duration of symptoms, the less likely infection is.

- If fever is long-standing, how often does it occur? Intermittent attacks suggest a non-infectious inflammatory process, eg familial Mediterranean fever or cyclical neutropenia.

- Weight loss should always be taken seriously and usually indicates serious infection or malignancy.

- A detailed systems enquiry is needed because specific symptoms may point to a focus of infection or abnormal organ system, eg cough, headache, rash, arthralgia, diarrhoea, dysuria or urethral discharge.

Exposure

- Occupation: vets and farmers are susceptible to Q fever and brucellosis; sewer workers to leptospirosis.

- Travel history: where? Think of malaria and visceral leishmaniasis if the patient has recently travelled to the tropics (see Sections 2.13.1 and 2.13.2). When? You need to know incubation periods. What was he exposed to? If unpasteurised milk, think of brucellosis; if freshwater exposure, think of schistosomiasis.

- Pets: if the patient has cats, think of toxoplasmosis and cat scratch disease (*Bartonella henselae*); if parrots, then consider psittacosis.

- Sexual history: is there a possibility of undiagnosed HIV?

- Dental/surgical procedures: well-recognised risk factors for endocarditis.

Additional clues

- Medication: prescribed and non-prescribed, both can result in drug fever.

- 'Foreign bodies': does the patient have any indwelling prostheses, eg heart valves, joint replacements or metalwork from previous surgery? These may be a focus of infection.

- Age: neoplasia and giant-cell arteritis/polymyalgia rheumatica are more common in the elderly.

Other relevant history

Immunocompromise, previous surgery and previous illnesses may be relevant.

Plan for investigation and management

Almost by definition patients with PUO do not have an obvious focus of infection, but you should not and cannot simply perform every available investigation. The history, examination and initial investigations should be used as pieces of a jigsaw puzzle to direct you towards an area in which to focus your diagnostic efforts. If the patient is generally well, investigation can be undertaken as an outpatient, but admission may be required for invasive procedures or, on occasion, to document the fever. Several rounds of investigation may be required with initial screening tests followed by more specific tests depending on the differential diagnosis, and with scans, biopsies and more invasive tests depending on the results and progress of the patient. In routine clinical practice it is often helpful to discuss difficult cases with colleagues and to review radiology and histology specimens, and in PACES you should say that you would do this in discussion.

Blood tests

- FBC and review of a blood film.

- Clotting screen.

- Urea and renal function tests.

- Liver function tests: some causes of hepatitis may present with PUO; in addition, liver function tests can provide a clue to occult biliary sepsis or hepatic infiltration with infection or malignancy.

- Thyroid function tests: may be abnormal in subacute thyroiditis. Hyperthyroidism is not associated with pyrexia but patients often complain of 'fever'.

- Erythrocyte sedimentation rate (ESR) or C-reactive protein (CRP): both are relatively non-specific markers of inflammation but, if abnormal, can be followed sequentially. In acute SLE, the CRP is often normal with a markedly elevated ESR. The CRP is raised during attacks of familial Mediterranean fever.

- Autoimmune screen where clinically indicated.

- Serum protein electrophoresis.

- Tumour markers, if clinically indicated.

- Serum angiotensin-converting enzyme is elevated in granulomatous disorders, but is non-specific and may be raised in TB and lymphoma as well as sarcoidosis.

Cultures and serology

- Blood cultures: essential in all cases.

- Urine dipstick, microscopy and bacterial culture: the presence of proteinuria and/or haematuria might indicate renal inflammation and support a diagnosis of autoimmune or vasculitic illness, but it would also be consistent with glomerulonephritis associated with infection, particularly endocarditis. Consider three early-morning urine samples for TB smear and culture if white cells are present in urine with no bacterial growth.

- Bacterial, TB and fungal culture of any biopsy specimens.

- Culture any wounds and other body fluids, eg cerebrospinal fluid (CSF), as clinically indicated.

- Serology: acute and convalescent samples as clinically indicated for Epstein–Barr virus, cytomegalovirus, HIV, *Coxiella burnetii*, *Mycoplasma pneumoniae*, toxoplasmosis, brucellosis and *Borrelia burgdorferi*.

Imaging

- CXR: look for evidence of infection, TB, lymphadenopathy or neoplasia.

- Ultrasonography, CT or MRI: look for occult abscesses, neoplasms or intra-abdominal lymphadenopathy. Chest and abdominal CT scans should be considered where lymphoma is suspected.

- Echocardiography: where endocarditis is suspected. It may also detect atrial myxoma, but will have a low yield if the cardiac examination is normal.

- CT pulmonary angiography/ventilation–perfusion scanning

or phlebography: where thromboembolic disease is suspected.

- Nuclear medicine imaging may be helpful in selected cases. Radiolabelled white cell scans may detect focal bacterial infection and inflammatory bowel disease. Gallium-67 injection labels macrophages and can detect chronic inflammatory lesions and granulomatous diseases.

Invasive procedures

Use in a targeted manner in response to finding an abnormality, eg intra-abdominal or thoracic mass. Consider biopsy of any involved organ, eg lymph node, liver or skin. Consider bone marrow biopsy. Always request both histology and culture (including TB) of specimens. Consider gastroscopy and/or colonoscopy if a gastrointestinal lesion is suspected.

> ⚠️ Before performing invasive tests, such as CSF analysis or tissue biopsies, check exactly what material is required in the laboratory. You do not want to have to repeat an investigation because the specimen was not handled properly.

Other tests

- Mantoux or Heaf test (see Section 3.2).

- Interferon-γ tests (see Section 3.2).

Further discussion

> 🔑 **Therapeutic trials**
>
> The temptation to treat PUO with empirical antibiotic therapy should be resisted unless the patient is severely ill. However, once a reasonably secure clinical diagnosis has been established, it is sometimes reasonable to give a trial of appropriate therapy.

Specific treatment of the patient with PUO depends on identifying the diagnosis and targeting therapy appropriately. Therapeutic trials should be avoided unless all other approaches have failed. It is important to recognise that a significant proportion of patients remain undiagnosed. Warn the patient of this at the onset of investigations. If this happens, fully review the case; if the patient is stable it is often best to stop investigations and carefully follow his or her progress. In general, the prognosis for prolonged PUO is good because infection and malignancy will usually declare themselves within a relatively short time.

1.1.4 Chronic fatigue

Letter of referral to infectious diseases outpatient clinic

Dear Doctor,

Re: Mr Daniel Parker, aged 29 years

Thank you for seeing this young man who has been complaining of severe fatigue for several months. He dates the onset to a viral illness he suffered last winter and feels he has an ongoing infection to explain his persistent symptoms. I have not found anything of note on investigation so far and wonder if he has chronic fatigue syndrome, but I do not want to miss anything else and would value your help.

Yours sincerely,

Introduction

Is this chronic fatigue syndrome (CFS)? This is essentially a diagnosis of exclusion, although there may be some 'positive' clues and the first priority must be to rule out significant treatable organic disease. Many patients will include fatigue as one of their symptoms, but in most cases there will be other more specific symptoms and a cause will be apparent. It is probably true to say that any illness can cause fatigue, and lists of conditions that can do so run the risk of simply becoming a catalogue of all known diseases (Tables 4 and 5). However, the first step in evaluating patients with fatigue is clearly a detailed history.

TABLE 4 NON-INFECTIVE CAUSES OF FATIGUE

Category	Examples	Category	Examples
Haematological	Anaemia Vitamin B_{12}/folate deficiency Lymphoreticular malignancy	Endocrine	Hypothyroidism Addison's disease Cushing's syndrome Hypopituitarism Diabetes mellitus
Sleep disorders	Sleep apnoea Narcolepsy	Metabolic	Hepatic or renal failure Hyponatraemia, hypokalaemia, hypercalcaemia
Neurological	Multiple sclerosis Myasthenia gravis	Psychological/ psychiatric	Depression/anxiety Substance abuse
Cardiorespiratory	Heart failure Chronic airway disease	Medication	Beta-blockers, benzodiazepines, neuroleptics Anticonvulsants, corticosteroid withdrawal
Neoplastic	Many cancers	Autoimmune/ inflammatory	Systemic lupus erythematosus, vasculitis, Crohn's disease, sarcoidosis

TABLE 5 INFECTIVE CAUSES OF CHRONIC FATIGUE

Type of infection	Examples
Viral	HSV, CMV, EBV Hepatitis B and C HIV Parvovirus B19
Bacterial	Occult abscess Osteomyelitis Chronic sinusitis Infective endocarditis Brucellosis Lyme disease Syphilis Tuberculosis
Fungal	Histoplasmosis and other dimorphic fungi
Parasitic	Toxoplasmosis Tropical parasites

CMV, cytomegalovirus; EBV, Epstein–Barr virus; HSV, herpes simplex virus.

History of the presenting problem

Many acute problems cause fatigue, but this man has persistent symptoms.

Pathological fatigue

Fatigue means different things to different people. The art here is to recognise everyday stress and avoid over-investigation, while not dismissing people with significant fatigue. Ask specific questions about the patient's level of activity and how it has changed.

- 'Are you still working?'

- 'Take me through what you do in a typical day.'

- 'Is there anything you are prevented from doing?'

Reason for tiredness

Patients often become worried that tiredness is a sign of serious disease and have not linked it to a change in lifestyle. Ask about occupation, home and social life.

- Is there a new baby?

- Relationship difficulties?

- Is he working two jobs to make ends meet?

- Is he partying all night?

- Medications, recreational drugs and alcohol?

Other relevant history

Depression

The symptoms of depression are very similar to CFS and depression may complicate the condition. Find out how well he is sleeping, and about his appetite, life events, stress and mood.

Serious underlying disease

Ask about weight loss, fever, sweats and any significant localising symptoms such as cough or early-morning joint stiffness. Patients with such symptoms do not have CFS.

Exposure to infective risk

Take a careful travel history (see Section 1.3.16), sexual history (see Section 1.1.5) and history of hepatitis risk factors. Ask about possible exposure to animals or chemicals.

Plan for investigation and management

Your aim is to detect and treat definable causes of fatigue. If none are found and the diagnosis of CFS is made, then the patient needs appropriate supportive management. Explain this at the outset, so that the patient is less angry than if you cannot find the 'infection' and give him or her the 'magic' cure. This scenario commonly appears in Station 4 of PACES (see Section 1.2.4), and may also emerge in routine clinical practice when you are taking the history – you should clearly be aware of this possibility and the examiners will be impressed if it is apparent that you are.

Fever, sweats or weight loss will accompany most infectious causes of chronic fatigue. Acute infections such as glandular fever have usually resolved by the time the patient comes to clinic. It is therefore quite unusual to make an infectious diagnosis in patients presenting with persistent fatigue.

Blood tests

Specific tests are dictated by clinical suspicion, but a typical core screen includes:

- FBC and blood film;

- electrolytes, renal and liver function tests, and calcium;

- C-reactive protein or erythrocyte sedimentation rate;

- glucose;

- thyroid function;

- testing for adrenal insufficiency;

- autoantibody screen, including rheumatoid factor, anti-nuclear antibodies, anti-neutrophil cytoplasmic antibodies and thyroid antibodies.

Cultures and serology

- Routine cultures are not helpful unless there are localising symptoms or fever.

- Serology for CMV, EBV and *Toxoplasma* spp. is worthwhile.

- Other serological tests may be indicated, eg *Brucella* with a history of travel to southern Europe or the Middle East; Lyme disease after a camping trip to an endemic area; hepatitis C if there is a history of past intravenous drug use; and HIV if risk factors are elicited.

Imaging

CXR, looking for TB, malignancy and lymphadenopathy. Other imaging should be as directed by clinical suspicion.

Management

If there are any abnormal findings and investigations or documented fever, patients should not be labelled as having CFS. If CFS has been diagnosed, do not send patients away with 'don't worry, there's nothing wrong' ringing in their ears. Tell them that:

- you can find no serious progressive disease;

- this is good news;

- this does not mean that you do not believe them;

- CFS is real.

See Section 1.2.4 for further information.

Further discussion

Chronic fatigue syndrome

The long-term outlook for most patients was thought to be good, with only 10% suffering long-term debility. However, recent reviews suggest median recovery rates of only 5%, with improvement in 40%, although this may reflect a bias towards severe cases.

No pharmacological intervention has been proven to work for CFS. Some small studies of antibacterial, antiviral or antifungal agents have been promising, but others show no benefit. Antidepressants are also ineffective in CFS, but may be worth considering if you suspect coexistent depression. If sleep disturbance is prominent, using a sedative antidepressant such as amitriptyline is preferable. Corticosteroids are not beneficial unless adrenal insufficiency is present. A small subgroup of patients with postural hypotension appear to benefit from mineralocorticoids. Many patients take numerous vitamins, minerals and other supplements, but the merits of these are unproven.

Non-medication treatments have been proven to work but are not always available. Bed-rest is detrimental, but a supervised graded exercise programme has been shown to speed up rehabilitation. This works best in conjunction with cognitive behavioural therapy, which is of proven benefit in CFS.

Lifestyle advice to the patient with chronic fatigue

- Limit excessive intake of tea, coffee, alcohol and recreational drugs.
- Take daily gentle exercise, building it up over time.

- Avoid over-exercise.
- Ensure a balanced diet.
- Lose weight if obese.
- Adjust work/social life to energy level.

Management of chronic fatigue syndrome

- Exclude other causes of fatigue.
- Tell the patient the diagnosis and prognosis.
- Provide support.
- Develop a rehabilitation plan.

1.1.5 A spot on the penis

Letter of referral to the genitourinary medicine clinic

Dear Doctor,

Re: Mr Peter Ketch, aged 34 years

This man, with no significant past medical history and taking no regular medications, complains of a lesion on his penis that he has noticed recently. He is worried that he might have a sexually transmitted infection.

Yours sincerely,

Introduction

The differential diagnosis is wide (Table 6). Is this a sexually transmitted infection (STI)? If so, your aim is not only to diagnose and treat the patient, but also to reduce the level of STIs in the community. Thus, you must assess exposure and the potential risk of transmission of this STI to others from this patient, and educate about safe sex. The advice of a genitourinary medicine physician will be required.

History of the presenting problem

When taking a sexual history in routine clinical practice, reassure the patient about confidentiality, explain why an accurate history is important and ensure that you have adequate privacy (See *Clinical Skills for PACES*).

Exposure

A detailed sexual history is required, which should cover the following risk factors for STIs.

- Have you recently changed your sexual partner?

- Do you have more than one sexual partner at the moment?

- When was the last protected/unprotected sexual intercourse?

- What type of sexual activity took place? Remember that STIs are not confined to the genitalia and oral or rectal lesions may be present.

- What contraception was used? In particular, did you use a condom?

- Who was it with? Casual encounters or contact with sex workers carry a higher risk.

- Do you pay/get paid for sex? Commercial sex workers are at high risk.

- Who else could be at risk now or in the past?

- Do you use drugs or alcohol during sex? Loss of control increases risk.

- Did you have sex abroad? People are often more sexually adventurous on holiday and may take fewer precautions. Ask about 'red light' districts. Some STIs, notably chancroid and granuloma inguinale are not endemic to the UK. Lymphogranuloma venereum in the classic form is also rare in the UK but has recently been seen

TABLE 6 DIFFERENTIAL DIAGNOSIS OF PENILE LESIONS

Condition		Features
Common infections	Herpes simplex	HSV-2 or HSV-1 Cluster of vesicles on penis, which progress to shallow painful ulcers Progressive ulceration in immunocompromised individuals
	Warts: human papilloma virus	Condylomata accuminata (Fig. 1): typically raised papillary lesions May extend into the urethra Flat verrucous forms also seen
	Molluscum contagiosum	1–3 mm papule with central umbilicus
Uncommon but increasing	Primary syphilis	Chancre (Fig. 2): usually single but kissing lesions where mucosal surfaces are opposed Papular and then ulcerates with a painless smooth raised edge and an indurated but clean base Regional lymphadenopathy Heals in 3–6 weeks
Uncommon	Secondary syphilis	Condylomata lata Moist papules in skin creases around genitals, groin and anus
	HIV seroconversion illness	Can include genital ulcers as well as generalised rash, lymphadenopathy and oral ulcers
	Chancroid	Painless papule rapidly progresses to painful 1–2 cm ulcer with raised irregular edges and a necrotic base. Usually acquired abroad
	Granuloma inguinale	Painless ulceration with beefy red base and tissue destruction. Endemic in the tropics
	Lymphogranuloma venereum	Caused by particular serovars of *Chlamydia trachomatis* Primary ulcer small and painless, healing without scarring Most characteristic lesion is gross inguinal lymphadenopathy ('bubo') Previously rare in the UK but seen in HIV-positive homosexual men, often as proctitis
	Non-infectious causes	Pearly penile papules, lichen planus, bowenoid papulosis, Kaposi's sarcoma and ulcers in Behçet's disease
	Carcinoma of the penis	Consider in any non-healing lesion Typically irregular ulcer with a necrotic base and tissue destruction

HSV, herpes simplex virus.

▲ **Fig. 1** Perianal condylomata accuminata caused by human papilloma virus.

in homosexual men, mostly HIV-positive, who have rectal infection.

- Past sexual history? Broadly speaking, the risk increases with the number of sexual partners.

- HIV risk factors? Any patient with an STI has, by definition, been at risk of HIV. Specific risks should also be explored, which include men having sex with men, intravenous drug use and sexual exposure in countries with a high HIV prevalence.

The lesion
If the information does not emerge spontaneously, ask about the following.

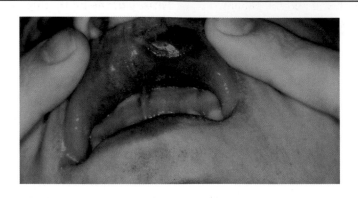

▲**Fig. 2** Chancre of primary syphilis appears at the site of inoculation and can be anywhere. After the genitalia and perianal region, the mouth is the most common site.

- Is it raised (papule/nodule), flat or an ulcer?

- How long has the lesion been present? Warts can be present for weeks/months before the patient presents; herpes lasts no more than 3 weeks (except in the immunocompromised); and the chancre of primary syphilis lasts for 3–6 weeks.

- Is there more than one lesion? Genital herpes often has multiple lesions, although single lesions can occur in recurrences.

- Is it painful? Herpes and chancroid usually are, but primary syphilis is not.

- How has it changed? A lesion that does not heal could be malignant.

- Did you injure yourself? Shallow ulcers are often the result of minor trauma.

Other relevant history

Genitourinary symptoms
Ask about local symptoms suggestive of other STIs, eg urethral discharge. People with one STI frequently are found to have others.

Relevant past history
Ask about previous STIs and where/how they were treated.

Recurrent infections such as oral candidal infection suggest immunodeficiency.

General health
Ask about associated symptoms suggestive of systemic involvement, such as fever, weight loss or rash. People with primary herpes usually have a 'flu-like illness. Generalised rash could point to concurrent syphilis or HIV seroconversion illness.

Plan for investigation and management
You should explain to the patient that in routine clinical practice you would need to do a genital examination and, as necessary, a more general examination. Following that you would proceed as follows.

Samples from the lesion
The samples that can be taken will depend on whether the lesion is an ulcer or solid (Table 7).

Male genitourinary infection screen
Explain that it is normal to test for other STIs if there is a risk of infection and perform a male genitourinary infection screen.

Male genitourinary infection screen

All patients

- Urethral swab: Gram stain and culture for gonorrhoea. DNA-based tests for *Chlamydia trachomatis* (chlamydial infection).
- Syphilis serology: if exposed to syphilis and serology is negative, repeat in 1 month.
- Hepatitis and HIV testing.

If there is relevant sexual exposure

- Rectal swab: culture for *Neisseria gonorrhoeae* (gonorrhoea).
- Throat swab: culture for gonorrhoea.

Blood tests
Routine haematology and biochemistry are rarely helpful. Check urine (dipstick for nitrite and culture) if there is a suspected urinary tract infection; check urine (dipstick for glycosuria) and blood glucose in candidal balanitis if diabetes is suspected. Serology

TABLE 7 TESTS FROM THE PENILE LESION	
Nature of lesion	**Test**
Ulcer	Swab for herpes culture or DNA test Dark-field microscopy of lesional scrape for spirochaetes in primary syphilis If the patient's history is suggestive, eg foreign travel, then take a specific culture for chancroid, and conduct a nucleic amplification test for chlamydia in lymphogranuloma venereum
Solid lesion	Warts diagnosed by typical appearance Biopsy if malignancy suspected

can be used to confirm syphilis (see Section 2.7.1) or HIV seroconversion illness, and it can also be of use in the uncommon condition of lymphogranuloma venereum.

Management

Treatment will depend on the diagnosis, which should be treated specifically.

- Syphilis (see Section 2.7.1).

- Chancroid: seek advice; a single dose of azithromycin 1 g is currently effective.

- Lymphogranuloma venereum: doxycycline 100 mg twice daily for 3 weeks.

- Herpes simplex: aciclovir 200 mg five times daily for 5 days is indicated in primary infection. Other dosing schedules are possible with famciclovir and valaciclovir, but these drugs are more expensive. Consider prophylactic aciclovir 400 mg twice daily if there are frequent recurrences.

- Condylomata accuminata: a variety of topical therapies, such as podophyllin or liquid nitrogen.

Further discussion

Contact tracing

Contact tracing must be handled with sensitivity. Sexually transmitted diseases are not notifiable. Reassure the patient about confidentiality, and refer to a health adviser who will organise contact tracing where appropriate.

Sexual health

Education is critical in attempting to reduce the risk of reinfection and improve long-term sexual health. Explain why this infection has occurred and how he can protect himself. Be explicit: there is no point

unless both you and the patient understand what is being said. Most clinics have a variety of health promotion leaflets, but these do not replace face-to-face education. Educate regarding condom use. Free condoms can be provided.

1.1.6 Penile discharge

Letter of referral to the genitourinary medicine clinic

Dear Doctor,

Re: Mr Reed Rogers, aged 27 years

This man complains of a penile discharge for the last week. He also has dysuria and is worried that he may have an infection.

Yours sincerely,

Introduction

Establish whether a urethral discharge is present and whether it is the result of a sexually transmitted infection (STI). There are many causes of urethritis (Table 8). Your aim is not only to diagnose and treat your patient, but also to reduce the level of the STIs in the community.

History of the presenting problem

A detailed sexual history

As in Section 1.1.5.

The discharge

- How long after sexual exposure did it start? Gonococcal urethritis normally has an incubation period of 1–5 days, although it can be 14 days or longer; chlamydia and non-gonococcal urethritis are usually more indolent, with an incubation period of 7–21 days.

- How much discharge and what colour? Gonococcal discharge is usually purulent (yellow or green); chlamydia and non-gonococcal urethritis discharge is usually thin and colourless/mucoid.

Other relevant history

Genitourinary symptoms

- Dysuria or haematuria? Dysuria is frequent in urethritis, but haematuria is uncommon and requires investigation for urinary tract disease. Dysuria in the absence of urethral discharge can still be due to an STI, especially in men under 35 years of age in whom urinary tract infection (UTI) is uncommon.

TABLE 8 CAUSES OF URETHRITIS

Frequency	Cause
Common causes	*Neisseria gonorrhoeae* *Chlamydia trachomatis* Non-gonococcal urethritis
Uncommon causes	Herpes simplex virus *Candida* spp.
Non-infectious	Trauma Chemical irritants Carcinoma Post-dysenteric Reiter's syndrome

- Pain on defecation or sitting down? Pain in the perineum or tip of the penis during defecation suggests prostatitis.

- Is there pain in the testicles? If present you would look for epididymo-orchitis in routine clinical practice.

- Systemic symptoms? Fever, rigors and loin pain suggest a bacterial UTI. Fever, a sparse pustular rash and arthralgia are seen in disseminated gonorrhoea. Reiter's syndrome may follow chlamydia urethritis and present with conjunctivitis, arthritis, keratoderma blenorrhagica and circinate balanitis.

Relevant past history
As in Section 1.1.5.

Plan for investigation and management
In routine clinical practice you would perform a full genital and general examination before proceeding to investigation.

Male genitourinary infection screen
As described in Section 1.1.5.

Urethral discharge
This is washed out by urination, so it is best if the patient has not urinated for 4 hours beforehand. Inspect the penile meatus, looking for spontaneous discharge or crusting. Staining of the undergarments may also be present. Note the volume and colour of any discharge.

The key to diagnosis and management is the urethral swab, which must be taken correctly. Currently, Gram stain (Fig. 3) and culture are the gold standards for the diagnosis of gonorrhoea. DNA amplification-based techniques are becoming more reliable and can be used on first-pass urine samples for both chlamydia and gonorrhoea. These techniques may soon replace culture as a tool for asymptomatic screening for gonorrhoea, but culture will be needed in symptomatic cases or as confirmation of a positive urinary screening test in order to establish the antibiotic sensitivity profile.

Taking a male urethral swab

1. The man should not have urinated for 4 hours.
2. Insert a swab 2–4 cm into the urethra and rotate for 5 seconds.
3. Roll the swab on a glass slide for Gram staining.
4. Plate onto chocolate agar and a specific medium, eg New York City medium.
5. Use a second specific swab for *Chlamydia trachomatis* (chlamydia) samples.

Management
Management based on the swab results is shown in the algorithm in Fig. 4. Specific antimicrobial therapy includes the following.

- Gonorrhoea (see Section 2.5.2).

- Chlamydia (see Section 2.8.4).

- Non-gonococcal urethritis is generally treated with doxycycline 100 mg twice daily for 7 days or azithromycin 1 g stat as first line and erythromycin as second line.

- Prostatitis requires therapy for 4 weeks.

- If *Neisseria gonorrhoeae* has been identified, repeat swabs (test of cure) should be taken if symptoms persist.

Epididymo-orchitis

- Pain and tenderness in testicle/epididymis.
- May complicate chlamydial and non-gonococcal urethritis.
- Less common complication of gonorrhoea.
- In older men (usually over 35 years old) it can be due to UTI.
- Can be difficult to distinguish from testicular torsion.
- Antimicrobial therapy for 2 weeks required.
- Chronic epididymo-orchitis in tuberculosis and brucellosis.
- Any persistent mass: consider testicular carcinoma.

For contact tracing and education, see Section 1.1.5.

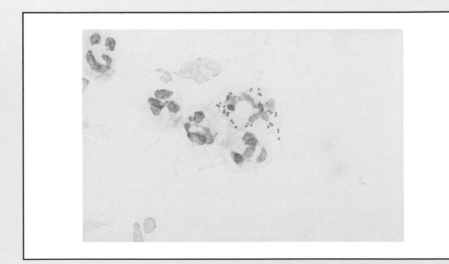

▲**Fig. 3** Gram-negative intracellular diplococci of *Neisseria gonorrhoeae*.

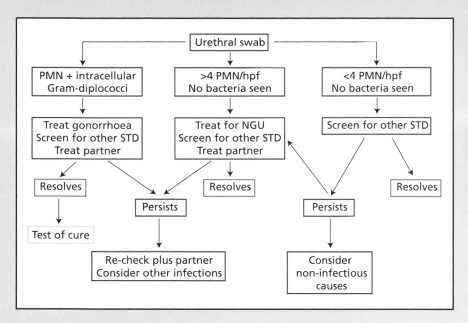

▲**Fig. 4** Algorithm showing the management of urethritis in males. hpf, high-power field; PMN, polymorphonuclear cells; NGU, non-gonococcal urethritis; STD, sexually transmitted disease.

1.1.7 Woman with a genital sore

Letter of referral to the genitourinary medicine clinic

Dear Doctor,

Re: Ms Sue Watson, aged 24

This woman complains of a sore place 'down below'. Could you please see and assess her, and in particular decide if this could be sexually transmitted?

Yours sincerely,

Introduction
Is this a sexually transmitted infection (STI)? The area is painful. Could this be genital herpes (Fig. 5)? The differential diagnosis can be quite wide (Table 9). Your aim is not only to diagnose and treat your patient, but also to reduce the level of the STIs in the community. Thus, you must assess exposure and the

potential risk of transmission to others, and educate about safe sex and contraception. The advice of an appropriate genitourinary medicine physician should be obtained.

History of the presenting problem

Exposure
A detailed sexual history is required, as described in Section 1.1.5.

Consider the possibility of a sexual assault and gently explore this where appropriate.

The sore area
Enquire about the following if the details do not emerge.

- How long has the pain been present?

- What was the area like at the start?

- How did she become aware of the problem?

- Is there one or more area that is sore?

- Is this the first episode?

- Is there a history of trauma?

The chancre of primary syphilis is usually painless, but can become painful if superinfected. Genital herpes starts as a cluster of small vesicles filled with clear fluid, but these soon progress to painful shallow ulcers. Recurrent episodes are strongly suggestive of herpes. Vulval candida is described as being itchy at first but can become quite sore if severe.

▲**Fig. 5** Extensive anogenital herpes simplex virus and warts in a patient with advanced HIV-related immunodeficiency.

Station 2: History Taking   **17**

TABLE 9 DIFFERENTIAL DIAGNOSIS OF VULVAL SORES		
Condition		**Features**
Common infections	Herpes simplex	HSV-2 or HSV-1 Cluster of vesicles on vulva or perineum, which progress to shallow painful ulcers Progressive ulceration in immunocompromised individuals
	Candida species	Vulval erythema with fissuring More common in pregnancy, diabetes and immunocompromised states
Uncommon but increasing	Primary syphilis	Chancre usually single but kissing lesions where mucosal surfaces are opposed Papular and then ulcerates with a painless smooth raised edge and an indurated but clean base Regional lymphadenopathy Heals in 3–6 weeks. Can overlap with secondary syphilis (Fig. 6)
Uncommon	HIV seroconversion illness	Can include genital ulcers as well as generalised rash, lymphadenopathy and oral ulcers
	Chancroid	Painless papule rapidly progresses to painful 1–2 cm ulcer with raised irregular edges and a necrotic base. Usually acquired abroad
	Granuloma inguinale	Painless ulceration with beefy red base and tissue destruction. Endemic in the tropics
	Lymphogranuloma venereum	Caused by particular serovars of *Chlamydia trachomatis*. Usually acquired abroad
Non-infective causes	Genital dermatoses	Lichen sclerosis et atrophicus, lichen simplex and eczema
	Ulceration	Behçet's disease, Crohn's disease
	Malignancy	Vulval carcinoma

HSV, herpes simplex virus.

Associated symptoms

Ask about the following.

- Vaginal discharge? This might suggest *Candida* as a cause. Also ask about change in vaginal odour and vulval symptoms.

- Dyspareunia? Is sexual intercourse painful and, if so, is the pain superficial or deep?

- Dysuria? This may indicate urethritis or a urinary tract infection (UTI), but is also common with genital herpes in women. Severe primary HSV may be associated with urinary retention.

- Abdominal pain, and back and leg pain?

- Systemic symptoms? Fever, headache and arthralgia are often present in genital herpes and constitutional symptoms may start 24 hours before the genital lesions develop. Some patients with primary HSV may develop aseptic meningitis.

- Menstrual cycle? When did her last period start? Has there been any blood loss, inter-menstrual bleeding or alteration in her cycle?

⚠ The woman presenting with a probable STI – could she be pregnant?

Other relevant past history

Enquire about previous STIs, including hepatitis, and how and where she was treated. Ask about previous UTIs. When was her last cervical smear and what was the result? Are there any underlying illnesses that might predispose to *Candida* spp. infection? Recurrent minor infections such as shingles may signify underlying immunodeficiency.

Sexually transmitted diseases and HIV infection

Consider the following.

- A coexistent STI increases the risk of HIV transmission.
- HIV prevalence is higher in STI clinic attendees.
- An STI may have atypical presentation in a patient HIV, eg increased reactivation of HSV or rapid progression of syphilis.

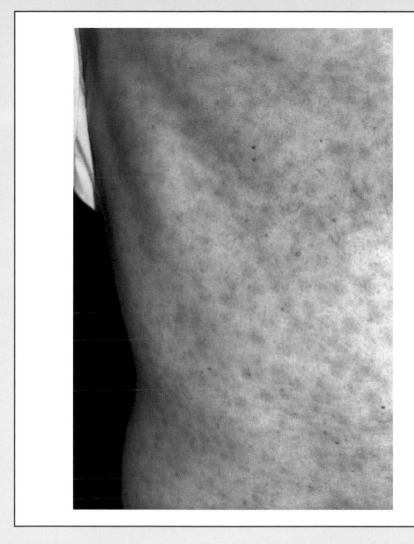

▲**Fig. 6** Rash of secondary syphilis.

Plan for investigation and management

You should explain to the patient that in routine clinical practice you would need to do a genital examination and, as necessary, a more general examination before performing the necessary tests.

Samples from the lesion

Appropriate samples should be taken from the affected area. If vesicles are present, vesicle fluid can be sent for culture for HSV, otherwise swab any ulcer. Electron microscopy on vesicle fluid can give a rapid diagnosis, but is impractical in routine situations. Screen for other sexually transmitted diseases.

As appropriate

- Rectal swab: culture for gonorrhoea.
- Midstream specimen of urine: bacterial culture.
- Throat swab: culture for gonorrhoea.
- Swab lesions: bacterial and viral culture.
- Serology for hepatitis C.

Blood tests

Routine haematology and biochemistry are rarely helpful. Check urine for glycosuria and blood glucose in patients with severe candidal vulvitis or recurrent UTI. Serology can be used to confirm syphilis or HIV seroconversion illness and can also be of use in the uncommon condition of lymphogranuloma venereum.

Management

The following are principles underlying management.

- Treat specific infections: topical (eg clotrimazole) or oral (eg fluconazole) antifungal in candidal infection.

- Partner notification and contact tracing where appropriate: screening and therapy of partners are essential for detecting undiagnosed infections. Partner notification and tracing can be difficult in situations where the woman feels at risk of abuse.

- Educate (see Section 1.1.5).

- Discuss contraceptive options and refer for family planning advice if appropriate.

- Make sure that follow-up for the cervical smear result has been arranged.

Female genitourinary infection screen

All women

- High vaginal swab: wet preparation can detect *Trichomonas* spp., bacterial vaginosis and *Candida* spp.
- Urethral swab: Gram stain, culture for gonorrhoea and DNA-based tests for *Chlamydia* spp.
- Endocervical swab: low-sensitivity Gram stain; culture for gonorrhoea; and chlamydia screen.
- Serology: for syphilis, hepatitis B and HIV.

Areas to cover in health promotion

- General education about the routes of transmission, symptoms and consequences of STIs.
- Safe sex: discuss the risks of different sexual activity, and the use of male and female condoms.
- HIV risk awareness.
- Cervical cancer and cervical screening programme.
- Contraceptive advice.

Further discussion

Female genital examination
Ensure that a properly trained person performs a thorough examination in the presence of a chaperone.

- Inspect the sore area to locate any discrete lesions (Table 9 and Fig. 7).

- Check for inguinal nodes.

- A speculum examination is mandatory because vaginal lesions may be hidden; look at the cervix for irregularity and mucosal abnormalities; and check for discharge from the urethra and cervix.

- A bimanual vaginal examination may detect uterine, fallopian or ovarian abnormalities.

- Have all the equipment to take screening swabs available to avoid unnecessary repeat vaginal examinations.

1.2 Communication skills and ethics

1.2.1 Fever, hypotension and confusion

Scenario

Role: you are a junior doctor working on a medical admissions unit.

You have admitted a 20-year-old female university student who presents with a 12-hour history of fever, chills and generalised aches and pains. On arrival she is extremely ill: confused, breathless, tachycardic and hypotensive (80/50 mmHg). You suspect that she has toxic shock syndrome or septicaemia. Initial

resuscitation is underway and arrangements are being made for her transfer to the intensive care unit.

The patient's mother has been phoned by the warden from the university hall of residence where her daughter lives. She has driven from her home town 80 miles away in a state of distress and has arrived on the medical admissions unit.

Your task: to explain the situation to the patient's mother.

Key issues to explore
The daughter is clearly very unwell with a life-threatening illness. The mother will undoubtedly want an explanation of the possible causes of the illness and your proposed investigation and management plan, but it will be important to find out if she has other concerns, eg about the possibility of spread of infection.

Key points to establish

- Likely diagnosis is toxic shock syndrome/septic shock.

- A clear plan for investigation and management is in place.

- Prognosis must be guarded as she is likely to develop multisystem disease.

- Risk to others is very unlikely unless she has meningococcal septicaemia, where prophylaxis would be offered to close personal contacts.

Appropriate responses to likely questions

Mother: how did this happen?

Doctor: at the moment we don't know why this has happened. It

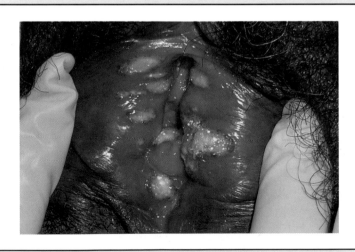

▲ **Fig. 7** Extensive introital ulceration due to HSV infection.

looks as though it is the result of an extremely serious infection and we are organising tests to try and find out the cause of the problem. However, we have already started treatment because she is too ill for us to wait for all the results to come back.

Mother: why wasn't she treated earlier?

Doctor: from what we know, she was perfectly well until about 12 hours ago. This is a condition that can occur without warning in a previously healthy person, and can develop extremely rapidly.

Mother: is she going to die?

Doctor: I'm not hiding anything when I say that I don't know. I'm afraid that your daughter is seriously ill, and there is a chance that she may die from her illness. We are treating the infection with antibiotics and helping to support her vital organs – giving fluids into the veins and giving oxygen; if she needs help with breathing we will put her on a breathing machine, a ventilator, and if the kidneys need help we will use a kidney machine, a haemofilter. We will know more when we see how she responds to treatment over the next few hours.

Mother: could she still die, even after receiving antibiotics?

Doctor: yes, I'm afraid that's still possible. Many of the serious complications of this condition are due to the effects of bacterial toxins on vital organs, and killing bacteria will not destroy all the toxins immediately. Much of the tissue damage has already occurred and cannot be prevented by antibiotics at this stage.

Mother: does anyone else need to take antibiotics?

Doctor: no, unless the tests show that she has one special form of infection, with a bug called a meningococcus, the risk to others is extremely small and antibiotics are not necessary for anyone else.

1.2.2 A swollen red foot

Scenario

Role: you are a junior doctor working on a general medical ward.

A 54-year-old patient of Indian origin is under your care. He has been admitted with cellulitis around a penetrating diabetic foot ulcer on his right heel. Deep wound swabs have grown meticillin-resistant *Staphylococcus aureus* (MRSA). He is currently being kept in a side room; staff are wearing aprons and gloves when they see him; he is being treated with intravenous vancomycin; and he is awaiting further investigation to rule out underlying osteomyelitis. If he does have osteomyelitis, it is likely he will require a below-knee amputation. The patient asks you to speak to his wife, who speaks reasonable English.

Your task: to explain the diagnosis of MRSA and its implications to the patient's wife.

Key issues to explore

As always you will start off by finding out what the patient's wife knows already, in particular:

- how much she knows about the problem with her husband's foot and the possible consequences of the ulcer;

- her understanding of MRSA.

Key points to establish

- The diagnosis is known and the patient is on the correct treatment.

- Further investigations to exclude complications are pending.

- The possible best- and worse-case outcomes (such as the possible need for amputation).

- The nature and implications of MRSA infection.

Appropriate responses to likely questions

Wife: when can my husband come home? We have a family wedding next week.

Doctor: I'm afraid that I don't know. Your husband has a serious infection in his foot, which we must treat properly. If we don't, it could get very bad indeed. The infection could spread throughout his body.

Wife: but he has to go to the wedding.

Doctor: I hear what you say. If it's at all possible we will try to make sure that he's able to go, even if only for a few hours or half a day. But I'm not hiding anything when I say that I can't promise: if he's not well enough, then it would be very unwise for him to go.

Wife: the nurses on the ward tell me he's got MRSA. What's that?

Doctor: it's the name of the bacteria, the bug, that's in his wound. It's a common sort of bug – *Staphylococcus aureus*, that's what the SA stands for – to cause wound infections, but I'm afraid that the one he's got is resistant to some of the standard antibiotics: the M stands for meticillin, that's one of the antibiotics, and the R stands for resistant. This is why we have to keep him in the side room and wear aprons and gloves when we see him – to try and stop it being spread to other patients.

Station 4: Communication Skills and Ethics

Wife: *where did he catch the MRSA?*

Doctor: I cannot say for sure. It's likely that he became colonised with the bug, the MRSA, during a previous hospital visit, but there are strains of MRSA in the community as well. People can carry the staphylococcal bacteria, including MRSA, on their skin or in their throat or nose without having any symptoms. The infection is only serious if it invades the body tissues or complicates surgery.

Wife: *if he's got MRSA, then will other people at home have it as well?*

Doctor: I don't know. It is possible that other members of the family are also carrying MRSA, but it is unlikely to be a problem for them unless they have open wounds that become infected. If anyone at home has a possible infection that is worrying them, then they should arrange to see their GP.

Wife: *are the antibiotics going to cure the problem?*

Doctor: I'm not sure. If the infection is only in the skin and soft tissues, then they should be able to. But if the bone is infected, and we're organising X-rays and scans to check for this, then I'm afraid that they might not.

Wife: *if the antibiotics aren't going to cure things, then what happens?*

Doctor: at the moment, we're hoping that the antibiotics will deal with things. But if it doesn't look as though they're going to, then we would plan to discuss the situation with our surgical colleagues. Sometimes it is necessary to operate to remove dead tissue and sometimes it is even necessary to amputate the foot. I'm not saying that we will definitely need to do so in your husband's case – as I said, we're hoping the antibiotics will cure the problem – but sometimes

amputation is the only way to get rid of the infection.

1.2.3 Still feverish after 6 weeks

Scenario

Role: you are a junior doctor working on a general medical ward.

A 49 year-old male teacher has been admitted for investigation of a 6-week history of malaise and fever. He has been in hospital for 4 days and a diagnosis has not been made. A wide range of tests have been normal or negative, including a urine dipstick, FBC, electrolytes, renal and bone function tests, serum immunoglobulins, autoimmune/vasculitic screen and CXR. Cultures of urine and blood have produced no growth after 2 days, but longer cultures are awaited. Liver blood tests show slight elevation of alanine aminotransferase; inflammatory markers show markedly elevated C-reactive protein. The results of other tests, eg viral serology, are awaited. Other tests, eg echocardiogram and CT scans of the chest/abdomen/pelvis, are planned.

The patient is not acutely very ill, but he is frustrated and angry about the lack of progress and has been shouting at the nurses. He wants to be started on treatment. The nurse in charge of the ward asks you to speak to him.

Your task: to explain the situation to the patient; in particular that it is necessary to establish a diagnosis before treatment can be given.

Key issues to explore

The patient will almost certainly be concerned about the fact that he is unwell and the doctors have not been able to work out why. But does he have any other concerns? Is he worried about anything in particular? It is unlikely that the patient's frustration and anger will be relieved unless such issues are explored and dealt with.

Key points to establish

- The complexity of differential diagnosis.

- Reassurance that the investigations are progressing in a logical fashion.

- Reassurance that as soon as definitive results are known they will be discussed with the patient and specific therapy commenced.

- That problems can be incurred by premature treatment, specifically the difficulty of further investigation should there be a failure to respond to initial treatment.

- Explanation that empiric therapy would be instituted should patient deteriorate.

Appropriate responses to likely questions

Patient: *why is all this taking so long?*

Doctor: I'm sorry it's taking a long time. I can understand why you're frustrated, but it's not obvious what the problem is. You've had a range of tests – blood tests, urine tests and an X-ray of the chest – and they haven't given us the answer. There's clearly something going on. One of the tests shows there's a high level of inflammation in the blood and another that the liver isn't working completely normally, but we don't yet know what the cause of the problem is.

Patient: the fever makes me feel very unwell.

Doctor: yes, the fever will make you feel unwell. We can give you a fan and medication to help that: paracetamol is very good. But the fever is not dangerous in itself: it is a sign that there's something going on in your body that we need to get to the bottom of.

Patient: why can't you just give me some treatment?

Doctor: because we don't know what's wrong. There are a number of possible diagnoses that all require different treatments, and it is possible that we could make things worse if we gave a 'best guess' treatment that was actually wrong. This might mask further progression of your illness or interfere with further investigation, making it more difficult or impossible to get the right diagnosis in the end.

Patient: if I was desperately ill, you'd give me something wouldn't you?

Doctor: yes, if that was the case we would make the best guess that we could and start you on treatment straight away. But as I said, this would have the risk of making it more difficult to get the right diagnosis and it wouldn't be the right thing to do at the moment.

Patient: could I have cancer?

Doctor: I'm not hiding anything when I say I don't know, but it is possible. Some cancers can cause fever and some of the tests we are planning are designed to check this out.

1.2.4 Chronic fatigue

Scenario

Role: you are a junior doctor working in a general medical outpatient clinic.

A 29-year-old man has been referred to the general medical outpatient clinic because of severe fatigue, which he has had for several months. He dates the onset to a viral illness he had last winter and feels he has an ongoing infection to explain his persistent symptoms. He does not have any symptoms to suggest that depression is the primary process. Following his first clinic attendance a standard range of tests are performed: FBC, inflammatory markers, electrolytes, glucose, renal/liver/bone function tests, autoimmune/vasculitic screen, thyroid function tests, serology for Epstein–Barr virus and cytomegalovirus, CXR and a short Synacthen test. All are normal or negative.

He now returns for a second clinic appointment. At the meeting with the consultant before the clinic it is agreed that the diagnosis is chronic fatigue syndrome, that no further investigations are required, that he should be encouraged to take gentle daily exercise, gradually building up over time, and that referral for cognitive behavioural therapy could be considered (although this is not likely to be readily or rapidly available).

Your task: to explain the diagnosis and treatment of chronic fatigue syndrome to the patient.

Key issues to explore

The patient is likely to have very clear-cut ideas about the cause of his problems, which need to be explored before the discussion can move on. Why is he convinced that an ongoing infection is responsible?

Key points to establish

- You can find no serious progressive disease.

- This does not mean that you do not believe the patient's symptoms.

- Chronic fatigue syndrome is real.

- There is no specific drug therapy but there are treatment options, including graded exercise and cognitive therapy.

Appropriate responses to likely questions

Patient: but doctor, I know there is something wrong with me.

Doctor: I haven't said that there isn't anything wrong with you. I know that chronic fatigue syndrome is a real illness that causes very real symptoms and problems for people who've got it. What we have been able to establish, and this is good news, is that there is no serious infection, cancer or anything like that to explain your symptoms.

Patient: you just think I'm depressed, don't you?

Doctor: no, I haven't said that. People with any severe illness are prone to get depressed, which can be a natural reaction in this situation. But I don't think that chronic fatigue syndrome is all due to depression or all in the mind, although sometimes depression can make it worse.

Patient: there must be some more tests you can do.

Doctor: yes, a doctor can always do more tests, but that wouldn't be the right thing to do here and we don't plan to do any more. We would only do more tests if the situation were to change in some way that made us think we should check something else out. But we have all discussed things, and we don't think that any more tests are necessary at the moment.

Patient: can I have a second opinion?

Doctor: yes, you can. Your GP could refer you to someone else and, if it was helpful, we could give your GP advice as to who they might refer you to. But I would be concerned that this might delay you getting started on appropriate treatment.

Patient: what treatment is there?

Doctor: chronic fatigue syndrome is not an easy thing to treat – I won't pretend that it is – but there are two treatments that are known to be effective. The first is graded exercise, where you aim to gradually improve your energy levels by increasing daily activities in a planned fashion. The second is cognitive behavioural therapy, where you explore reasons and triggers for your illness with a therapist and determine appropriate responses to those triggers. Either we or your GP could make a referral for you to visit someone who can help you with cognitive behavioural therapy, but it isn't always easy to get access to this treatment.

Patient: what about vitamins or medications?

Doctor: I am afraid that there aren't any vitamins or medications that help this condition. Antidepressants are sometimes used if we feel that there is coexistent depression, and they may help if someone has a sleep disorder.

1.2.5 Malaise, mouth ulcers and fever

Scenario

Role: you are a junior doctor working on a general medical ward.

A 54-year-old gay man is admitted on the medical take complaining of malaise, rash, mouth ulcers and pyrexia. You suspect HIV infection and want to encourage him to take the test but he is reluctant.

Your task: explore the reasons for the man's reluctance to test for HIV and explain why you think he should agree to be tested.

Key issues to explore

Why is he reluctant to test? You will begin by asking him open-ended questions, but if the reasons are not forthcoming you will need to probe regarding common reasons for reluctance, including:

- fears about confidentiality;

- misconceptions about the prognosis of HIV;

- concern that he may lose his mortgage/insurance as a result of being found HIV-positive, or even through the act of testing for HIV.

It will also be appropriate to discuss the following.

- What will he feel like if he fails to test but subsequently develops a severe illness?

- What about his partners? Shouldn't they be given the information that they may be at high risk of HIV?

Key issues to establish

- Reassure the patient about confidentiality: you have a duty of care which includes confidentiality.

- Explain that with modern antiretroviral therapy (see Section 2.11) the prognosis of HIV is very good and management has become that of a chronic condition in which patients mostly feel very well. People now rarely die of AIDS in the UK.

- Taking an HIV test will not affect any current insurance or mortgage, even if the test is positive.

- His partners may be asymptomatic and yet still could be HIV-positive and therefore are best told of any risk.

Apropriate answers to likely questions

Patient: I would rather not know the diagnosis. There is nothing you can do about HIV anyway, is there?

Doctor: I am pleased to say that that's not true: there are several good reasons why you should know the diagnosis. If you have HIV, we can do tests to see how badly your immune system has been affected: the CD4 count. If the count is low you would need to go on treatment, and modern treatment is very safe and effective. Even if you don't need treatment, we can monitor your health with regular blood tests and start treatment when the time is right; this would stop you becoming ill. If managed in this way, most patients in the UK with HIV infection will live for many decades and possibly have a near-normal lifespan if they get the right treatment.

Patient: I would rather wait until I become more ill. Isn't that the best time to take treatment?

Doctor: no, I don't think so. As the disease progresses it damages the immune system more and more, and if it becomes so badly damaged that the person becomes ill with a very severe infection or cancer it may be too late to save their life. For HIV treatment to work properly, so that people with the disease can live for a long time, it is best to start it before they become seriously ill.

Patient: *I am worried about confidentiality. Won't people find out about me?*

Doctor: I can understand why you are worried about this, but all healthcare workers are bound by a duty of confidentiality. If any healthcare worker is discovered to have breached confidentiality without good reason they will be punished, and they may lose their job. HIV units are especially aware about maintaining confidentiality, but it is often in the patient's best interest that other people are told. For instance telling the GP means that someone doesn't get the wrong treatment if the GP is aware of that person's HIV status. Many people also find that it is good to tell close friends and join community HIV support groups as they can help the person talk through the problems they face, but this would be your decision.

Patient: *do you have to tell my partner?*

Doctor: if your partner was my patient, then I would have a clear duty of care to him and would have to tell him; but he is not my patient, so I don't have to tell him. However, in some circumstances doctors are allowed to break confidentiality, for instance if they think that a patient is putting the lives of other people at risk. If you are HIV positive, and we don't know if you are yet, then I would strongly advise that you do tell your partner. I could help you

do this if that would be helpful, because if he is positive then he would benefit from being diagnosed and monitored or treated in the same way that I think you would. I am sure that you wouldn't want to be responsible for denying him the opportunity to make his own decisions about this, would you? I must also say to you that if you have unprotected sex with your partner and he finds out about the HIV later from someone else, then he could have you prosecuted for endangering his health. People have been sent to prison for this.

Patient: *won't I be financially disadvantaged if people like my insurance company find out that I am HIV-positive?*

Doctor: any existing insurance and mortgage policies will not be affected and will continue in the normal way. If you are positive you are right that you will find it more difficult to get insurance, but there are companies that will offer insurance to people with HIV, especially as the prognosis has improved so much. If you test HIV-negative, then this won't affect any current insurance policies either and a negative test also won't have any effect on your future insurance chances. The insurance companies now accept an HIV test as being a 'routine' test and are more interested in your future risks based on the information you give them on the application form.

> **HIV testing**
> - In the mentally competent this must always be performed with consent.
> - Testing without consent is only acceptable if the patient is *not* competent *and* the test is in their best interests.
> - Pre- and post-test discussion should be available.

1.2.6 Don't tell my wife

Scenario

Role: you are a junior doctor working in a medical outpatient clinic.

A 38-year-old man is referred to the outpatient clinic because of weight loss. On examination he has oral candida. After appropriate discussion he consents to testing for HIV. The result is positive. He returns to the clinic and accepts advice that he should start antiretroviral therapy, but is not willing to accept that his wife should be told about the diagnosis.

Your task: to explain to the man why his wife should be told.

Key issues to explore

The man has just tested positive for HIV and a common reaction is to want no one else to know. The discussion is likely to be difficult, but important things to find out include the following.

- What does he understand about how HIV is transmitted, how it can be treated and what the prognosis is with treatment? His views about informing his wife and others may be based on significant misconceptions.

- What are his fears about revealing the diagnosis to his wife?

- What would he feel like if his wife became ill and this could have been prevented if she had been told about the HIV?

- What happens if his wife finds out through other means? What will that do to their relationship?

- Does he have children? If his wife is also positive then they are also at risk and need to be tested.

- Does he have other sexual partners who may also be at risk?

Key issues to establish

- Make it clear that his care is your main priority and that your aim is to help him to understand HIV and what options will be open to him.

- Facts regarding the transmission of HIV and its prognosis with appropriate monitoring and treatment.

- Reassure him about confidentiality: you have a duty of care to him which includes confidentiality. However, if his wife is also your patient, then inform him that you have a duty of care to her and that if he doesn't tell her then you will do so.

- If his wife is not your patient, then your duty to her is less clear-cut, but you should inform him that if he has unprotected sex with her and she finds out about the HIV later from someone else then she could have him prosecuted for endangering her health, and that people have been sent to prison for this.

Apropriate answers to likely questions

Patient: my wife looks healthy enough so she can't have HIV, can she?

Doctor: I'm afraid we can't be sure of that. People with HIV can remain healthy for many years, so you can't tell just by looking at them and so she might be positive. If she is, then we would advise her about the proper tests and treatment that

would prevent her becoming ill in the future. If she is negative, then we can do our best to make sure that she and any children you may have in the future will remain negative.

Patient: if I tell my wife about the HIV test she might leave me. As long as I use condoms she won't be at risk, will she?

Doctor: I'm afraid that can't be guaranteed. You may have been HIV positive for many years and your wife could have become infected at any time during this period. You are right that condoms are very good protection against HIV if used properly, but they sometimes break or come off, and if your wife is HIV-negative now she would be at risk of catching the infection each time this happens. This risk can be greatly reduced by giving immediate treatment called postexposure prophylaxis if a condom fails, but if she doesn't know about the HIV then she wouldn't know to take this treatment.

Patient: will you tell my wife, even if I don't give my permission?

Doctor: if she attends the clinic and is my patient, then I will have to tell her because I know she is at risk of catching the infection and my duty as a doctor is to protect my patients from harm. But I would prefer that you tell her as that shows your trust in her. If she is not my patient, the rules of confidentiality mean that I don't have to find her and tell her if you refuse permission, but I cannot lie if she or her GP ask me directly. I certainly would feel unhappy that she hasn't been told: it is best for everyone if she is told, and there are many people who are experienced in HIV who can help you do this. Also, I have to tell you that if you have unprotected sex with her and she finds out about the HIV later from someone else, then she could have

you prosecuted for endangering her health and people have been sent to prison for this.

Patient: I have had unprotected sex with my wife for many years. What are the chances she is still negative?

Doctor: transmission of HIV between couples is variable and depends on many factors. We very frequently find couples where one partner is positive and the other negative after many years together, so you can't assume that your partner is positive. Furthermore, if she is negative now, then she can still catch the infection from you in the future. You are potentially putting her at risk if you have unprotected sex with her now that you know you are positive, and there is a growing number of people who have been prosecuted and sent to prison for having unprotected sex when they knew they were HIV-positive and their partner was at risk of catching the infection. It is therefore best to tell her before putting her at risk and before she finds out some other way: for instance, if she becomes pregnant then she will be offered an HIV test and might find out that way.

Patient: I have two children aged 2 and 10 years old. What are the chances of them being positive?

Doctor: your children cannot catch HIV from you unless you were to bleed heavily and they were to be covered in your blood. Things such as kissing or sharing a toothbrush are not a risk, but if your wife is HIV-positive then your children might have caught it from her at birth or from breast-feeding if she wasn't tested for HIV when she was pregnant. Children who are HIV-positive can sometimes remain well for many years, but then eventually can become very ill or die unless diagnosed early and given the right treatment. If you tell your wife about your condition, you can then find out if your children need a test according to her result.

Patient: if I die, will you tell my family about the HIV?

Doctor: it is a legal responsibility for the doctor to put the accurate cause of death on the death certificate, so if you die of HIV then this has to be mentioned on the death certificate. The person registering your death, who is normally one of your close family members, will see this. Although my duty of confidentiality to you continues after death, under these circumstances it is likely that I will meet your wife and I would have to tell her that she is at risk of being infected, even if I can't tell her your medical history without your previous consent.

Patient: can I bring my wife here for you to test her without telling her what the test is?

Doctor: no, we can't do that. We cannot do any test without informed consent, which means that we would have to tell your wife she is having an HIV test.

1.3 Acute scenarios

1.3.1 Fever

Scenario

A 43-year-old man who is feeling feverish and unwell comes to the Emergency Department. The casualty officer asks you to review him.

Introduction

Fever has a complex pathogenesis and is a frequent presenting feature of illness. Infections are by far the most common cause of fever and would be the most likely cause of the problem in this case, but it shouldn't be forgotten that non-infectious causes are also possible (see Section 1.1.3). In view of the wide range of possible diagnoses, there is no substitute for a detailed history and complete physical examination. It is a useful exercise to formulate two differential diagnoses, first infectious and then non-infectious. If you know or suspect that the patient is immunocompromised, generate separate differential diagnoses, first for an immunocompetent and then for an immunocompromised individual.

During your assessment, keep in mind the key questions that will direct the initial management of a patient with suspected infection.

- What is the site of infection?

- What is the likely infecting organism(s)?

- What has the patient been exposed to?

- Is empirical therapy appropriate?

History of the presenting problem

Documentation of fever
In many illnesses, fever is not continuous. In keeping with the normal circadian temperature rhythm, fever usually peaks in the evening. At the time you see the patient, fever may be absent, especially if he has taken antipyretic medication. Ask the following questions.

- Have you been feeling hot and cold? These subjective sensations are commonly reported by patients who are well and subsequently found not to have fever. Exactly what does the patient mean by 'fever'?

- Have you measured/how did you measure your temperature? Digital thermometers are the most reliable; mercury thermometers are easily misread; and thermal paper strips are hopeless.

- Have you been having sweats? Drenching sweats, commonly at night, are an objective symptom and indicate significant pathology. Ask about having to change the sheets as a result of sweats.

- Have you been having shivers/chills? Ask specifically about rigors, ie uncontrollable shaking of the whole body, often with teeth chattering and lasting for minutes. Rigors are particularly, but not exclusively, associated with bacterial sepsis or malaria.

- How long have you noticed the fever? In general, as the duration of fever increases, the likelihood of an infectious cause decreases. You will gain little by trying to analyse the fever pattern, unless the patient has recently been to an area endemic for malaria and has a typical 'tertian' or 'quartan' fever pattern.

Site of infection
What else have you noticed? The key aim is to gain a clue that can be used to target appropriate examinations and investigations. A detailed history of symptoms associated with the fever is required. Give particular weight to volunteered symptoms and perform a detailed systematic enquiry in relation to all organ systems. By definition, common things are common, so ask about the following.

- Urinary symptoms: dysuria, frequency, smelly urine, suprapubic pain and loin pain.

- Chest symptoms: breathlessness, pleuritic pain and sputum production.

- Spots/boils/abscesses/rashes.

- Sinuses, teeth, throat and ears (particularly children).

- Known heart murmurs.

- Prosthetic devices, heart valve replacements, artificial joints and arterial grafts.

- Diarrhoea/vomiting.

- Meningitic symptoms: severe headache, photophobia, neck stiffness and rash.

Remember that fever of any cause may be accompanied by a constellation of symptoms, including anorexia, myalgia and mild headache.

> ⚠ Serious infections such as bacterial sepsis or malaria may present with 'false localising' symptoms and signs such as headache, breathlessness, vomiting or diarrhoea.

Other relevant history

Drug history
Pay special attention to the following:

- immunosuppressive drugs, eg steroids;

- recent antibiotics;

- adverse reactions to antibiotics;

- alternative and ethnic medicines.

Exposure history
Ask carefully about what the patient has been doing as this may suggest certain infections.

- Has anyone whom you know had a similar illness?

- Have you travelled abroad? (See Section 1.3.16.)

- What do you do in your job?

- Do you have any particular hobbies?

- Do you have any pets or have you been exposed to animals?

- Have you participated in recreational drug use?

- Sexual contacts: a sexual history is an important aspect of the assessment of suspected infection and if the cause of the problem is not immediately apparent, you should not avoid the subject out of a misplaced sense of politeness. Tact and care are required (see Section 1.1.5).

Relevant past history
Very many conditions, not only obvious immunosuppression, are associated with a particular risk of infection, and so a detailed past history is required. A history of previous infections may suggest the patient is immunocompromised. A previous history of tuberculosis (TB), possibly from many years ago, may be relevant as reactivation might have taken place.

> 🔑 When the cause of fever is not obvious, consider the following:
>
> - primary and secondary immunodeficiencies;
> - structural abnormalities such as an abnormal heart valve, indwelling prosthetic material or a chronic urinary catheter;
> - non-infectious causes.

Examination
Is the patient pyrexial (Fig. 8)? A full examination of the patient

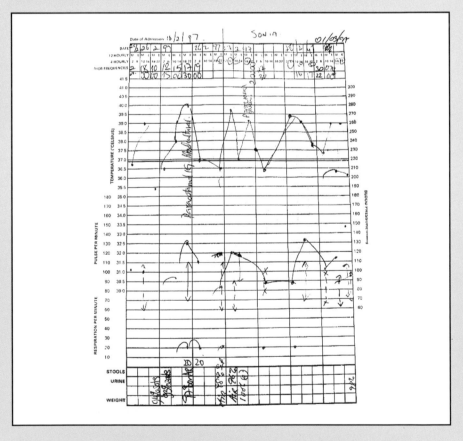

▲**Fig. 8** Temperature chart from a patient with TB. Temperature recording is essential to establish the presence or absence of a fever, but the pattern of fever cannot reliably distinguish between bacterial, viral, parasitic, fungal and non-infectious causes of fever.

is required. Your primary survey should ensure that breathing and circulation are adequate, followed by a detailed examination of each system. Is the patient well, ill, very ill or nearly dead? Your general impression is critically important in deciding whether to give 'best guess' empirical antimicrobial treatment or to wait for the results of tests.

Each system should be examined in detail.

- Skin and general examination: skin rashes, lymphadenopathy, clubbing, stigmata of subacute bacterial endocarditis, signs of liver disease, sore throat and tonsillar exudate, etc.

- Cardiovascular system: presence of heart murmurs, vascular disease and vascular grafts.

- Respiratory system: chest signs to suggest pneumonia, TB and underlying lung disease.

- Abdomen: hepatosplenomegaly, enlarged or tender kidneys, palpable masses or lymphadenopathy. Also examine the patient's genitals if sexually transmitted infections are a consideration.

- Central nervous system: signs of meningitis and focal neurological signs.

- Locomotor system: painful or swollen joints, back pain and sacroiliitis.

Investigation

Initial investigations should include the following.

Blood tests

- FBC.

- Electrolytes, renal/liver/bone function tests and C-reactive protein/plasma viscosity/ erythrocyte sedimentation rate.

- Serum: ask microbiology or virology to save a sample.

Cultures

Blood and urine cultures should be performed in all cases. Ideally several sets of blood cultures should be sent at different times before commencing antibiotics. Other specimens should be sent according to the clinical picture.

Imaging

A CXR is needed in all patients with no obvious cause of fever to look for areas of consolidation and mediastinal lymphadenopathy. Other imaging will depend on the clinical picture and suspected site of infection.

Management

In general, it is not necessary to abolish fever except for giving symptomatic relief. You may be clear about the likely site of infection from your initial assessment of the patient, in which case you can then initiate specific management, including antimicrobial therapy if appropriate.

Most hospitals have guidelines for the initial antibiotic treatment

of infections. You will probably find these helpful in guiding your selection of antibiotics, but remember that you must apply them thoughtfully to ensure that you choose the appropriate treatment for individual cases. Usually, the choice of empirical antibiotic therapy is a matter of probability (Fig. 9). For patients who are reasonably well, you should choose antibiotics that treat the most likely organisms. However, if you judge that a patient is seriously ill, you should seek expert advice and use an antimicrobial regimen that also treats less likely, but possible, pathogens.

As results become available, especially from the microbiology laboratory, you may be able to target antimicrobial treatment more precisely. You will also need to consider modifying antimicrobial treatment if the illness fails to respond to the initial regimen.

Further comments

Fever of unknown cause

If a positive diagnosis cannot be made, management depends on your judgement of the most likely

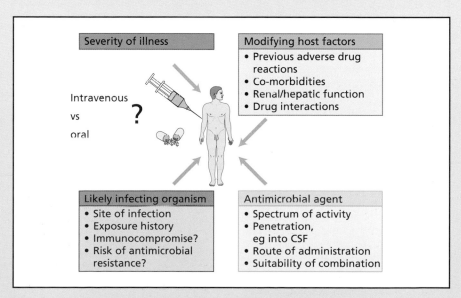

▲ **Fig. 9** Factors influencing choice of empirical antimicrobial therapy. CSF, cerebrospinal fluid.

diagnoses and how severely ill the patient is. Those whom you judge to be (or at risk of becoming) seriously unwell should be given 'best guess' empirical antimicrobial therapy once specimens for culture have been obtained. In other cases, it will almost certainly be more appropriate to wait for the results of further investigations.

Persistent fever despite antimicrobial therapy

If this occurs, consider the following.

- The antimicrobial spectrum does not include the infecting organism.
- The infecting organism has developed antimicrobial resistance.
- Failure to achieve adequate drug concentrations at site of infection, possibly because of compliance, dose, absorption or penetration into a sequestered site.
- Non-infectious cause of the fever.
- Antibiotic-induced (drug) fever.
- Nosocomial or device-related infection.

1.3.2 Fever, hypotension and confusion

Scenario

A 20-year-old female university student presents with a 12-hour history of fever, chills and generalised aches and pains. On arrival she is confused, breathless, tachycardic (110 bpm) and hypotensive (80/40 mmHg).

Introduction

The diagnosis is septic shock until proved otherwise.

You must act quickly. The immediate priority has to be resuscitation. Once resuscitation is underway (intravenous 0.9% saline/colloid

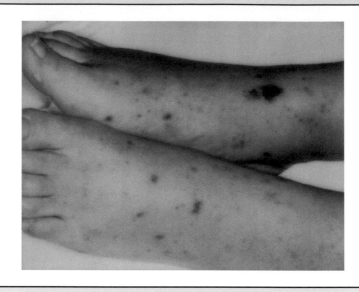

▲ **Fig. 10** Petechial/purpuric rash associated with meningococcal bacteraemia. A similar rash can occur with disseminated intravascular coagulation resulting from other infectious agents, although in the UK it is most commonly seen in meningococccal disease.

and oxygen therapy; see *Acute Medicine*, Sections 1.2.2 and 1.2.11), you need to identify the source of infection. If none is obvious, then consider meningococcal septicaemia or toxic shock and look thoroughly for the purpuric/petechial rash of meningococcal disease (Fig. 10) or the more diffuse erythema associated with toxic shock syndrome.

Differential diagnoses of septic shock

- Toxic shock syndrome: a severe illness caused by toxin-producing staphylococci. It occurs particularly in women in association with tampon use. Onset is acute with high fever, myalgia and shock. An erythematous sunburn-like rash and renal impairment are both common. Palmar desquamation is common after toxic shock (Fig. 11).
- Group A streptococcal toxic shock syndrome may follow invasive streptococcal infection. Look for evidence of streptococcal throat or skin infection and ensure that blood cultures are taken prior to treatment.

- Meningococcal septicaemia: occurs mainly in children and young adults, and may occur in the absence of meningitis. Look for the characteristic petechial/purpuric rash (Fig. 10), although this is not always present.
- Non-meningococcal septic shock: look for focus of infection, eg cutaneous, pulmonary, urinary tract or intra-abdominal (such as cholangitis).

History of the presenting problem

In anyone who is severely ill, resuscitate first, ask questions afterwards.

It may be difficult to obtain any history from this woman, but while beginning to resuscitate get as much information as possible from her and from any friends or family who are available.

When, where and how

Try to assess the severity/rate of progression of the illness, along

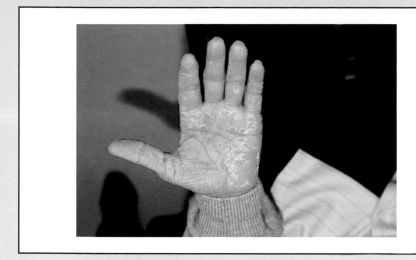

▲ **Fig. 11** Palmar desquamation after staphylococcal toxic shock. This may also occur with scarlet fever, Kawasaki's disease or drug reactions.

with the likely focus and aetiological agent.

- When did the symptoms start?

- How did the illness start and how have the symptoms changed? In bacterial sepsis, the rapid progression of symptoms indicates severe disease.

- Any rashes? If so, where did the rash start and how has it progressed?

Associated symptoms

These symptoms may help to localise the site of infection but can also be misleading, eg diarrhoea is frequently seen in bacterial sepsis and does not necessarily indicate an intra-abdominal focus of infection.

- Cough, chest pain and sputum production.

- Nausea and/or vomiting: common but non-specific, eg occurring with meningitis, intracerebral events and migraine.

- Earache, sinusitis or cough: pneumococci are more likely as the aetiological agent.

- Focal neurological signs or diplopia: if present you need to exclude brain abscess.

- Genitourinary symptoms such as vaginal discharge.

Other relevant history

Pursue features that might suggest a particular underlying infection.

- When was her last menstrual period? If she is currently menstruating, could she have left a tampon *in situ*? Think of toxic shock syndrome.

- Has she been in contact with anyone with meningococcal infection?

- Has she recently travelled abroad? Think of malaria. Consider viral haemorrhagic fever if she has returned from an endemic area within 3 weeks (see Section 1.3.16).

- Has she recently been bitten by a dog: consider *Capnocytophaga canimorsus*.

Relevant past history

The following could be relevant.

- Immunocompromised, eg immunosuppressive therapy, risk factors for HIV infection, immunosuppressive diseases and a history of recurrent infection.

- Intravenous recreational drug use makes endocarditis and infection with *Staphylococcus aureus* more likely.

- Recent hospitalisation: this raises the possibility of antibiotic-resistant infection.

- Previous surgery and indwelling prosthetic material.

Examination

A full general examination should be performed, taking particular note of the following.

- Vital signs: pulse, BP, respiratory rate, temperature and pulse oximetry.

- Glasgow Coma Scale score: to establish baseline condition.

- Rash: in the setting of shock, a petechial/purpuric rash is highly suggestive of meningococcal septicaemia and an erythematous rash suggests toxic shock.

- Any peripheral signs: to support a diagnosis of bacterial endocarditis.

- Needle marks suggesting intravenous drug use makes *Staphylococcus aureus* infection more likely.

- Evidence of meningism, ie neck stiffness and Kernig's sign.

- Throat: for evidence of source of infection.

- Cardiac murmurs that might indicate bacterial endocarditis.

- Chest: for evidence of pneumonia.

- Abdomen: for organomegaly and tenderness that might be evidence of the source of infection.

- Ears: for evidence of the source of infection.

- Fundoscopy: for signs of elevated intracranial pressure or focal signs of infection, ie endophthalmitis or Roth's spots.

Investigation

In the patient who is very ill, resuscitation should be started immediately, with investigations initiated as soon as this is underway. Investigations are performed to identify the site and nature of the infection and to monitor disease severity/complications.

Blood tests

- FBC and differential: neutrophilia is common in bacterial sepsis but in severe cases the white cell count may be normal or low; thrombocytopenia may occur as part of disseminated intravascular coagulation (DIC) in septicaemia.

- Electrolytes and renal function tests: renal failure may occur in septicaemia and is common in toxic shock syndrome.

- Liver function tests: these can be non-specifically raised in bacterial sepsis, but may also indicate a hepatic source, particularly cholangitis.

- Blood glucose: to exclude hyperglycaemia/hypoglycaemia; hypoglycaemia can complicate severe sepsis and is a poor prognostic sign.

- Clotting and fibrin degradation products (DIC in meningococcal septicaemia).

- Creatine kinase: for evidence of muscle involvement.

- Save serum.

- Arterial blood gases are required to assess hypoxia and acidosis.

Febrile breathless patients need arterial blood gas measurement. In bacterial sepsis, breathlessness is often the result of lactic acidosis and may be the only sign of severe disease early in meningococcal septicaemia.

Cultures

- Blood cultures are essential in all cases before giving antibiotics (see Section 3.2).

- Urine culture.

- Culture other body sites as clinically indicated, eg high vaginal swab in this case.

Imaging

- CXR: exclude pneumonia and look for evidence of adult respiratory distress syndrome.

- Liver ultrasonography: if cholangitis is suspected as source of sepsis.

- Ultrasonography/CT scan: as indicated for focal infection, eg cranial CT scan in suspected intracranial infection.

Other tests

A lumbar puncture will need to be considered if meningitis or encephalitis is suspected, but is contraindicated in patients with meningococcal sepsis and a haemorrhagic rash.

Management

The management of severe bacterial sepsis is based on identification and treatment of the likely causative organism and intensive support of organ function. In this case the two most likely diagnoses are toxic shock syndrome and streptococcal/meningococcal septicaemia.

Resuscitation

Resuscitation of the patient with profound hypotension

- Check airway, breathing and circulation.
- Call for assistance.
- Give high-flow oxygen.
- Establish intravenous access: place large-bore drips in both antecubital fossae or insert a femoral venous line.
- Give colloid or 0.9% saline as fast as possible until BP is restored or JVP is clearly visible.
- Establish diagnosis and treat if possible.

For detailed discussion of how to resuscitate the patient with profound hypotension, see *Acute Medicine*, Section 1.2.2.

Toxic shock syndrome

- Resuscitation and supportive treatment.

- Removal of tampon or drainage of pus.

- Intravenous flucloxacillin 1–2 g four times daily.

Meningococcal septicaemia

- Resuscitation and supportive treatment.

- Antibiotics as for meningococcal meningitis (see Section 1.3.11).

- Notification to Consultant in Communicable Diseases Control (CCDC) and prophylaxis for those coming into prolonged close contact with the patient (see Section 1.3.11).

Sepsis with unknown source

- Resuscitation and supportive treatment.

- High-dose intravenous antibiotics based on the clinical setting.

1.3.3 A swollen red foot

> ### Scenario
>
> A 32-year-old man accidentally cut his left foot with a fork while gardening. Three days later he presents to the Emergency Department with redness and swelling surrounding the injury and a high fever.

History of the presenting problem

The working diagnosis must be cellulitis with the possibility of septicaemia. Confirm the following.

- Site of the injury and how it occurred.

- Duration of symptoms.

- Pain, redness and swelling.

- Is it spreading?

- Associated systemic upset: if this is out of proportion to the cellulitis, necrotising fasciitis must be considered.

Other relevant history

There may be specific risk factors for particular soft-tissue infections, in which case careful enquiry may help to identify the likely pathogen (Table 10).

- Soil contamination of wound (as in this case): consider *Clostridium perfringens*, the cause of gas gangrene.

- Injury in salt water (warm climate): consider *Vibrio vulnificus* as a possible causative agent, particularly in patients with underlying liver disease.

- Injury while swimming in fresh water: consider *Aeromonas hydrophila*.

- Animal or human bite: may inoculate pathogens; bites are associated with a high incidence of infection.

- Could there be a foreign body within the wound?

- Coexistent illness, eg diabetes mellitus

Also check that the patient has been immunised with tetanus toxoid within the last 10 years.

Examination

General features

As described in Sections 1.3.1 and 1.3.2.

Cellulitis

- Note area of redness and draw a line around the edge with a pen: this will make progression easy to monitor.

- Is there evidence of lymphangitis? A red line tracking up the limb along the line of the lymphatic drainage confirms the presence of distal infection.

- Is there tender lymphadenopathy at the proximal end of the affected limb?

- Are there any areas of necrosis? If present you must immediately suspect necrotising fasciitis. This may not be immediately apparent in the early stages, but is suggested by very severe pain accompanied by discoloration and blistering of the skin.

- Any evidence of crepitus within the affected area suggests gas within the tissues, indicating gas gangrene/necrotising fasciitis.

- Athlete's foot in lower limb cellulitis: this is often a portal of entry for organisms, and recurrent infection will result unless treated appropriately.

> ⚠️ **Deep venous thrombosis**
>
> Deep venous thrombosis (DVT) is a common differential diagnosis of cellulitis. Both conditions are associated with fever, leg swelling, redness and pain, and they can be difficult to distinguish clinically. However, DVT is associated with a woody texture and tenderness to the posterior calf. In cellulitis the fever and redness are typically more pronounced, the tenderness is circumferential, and lymphangitis and lymphadenopathy are commonly present.

TABLE 10 AETIOLOGICAL AGENTS OF CELLULITIS	
Scenario	**Likely pathogens**
Most common	*Streptococcus pyogenes*
Common	*Staphylococcus aureus*
Uncommon	*Clostridium perfringens*: cellulitis or gas gangrene Other *Streptococcus* spp. such as group C or G
Saltwater injury	*Vibrio* spp., particularly *V. vulnificus*
Freshwater injury	*Aeromonas hydrophila*
Hospital-acquired infection	Staphylococci: consider antibiotic resistance, ie meticillin-resistant *Staphylococcus aureus* (MRSA), Gram-negative bacilli
Patient with diabetes	Streptococci and staphylococci plus Gram-negative bacilli and anaerobes
Bites (animal or human)	Many potential pathogens including *Pasteurella multocida*, *Capnocytophaga canimorsus*, anaerobes, *Streptococcus viridans*, *Eikenella corrodens*

> **Necrotising fasciitis/gas gangrene**
>
> - Cellulitis with evidence of skin necrosis, including discoloration and blistering (but note that necrosis may be deep to the skin and not visible).
> - Severe pain.
> - Rapid progression.
> - Gas detectable in tissues on examination and/or radiologically.
> - Typically the patient is more systemically unwell than the degree of skin involvement would suggest.

Investigation

This will be dictated by the severity of the illness.

Severe sepsis

Investigation should occur at the same time as resuscitation if there are signs of severe sepsis, as described in Section 1.3.2, with the addition of specific imaging: take a radiograph of the affected limb to look for gas in the subcutaneous tissues if gas gangrene or necrotising fasciitis is suspected. A radiograph may reveal osteomyelitis in chronic infection.

Cellulitis without severe sepsis

- FBC: neutrophilia usually present.

- C-reactive protein: to assess inflammatory response.

- Electrolytes and renal function tests: to establish baseline renal function.

- Blood cultures: may yield the organism responsible.

- Swab for bacterial culture of any open wound around or within the cellulitis.

Management

The aims of management are to control the infection, reduce swelling and monitor for evidence of tissue necrosis. Rarely surgical intervention may be required.

Keep the affected limb elevated while resting (this reduces oedema and speeds healing) and administer analgesia as required.

Appropriate antibiotics are given orally if the patient has mild illness or intravenously if severe.

- Streptococci/staphylococci: intravenous benzylpenicillin 1.2–2.4 g four times daily will cover a streptococcal cellulitis, but flucloxacillin 0.5–1.0 g four times daily may be added if a staphylococcal aetiology is suspected. Oral co-amoxiclav is a good alternative for mild cases and for infection following human or animal bites. If the patient is allergic to penicillin, use a macrolide (such as erythromycin) or clindamycin. Give broad-spectrum antibiotics if mixed infection is considered eg diabetic ulceration and cellulitis and necrotising fasciitis.

- *Aeromonas hydrophila*: use ciprofloxacin or gentamicin.

- *Vibrio vulnificus*: use tetracycline or doxycycline.

Immunise the patient with tetanus toxoid if this has not been done in the last 10 years.

Further comments

Necrotising fasciitis

Treatment of this condition is an emergency so do not waste any time.

- Surgical exploration and débridement of all dead tissue is mandatory.

- Give the patient high-dose intravenous antibiotics to cover *Streptococcus pyogenes* and other possible aerobic and anaerobic bacteria.

Gas gangrene

This is caused by *Clostridium perfringens* and other *Clostridium* spp. (see Section 2.5.1). Treat with:

- aggressive surgical débridement;

- high-dose intravenous benzylpenicillin and clindamycin;

- hyperbaric oxygen therapy if available.

1.3.4 Fever and cough

> ### Scenario
>
> A 44-year-old smoker presents to the Emergency Department with a 4-day history of fever and cough.

Introduction

The important things to establish initially are whether this is likely to be an upper respiratory tract infection (URTI) or a lower respiratory tract infection (LRTI), and whether it is likely to be bacterial or viral. A URTI does not usually require antibiotic treatment. The term 'chest infection' should be avoided because it is too non-specific.

Is this an upper or lower respiratory tract infection?

URTIs are not an immediate danger, but they predispose to subsequent LRTIs and can also precipitate severe bronchospasm. A URTI is suggested when the patient:

- appears clinically well;

- has a sore throat and/or rhinorrhoea;

- has an unproductive cough, or a cough productive of clear or white sputum;

- has no chest signs.

An LRTI is clearly of more concern than a URTI because pneumonia can be life-threatening. An LRTI is suggested by the following.

- Dyspnoea (in the absence of wheeze).

- Pleuritic chest pain: must be LRTI.

- Haemoptysis: consider also the possibility of underlying carcinoma or of pulmonary embolism.

- Cyanosis.

- Focal chest signs.

What are the common microbial causes of an acute LRTI?

Many organisms can cause an LRTI (Table 11), and a careful history is required to spot risk factors predisposing to the more unusual causes.

History of the presenting problem

Clues in the history may include the following.

- Was the onset sudden or gradual over a few days? Sudden onset with high fever, purulent sputum, pleuritic chest pain and/or dyspnoea is suggestive of pneumococcal pneumonia. Gradual onset with prodrome of fever and malaise lasting a few days followed by dry cough suggests an atypical organism.

- What is the colour of the sputum? Green suggests bacterial infection; a dry cough or white or clear sputum suggests viral or atypical infection.

- Has the patient recently travelled abroad? An air-conditioned hotel room suggests Legionnaire's disease. Caving in North America may lead to acute histoplasmosis.

- Does the patient have any pet birds at home and, if so, are they ill? Consider psittacosis.

- Has there been any recent contact with farm animals? Consider Q fever (*Coxiella burnetii*).

- Preceding 'flu-like illness? Consider secondary bacterial pneumonia, particularly *Staphylococcus aureus*.

- Systemic symptoms? Diarrhoea, jaundice and confusion are more common in Legionnaire's disease. Severe earache suggests *Mycoplasma* spp.

Other relevant history

Many conditions predispose to LRTI.

- Smoking history: even in the absence of chronic lung disease, smoking increases the risk of pneumococcal disease and increases the severity of many pulmonary infections.

- Long-standing respiratory symptoms in a smoker suggest a diagnosis of chronic obstructive pulmonary disease (COPD). Although *Streptococcus pneumoniae* is still the most common cause of an LRTI in this setting, organisms such as *Haemophilus influenzae* and *Moraxella catarrhalis* are more common than in the general population.

- Bronchiectasis or cystic fibrosis: consider organisms such as *Staphylococcus aureus*, *Pseudomonas aeruginosa* and *Burkholderia cepacia*.

- Immunocompromise such as HIV: bacterial pneumonia is significantly more common in HIV-infected patients, but don't forget tuberculosis (TB), *Pneumocystis carinii* and fungal infection (see Section 2.11).

- A past history of TB, although TB usually presents more insidiously (see Section 1.1.3).

- Possibility of aspiration pneumonia: recent coma, swallowing difficulties and binge drinking.

Examination

Is the patient well, ill, very ill or nearly dead? For details of the clinical approach to the patient who is very breathless, see *Acute Medicine*, Section 1.2.5.

Look for evidence of respiratory failure and signs of acute or chronic lung disease. Pay particular attention to the following.

- Vital signs: pulse rate, BP, respiratory rate and temperature.

- Central cyanosis.

- Exclusion of pneumothorax.

TABLE 11 AETIOLOGY OF COMMUNITY-ACQUIRED PNEUMONIA

Frequency	Pathogen
Most common	*Streptococcus pneumoniae*
Common	*Haemophilus influenzae*
	Moraxella catarrhalis
	Mycoplasma pneumoniae
	Chlamydia pneumoniae
Less common	*Legionella pneumophila*
	Chlamydia psittaci
	Coxiella burnetii
	Staphylococcus aureus
	Influenza virus (frequent during epidemics/pandemics)

- Focal lung signs: consolidation, pleural rub or pleural effusion/empyema.

- Check peak flow rate and monitor arterial oxygen saturation (pulse oximetry).

- Look at the sputum (and make sure that it is sent for culture).

Note that wheeze signifies bronchospasm, probably as a result of exacerbation of COPD or asthma in this context, but it can also be generated by pulmonary oedema. Look for evidence of finger clubbing, suggesting chronic suppurative lung disease or an underlying bronchial carcinoma. This is unlikely, but you'll miss it if you don't look.

> ⚠ A normal respiratory rate is 10–16 breaths/minute. When near death the respiratory rate will fall as the patient becomes more exhausted, reaching zero when he or she dies.
>
> Always think 'Is this person looking exhausted?' If so, call for help from the intensive care unit (ICU) sooner rather than later.

Investigation

Blood tests

- FBC: a marked neutrophilia suggests bacterial pneumonia. In pneumococcal pneumonia a low white cell count is a poor prognostic sign. The white cell count is often normal in cases of atypical pneumonia, with the exception of Legionnaire's disease where a neutrophil leucocytosis is seen. Low haemoglobin may be the result of haemolysis, eg *Mycoplasma pneumoniae*.

- Electrolytes and renal function: renal impairment and

hyponatraemia are markers of severe disease, the latter being particularly likely in Legionnaire's disease.

- Liver function tests: mild hepatitis may occur in infection as a result of *Mycoplasma pneumoniae*, *Legionella pneumophila*, *Coxiella burnetii* and *Chlamydia psittaci*.

Check arterial blood gases in any patient with oxygen saturation <95% on pulse oximetry, who is very unwell or who looks as though he or she might retain CO_2. Significant metabolic acidosis is a poor prognostic factor and an indication for intensive care.

Microbiological tests

- Respiratory tract: sputum for bacterial culture. Always perform a diagnostic aspirate on any pleural effusion to exclude an empyema. Pleural biopsy may be helpful if there is suspicion of TB

(or malignancy). Bronchial lavage is appropriate in selected cases.

- Blood cultures: may yield the responsible organism.

- Serology: acute and convalescent for atypical organisms if these are suspected. Rapid diagnostic tests for *Legionella* spp. can be performed on urine and blood.

Imaging

On the CXR, look for evidence of consolidation, cavitation and lymphadenopathy. However, do not forget that although changes on a CXR may suggest certain diagnoses, they are not diagnostic of specific pathogens (Fig. 12).

> 🔑 Don't forget that atypical pneumonias commonly present with a gradual onset, dry cough and without any focal chest signs. Always perform a CXR if you suspect atypical pneumonia (Fig. 13).

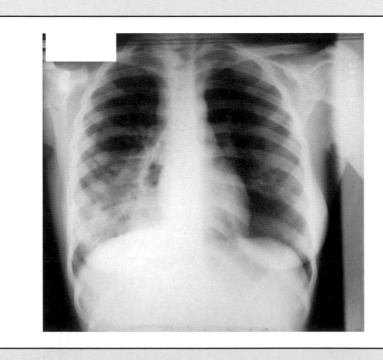

▲**Fig. 12** CXR from a patient admitted with right lower lobe consolidation and treated for bacterial pneumonia. When the patient failed to respond to antibiotics, an acid-fast sputum smear was positive, indicating TB.

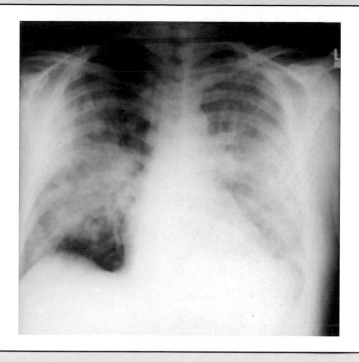

▲ **Fig. 13** CXR from a patient with severe Legionnaire's disease. The patient was a smoker who had recently returned from a package holiday in Europe. His chest was clear on examination, but he was markedly hypoxic and the radiograph shows extensive consolidation.

Management

Patients may die from respiratory failure or failure to control infection: management must be aimed at both aspects.

You need to act quickly if the patient looks very unwell, is centrally cyanosed, is very tachypnoeic (30 breaths/minute) or looks as though he or she is becoming exhausted. For discussion of the management of the patient who is very breathless and has respiratory failure, see *Acute Medicine,* Section 1.2.5.

Immediate management of the very breathless patient

- Check airway, breathing and circulation.
- Exclude tension pneumothorax.
- Sit patient up and give high-flow oxygen.
- Give nebulised bronchodilator.
- Monitor with pulse oximetry.
- Check blood gases.
- Establish diagnosis and treat if possible.
- Call for help from the ICU sooner rather than later.

Definition of severe pneumonia

The British Thoracic Society (BTS) has described the CURB 65 score for identifying patients with severe pneumonia. Two or more features indicate severe disease, and scores of three or above are associated with high mortality and need for ICU treatment.

CURB 65 criteria

- Confusion.
- Urea elevated >7.0 mmol/L.
- Respiratory rate >30 breaths/minute.
- BP ≤90 mmHg systolic, ≤60 mmHg diastolic.
- Age >65.

Supportive care

The following are important aspects.

- Give high-flow oxygen, monitoring oxygen saturation with pulse oximetry and repeating blood gases if there is deterioration or any chance of CO_2 retention.

- Give intravenous fluids.
- Give adequate analgesia if coughing is painful.

Antibiotic therapy

Antimicrobial therapy is based on the assessment of the probable aetiological agent and the severity of the illness. The BTS guidelines recommend an extended-spectrum penicillin or macrolide alone for uncomplicated LRTI, with a second- or third-generation cephalosporin plus a macrolide for more severe disease. When a patient fails to respond to first-line therapy, consider the possibility of underlying immunocompromise, TB, lung cancer, bronchial obstruction, lung abscess or empyema formation.

BTS guidelines for the treatment of community-acquired pneumonia

- Mild-to-moderate infection: extended-spectrum penicillin (amoxicillin) alone or plus a macrolide (erythromycin). In mild cases and in patients with penicillin allergy, a macrolide alone may be sufficient. Give oral therapy unless it is not possible to use the oral route.
- Severe pneumonia: parenteral therapy with co-amoxiclav or a second- or third-generation cephalosporin plus a macrolide (oral or intravenous).
- Suspected Legionnaire's disease: high-dose parenteral erythromycin 1 g 6-hourly; plus consider adding oral rifampicin.

1.3.5 Fever, back pain and weak legs

Scenario

A 54-year-old Somalian refugee complains of back pain and weak legs. He gives a 3-month history of weight loss and night sweats.

Introduction

For any patient who presents with leg weakness and back pain, your first thought must be of spinal cord compression. This is a medical emergency and an immediate assessment should be made (see *Acute Medicine*, Section 1.2.28; and *Neurology*, Section 1.4.1). Weight loss and night sweats make infection or malignancy high probabilities in the differential diagnoses, and the knowledge that the patient is from Somalia suggests tuberculosis (TB). However, it is important to consider other possibilities, both infectious (Table 12) and non-infectious, such as trauma, malignancy or a ruptured aortic aneurysm. Do not exclude the possibility of immunocompromise and HIV infection in this patient.

History of the presenting problem

A detailed description of the symptoms is required.

- The pain: where is it, is there any radiation, how long has it been present, is it constant and is it present at night?

- The weakness: is there true loss of power, or is movement restricted by pain? Was it of sudden or gradual onset? Is it bilateral? What activities are interfered with?

- Associated symptoms: ask specifically about bowel and bladder function. Is there incoordination? Are there associated sensory symptoms?

- Features of systemic disease including night sweats: has he measured his temperature or had rigors? Any weight loss or symptoms in other body systems may point to an additional focus of infection or site of primary/secondary malignancy.

- Is there any past history of neurological problems or malignancy?

Other relevant history

Ask about other risk factors for infection.

- How long has he been in the UK?

- Is there a past history of TB or known contacts with others who have the disease?

- HIV: remember that HIV is essentially a heterosexual disease in Africa and his place of origin is in itself a risk factor. Are there any other features in the history that are suggestive, eg chronic diarrhoeal disease, long-standing weight loss or recurrent infections?

Examination

General features

First impressions are important. If this man is a fit, healthy-looking individual moving about the bed, you will think differently than if he were wasted with oral thrush, widespread lymphadenopathy and unable to move his legs. A complete general examination, including rectal examination, is required. The following might suggest immundeficiency:

- obvious weight loss and cachexia;

- generalised lymphadenopathy;

- oral lesions (look for *Candida*, herpes simplex virus, hairy leucoplakia and Kaposi's sarcoma);

- rashes and skin lesions;

- hepatosplenomegaly;

- genital pathology, eg testicular masses.

Look specifically for other features that might suggest an infective cause for his symptoms:

- infective endocarditis (peripheral stigmata and cardiac murmurs);

- TB (abnormal chest signs).

Neurological

Your priority is clearly to make an assessment of this man's leg weakness. Does he have clinical evidence of cord compression? (See *Acute Medicine*, Section 1.2.28 and *Neurology*, Section 1.4.1.) Examine his back: is there an obvious deformity or abscess? Does he have an area of localised tenderness?

TABLE 12 CAUSES OF VERTEBRAL OSTEOMYELITIS AND DISCITIS

Frequency	Cause	Comment
Common	*Staphylococcus aureus* *Mycobacterium tuberculosis*	>50% pyogenic vertebral osteomyelitis
Less common	Coliforms	Risk factors include intravenous drug use and urinary tract infections; more common in the elderly
	Streptococci	Especially in association with infective endocarditis
	Brucellosis	Consider if the patient has a relevant travel history

---

Back pain and weak legs

- Perform a full neurological examination: is there spinal cord compression? Look for increased tone in the legs, weakness, up-going plantars and a sensory level.
- Examine the back.
- Look for other septic foci.

Back pain, fever and weak legs

- The absence of neurological signs does not mean that there isn't a lesion that needs urgent intervention. The patient may go on to develop cord compression or suffer cord infarction after spinal artery thrombosis in association with a spinal epidural abscess.
- Do not be complacent. Aggressive investigation and management before an irreversible neurological event is preferable to waiting for something to happen. If in doubt, always perform urgent spinal imaging and obtain a surgical opinion.

HIV testing in tuberculosis

- HIV testing should be considered in *all* cases of TB infection as co-infection is common, particularly in sub-Saharan Africa.
- TB is now one of the most common AIDS-diagnostic conditions in HIV-positive patients in the UK.
- HIV is a treatable disease and failure to diagnose it can have serious clinical and medico-legal consequences.
- Enquiring about risk factors for HIV is often unrewarding and a more practical approach is to offer the test to all patients with suspected or confirmed TB.

Investigation

Blood tests

- Blood cultures: these are essential, and preferably done on more than one set of blood samples.
- FBC: is the white cell count raised? Is the total lymphocyte count abnormally low? A low lymphocyte count is common in disseminated TB or may be a sign of HIV infection.
- Electrolytes and renal/liver/bone function tests.
- Inflammatory markers: C-reactive protein and erythrocyte sedimentation rate.
- Serum immunoglobulins: myeloma does not seem at all likely in this context, but it is a bad diagnosis to miss!
- Vitamin B_{12} and folate levels.
- HIV testing (after appropriate discussion; see Section 1.2.5).
- Take serum for storage, which can be used later for serology if necessary.

Imaging

- CXR: look for evidence of old or active TB, hilar lymphadenopathy and a paraspinal mass, especially if the back pain is thoracic.
- Radiographs of the spine (anteroposterior and lateral) (Fig. 14a): look for bony destruction, wedge fractures and lytic or sclerotic lesions.
- CT or (preferably) MRI of the spine (Fig. 14b): this must be performed urgently (same day) if spinal cord compression is suspected. An MRI scan can exclude osteomyelitis, a paraspinal mass or an abscess, and can detect cord compression.

Other diagnostic tests

- In the event of a diagnosis of a mass lesion, irrespective of the need for débridement, drainage or decompression, there is a need to obtain tissue for histology and microbiology.
- Sputum and urine for mycobacterial detection and culture.

- Tuberculin skin testing (Heaf or Mantoux test) and interferon-γ blood tests (T spot-TB and QuantiFERON tests) may be helpful in cases of suspected TB.
- Echocardiogram in suspected subacute bacterial endocarditis.
- Whole-body CT scan if malignancy is suspected.
- Tumour markers if a particular malignancy is suspected.

Management

Paraspinal abscess

Management is directed towards the underlying cause and preserving spinal cord function. Urgent drainage is required, with microscopy and Gram and auramine staining of pus. Every attempt should be made to obtain histological and microbiological samples before commencing antimicrobial therapy, but antimicrobial therapy can be started after taking blood cultures if this is not possible. The empirical regimen will depend on the immunological status of patient and the likely cause. Discussions with colleagues in microbiology and infectious diseases departments may be helpful. For an immunocompetent individual with a pyogenic abscess, consider empirical treatment with a third-generation cephalosporin plus flucloxacillin and metronidazole. To obtain good penetration into bone, high-dose parenteral antibiotics are required. Antituberculous and antibrucella therapy should be considered where clinically appropriate.

Vertebral osteomyelitis

- Early surgical intervention is often needed for diagnosis or decompression.

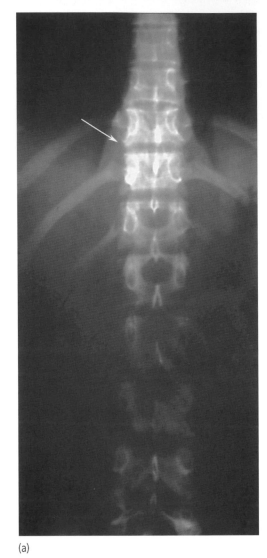

(a)

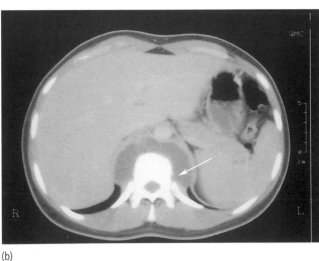

(b)

▲**Fig. 14** **(a)** Plain radiograph demonstrating a paraspinal soft tissue mass (arrow). **(b)** CT scan from the same patient demonstrating a paravertebral collection (arrow). This was aspirated and confirmed to be TB. (Copyright of Dr C. Conlon.)

- Tissue/pus should be sent for histology or cytology, and culture for standard bacteria, mycobacteria and brucellosis. If the patient is immunocompromised, also request nocardia and fungal culture.
- Consider radiotherapy and steroids for patients with compressive lesions due to malignancy.

Vertebral osteomyelitis and discitis

A tissue biopsy is essential for a definitive diagnosis and should be obtained before commencing antimicrobial therapy. Débridement and spinal stabilisation may be needed, and should be considered urgently if there are neurological signs. In pyogenic infection, give an initial 4–6 weeks of parenteral antibiotics followed by a further 6 weeks of oral therapy, as guided by the microbiology. Tuberculosis and brucellosis require specific regimens (see Sections 2.5 and 2.6.1).

1.3.6 Drug user with fever and a murmur

Scenario

A 34-year-old intravenous drug user arrives in the Emergency Department short of breath. On examination he is febrile and has a loud early diastolic murmur in the aortic region.

Introduction

The differential diagnosis of infection in intravenous drug users is wide. The cardiac murmur places endocarditis high on the list, but do not be blinkered and miss another obvious focus of infection. For instance, could he have pneumonia and long-standing aortic regurgitation (probably from previous endocarditis)?

History of the presenting problem

Breathlessness

The most obvious explanations for breathlessness are pulmonary oedema due to aortic valve dysfunction or pneumonia. The length of history and the severity of symptoms are important. Ask the following.

- How long has he been breathless?

- Was it of sudden onset or gradual?

- How severe is the problem? What is he restricted in doing?

Cardiac failure resulting from acute valve rupture secondary to endocarditis will have a sudden onset, whereas the less dramatic development of aortic incompetence or a pneumonic process may have a longer history.

Other symptoms

- Has he had fevers, rigors or night sweats? These could be found in endocarditis or pneumonia, but rigors would be in favour of the latter.

- Are there any respiratory symptoms? Chest pain, productive cough or haemoptysis would suggest pneumonia in this context, as would any history compatible with aspiration. Also consider infected pulmonary emboli, particularly if he has been injecting into leg veins.

- Is he more breathless lying down? No one who is severely short of breath will want to lie down, but a clear history of orthopnoea favours pulmonary oedema.

Drug use

Is he still injecting? Where does he inject and has he had any complications at the injection sites? What has he been mixing the drugs with, and does he lick the needles? This is a common practice and increases the likelihood of infection with oral organisms. Has he ever shared needles or equipment? Do not forget the possibility of HIV or hepatitis B or C co-infection.

Relevant past history

It is important to try to establish whether the murmur is old or new.

- Has he had endocarditis in the past?

- Has he ever been admitted to hospital for a long course of antibiotics before (and where, so that records can be sought)?

- Has he previously been told he has a heart murmur/funny sound?

Also ask if he has been tested for hepatitis and/or HIV in the past.

> ⚠️ Remember that a past history of endocarditis is a risk factor for further episodes, but do not gain a false sense of security from being told that a murmur has been noted before.

In the febrile, breathless intravenous drug user consider the following.

- Endocarditis: intravenous drug use is associated with a high risk of endocarditis, most commonly right-sided.
- Cardiac failure: secondary to valvular incompetence.
- Pneumonia: community-acquired pneumonia; drug use increases risk of aspiration pneumonia.
- Pulmonary emboli: either septic emboli in association with right-sided endocarditis or secondary to a venous thrombosis. Femoral injection increases the risk of thrombosis, infected or otherwise.
- Immunosuppression: intravenous drug use is a risk factor for HIV. Is the patient known to be HIV positive?

Examination

As described in Sections 1.3.1 and 1.3.2. Is the man well, ill, very ill or nearly dead? Does he need immediate resuscitation? See *Acute Medicine*, Section 1.2.2 for details of the approach to the patient who is very ill or worse.

A full physical examination is required, concentrating particularly on looking for evidence of the following.

- Injection sites: do any of these look obviously infected?

- Bacterial endocarditis: peripheral stigmata and cardiac murmurs.

- Pneumonia: signs of consolidation.

- Pulmonary oedema: gallop rhythm and basal crackles.

- HIV infection (see Section 1.3.20).

- Deep vein thrombosis/septic thrombophlebitis.

Peripheral stigmata of endocarditis

- Splinter haemorrhages.
- Janeway's lesions: transient, non-tender and macular patches on the palms or soles (very rare).
- Osler's nodes: indurated, red and tender lesions, usually in the pulps of fingers or toes.
- Peripheral emboli.
- Conjunctival petechial haemorrhages (Fig. 15).
- Infective endophthalmitis.
- Roth's spots: fundal haemorrhages with pale central area.
- Splenomegaly.
- Microscopic haematuria.

Remember that peripheral signs are not present in all cases, particularly if the valve lesion is right-sided.

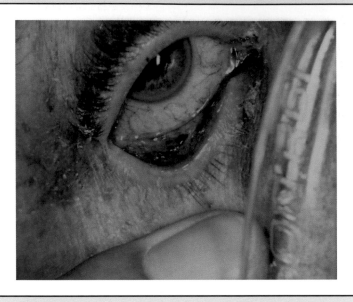

▲**Fig. 15** Peripheral stigmata of endocarditis: subconjunctival haemorrhages.

⚠ Cardiac failure developing in the context of an early diastolic murmur suggests acute aortic valve insufficiency. This is a medical emergency and the patient should be immediately referred for a cardiothoracic surgical opinion.

Imaging

- CXR: is there pulmonary oedema or obvious pneumonia? Diffuse patchy changes or abscesses would be in keeping with septic emboli secondary to right-sided endocarditis. Look at the apices and remember tuberculosis in this population. If the patient is breathless but the CXR is normal, think of pulmonary emboli and consider proceeding to CT pulmonary angiography or ventilation–perfusion scanning.

- Echocardiography: an essential investigation to assess valve function and look for supportive evidence of endocarditis (Figs 16 and 17). However, remember that echocardiography cannot exclude endocarditis and the transthoracic approach is less sensitive than the transoesophageal, particularly when looking at the right side of the heart and the aortic root.

Investigation

ECG

Particularly note conduction abnormalities, eg long PR interval, because these are associated with aortic root abscess. Look for right heart strain in pulmonary embolism.

Blood tests

- Blood cultures: these must be taken before antibiotic therapy; ideally three sets separated in space and time. The isolation of the aetiological agent (Table 13) is the key to best management of infective endocarditis.

- FBC, electrolytes, renal and liver function, C-reactive protein and erythrocyte sedimentation rate.

- HIV and hepatitis B and C: to be considered (with consent from the patient).

- Arterial blood gases: if the patient is very ill.

TABLE 13 AETIOLOGICAL AGENTS IN INFECTIVE ENDOCARDITIS		
Heart valve affected	**Occurrence and frequency**	**Aetiological agents involved**
Native valve	Common	Viridans streptococci *Staphylococcus aureus*
	Less common	Enterococci HACEK group of organisms β-Haemolytic streptococci Coliforms, pneumococci, fungi, *Brucella* spp., *Bartonella* spp., *Coxiella* spp. (Q fever), *Chlamydia* spp.
Prosthetic valve	Early after surgery	*Staphylococcus epidermidis* *Staphylococcus aureus*
	Late, ie >1 year postoperatively	As with native valve
Intravenous drug users	Common	*Staphylococcus aureus*
	Less common	Gram-negative bacilli, *Haemophilus* spp., *Bacillus* spp., *Corynebacterium* spp., fungi

HACEK, *Haemophilus* spp., *Actinobacillus* spp., *Cardiobacterium* spp., *Eikenella* spp. and *Kingella* spp.

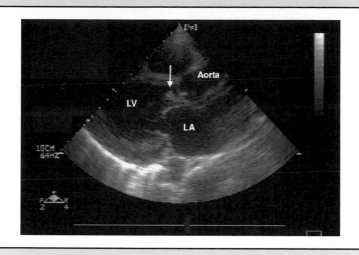

▲**Fig. 16** Transthoracic echocardiogram showing a vegetation on the aortic valve (arrowed). LA, left atrium; LV, left ventricle.

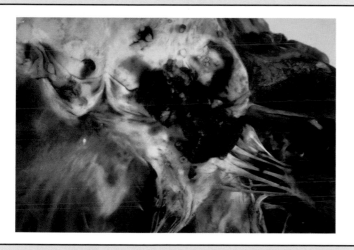

▲**Fig. 17** Pathology specimen showing a vegetation on the aortic valve.

Serial echocardiography may detect complications that require surgical intervention such as progressive valve destruction and intramyocardial abscess formation.

> An echocardiogram can support a diagnosis of endocarditis, but it can never exclude it.

Diagnosis of endocarditis

The diagnosis of infective endocarditis is clinical and based on the combination of cardiac, embolic and infective features, along with isolation of an appropriate organism from the blood (Table 14).

Management

Management of the patient who is very ill with pneumonia (see Section 1.3.4) or severe bacterial sepsis (see Section 1.3.2) is covered elsewhere.

Treat hypotension and heart failure urgently, and then consider treatment of endocarditis.

Endocarditis

The aim of antimicrobial treatment is to eradicate valvular infection, which requires prolonged intravenous bactericidal therapy. Combination therapy, with two drugs for synergy, is proven to be better than monotherapy for streptococci. Close liaison with diagnostic microbiology is essential: in addition to standard antimicrobial susceptibility testing, the minimal inhibitory concentration (MIC) of the infecting organism should be measured to guide treatment and length of therapy (Table 15). Culture-negative endocarditis poses a particular

TABLE 14 DUKE CRITERIA FOR THE DIAGNOSIS OF ENDOCARDITIS: DEFINITE DIAGNOSIS REQUIRES TWO MAJOR, ONE MAJOR AND THREE MINOR, OR FIVE MINOR CRITERIA

Grade	Criteria

Major	Positive blood culture
	    Typical organism, eg *Staphylococcus aureus* or viridans streptococci
	    Persistently positive cultures (two 12 hours apart, or three over >1 hour)
	    with compatible organism
	Endocardial involvement
	    New regurgitant murmur
	    Positive echocardiogram for infective endocarditis

Minor	Predisposing cardiac lesion or intravenous drug use Fever Vascular phenomena: petechiae, emboli, mycotic aneurysms Immunological phenomena: glomerulonephritis, Roth's spots, etc. Echocardiogram consistent with infective endocarditis, but not meeting major criteria Positive blood cultures, but not meeting major criteria, or serological evidence of active infection with plausible organism

TABLE 15 ANTIMICROBIAL THERAPY OF COMMON CAUSES OF ENDOCARDITIS

Organism	Therapeutic options	Duration (weeks)
Viridans streptococci: highly susceptible to penicillin	Benzylpenicillin 12–16 g/day Benzylpenicillin + gentamicin 3 mg/kg daily[1] Vancomycin 15 mg/kg twice daily[1]	4 2 4
Viridans streptococci and *Streptococcus bovis*: partially penicillin resistant, with MIC >0.1 mg/L	Benzylpenicillin + gentamicin[1]	4, stopping gentamicin after first 2
Enterococci	Vancomycin[1] Ampicillin or benzylpenicillin + gentamicin Vancomycin + gentamicin	4 4–6[2] 4–6[2]
Vancomycin-resistant enterococci	Seek specialist advice urgently	
Staphylococcus aureus: sensitive to flucloxacillin	Flucloxacillin 8–16 g/day; also consider adding a second agent	4–6 4–6
Meticillin-resistant *Staphylococcus aureus*	Vancomycin[1]	

1. Monitor therapeutic drug levels.
2. Increased risk of renal toxicity and ototoxicity.

therapeutic challenge: initial therapy should be based on the clinical picture with specialist advice.

Surgical intervention is indicated for failure of medical therapy, severe valve damage or intracardiac abscess formation, and where systemic emboli continue despite adequate medical therapy. Surgical removal of the valve is more often required in endocarditis on a prosthetic valve, in an infection resulting from fungi or *Brucella* spp., or in Q fever.

Septic thrombophlebitis

Incise and drain any collections. Anticoagulation and prolonged antibiotic therapy may be required for infected thrombus. Rarely, surgical intervention is required for prolonged sepsis and embolisation.

1.3.7 Fever and heart failure

Scenario

A 19-year-old woman has a 'flu-like illness followed by breathlessness and chest pain. On examination there is a scratchy pericardial rub and evidence of biventricular failure.

Introduction

When dealing with any patient presenting with chest pain, the first priority is to exclude life-threatening causes such as myocardial infarction, aortic dissection and pulmonary embolism. However, both myocardial infarction and aortic dissection would be extremely improbable in a woman of this age. Pulmonary embolism would be more likely, but in this patient the presumptive diagnosis

must be viral myopericarditis. This is a difficult diagnosis to prove definitively, so the priority must be to exclude other treatable causes.

History of the presenting problem

When taking the history, consider other causes of chest pain (see *Cardiology*, Sections 1.4.3 and 1.4.6; and *Acute Medicine*, Section 1.2.2), but bear in mind the causes of myocarditis (Table 16). It is very important to establish when the disease started: this enables interpretation of serology and helps put progression into context, which is important for identifying those with a poor prognosis.

Symptoms suggesting an infectious cause

Systemic symptoms such as fever, rigors, weight loss and lethargy suggest an infectious aetiology. Ask about other features of viral infection, including rash, sore throat, headache and diarrhoea, although these features are clearly very non-specific. Joint pains are common, but arthritis is more suggestive of connective tissue disease. Severe muscle pain or marked weakness may be the result of infective myositis, but consider primary muscle disease.

Symptoms suggesting pulmonary embolism

Could this woman have had a pulmonary embolus? Ask about risk factors, pleuritic chest pain (which can be difficult or impossible to distinguish from pericarditic pain), haemoptysis and leg pain/swelling.

Symptoms suggesting myocardial involvement

Fever and chest pain could be the result of uncomplicated pericarditis (see *Cardiology*, Section 2.6.1), but the development of heart failure indicates probable myocardial involvement. It is therefore important to document these symptoms, both to confirm the diagnosis and to form a baseline against which to judge disease progression. Ask about breathlessness, orthopnoea, palpitations, ankle swelling and syncope.

Other relevant history
Take note of the following.

- Alcohol and recreational drugs, particularly cocaine, which can lead to cardiac failure.

- Travel history: a number of unusual infections can lead to myocarditis (Table 16).

- HIV risk factors (see Section 1.1.5).

- Previous history of illness suggesting Kawasaki's disease.

- Previous cancer treatment, both chemotherapy and radiotherapy, which can lead to delayed cardiomyopathy, but fever would be unusual.

- Current and past drug therapy.

- Risk factors for coronary artery disease.

- Family history, particularly of muscle and connective tissue diseases.

> ⚠️ **Chest pain in a young woman**
> - Acute myocardial infarction is unlikely but can occur at this age as a result of either inherited lipid disorders or autoimmune/vasculitic disorders such as SLE, PAN or Behçet's disease.
> - Consider aortic dissection if features of Marfan's syndrome are present.

Examination

General features
As described in Sections 1.3.1 and 1.3.2. Is the woman well, ill, very ill or nearly dead? Does she need immediate resuscitation? See *Acute Medicine*, Section 1.2.2 for details of the approach to the patient who is very ill or worse.

A full physical examination is required, with particular attention to the following.

- Rash: suggests an infectious aetiology or vasculitis.

- Throat: inflammation suggests a viral aetiology (eg coxsackie virus); consider the possibility of streptococcal infection, and also diphtheria in patients with appropriate travel/contact history.

- Lymph nodes/liver/spleen.

- Joints: looking for synovitis.

- Features of acute rheumatic fever.

Cardiovascular
Look specifically for the following.

- Tachycardia: may be out of proportion to the degree of fever in myocarditis.

- Pericardial friction rub: indicates pericarditis.

- Cardiac murmurs: functional mitral regurgitation is common in myocardial failure.

- Signs of heart failure: high JVP, displaced apex, gallop rhythm, basal crackles, hepatomegaly (pulsatile if tricuspid regurgitation) and peripheral oedema.

- Cardiac tamponade: tachycardia, very high JVP and pulsus paradoxus (inspiratory fall in systolic BP of >10 mmHg).

TABLE 16 CAUSES OF MYOCARDITIS		
Type		**Examples**
Infectious	Viral	Common: enteroviruses, eg coxsackie virus A and B, poliovirus, echovirus Less common: influenza, CMV, EBV, hepatitis B, HIV
	Bacterial	Lyme disease Myocarditis can rarely complicate systemic staphylococcal, streptococcal, meningococcal, mycoplasma and rickettsial infections Bacterial toxin-mediated, eg diphtheria
	Parasitic	Toxoplasmosis (immunocompromised host), American trypanosomiasis (Chagas' disease), trichinosis
	Fungal	Histoplasmosis and disseminated fungal infections in an immunocompromised host
Non-infectious	Autoimmune rheumatic/ vasculitic diseases	SLE, dermatomyositis, PAN, rheumatoid arthritis
	Idiopathic	Sarcoidosis, Kawasaki's disease, giant-cell myocarditis
	Toxins	Scorpion bite
	Drugs	Alcohol, cocaine, daunorubicin, cyclophosphamide, doxorubicin
	Endocrine	Thyrotoxicosis, phaeochromocytoma

CMV; cytomegalovirus; EBV, Epstein–Barr virus; PAN, polyarteritis nodosa; SLE, systemic lupus erythematosus.

Diagnosis of tamponade

The three critical signs are:

- tachycardia;
- very high JVP;
- pulsus paradoxus.

Investigation

The aim is to assess and treat myocardial dysfunction while looking for treatable underlying diseases. There is no specific antimicrobial therapy for most of the infectious causes of myocarditis.

Blood tests

- FBC: most viral infections will show modest lymphocytosis, sometimes with atypical lymphocytes. Bacterial infection is associated with neutrophil leucocytosis, and there may be marked eosinophilia in parasitic infections.

- Inflammatory markers: C-reactive protein (CRP), erythrocyte sedimentation rate (ESR) and plasma viscosity. Viral infections usually cause mild to modest elevation of CRP. A high ESR points to an inflammatory process but is very non-specific.

- Biochemical profile including cardiac enzymes: cardiac enzymes may be elevated and mimic myocardial infarction. Beware of skeletal muscle involvement, which may increase total creatine phosphokinase in the absence of myocardial disease, and check myocardial-specific tests, such as the creatine kinase (CK) fraction CK-MB or troponin I, and follow sequential measurements. In myocarditis the enzymes will tend to remain elevated or rise, whereas in acute myocardial infarction the enzymes will fall after the acute event. Renal

impairment indicates a poor prognosis.

- Autoantibodies such as antinuclear antibody, double-stranded DNA and antineutrophil cytoplasmic antibody as appropriate.

Cultures and serology

- Blood cultures in all cases, along with culture of pleural or pericardial fluid if available.

- Serology: take an acute sample and make sure the date of onset is clear to the laboratory. Single elevated titres may be indicative of infection with coxsackievirus or influenza. IgM tests are available for CMV and EBV. Raised anti-streptolysin O titre indicates recent streptococcal infection. Rickettsial infection (in the appropriate setting of foreign travel) can be diagnosed on the basis of an elevated IgM level, but this test will not be available immediately in most hospitals in the UK. Make sure that arrangements are in place to take a follow-up sample after 10–14 days to confirm a rise in titre.

- Viral culture/polymerase chain reaction (PCR): throat swabs sent in viral culture fluid and faeces samples for virology may be helpful in diagnosing enterovirus infection.

ECG

There may be widespread ST-segment changes in myocarditis, along with T-wave inversion. These do not follow the normal evolution of changes seen in myocardial ischaemia and may last for weeks.

Imaging

- CXR: may reveal a large heart, resulting from either dilatation or

pericardial effusion, and pulmonary congestion/oedema.

- Echocardiogram: should be obtained urgently to assess the degree of ventricular dilatation and dysfunction, and also to look for a pericardial effusion. Serial echocardiography can monitor disease progression and response to therapy.

- If there is clinical suspicion of pulmonary embolism, CT pulmonary angiography or ventilation–perfusion scanning will be required.

Histology

The gold standard for diagnosis of myocarditis is an endomyocardial biopsy, but this is very rarely performed. Histology may reveal inflammatory changes accompanied by lymphocytic infiltration (Fig. 18), and can also be used to provide tissue for analysis for viral genome by PCR or *in situ* hybridisation.

Management

If the woman is very ill, then immediate management will be as described in Section 1.3.2.

In viral myocarditis the appropriate treatment is supportive: no antiviral therapy has been shown to be effective. The treatment of ventricular failure will depend on its severity. The use of corticosteroids is controversial: there are no clear data showing efficacy and in acute viral myocarditis they may accelerate disease progression. Most cases will resolve spontaneously over weeks or months, but a minority may progress to severe cardiac failure and death unless heart transplantation is considered. The long-term prognosis following fulminant myocarditis is generally good and aggressive supportive care

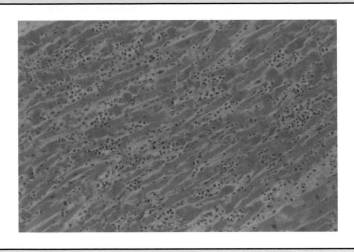

▲**Fig. 18** Cardiac histology from a fatal case of viral myocarditis in a 48-year-old man. High-power view showing disordered and apoptotic myocytes with a marked lymphocytic infiltrate. (Courtesy of Dr M. Falzon, Ealing Hospital.)

is justified. Some patients develop a chronic dilated cardiomyopathy, but although this has an inflammatory basis there is no benefit shown from trials of immunosuppression.

> ⚠ Do not miss rare cases of autoimmune myocarditis. Always consider this diagnosis and investigate accordingly, because immunosuppression may reverse the condition or prevent further deterioration.

1.3.8 Persistent fever in the intensive care unit

Scenario

You are asked to see a 20-year-old man who is being ventilated on the intensive care unit (ICU). He was involved in a severe road traffic accident 4 weeks earlier and now has a persistent fever and elevated white cell count.

Introduction

Infection will clearly be the most likely cause of fever and leucocytosis, but do not ignore non-infectious problems such as gut ischaemia or adverse drug reactions. The EPIC one-day snapshot of European ICUs revealed a point prevalence of infection of 16%.

Why not just prescribe blind broad-spectrum antibiotics?

The challenge when managing patients such as the one described in this scenario is to locate and treat serious infection, while not overusing empirical broad-spectrum antimicrobial agents that increase the risk of antibiotic resistance and fungal superinfection.

History of the presenting problem

History-taking in this situation is very different from that in usual general medical practice: most patients are unconscious and most of the relevant information comes from events that have happened after hospitalisation. As you look for clues, consider the following possibilities.

- Nosocomial pneumonia: hospital-acquired pneumonia is a common cause of fever in the ventilated patient. Organisms include *Streptococcus pneumoniae*, *Staphylococcus aureus*, Enterobacteriaceae and *Pseudomonas aeruginosa*.

- Nosocomial urinary tract infection (UTI): *Escherichia coli* is the most common associated organism, but infection with *Proteus* spp., enterococci, *Klebsiella* spp. and *Pseudomonas* spp., and *Candida* spp. also occurs.

- Wound infection: you may well be the only person to take the trouble to uncover the wound.

- Intravascular line infection: sick patients often have multiple cannulae, which are a common source of fever in the ICU (Fig. 19). Organisms include *Staphylococcus aureus* and *Staphylococcus epidermidis* (coagulase-negative staphylococci), but the range is wide.

- Infection of a prosthesis: any foreign body is at risk of infection.

- Sinusitis: this may complicate nasogastric tube feeding.

- Fungal infection: can explain persistent fever and deterioration despite broad-spectrum antibiotics.

- *Clostridium difficile* infection.

- Thromboembolic disease: deep vein thrombosis (DVT) or pulmonary emboli may occur in an immobilised patient despite prophylaxis.

- Drug fever.

Medical records

Thoroughly review the medical notes, intensive care charts and investigation results. These will tell you how long the fever has been present and give important information regarding procedures and complications, eg in this case you may discover that the patient

▲ **Fig. 19** Pus coming from a peripheral venous cannula site when the cannula was removed. The patient had been admitted with epilepsy and developed fever as he was discharged from the ICU to the ward. Meticillin-resistant *Staphylococcus aureus* was cultured.

had a base of skull fracture and may have meningitis, or that blood transfusion-related infections must be considered.

Other staff

Talk to the nurses looking after the patient and ask specifically about changes in the skin (it is easy to miss the pressure areas), diarrhoea (*Clostridium difficile*) and the quantity/quality of the sputum that they may be aspirating from his chest. When were his various invasive lines placed or last changed? Also ask whether there have been any recent outbreaks of infection within the unit. If necessary, track down the various medical and surgical teams involved in his care, because important information is often not in the notes.

Other relevant history

Previous medical/surgical conditions and severe immunocompromise can be relevant. You may need to talk to a family member or phone the patient's GP. Often it may be necessary to consult with the

referring team outside the ICU or the referring hospital.

Examination

The patient's vital signs will be closely monitored within the ICU, but you should perform as full a physical examination as possible. This will often have been omitted by your colleagues on the ICU, perhaps in the erroneous belief that all the monitoring paraphernalia render it unnecessary. However, no monitor has been devised that will detect an abscess on someone's buttock.

Take careful note of the following.

- Skin: for cellulitis around lines; check all wounds and pressure areas.

- Lungs: for consolidation or pleural fluid.

- Heart: for new murmurs suggesting endocarditis.

- Legs: for swelling suggestive of DVT.

- Abdomen: new-onset ileus can indicate gut ischaemia or infective

colitis; a palpable gallbladder suggests acalculous cholecystitis.

- Ears, throat and sinuses: for evidence of infection.

- Fundoscopy, preferably with dilated pupils: may reveal *Candida* endophthalmitis.

- Urine: if cloudy, consider catheter-associated UTI.

Investigation

Fever in the ICU

Consider the 'usual suspects': infection of the respiratory tract, urinary tract, pressure areas and sites of surgery. If there is no apparent focus of infection and the patient is not haemodynamically compromised, consider stopping all antibiotics and reculturing.

In many ways the process is similar to that described for the patient with pyrexia of unknown origin in Section 1.1.3, with investigations looking for areas of abnormality to focus imaging and other diagnostic tests. The care of patients on the ICU should always be multidisciplinary, with the results of investigations being reviewed with the relevant specialists.

Routine blood tests

These will often be persistently abnormal in intensive care, so concentrate on newly abnormal results and look for trends, particularly in acute inflammatory markers (C-reactive protein, plasma viscosity and erythrocyte sedimentation rate). This is a complicated situation and there may be many explanations for an abnormal value, eg a rising alkaline phosphatase may be the result of acalculous cholecystitis, cholangitis, liver abscess or transfusion-acquired viral infections, or may simply be caused by drug-related cholestasis and be unrelated to the fever. Monitor organ function and acidosis because these will indicate the development of severe sepsis that requires urgent therapy.

Microbiological tests

Review all the culture results from this admission with the microbiologist, and reculture all possible sources of infection.

- Blood cultures: essential in all cases. If a central line is *in situ*, take a set through the line and a further set peripherally (see Section 3.2). Consider specific fungal blood cultures.

- Lower respiratory samples: these can be obtained by endotracheal aspiration or bronchoscopy in the ventilated patient. Such patients are usually colonised with bacteria, hence the results must be interpreted with caution. Do not forget tuberculosis, which can reactivate in debilitated ICU patients.

- Urinary microscopy and culture, but do not assume that simply because the urine culture is positive this is the cause of the fever.

- Take swabs from any wounds that appear infected.

- Culture any drain fluid and other body fluids as indicated.

- Culture any line tips that are removed.

> Trauma patients often receive multiple blood products. These can transmit cytomegalovirus and parvovirus as well as hepatitis, so consider these possibilities in cases of persistent unexplained fever, particularly where the patient is leucopenic or has evidence of hepatitis.

Imaging

- CXR: can be very difficult to interpret, particularly if the patient has adult respiratory distress syndrome, but any change from previous films should be taken seriously.

- Abdominal ultrasonography: technically difficult to perform in an intensive-care environment, but may detect cholecystitis and occult abscesses.

- CT scan of the chest and abdomen: increasingly used in ICU to detect infectious foci.

- Echocardiography: if endocarditis is suspected, but this will only help to confirm a clinical diagnosis and cannot exclude the condition (see Section 1.3.6).

Management

If the patient is stable with no obvious focus of infection

- Stop all antibiotics.

- Reculture blood, urine and endotracheal aspirates.

- Remove all unnecessary intravascular lines and change others if possible (often line-related fever will abate).

If patient is clinically unstable and developing severe sepsis

- Reculture.

- Consider empirical antibiotics: the choice is difficult and needs to be made in the light of the suspected site of infection, past and current therapy, local antibiotic policies and antimicrobial resistance patterns. Always take advice from the local microbiology laboratory.

- Consider antifungal therapy: fungal infection is becoming more common in intensive care and

adding empirical antifungal therapy, with amphotericin B, should be considered where the patient is deteriorating despite appropriate antibacterial therapy.

Further comments

One important mistake to avoid is non-surgical treatment of a surgical problem: do not hesitate to seek surgical advice.

> ⚠ **Need for surgical intervention**
> Deep-seated abscesses are unlikely to resolve without drainage, either percutaneously or operatively. When such patients are deteriorating despite antibiotics, you may need to push for surgical intervention. Do not accept the argument that 'they are too sick for an operation': they are more likely to die without one if they have an undrained collection.

1.3.9 Pyelonephritis

Scenario

> A young woman with high fever, rigors and loin pain is sent to the Medical Admissions Unit, where you are asked to review her.

Introduction

The presence of loin pain points to a diagnosis of pyelonephritis, but care must be taken to exclude other intra-abdominal and retroperitoneal pathologies. However, if the patient is unwell with presumed bacterial sepsis, 'blind' antimicrobial therapy is essential.

History of the presenting problem

If the patient has had a previous episode, this information is likely to be volunteered, but always ask. Typical urinary symptoms (frequency, dysuria, change in smell, urgency) are clearly useful pointers, but these are not always present, particularly in the elderly, people with diabetes, the immunocompromised or those who have been partially treated.

> ⚠️ Patients with symptoms of lower urinary tract infection (UTI) may also have infection of the upper urinary tract. Patients can have upper UTI without lower urinary tract symptoms.

Severity of illness

This is a key question in determining the intensity of investigation and treatment. Were these true rigors, where the patient could not control the shaking? Is there confusion or cardiovascular collapse, which is likely to indicate bacteraemia in this context? Nausea and vomiting are common features of any infection and may preclude oral therapy.

Was the pain coming from the kidney?

Site, type, radiation and intensity are essential features of the pain. Although described as loin pain, is this really the case? The strong presumption from the details given is that it is coming from the kidney, but pain in the general area of the loin could be the result of bony pain, superficial pain in the skin or soft tissue, radiated pain from the retroperitoneum, or even a basal pneumonia. Colicky pain could be caused by bowel or biliary tract disease. Other important causes of pain include pancreatitis and renal tract stones.

Other relevant history

The important aspects to cover are previous urinary or abdominal problems. Has the woman had

TABLE 17 CONDITIONS THAT INCREASE THE FREQUENCY OF UTI

Condition	Examples
Diabetes mellitus	
Pregnancy	
Mechanical problems of the urinary tract	Prostatic hypertrophy/cancer
	Urinary tract stones
	Congenital malformations
Increased/new sexual activity in women	'Honeymoon cystitis'
Immunocompromise	Multiple myeloma, HIV

previous UTIs, renal stones, instrumentation of the urinary tract or trauma and neurological diseases that may affect bladder function? Ask about conditions that can increase the risk of UTI (Table 17).

Prior antibiotic use may increase the risk of antibiotic resistance. Allergies must not be forgotten.

> 🔑 **UTI in pregnancy**
>
> The consequences of UTI are more significant in pregnant women, and also have implications for radiological investigations and antibiotic therapy.

Examination

Severity of illness

Is the patient shocked, breathless or confused? These are all signs of severe sepsis that can complicate focal urinary infection or bacteraemia. Check pulse, BP, peripheral perfusion and respiratory rate. For details of the management of the patient with profound hypotension/septicaemia, see Section 1.3.2.

The source of the pain

As the complaint is of loin pain, sit the patient up and examine the renal angle and back.

- Is there tenderness in the renal angle?

- Is there bony tenderness?

- Is there swelling or erythema, suggesting a local soft tissue problem?

- Is there a rash, eg the vesicles of shingles?

- Are there signs of basal pneumonia?

- Are there signs of endocarditis? A renal embolus may mimic pyelonephritis. This is extremely unlikely, but you'll never make the diagnosis unless you consider it.

You will clearly perform a careful abdominal examination to look for scars and swellings, examine for local tenderness (is there peritonism?), palpate for organomegaly, listen for bowel sounds and (in men) perform a digital examination of the prostate.

> ⚠️ Do not forget shingles as a cause of unilateral pain starting in the back and radiating forward (Fig. 20). The pain usually precedes the rash, so look carefully for a few spots.

Investigation

Urine dipstick

The presence of urinary nitrites and leucocytes are specific and sensitive for urinary infection, and they should be positive in most cases of pyelonephritis.

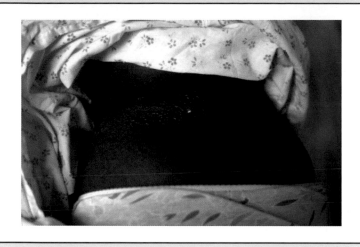

▲ **Fig. 20** T12/L1 shingles. The prodromal pain before the rash can be mistaken for renal pain.

is severely unwell or not responding to therapy. A plain radiograph may reveal a renal stone or rarely gas around the kidney (Fig. 21), but renal tract ultrasonography is the first-line modality. In suspected perinephric abscess, a CT scan may provide more detail.

Renal obstruction with infection

- This is a medical emergency.
- Urgent relief of obstruction is essential.
- Antegrade nephrostomy is usually the preferred technique.

If the diagnosis is not clear-cut, a CXR is needed to avoid missing a lower-lobe pneumonia (Fig. 22).

Microbiological investigations

Take cultures of urine and blood (see Section 3.2). Send a midstream urine (MSU) specimen for microscopy and culture before antimicrobial therapy is started, except in those patients with severe sepsis in whom therapy is urgent. At least one set of blood cultures should be taken in any ill patient with fever, again prior to antibiotic administration.

Other laboratory tests

- FBC: a raised white cell count suggests bacterial infection.

- Electrolytes and renal function: impaired renal function may be due to severe sepsis or concurrent/chronic renal disease.

- Liver function tests: impairment may be due to severe sepsis or concurrent liver disease.

- Glucose: undiagnosed diabetes.

- Inflammatory markers: high C-reactive protein suggests bacterial infection or other severe inflammatory disease.

- Amylase: to exclude pancreatitis.

Imaging

Imaging is not required immediately in uncomplicated pyelonephritis, but should be performed urgently if there is renal impairment or if the patient

Management

Initial therapy will usually be given blind, unless there is a culture result

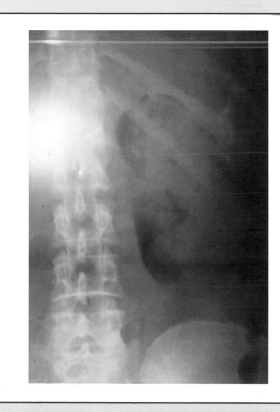

▲ **Fig. 21** Plain radiograph showing gas in and around the left kidney as a result of emphysematous pyelonephritis in a 43-year-old woman with diabetes. *Escherichia coli* was isolated from the blood and urine, and a left nephrectomy was required despite attempts to conserve the kidney.

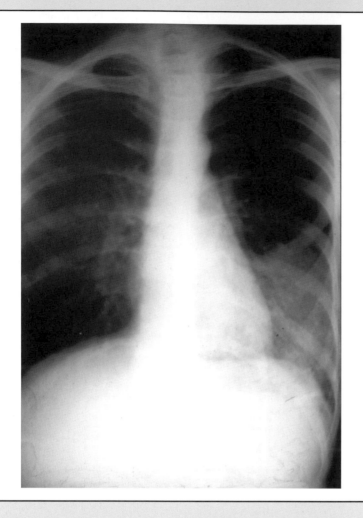

▲**Fig. 22** CXR showing left lower-lobe pneumonia, which may present as upper abdominal/loin pain.

- Structural renal tract abnormality: *E. coli* is still common, but there is an increased incidence of other enteric Gram-negative bacilli, *Pseudomonas aeruginosa* and enterococci. Treat for a minimum of 14 days.
- Recurrent UTI: suspect antimicrobial resistance; evaluate the patient for underlying diabetes or a renal tract abnormality.
- Always obtain urine culture prior to starting antibiotics: be aware of the emergence of multiresistant, extended-spectrum, β-lactamase-producing organisms.

⚠ Antibiotic resistance

The prevalence of resistance against many common antibiotics among *E. coli* in the community is increasing. Ampicillin or trimethoprim have become a poor choice for blind therapy of UTI/pyelonephritis. Make sure that local antibiotic guidelines are followed.

available from a recent urine sample. Antibiotic regimens will vary according to local policies, but consider the following.

Uncomplicated UTI

Commonly caused by *Escherichia coli*, less commonly by other Gram-negative organisms, enterococci and staphylococci. Keep the duration of therapy (eg with cefalexin 500 mg bd po) to a minimum, ie 3 days in women and 7 days in men. Longer therapy is indicated for diabetics or those with an abnormal renal tract.

Pyelonephritis

Commonly caused by *E. coli* and occasionally by other Gram-negative bacilli. Most patients with pyelonephritis will need hospital admission, intravenous rehydration and intravenous antibiotics. Treat according to the local antibiotic sensitivity profile and hospital guidelines (eg co-amoxiclav 625 mg tds plus ciprofloxacin 250–500 mg bd po in mild cases, or co-amoxiclav 1.2 g tds plus gentamicin 5 mg/kg iv once daily in severe cases) for 10–14 days.

🔑 Complicated UTIs

- Urinary catheter *in situ*: *E. coli* is still common, but the incidence of other enteric Gram-negative bacilli, *Pseudomonas aeruginosa* and enterococci is higher. Treat for a minimum of 5 days unless there is evidence of upper tract disease.

Failure to respond

If the diagnosis of pyelonephritis is correct, symptoms should resolve rapidly. If they do not, then reconsider the diagnosis and think about the possibilities of antibiotic failure (what are the sensitivities of any organism cultured from the MSU taken at presentation?), local abscess formation or an obstructed kidney. Priorities then are to reculture blood and urine, and arrange for urgent ultrasonography or CT.

1.3.10 A sore throat

Scenario

A 32-year-old man developed a sore throat for which he took simple analgesia. The pain worsened over the next 2 days and he consults you, requesting antibiotics.

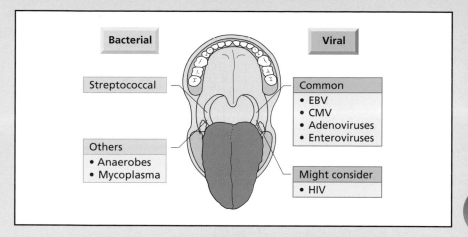

▲ **Fig. 23** Differential diagnosis of sore throat. CMV, cytomegalovirus; EBV, Epstein–Barr virus.

Introduction

The differential diagnosis lies between bacterial and viral infections (Fig. 23). These may be distinguished clinically, but also overlap substantially and culture or serology is really required to make a definitive diagnosis. Throat infections are often trivial and settle spontaneously, but more serious conditions, including pharyngeal abscess, epiglottitis and neutropenic sepsis, need to be considered.

History of the presenting problem

Severity

This is important not only for diagnosis and in guiding treatment, but also for basic supportive measures. With increasing tonsillar and local tissue swelling some patients may become unable to eat or drink, finally developing stridor and even requiring tracheostomy in extreme cases.

Systemic symptoms

Most patients with a sore throat will have a fever. Marked systemic symptoms with myalgia and neck pain are common in streptococcal throat infection. Viral infections are also commonly associated with systemic symptoms, which may include those related to hepatitis (nausea and lethargy) or (rarely) neurological problems.

Source of infection

There is often no obvious source, despite the fact that the common viral infections are passed from person to person by saliva. Both CMV and EBV are often asymptomatic if acquired young, but cause local and systemic disease in adulthood. HIV seroconversion may present with sore throat. Coxsackievirus infections may occur in outbreaks.

Sexually transmitted infection

Neisseria gonorrhoeae can present with a sore throat and exudative pharyngitis.

⚠ **Diphtheria**

- Consider if there has been recent travel from Eastern Europe or a developing country.
- Look for a grey pseudomembrane in the posterior pharynx.
- The patient is usually very toxic.

Other relevant history

Some patients have recurrent bacterial throat infections, and this may simply be another presentation of the same syndrome. A past history of 'glandular fever' might make EBV unlikely, although in the absence of documented serology you should not be put off this diagnosis.

Examination

Examine the whole patient, not just the throat. A corollary of this is not to forget to examine the throat carefully in patients with systemic disease.

It is not likely that this man will be very ill, but note his vital signs (temperature, pulse, BP and respiration) and respond appropriately if they are severely abnormal (see Section 1.3.2).

Airway

Is there stridor? Is the patient able to swallow? Is he dribbling? If so, get urgent assistance from an ear, nose and throat specialist or anaesthetist (see *Acute Medicine*, Section 1.2.13; and *Respiratory Medicine*, Section 1.4.6).

The throat

Pharyngitis is very non-specific. Pus or exudate does not reliably differentiate between viral and bacterial infections. Severe unilateral tonsillar swelling with a pointing lesion ('quinsy') suggests local bacterial infection. The presence of small petechiae on the palate may indicate viral infection, as do vesicular lesions that are typical of 'herpangina' caused by coxsackieviruses. White plaques suggest candidiasis. Oral *Candida* infection is not associated with fever, but is a sign of underlying immunodeficiency and needs to be taken seriously in this context.

The neck

Feel for local lymph nodes and note their size and tenderness. Look for a tender swelling associated with internal jugular vein thrombosis in Lemierre's syndrome.

Evidence of systemic disease

- Rash: streptococcal infections may be associated with the rash of 'scarlet fever' (fine erythematous macules, mainly over the body, that are associated with circumoral pallor and a coated 'strawberry' tongue). Both CMV and EBV may produce a fine macular rash, although the most striking rash associated with EBV is that produced after amoxicillin therapy, which for this reason should never be given as treatment for a sore throat. This is not associated with allergy to other penicillins.

- Splenomegaly: a feature of EBV and CMV infection.

> ⚠ Lemierre's disease is caused by polymicrobial infection of the posterior pharyngeal space and is characterised by the isolation of *Fusobacterium necrophorum*. Local throat disease is associated with thrombosis of the internal jugular vein and metastatic spread of infection, particularly to the lungs.

Investigation

The intensity of investigation will largely depend on how unwell the patient is, but also to some degree on his or her desire to obtain an accurate diagnosis. The following tests should be considered.

Cultures

Send throat swab for bacterial culture (see Section 3.1). Routine viral swabs are not performed but can yield enteroviruses, and viral culture is important when mouth ulcers are present to detect herpesviruses, which may also be detected by polymerase chain reaction. Blood cultures are required if there are severe systemic symptoms or if the patient is neutropenic.

Blood tests

- FBC: will reveal neutrophilia in bacterial infections, and atypical lymphocytes in acute EBV or CMV infection. Haemolysis may complicate EBV.

- Inflammatory markers: a high C-reactive protein is most consistent with bacterial infection.

- Liver function tests: may show a hepatitic picture with EBV and CMV.

- Monospot and Paul–Bunnell tests: these can rapidly diagnose EBV infection. Positives may also occur with other viral infections, including CMV and hepatitis B. Serology is essential if the diagnosis is not clearly bacterial (Table 18).

> ⚠ Neutropenic sepsis often presents with fever and a sore throat, and should be considered in all cases. Has the patient recently been started on a new medication that might cause neutropenia? See *Haematology*, Section 1.4.2.

Imaging

This is only necessary when stridor, severe dysphagia or marked neck swelling is present. A lateral neck radiograph can assess the epiglottis and detect retropharyngeal swelling. A CT or MRI scan of the neck is indicated to assess retropharyngeal abscess or Lemierre's syndrome.

Management

There is little evidence that antimicrobial therapy is of more than modest benefit in uncomplicated viral or bacterial pharyngitis, and over-prescribing encourages antibiotic resistance. The patient should be given symptomatic advice and warned to return if his condition deteriorates.

Antibiotics are indicated for marked local disease with proven or suspected streptococcal

---

TABLE 18 SEROLOGICAL INVESTIGATIONS OF USE IN PHARYNGITIS

Organism	Test	Interpretation
Streptococci	ASOT	Titres >1 in 800 significant. May be higher in children and normal in acute illness: check acute and convalescent samples
	DNAase	Less commonly positive in pharyngeal infection
EBV	GF test	Positive in acute EBV
	EBNA	Suggests past infection
	EBV IgM[1]	Positive in acute EBV
Cytomegalovirus	CMV IgM[1]	Positive in acute CMV

1. Occasional cross-reactivity.
ASOT, anti-streptolysin O titre; EBNA, Epstein–Barr nuclear antigen; GF, glandular fever.

infection. Ampicillin should be avoided in empirical therapy. Phenoxymethylpenicillin 250 mg four times daily for 10 days would be the standard treatment, with erythromycin or clindamycin as alternatives in penicillin allergy.

Retropharyngeal abscess and Lemierre's disease are treated with broad-spectrum antibiotics including metronidazole. Surgical intervention may be required.

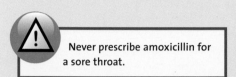 Never prescribe amoxicillin for a sore throat.

Further comments
EBV is associated with a number of clinical syndromes (see Section 2.10.4). Look for hepatic, neurological and haematological complications. CMV may produce a similar pattern. The systemic consequences of group A streptococcal disease include scarlet fever, acute glomerulonephritis, acute rheumatic fever and guttate psoriasis (Fig. 24).

1.3.11 Fever and headache

Scenario

A 23-year-old woman presents with a 12-hour history of fever, headache and photophobia.

Introduction
Fever, headache, photophobia and neck stiffness are features of meningitis. This is a medical emergency: you must act quickly. Your main concern is to resuscitate the patient and to identify and treat the causative organism (Table 19). Antibiotics should be administered as soon as the diagnosis of bacterial meningitis is suspected and should not be delayed until results of investigations are available. GPs are encouraged to treat with antibiotics before referring such patients to the hospital, although recent studies have questioned the value of out-of-hospital antibiotics.

You must also:

- look for signs of haemorrhagic rash and shock because she may develop fulminant sepsis (see Section 1.3.2);

- consider other common causes of headache and photophobia, such as subarachnoid haemorrhage (SAH) and migraine.

History of the presenting problem
If the patient cannot give a lucid history because he or she is extremely unwell or drowsy, it is vital to seek information from relatives or friends.

Headache and fever

- When did the symptoms start? If more than 5–7 days previously, consider causes of chronic meningitis such as tuberculosis (TB), Lyme disease and fungi, and non-infectious conditions such as sarcoidosis or malignancy.

- Where is the headache and how did it start? Sudden-onset headache, particularly during physical exertion, means that SAH must be excluded, although the headache of meningitis can also have an abrupt onset. SAH typically causes occipital headache.

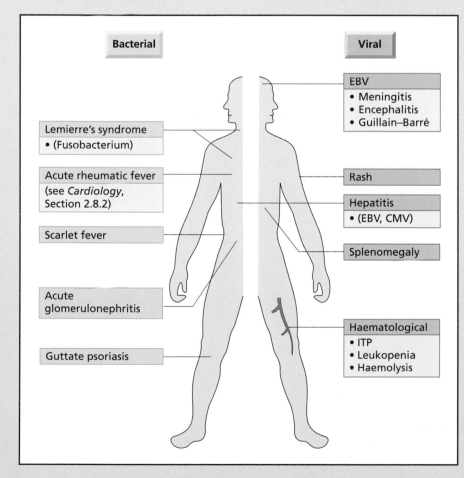

▲**Fig. 24** Systemic complications of throat infections. ITP, idiopathic thrombocytopenic purpura.

TABLE 19 INFECTIVE CAUSES OF MENINGITIS IN ADULTS

Type of infection	Frequency	Examples
Viral	Common	Enteroviruses
	Less common	Mumps and adenoviruses HSV, VZV and HIV
Bacterial	Common	*Neisseria meningitidis* *Streptococcus pneumoniae*
	Less common	*Staphylococcus aureus* *Listeria monocytogenes* *Mycobacterium tuberculosis* Leptospirosis *Borrelia burgdorferi* *Treponema pallidum*
Rickettsial	Uncommon	*Rocky Mountain spotted fever*
Fungal	Rare unless immunocompromised	*Cryptococcus neoformans* Coccidioidomycosis

HSV, herpes simplex virus; VZV, varicella-zoster virus.

Associated symptoms

- Rash: purpuric or haemorrhagic rash supports the diagnosis of meningococcal meningitis/septicaemia. A macular or petechial rash could indicate early meningococcal sepsis, but are more suggestive of a viral infection.

- Nausea and/or vomiting: common but non-specific because it occurs with meningitis, SAH and migraine.

- Associated earache, sinusitis or cough: these make pneumococci more likely to be the aetiological agent (Fig. 25).

- Any focal weakness, confusion or diplopia? If so, consider cerebral oedema, encephalitis, brain abscess and TB.

Other relevant history

History of specific exposure

- Recent contact with anyone suffering from meningitis, particularly meningococcal.

- Contact with fresh water or working as a farmer: consider leptospirosis.

- Tick bite or camping trip to an endemic area: consider Lyme disease.

- Travel: coccidioidomycosis is endemic in the western USA; meningococcal outbreaks may be associated with travel, eg pilgrims to the Haj festival in Mecca.

- Unpasteurised dairy products: consider *Listeria* and *Brucella* spp.

- HIV infection: consider the possibility of underlying HIV infection complicated by *Cryptococcus*/TB/treponemal infection/cytomegalovirus.

Additional clues

- Is she pregnant? Consider *Listeria* spp. in pregnancy and in immunocompromised individuals.

- Season: meningococcal disease is more common during winter and enteroviral outbreaks are more common in the spring and summer.

- Is there a local outbreak, particularly of meningococcal infection?

- Has the patient received meningococcal vaccine? This protects against a and c strains of meningococcus, but does not protect against meningococcus group b infection.

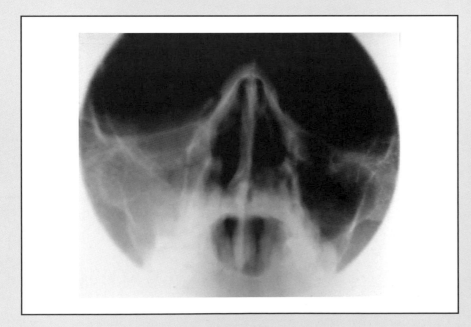

▲**Fig. 25** Right maxillary sinusitis in a patient with pneumococcal meningitis.

Relevant past history

- Does she have a previous history of meningitis? Recurrent pneumococcal meningitis may occur as a result of a persistent cerebrospinal fluid (CSF) leak. Mollaret's meningitis is a rare recurrent condition caused by HSV-2. Deficiency in the terminal complement pathway increases the risk of meningococcal disease (see *Rheumatology and Clinical Immunology*, Section 2.1.5.)

- Does she have a history of neurosurgery, a ventriculoperitoneal shunt or head trauma?

- Is she immunocompromised? If so, then a much broader differential must be considered, including cryptococcal meningitis.

- A history of congenital heart disease or suppurative pulmonary disease increases the risk of pyogenic brain abscess.

Examination

A full physical examination is required, but take particularly careful note of the following.

- Vital signs: temperature, pulse, BP and respiratory rate for evidence of septic shock. Assess skin temperature and capillary return: cool skin and delayed capillary return may be an early indication of meningococcal sepsis. Hypertension with bradycardia suggests raised intracranial pressure.

- Rash: look very carefully over the whole body, including the conjunctivae and buttocks, for the petechial/purpuric rash of meningococcal disease, which may be maculopapular at an early stage.

- Level of consciousness (Glasgow Coma Scale) and Mini-Mental Test Score.

- Neck stiffness or positive Kernig's sign, indicating meningism.

- Conduct a detailed neurological examination, looking for focal neurological signs and evidence of raised intracranial pressure. Fundoscopy is important to exclude papilloedema.

- Otitis media or pneumonia: these make *Streptococcus pneumoniae* infection more likely.

- Evidence of infective endocarditis: septic emboli can enter the cerebral circulation.

Fever and headache

- Look thoroughly for a petechial/purpuric rash: this is virtually pathognomonic of meningococcal infection in meningitis in the UK.
- Treatment must be instituted without delay in bacterial meningitis.

⚠ Bacterial meningitis is deadly. Even if the patient looks reasonably well, meningitis is potentially life-threatening and can progress at frightening speed.

Investigation

'Shoot first, ask questions later'

- You cannot reliably differentiate viral from bacterial meningitis on clinical grounds alone. Lumbar puncture is essential unless there are contraindications or the patient has a petechial/purpuric rash (in which case the agent is almost certainly *Neisseria meningitidis*).
- Do not delay antimicrobial therapy while awaiting investigation results.

Microbiology

- Lumbar puncture: CSF analysis (Table 20) is the only way to establish a secure diagnosis and should be performed unless there are contraindications or if the patient has a petechial/purpuric rash. CT is essential before lumbar puncture if there is decreased consciousness, focal neurological signs, fits, strong suspicion of SAH or any suspicion of elevated intracranial pressure.

- Blood cultures.

- Throat swab and stool for viral culture: these have a higher yield than CSF culture.

- Throat swab for bacterial culture: particularly important for detecting meningococci.

- If a petechial rash is present, disrupt a lesion for Gram stain and culture.

- Blood sample (in EDTA tube) for meningococcal polymerase chain reaction (PCR).

- Clotted blood for acute viral/meningococcal serology: a further convalescent sample will be needed to confirm a significant rise in antibody titre, indicating recent infection.

Contraindications to lumbar puncture

- Presence of petechial or purpuric rash.
- Decreased conscious level or other symptoms or signs suggestive of raised intracranial pressure: the absence of papilloedema does not exclude this.
- Epileptic seizures.
- Focal neurological signs.
- Local infection around the lumbar puncture site.
- Septic shock.
- Coagulopathy.

TABLE 20 INTERPRETATION OF CSF FINDINGS IN MENINGITIS

Condition	CSF	Cells/mL	Protein (g/L)	Glucose	Microbiology tests
Normal	Clear	0–5 lymphocytes	0.15–0.45	60% of plasma	–
Bacterial	Cloudy, purulent or clear	500–2,000 mainly polymorphs	0.5–3.0	Low	Gram stain and culture Bacterial antigen detection for common pathogens PCR for meningococci
Viral	Clear	15–500 mainly lymphocytes	0.15–1.0	Normal	PCR available for enteroviruses and herpesviruses
Fungal	Clear or cloudy	0–500 lymphocytes Absent in severe immunocompromise	0.5–3.0	Low	India ink stain and cryptococcal antigen
Tuberculous	Clear	30–500 mixed lymphocytes and polymorphs	1.0–6.0	Low	Ziehl–Neelsen smear positive in <5% and PCR in 30–40% of TB meningitis

Blood tests

- FBC and film: neutrophilia suggests bacterial infection, but fulminant meningococcal disease may present with leucopenia and thrombocytopenia. Reactive lymphocytes may be seen in viral meningitis.

- Coagulation screen in patients with suspected meningococcal disease: there may be evidence of disseminated intravascular coagulation.

- Electrolytes, renal/liver/bone function tests, glucose and (possibly) arterial blood gases will also be required in any patient presenting with meningitis.

Imaging

- CXR: primarily to exclude pneumonia.

- CT or MRI of brain: required whenever there is decreased conscious level or focal neurolgical signs; may also detect brain abscess and sinusitis.

Management

Meningitis: telephone advice to patient's GP

- Benzylpenicillin 1200 mg (2 MU) iv or im immediately in suspected meningococcal disease and arrange urgent hospital admission.
- Cefotaxime (or ceftriaxone) 1 g if history of anaphylaxis to penicillin.

Resuscitation

If there is circulatory compromise, resuscitation must begin immediately while the history and examination are being completed (see Section 1.3.2). The following are key aspects.

- Check airway, breathing and circulation.

- Ensure airway and give high-flow oxygen.

- Obtain venous access.

- Give colloid/0.9% saline iv rapidly until BP is restored or JVP is clearly visible.

- Call for help from the intensive care unit sooner rather than later.

Empirical antibiotics

These will depend on the clinical context.

- If meningococcal meningitis is suspected (typical rash or shocked), immediately administer high-dose intravenous cefotaxime or ceftriaxone, but take blood cultures first.

- If recent head injury, neurosurgery or a ventricular shunt is present, add flucloxacillin to cover *Staphylococcus aureus*.

- If the patient is pregnant, aged over 55 years or moderate/ severely immunocompromised, then add ampicillin to cover *Listeria* spp.

- Consider adding aciclovir if there are features of encephalitis (see Section 1.3.12).

- If the patient is HIV positive or has any other cause of severe immunocompromise, seek expert advice.

> **Antibiotic resistance to meningitis**
>
> In 2000, 7% of blood isolates of *Streptococcus pneumoniae* were penicillin resistant in England and Wales. In southern Europe and the USA this figure is much higher, and some isolates are also cephalosporin resistant.

> **Meningitis: no pathogen identified and not responding**
>
> • Wrong empirical therapy, eg unusual organism.
> • Parameningeal focus, eg epidural abscess.
> • Antibiotic resistance.
> • Non-infectious cause, eg sarcoidosis, vasculitis or malignancy.

Specific antimicrobial therapy

• *Neisseria meningitidis, Streptococcus pneumoniae* or *Haemophilus influenzae* (very unlikely in this age group): intravenous cefotaxime 2 g 4-hourly or ceftriaxone 2–4 g in 24 hours. High-dose penicillin or ampicillin can be substituted when sensitivities are available. Duration of treatment is 5–7 days for *N. meningitidis* and *H. influenzae*, but 14 days for *Strep. pneumoniae*. The addition of corticosteroids to initial therapy has been shown to improve outcome in *Haemophilus* and pneumococcal meningitis.

• *Listeria monocytogenes*: intravenous ampicillin 2 g 4-hourly for 14–21 days; consider adding gentamicin.

• Tuberculous: rifampicin, isoniazid, pyrazinamide and ethambutol for 2 months, followed by rifampicin and isoniazid for a further 10 months. The addition of corticosteroids to initial therapy has been shown to improve outcome in tuberculous meningitis.

• Aseptic meningitis: conservative treatment. Aciclovir for HSV infection.

Other issues

• After any bacterial meningitis, perform audiometry during follow-up.

• In recurrent meningococcal meningitis, or if there is family history of the condition, measure complement levels, immunoglobulins and IgG subclasses. Immunise with ACYW135 meningococcal vaccine. In recurrent pneumococcal meningitis, investigate for a CSF leak.

Further comments

Notification and contact tracing

Meningitis is a notifiable disease. If meningococcal infection is confirmed or likely, notify your microbiologist and the local Health Protection Agency (HPA) consultant by phone immediately. This serves several purposes and provides:

• a point of contact for questions, advice and education for healthcare professionals and the public;

• administration of chemoprophylaxis and immunisation;

• management of outbreaks and reassurance to those not at immediate risk.

> **Carriage of meningococci**
>
> Humans are the only natural host for meningococci. At any one time, about 10% of the population will be carrying the organism in the nasopharynx. The mean duration of carriage has been estimated from community studies as about 9 months. Little is known about the factors that influence progression to invasive disease or maintenance of a carrier state, but analysis of bacterial population structure and genetics shows that there are certain hypervirulent strains of meningococci associated with invasive disease.

> **Risk to household contacts**
>
> People who live in the same household as an individual with meningococcal disease are at higher risk of developing the condition than other members of the community. The attack rate in the month after the index case has occurred is increased by about 500–1,200 times, ie to a risk of around 1% per household. This probably reflects the epidemiology of strain carriage, but also the genetic susceptibility of household members.

Chemoprophylaxis

Chemoprophylaxis is an attempt to reduce risk by eliminating carriage from the network of contacts, thereby reducing the risk of invasive disease in other susceptible family members and close contacts. Many antibiotics that are useful in treating meningococcal disease are ineffective in eradicating carriage, so do not forget to treat the index case with chemoprophylaxis if a penicillin-based agent has been used. It is not necessary to give additional antibiotics if the index patient has been treated with a third-generation cephalosporin (cefotaxime or ceftriaxone).

The following are effective agents for meningococcal chemoprophylaxis (adult doses shown):

• rifampicin 600 mg po twice daily for 2 days;

- ciprofloxacin 500 mg po single dose;

- ceftriaxone 250 mg im single dose.

Chemoprophylaxis of meningococcal disease

Side effects should be explained, including the reduction in the efficacy of the oral contraceptive pill when taking rifampicin.

Notification and prophylaxis of meningococcal disease

- The HPA should be notified of all suspected and confirmed cases of meningococcal disease.
- Steps should be taken to confirm the diagnosis.
- Chemoprophylaxis is recommended for close household contacts or other intimate (kissing) contacts as soon as possible after the diagnosis of the index case.
- Healthcare workers need prophylaxis only if they have performed mouth-to-mouth resuscitation.
- Immunise household contacts of meningococcal serogroup C or A (unless previously immunised).

1.3.12 Fever with reduced conscious level

Scenario

You are asked to see a 29-year-old man who has been admitted under a psychiatric section, having been found wandering in the street. On admission, he was found to have a temperature of 39°C and his conscious level has fallen since admission.

Introduction

The differential diagnosis for this scenario is broad, but the falling level of consciousness means that urgent action is required. The airway must be protected, high-flow oxygen given and readily treatable causes of impaired consciousness excluded immediately, eg hypoglycaemia and drug intoxication (opiates and neuroleptics, etc.) (see *Acute Medicine*, Section 1.2.31). The patient will not be able to give a useful history, so attempt to obtain as much information as possible from friends, relatives or observers. Given the high fever, it is critically important to consider infection, particularly meningitis, encephalitis (Table 21) and brain abscess. Less common (in the UK) travel-related infections include cerebral malaria, rickettsial infections, African trypanosomiasis and typhoid. Remember that confusion may complicate severe sepsis and encephalopathy can occur in metabolic derangement, in the period following drug use (eg neuroleptic agents), in malignant conditions and in cerebral vasculitis.

History of the presenting problem

The history, if available, will be from a friend or relative, or via previous medical records.

- Duration of illness: was there any prodromal illness suggestive of a viral infection?

- Has he experienced headache, neck pain or photophobia suggestive of meningitis? See Section 1.3.11.

- Is there a history of tuberculosis (TB) or close contact with TB? Remember that most patients from Asia and Africa will have been exposed to TB, and TB meningitis can present subacutely with personality or psychiatric changes leading to reduced conscious level with or without focal signs.

- What has his behaviour been like? In encephalitis patients typically start acting strangely, become confused and then develop coma.

- Is there a possibility of trauma?

TABLE 21 INFECTIOUS CAUSES OF ACUTE ENCEPHALITIS

Scenario	Organisms
Immunocompetent adult	HSV[1] Enteroviruses Influenza[1] EBV HIV seroconversion[1] West Nile virus *Mycoplasma pneumoniae*[1] *Legionella pneumophila*[1]
Travel related	Japanese B encephalitis Tick-borne encephalitis Various flaviviruses (eg West Nile virus)
Severe immunocompromise	VZV[1], CMV[1] (HSV[1] less common) HIV[1] Toxoplasmosis[1]

1. Treatable causes.
CMV, cytomegalovirus; EBV, Epstein–Barr virus; HSV, herpes simplex virus; VZV, varicella-zoster virus.

- Has he had a fit or convulsion?

- Does he suffer from any medical conditions?

- Ask about his premorbid mental state, and drug and alcohol use: is there any possibility of an overdose?

Other relevant history

Travel history

Recent travel raises the possibility of exposure to many organisms (see Section 1.3.16). If relevant, obtain precise details of the area involved and seek expert advice on possible exposure. Consider the following.

- Malaria, typhoid and trypanosomiasis.

- Specific encephalitis viruses, eg Japanese B encephalitis in South-east Asia, eastern equine encephalitis in North America, West Nile virus in many parts of the USA (and recently reported in Western Europe) and tick-borne encephalitis in Eastern Europe (in summer).

Relevant past history

- Diabetes mellitus (hypoglycaemia or hyperglycaemia).

- Drug overdose or depression.

- Use of alcohol or recreational drugs.

- Regular medication such as neuroleptics.

- Immunocompromise such as HIV infection or recent chemotherapy.

⚠ Confusion may occur in any severe systemic infection, particularly in the elderly. Always consider encephalitis and meningitis and, if in doubt, perform a CT scan and lumbar puncture.

Examination

Take particular note of the following.

- Vital signs: temperature, pulse, BP and respiratory rate.

- Glasgow Coma Scale score and Mini-Mental Test Score: follow these over time; falling consciousness requires immediate review.

- Look for signs of trauma.

- Look for a Medic-Alert bracelet or other useful 'clues', eg medication (insulin or anticonvulsants).

- Skin: an erythematous maculopapular rash is non-specific, occurring in mycoplasma and enteroviral infection. Is there a meningococcal rash? In travellers, hunt for an eschar or tick.

- Neck stiffness: signs of meningism are usually absent in encephalitis, but remember that the distinction is not always absolutely clear and meningoencephalitis may be present.

- Focal neurological signs: these may occur in viral encephalitis, but consider cerebral abscess and other space-occupying lesions.

- Ocular fundi: papilloedema indicates raised intracranial pressure in this context, although its absence does not exclude it. In advanced HIV infection, CMV retinitis may indicate coexistent CMV encephalitis.

- Muscle rigidity: present in neuroleptic malignant syndrome.

- Cardiac murmurs: consider infectious endocarditis with septic embolus to the brain.

Investigation

Urgent imaging

Urgent cranial imaging is needed for this man, whose conscious level is falling. Waiting until the next day could be fatal if he has a space-occupying lesion.

- A CT scan of the brain will readily exclude space-occupying lesions, such as brain abscess, and gauge whether lumbar puncture is unsafe. CT may show parenchymal features of encephalitis, but MRI is more sensitive. Changes in many cases are non-specific, but temporal lobe involvement suggests HSV encephalitis. Patients often need both imaging modalities.

- Early imaging is often normal, with typical encephalitic changes appearing later in the course of the illness. Initial scans may therefore need to be repeated.

Cultures and serology

- Blood cultures.

- Cerebrospinal fluid (CSF) analysis (if safe, see Section 1.3.11): in encephalitis the opening pressure is commonly raised (>200 mm CSF); the CSF itself may be normal but a mild lymphocytosis is common. Polymerase chain reaction (PCR) is now the gold standard for recognising the infectious agent, ie enteroviruses, HSV, EBV, CMV, VZV, mumps and *Mycoplasma* spp. (Fig. 26). TB culture and PCR should be sent if TB is suspected. CSF cytology may be helpful in malignant meningoencephalitis.

- Viral cultures from throat swab and faeces may identify an enterovirus infection.

- Acute serology should be saved for paired testing later.

- Consider an HIV test: this may be performed in an incompetent patient without consent if you believe that the result will benefit the patient (see Section 1.2.5).

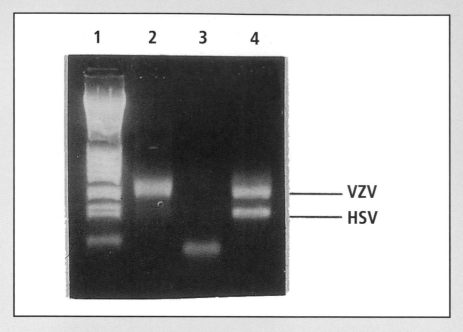

▲**Fig. 26** PCR of CSF from a patient with AIDS revealing VZV DNA. Lane 1, DNA ladder; lane 2, CSF from patient; lane 3, negative control; lane 4, positive control. (Courtesy of Dr C. Bangham.)

Blood tests

- FBC.

- Check thick and thin malaria films if the patient has travelled to an endemic area within the last 3 months: falciparum malaria usually presents within 6 weeks.

- Biochemical profile, including electrolytes, renal and liver function, glucose and creatine kinase if neuroleptic malignant syndrome is possible.

- Consider toxicology screen.

- Consider autoimmune/vasculitis profile to exclude acute cerebral vasculitis.

Other imaging

- CXR: to exclude atypical pneumonia in association with encephalitis.

- Echocardiogram: if there is any suspicion of bacterial endocarditis.

Other tests

The following may be indicated in some cases.

- Electroencephalography: temporal lobe changes strongly suggest HSV encephalitis.

- Brain biopsy: now rarely performed for encephalitis since the development of MRI and PCR.

Management

Immediate management

- Secure the airway, control seizures and commence empirical therapy as soon as possible.

- Patient with coma (see *Acute Medicine*, Section 1.2.31).

- Patient with meningitis (see Section 1.3.11).

- Until a specific diagnosis is confirmed, treat for both meningitis and encephalitis.

Encephalitis

Once you suspect encephalitis, you must consider the likely aetiological agents (see Table 21), particularly the treatable ones. In the UK, the most common identifiable agent in a patient with encephalitis is HSV.

Other treatable causes include *Mycoplasma pneumoniae*, VZV and HIV infection. Empirical therapy before an aetiological agent is identified should include parenteral aciclovir 10 mg/kg three times daily for 10 days (dose reduced in renal failure), together with a macrolide. It is important to start therapy early for HSV because death or severe brain damage is likely once the Glasgow Coma Scale score has fallen below 8.

Have a high index of suspicion for TB meningitis, particularly if there is a lymphocytosis in the CSF. It is unusual to see acid-fast bacilli in the CSF and empirical treatment may be required while you are awaiting culture results.

⚠️ **Emerging infections**
Outbreaks can occur out of the blue, as happened in New York in 1999 when cases of encephalitis, caused by a West Nile-like virus previously undescribed in the USA, suddenly appeared.

1.3.13 Fever in the neutropenic patient

Scenario

A 24-year-old man develops a high fever 3 weeks after bone-marrow transplantation for acute myeloid leukaemia. You are asked to assess him urgently.

Introduction

The patient is highly immunosuppressed and neutropenic. He is at high risk of serious sepsis and treatment must not be delayed. There is usually a protocol, based on local antimicrobial sensitivity patterns, to

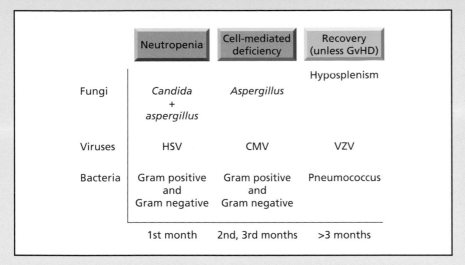

	Neutropenia	Cell-mediated deficiency	Recovery (unless GvHD)
Fungi	*Candida* + *aspergillus*	*Aspergillus*	Hyposplenism
Viruses	HSV	CMV	VZV
Bacteria	Gram positive and Gram negative	Gram positive and Gram negative	Pneumococcus
	1st month	2nd, 3rd months	>3 months

▲**Fig. 27** Risk of infection following bone-marrow transplantation. The early phase with chemotherapy-related mucositis and neutropenia is dominated by bacterial and fungal infections. CMV, cytomegalovirus; GvHD, graft-versus-host disease; HSV, herpes simplex virus; VZV, varicella-zoster virus.

guide urgent therapy in haematology units (see *Haematology*, Section 1.4.2), but this should not prevent a rational diagnostic approach.

History of the presenting problem

This patient will have been monitored very closely and so a lot of information should already be available. The time-scale after the graft is important in guessing likely pathogens (Figs 27 and 28). In the first month or so neutropenia is the main concern; thereafter the main defects are in cell-mediated immunity, and the opportunistic infections in the second and third months are similar to those in solid organ transplants or HIV infection. After the third month, immune reconstitution is sufficient and so opportunistic infections are less of a problem, although patients remain hyposplenic.

Site of infection

It is often difficult to determine the site of infection in neutropenic patients, who fail to 'localise' infections in the same way as the immunocompetent. Commonly, infection enters because of a decrease in the normal barrier function of the mucosae, so the portal of entry may not be obvious. Nevertheless, assess symptoms relating to individual systems carefully. Discuss the case with the nurses on the unit who often notice relevant changes in the patient.

Indwelling lines

Rigors and fever are occasionally associated with the infusion of fluids or drugs. A drug fever is obviously a possibility here, but consider also a line infection. Rarely, the infusion fluids themselves may become contaminated. If this is suspected, retain the fluid and contact the microbiology unit for advice.

Routine surveillance

According to local protocol, surveillance cultures or CMV studies (polymerase chain reaction or antigen detection) may be ongoing. Review all results with the microbiologist, and also ask about recent infections in other patients within the unit. If the patient is CMV IgG antibody negative (pre transplantation), has he received exclusively CMV-negative blood products?

Antimicrobial prophylaxis

Antibacterial, antifungal, antiprotozoal and antiviral prophylaxis may have been used according to protocol, based on pretransplantation serology and past infections. Review what has been prescribed and administered. Drug reactions may have led to cessation of prophylaxis, putting the patient at greater than usual risk of those infections that the prophylaxis was designed to prevent.

⚠ Leucocyte-depleted blood reduces CMV transmission, but protection is not complete. Primary CMV disease in the bone-marrow transplant recipient is very severe if not treated aggressively and early.

Neutropenia <10d
Autologous BMT

Neutropenia 10–21d
Mucositis
Previous lung disease

Neutropenia >21d
Allogeneic BMT
Bacteraemia treated previously

Low   Intermediate   High

Increasing risk of fungal disease

▲**Fig. 28** Fungal infection in bone-marrow transplantation (BMT).

Examination

Is the patient cardiovascularly stable? If not, resuscitate (see Section 1.3.2) and call for assistance from the intensive care unit sooner rather than later.

A full examination is required, but physical signs may be subtle or absent in neutropenic patients as a result of the lack of an inflammatory response. Pay particular attention to the following.

- Intravenous line site(s).

- Skin: looking for lesions of disseminated bacterial (Fig. 29) or fungal infection, pressure sores or other sites of skin breakdown.

- Perianal area: a common site of cellulitis.

- Oral cavity: looking for mucositis, candidal and herpetic infection.

- Fundoscopy: for evidence of fungal or viral infection.

Investigation

> ⚠️ **Neutropenic sepsis**
>
> Do not await culture results before treatment. Take cultures and treat immediately according to local protocols.

Microbiological tests

- Blood culture (all cases): ideally these should be taken peripherally because central line cultures have a poor positive predictive value. A paired line and peripheral culture may be taken if line sepsis is possible.

- Urine culture (all cases).

- Stool culture: if diarrhoea is present.

- Cerebrospinal fluid (CSF) culture: if there are meningeal or neurological symptoms. Test for cryptococcal antigen in blood and CSF if central nervous system infection suspected.

- Respiratory samples: these are essential if there are respiratory symptoms or an abnormal CXR, or if hypoxia is present. Send sputum for bacterial, fungal and mycobacterial culture. Bronchoscopy and lavage may be required to obtain an adequate specimen and to detect respiratory viruses or *Pneumocystis carinii*. Mouth washings or nasopharyngeal aspirate for respiratory virus culture and immunofluorescence can be useful.

- Vesicular lesions: should be sampled and sent to virology for electron microscopy, polymerase chain reaction (PCR) or culture for herpesviruses. Other skin lesions may be biopsied and cultured for bacteria and fungi.

Other blood tests

- Check FBC, clotting, electrolytes, and renal and liver function. What is the degree of neutropenia at this stage of treatment?

- Send blood for detection of CMV by antigen testing or PCR: increasingly, CMV viral load is monitored by quantitative PCR. *Candida* or *Aspergillus* antigen detection (galactomannan test) is available in some centres and may be useful.

Imaging

- CXR (all cases): to exclude obvious disease.

- Consider chest CT: this is more sensitive than plain radiography in detecting pulmonary infection, particularly the peripheral lesions of aspergillosis (Fig. 30).

- Consider other imaging as determined by clinical suspicion: ultrasonography, CT and MRI are valuable in localising focal sites of infection.

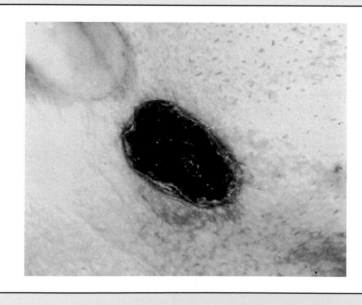

▲**Fig. 29** Ecthyma gangrenosum in a neutropenic patient. Focal areas of necrosis start as dark-red patches and quickly turn black. This lesion occurs only in neutropenia and is almost always the result of metastatic *Pseudomonas aeruginosa*.

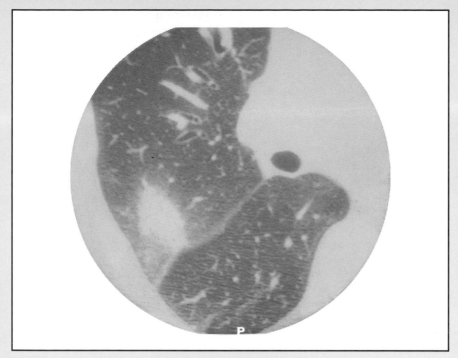

▲ Fig. 30 Pulmonary CT scan showing an area of dense peripheral consolidation caused by invasive aspergillosis. (Courtesy of Dr C. Conlon.)

Invasive procedures

Tissue biopsies, guided by imaging techniques, may establish the diagnosis of deep-seated infection, eg hepatosplenic candidiasis, but can be difficult in the face of thrombocytopenia or coagulation abnormalities. Have a low threshold for bronchoscopy if respiratory symptoms are present, or for upper and lower gastrointestinal endoscopy if there are appropriate symptoms. Send samples to both microbiology and cytology/histology.

Management

Aggressive supportive care will almost certainly be required (see Section 1.3.2).

Empirical antimicrobial treatment

This must be instituted immediately in a 'blind' manner to cover the likely pathogens according to protocol (see *Haematology*, Section 1.4.2). Most regimens start with antibacterial cover, including *Pseudomonas* spp., and escalate

therapy in a sequential manner. If initial antibacterial therapy fails, then the likelihood of fungal infection (*Candida* or *Aspergillus* spp.) is increased, and blind antifungal therapy in the form of amphotericin is usually added at 72–96 hours if there is no response.

> Gram-positive bacterial infections and antimicrobial resistance have been increasing in frequency in the neutropenic population. Consider this when formulating treatment protocols.

> ⚠ Although *Candida albicans* is susceptible to fluconazole, other *Candida* spp. may not be. There has been an increase in non-*albicans* candida infection, possibly related to the use of fluconazole prophylaxis: these require antifungal therapy, eg with amphotericin.

Specific therapy

If a specific pathogen is isolated, adjust the antimicrobial regimen with microbiology advice. There is a great temptation to leave the patient on multiple different antimicrobial agents, which increases the risk of adverse reactions.

> **Review . . . and review . . . and review**
>
> Keep reviewing the patient's clinical state and investigations. If necessary, re-image or take further invasive samples.

Line infection

If an intravascular line, eg a tunnelled Hickman catheter, is a potential site of infection, it is often possible to treat without having to remove it. However, removal should be considered if the patient remains septic, in suspected endocarditis (rare in neutropenia), when there is venous thrombosis around the line or if the line tunnel becomes infected.

Immunomodulation

If neutropenia persists, the outlook, particularly from invasive fungal infection, is poor. Efforts should be directed towards trying to restore bone marrow function as soon as possible with the use of colony-stimulating factors (see *Haematology*, Section 2.9).

1.3.14 Fever after renal transplant

Scenario

A 64-year-old man presents with a temperature of 39°C 6 weeks after a successful renal transplant. You are phoned from the renal transplant unit to come and assess him.

MMC Core Curriculum   **65**

Introduction

This patient has significant immunosuppression, in particular of cell-mediated immunity (helper T cells, killer T cells and macrophages; see *Immunology and Immunosuppression*). The differential diagnosis is wide, requiring careful evaluation and investigations. Cytomegalovirus (CMV) must be high on the list of probabilities (depending on the CMV status of the donor and recipient), but bacterial infection, eg urinary tract infection, must be excluded. If the patient is severely ill, treatment must be initiated immediately on a 'covering the possibilities' basis while waiting for the results of investigations. However, if the patient is not in such a desperate state it is preferable to establish the diagnosis before starting on specific therapy.

History of the presenting problem

What immunosuppression has the patient received? If he was at high risk of rejection (eg because he was highly sensitised) or had suffered graft rejection, he is likely to have received more immunosuppression than would otherwise be the case. Agents such as antithymocyte globulin increase the risk of invasive CMV disease.

Site of infection

A detailed history searching for an infective focus is essential.

- Localising symptoms: take respiratory, urinary, gastrointestinal and neurological symptoms particularly seriously.

- Prosthetic material: central venous haemodialysis catheters, Tenckhoff catheters for peritoneal dialysis, arteriovenous connections for haemodialysis with Gortex or similar materials, ureteric stent inserted at the time

of transplantation. Any of these could be a focus of infection.

Other relevant history

- Hospital-acquired infection: is there an outbreak on the ward (see Section 2.3)?

- Is there a history of previous infections, eg tuberculosis (TB) or *Aspergillus*?

- What happened around the time of the transplantation? Could this be transfusion-acquired CMV or viral hepatitis?

- Medication: drug fever is often overlooked and, once blind antibiotic therapy is started, is difficult to disentangle. What antimicrobial prophylaxis has been taken?

- Travel history: reactivation of TB is common in renal failure or transplantation. *Strongyloides* hyperinfection syndrome may occur when immunosuppression is commenced many years after the initial infection (see Section 2.14.2).

Examination

Monitor vital signs regularly for evidence of shock or organ dysfunction necessitating urgent intervention. A full general examination is required, paying particular attention to the following.

- Skin: examine the operation site for redness, tenderness, exudate or necrosis. Check all lines, fistulae and dialysis catheter sites. Vesicles suggest herpes simplex or herpes zoster (see Section 2.10.2). Fungal infection may present with scattered maculopapular lesions (see Section 2.9).

- Respiratory: classic chest signs may be masked by immunosuppression. *Pneumocystis carinii* and CMV

pneumonitis often present with cough, breathlessness and oxygen desaturation, but with no abnormalities on auscultation (see Section 1.3.21).

- Abdomen: localised signs or ileus may be the result of surgical complications, gut ischaemia or intra-abdominal abscess. Infectious diarrhoea may represent nosocomial infection, especially *Clostridium difficile* in a patient who has received previous antibiotics. Bleeding or diarrhoea may be caused by CMV colitis.

- Neurology: change in mental state, headache, photophobia or localised neurological signs require urgent investigation. Signs of meningism are often mild/absent in severe immunocompromise.

CMV disease in renal transplant recipients

- Primary or secondary (reactivation) is common after solid organ transplantation.
- Multisystem infection can involve the lungs, eyes, gut, liver, bone marrow or brain.
- Most common 1–3 months after the transplantation.
- More common and severe if a CMV-negative patient receives a CMV-positive graft.
- Risk is related to the intensity of immunosuppression: it is particularly high immediately after antithymocyte globulin.
- Regular monitoring, with blood CMV antigen or polymerase chain reaction (PCR) detection/quantification, allows pre-emptive therapy.

Investigation

Keep in mind the wide differential diagnosis (Figs 31 and 32) and remember that immunocompromised

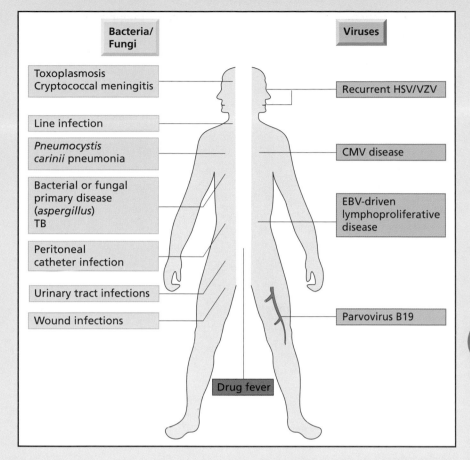

▲ **Fig. 31** Potential causes of fever in renal transplantation. EBV, Epstein–Barr virus; HSV, herpes simplex virus; VZV, varicella-zoster virus.

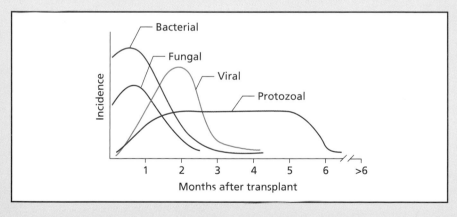

▲ **Fig. 32** Timing of infections after transplantation.

patients may be infected by more than one pathogen.

> • Examine, culture, image and biopsy until you have obtained a diagnosis.
> • If the patient looks very ill, give broad-spectrum antibacterial cover immediately.

Cultures

These should be directed by specific symptoms, but should include culture of blood, urine, stool and infected sites. Note the following.

• CMV: test for viraemia by PCR or antigen detection.

• Sputum culture: has a low yield for bacterial pathogens but may

detect TB. Induced sputum and/or bronchial lavage is indicated for the diagnosis of *Pneumocystis carinii* pneumonia, TB, fungi, CMV and respiratory viruses (see Section 3.1).

• Stool: culture, *Clostridium difficile* toxin measurement, and stain for cryptosporidia if there is diarrhoea. If there is a history of foreign travel, request microscopy for ova, cysts and parasites.

• *Candida* or *Aspergillus*: antigen tests are not universally available, but may prove useful in the future to aid early diagnosis and therapy.

> ⚠ Have a low threshold for bronchoscopy if there are respiratory symptoms, desaturation or abnormal imaging – bronchoscopy may not be possible as a result of worsening hypoxia if you delay.

Blood tests

Check the FBC, electrolytes, renal and liver function, glucose, clotting and (possibly) arterial blood gases. Neutropenia will change the clinical approach (see Section 1.3.13). Leucopenia may suggest CMV and anaemia is common in parvovirus B19 infection, but these could simply be an effect of drugs, eg azathioprine and mycophenolate mofetil.

Imaging

A CXR is mandatory. Other imaging should be as indicated by clinical or laboratory findings. Ultrasonography, CT and MRI are increasingly used to image the chest/abdomen in transplant recipients with pyrexia of unknown origin (see Sections 1.1.3 and 1.3.8) and to direct aspiration/ biopsy of suspect lesions. Nuclear medicine imaging, such as indium-111-labelled white cell or gallium-67 scanning, may occasionally localise inflammation in difficult cases.

Histology

This can often establish the diagnosis and is required for the formal diagnosis of invasive fungal or CMV disease. It may also detect malignancy, so send samples for both microbiology and cytology/histology.

Transplant-associated lymphoproliferative disease

- Increased incidence of EBV-related non-Hodgkin's B-cell lymphoma after transplantation.
- Commonly presents with unexplained fever.
- Often extranodal and high rate of central nervous system involvement.
- Management is by reducing immunosuppression.
- Responds poorly to chemotherapy.

Management

The level of supportive care required will be determined by the severity of haemodynamic or respiratory disturbance (see Section 1.3.2). A full discussion of therapy for individual infections is included in Section 2 of this module, but your first decision in this regard is whether empirical antimicrobial treatment is needed.

- Base this judgement on your clinical findings, exposure history and local policies.

- Review the patient regularly: rapid deterioration can occur.

- If empirical treatment is needed, you cannot cover every possible organism: concentrate your efforts on the most likely and most dangerous causes while continuing with investigations.

Further comments

These cases are not straightforward: if treatment is started, review regularly and consider possible causes of treatment failure.

Failure of fever to respond to treatment

If this occurs consider:

- wrong diagnosis;
- drug resistance;
- malabsorption or drug interactions;
- a second infection;
- drug reaction;
- malignancy (EBV-related lymphoma).

1.3.15 Varicella in pregnancy

Scenario

A 23-year-old pregnant woman is referred urgently by her GP with chickenpox. You are called to review her.

Introduction

The rash is usually characteristic and the diagnosis of chickenpox clear. Although a relatively benign illness in children, severe disease is not uncommon in adults. Life-threatening complications such as pneumonitis are more common in people who smoke, are immunocompromised or who are pregnant (when there is also the fetus to consider). These groups therefore need urgent assessment and therapy.

Complications of chickenpox

- Pneumonitis.
- Secondary bacterial infection of skin lesions.
- Hepatitis.
- Postinfectious cerebellar encephalitis: more common in children, occurring in 1 in 6,000 cases.
- Effect on the fetus.

History of the presenting problem

- Duration of illness: the earlier treatment is started the better.

- Dyspnoea, cough or haemoptysis: must consider varicella pneumonitis; cough is typically non-productive or produces clear sputum streaked with blood; and purulent sputum suggests secondary bacterial infection.

- Stage of pregnancy: risk of fetal abnormalities is highest (about 2.2%) if maternal infection occurs before 20 weeks' gestation. If maternal chickenpox develops within 7 days of delivery, the neonate may develop severe chickenpox up to 3–4 weeks after birth. The highest risk of pneumonitis to the mother is in the third trimester.

Other relevant history

Immune dysfunction increases the risk of severe complications, particularly if there is cell-mediated immune deficiency, eg after transplantation, immunosuppressive therapy or HIV infection (see Sections 1.3.14 and 1.3.21). Smokers are more likely to develop pneumonitis.

Examination

Aside from assessing how ill the woman is, key issues to check include the following.

- Skin: for vesicles, and for evidence of secondary bacterial infection.

- Breathing: central cyanosis, increased respiratory rate and focal chest signs would suggest pneumonitis.

⚠ Rash of varicella

Starts as crops of vesicles containing clear fluid on an erythematous base. These evolve into pustules and then scabs. The lesions start on the trunk and spread peripherally. Examine the mouth for lesions (Fig. 33): these may be so severe as to interfere with eating and drinking.

Investigation

The diagnosis is usually obvious clinically. Tests may be required to confirm the diagnosis in atypical cases and to assess the severity of disease.

Cultures and serology

- Vesicle fluid for electron microscopy, viral and bacterial culture and/or viral polymerase chain reaction (see Section 3.1).

- Anti-varicella IgM antibodies: available in some hospitals to confirm the diagnosis.

- Blood and sputum cultures: because bacterial superinfection is common.

Other tests

- FBC, electrolytes and renal function: hyponatraemia is common in severe varicella.

- Liver function tests to detect varicella hepatitis.

If the patient is very unwell or there is reduced oxygen saturation on pulse oximetry, check arterial blood gases.

Imaging

CXR is required in any pregnant woman referred to hospital with chickenpox. In pregnancy the radiation risk of a CXR (minimal with shielding) is far outweighed by the mortality of pneumonitis (Fig. 34).

Management

- Assess for maternal complications such as pneumonitis.
- Review the potential fetal risk.
- Decide on therapy.

The patient

Give supportive care as required (see Section 1.3.2).

- Isolate: transmission is by respiratory droplets and hospitalised isolation in a single room is essential.

- Antiviral treatment: adults presenting within 72 hours of developing skin lesions should be treated with aciclovir (valaciclovir and famciclovir are suitable alternatives). Intravenous therapy with aciclovir 10 mg/kg three times daily (adjusted depending on renal function) is indicated for severe disease, pneumonitis, hepatitis or acute encephalitis, or in significant immunocompromise.

- Consider secondary bacterial pneumonia, bacteraemia or cellulitis and treat appropriately.

- Note that hyperimmune anti-varicella immunoglobulin (VZIG) has no role in therapy of the mother at this stage (but see Contacts below).

The fetus

Inform obstetricians because of the possibility of premature labour. There is a small risk of spontaneous abortion or fetal abnormality up to 20 weeks' gestation, and even beyond this. Aciclovir is not associated with any known teratogenic effects. There is a high risk (30%) of disseminated varicella, encephalitis and death if the child is born before maternal immunity to varicella has developed. Neonates born between 5 days before and 3 days after the onset of maternal chickenpox should be treated with VZIG.

Contacts

Varicella non-immune pregnant women who are exposed to

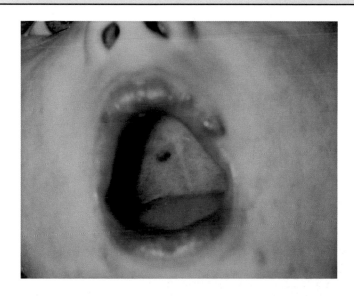

▲ **Fig. 33** Child with typical palatal lesion of chickenpox.

MMC Core Curriculum **69**

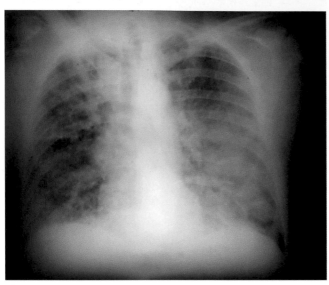

(a)

(b)

▲ **Fig. 34** (a) CXR of a 43-year-old smoker presenting 5 days after the onset of the rash with cough and breathlessness. Widespread interstitial shadowing is present throughout the lungs. This may progress to form calcific nodules in survivors. (b) Lung of the same patient *post mortem*. The haemorrhagic lesions of varicella can be seen on the lung surface.

chickenpox should be referred for assessment. If varicella IgG negative, thereby confirming non-immune status, consider administering VZIG to the mother. VZIG supplies are limited and organised usually through microbiology or virology departments. VZIG should also be considered for any immunocompromised contacts.

Fetal varicella syndrome

- Occurs in 2.2% of pregnant women infected before 20 weeks' gestation, but may occur beyond this time.
- Causes microcephaly, cicatricial limb deformities and skin scarring, cataracts, and eye defects.

Varicella pneumonitis

Smoking, pregnancy and immunocompromise increase the risk of pneumonitis. Patients may deteriorate very rapidly and their clinical condition, including oxygen saturation, should be monitored.

1.3.16 Imported fever

Scenario

A 19-year-old student has been feeling hot and cold for the last 3 days and is found to have a temperature of 39°C. Ten days ago he returned from a round-the-world trip.

Introduction

This is malaria until proven otherwise.

Your aim is, as always, to prevent morbidity and mortality from treatable disease, but also to consider transmissible infections of public health importance. Analyses of the final diagnosis in patients with fever after travel to the tropics reveal that about half are the result of tropical disease (Table 22). In assessing an individual patient, formulate two differential diagnoses, first including and then excluding the travel history. Your primary

TABLE 22 IMPORTANT INFECTIOUS CAUSES OF FEVER AFTER TRAVEL TO THE TROPICS		
Tropical	Common	Malaria (N)
		Diarrhoeal illness[1] (N)
		Dengue fever
		Enteric fever[1] (N)
		Acute viral hepatitis[1] (N)
	Less common	Rickettsial infection
		Amoebic abscess
		Filariasis
		Acute HIV infection[1]
	Must consider	Viral haemorrhagic fevers[1] (N)
Cosmopolitan		Respiratory infection
		Urinary tract infection
		Pharyngitis
		Tuberculosis[1] (N)
		Meningitis[1] (N)

1. Transmission of public health significance.
N, notifiable.

concern is early recognition of malaria: this is the most common single diagnosis and can kill, death being associated with delay in diagnosis. Remember that non-travel-related acute infections can also be serious in young people.

 Failure to report notifiable infections is an offence.

History of the presenting problem

Possibility of malaria

There are no clinical features that are specific for malaria (see Section 2.13.1). You must consider this diagnosis immediately in any febrile traveller who may have been exposed within the last 6 months. The life cycle of the malaria parasite takes at least 8 days from the moment of inoculation by an infected mosquito to the appearance of clinical symptoms, so any fever arising within the first week of potential exposure cannot be due to malaria. Almost all cases (90%) of

malaria occur within 1 month of exposure, but *Plasmodium vivax* and *Plasmodium ovale* infection can occasionally present weeks or months after exposure.

Malaria pitfalls

- Malaria typically presents with abrupt onset of fever accompanied by myalgia and headache, but there can be misleading localising features such as abdominal pain, diarrhoea, breathlessness or jaundice.
- Brief exposure is sufficient to acquire malaria; a single bite from an infected mosquito will suffice. The patient may be unaware that he has visited a malarious area or been reassured that there was no risk. If in doubt, assume potential exposure.
- Malaria chemoprophylaxis does not exclude malaria: it is at best 70–90% effective and compliance is poor.

Other symptomatology

A detailed history of symptoms associated with the feverishness is

required. Give particular weight to those that are volunteered, but also perform a systematic enquiry in relation to all organ systems. You will gain little by trying to analyse the fever pattern.

Other relevant history

Travel history

A comprehensive travel history is required to assess exposure to malaria (and other infections).

Where exactly did he go, when exactly was he there and what did he do?

- Ask for specific countries, regions and descriptions (city or rainforest, etc.).

- Did he stay in a hotel, hostel or tent?

- Exactly when was he in each place? The incubation period limits the differential diagnosis.

- Was it holiday or work, such as disaster relief or a zoological expedition?

- Did he have any contact with fresh water? If so, there is risk of schistosomiasis, amoebiasis or leptospirosis.

- Did he come into close contact with animals? If so, there is risk of anthrax and other zoonoses (Q-fever, tularaemia and avian influenza).

- Did he eat unpasteurised dairy products or undercooked food? If so, there is risk of enteric pathogens and brucellosis.

- Was the water he was drinking local, bottled or sterilised? Its source could suggest a risk of enteric pathogens.

- Did he have sex while abroad?

- Did he do any unusual activities, eg caving? There is a risk of histoplasmosis if this was done in the Americas.

- Did he experience any illness or treatment while away?

Precautions
Did he take any precautions?

- Pre-travel immunisations.

- Malaria prophylaxis and insect bite deterrents.

- Safe sex: HIV seroconversion and other sexually transmitted diseases should always be considered in sexually active travellers in the absence of another explanation.

Contact history
Have you been in contact with other sick people? This might reveal common source outbreaks (eg leptospirosis in adventure travel expeditions) or potential source cases (eg meningococcal disease).

Viral haemorrhagic fevers

Viral haemorrhagic fevers are not a major threat to public health, but some (Lassa, Marburg, Ebola and Congo–Crimean haemorrhagic fever) can be transmitted to nursing, medical and laboratory staff and carry a high case-fatality rate. Lassa fever should be considered if the patient has travelled to rural, sub-Saharan West Africa. Congo–Crimean haemorrhagic fever is distributed sporadically in Africa, the eastern Mediterranean, the Middle East and parts of southern Asia.

Viral haemorrhagic fevers are rare in travellers, but difficult to distinguish from other febrile illnesses so you need to maintain vigilance. Case identification depends on the recognition of risk factors. Take a careful travel history and enquire about any contact with known or suspected human cases. The upper limit of the incubation period is 21 days, beyond which these diseases are effectively excluded.

Examination
As always, your primary survey should ensure that breathing and circulation are adequate, and your general impression of how ill the patient is will determine whether you start immediate empirical treatment. Take particular note of the following.

- Lymphadenopathy; not a feature of malaria.

- Jaundice: occurs in viral hepatitis, and secondary to haemolysis in severe malaria.

- Hepatomegaly and/or splenomegaly

- Rash, eg look carefully for the eschar of a tick bite or the generalised rash of dengue fever (Fig. 35).

Investigation

Blood tests
Check the FBC, thick and thin malaria films (see Sections 2.13.1, and 3.2), renal and liver function tests, and C-reactive protein. Creatine kinase may be elevated in leptospirosis or severe septicaemia. Save serum for serological tests.

Malaria films

- The timing of the blood sample in relation to the fever is not important.
- A single negative malaria film does not exclude the diagnosis: repeat every 12–24 hours in a patient at risk.
- Malaria is highly unlikely after three negative films, but remains a possibility until the illness resolves or an alternative diagnosis is confirmed.
- Rapid diagnostic tests for malaria can be helpful if available (see Section 2.13.1).

Cultures
Take blood, throat swab, urine and stool for microscopy (if appropriate) and culture. Other body sites should be cultured if clinically appropriate.

Imaging

- CXR (all cases): look for consolidation and mediastinal lymphadenopathy. A raised right hemidiaphragm suggests the possibility of an amoebic abscess (Fig. 36).

- Ultrasonography and/or CT: if a liver abscess or other

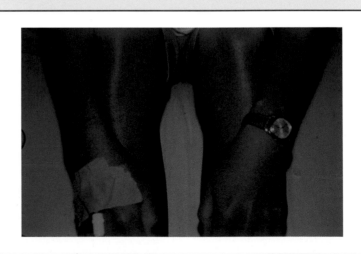

▲ **Fig. 35** Evanescent macular rash of dengue fever. The rash resembles scarlet fever or a toxic drug reaction, but may be difficult to see. (Courtesy of T. Loke.)

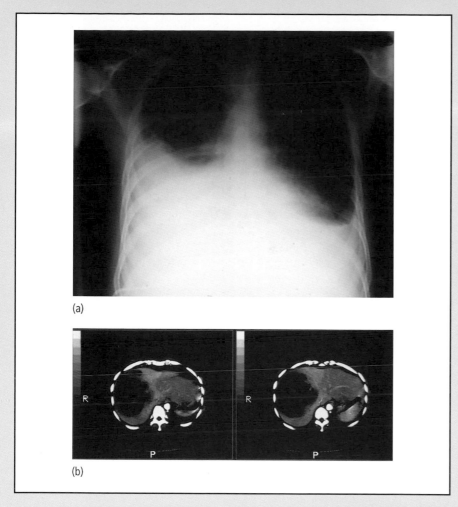

(a)

(b)

▲**Fig. 36** **(a)** CXR of a patient from India presenting with fever and right upper quadrant pain. **(b)** CT scan from the same patient revealing a large liver abscess later confirmed as amoebic.

intrathoracic/intra-abdominal collection is suspected.

Management

Resuscitate if needed (see Section 1.3.2).

Malaria

The first priority in this clinical context is always to exclude malaria. If malaria films are positive, institute therapy and seek specialist advice in those with severe disease (see Section 2.13.1). Benign malaria can be treated as an outpatient but all patients with *Plasmodium falciparum* malaria or in whom falciparum malaria cannot be reliably excluded (eg in mixed infections) should be admitted.

Other known diagnosis

If another specific diagnosis is made, treat appropriately.

Fever of unknown cause

The challenge is the febrile traveller without a diagnosis! Always consider the possibility of viral haemorrhagic fever in those returning from an endemic area with negative malaria films. If in doubt, discuss urgently with colleagues in infectious/tropical diseases.

- Is admission required? Your management depends on judgement of the most likely diagnoses and how ill the patient is. Review the history, examination and investigations

carefully. If the patient is well enough to be discharged, then make arrangements for repeat malaria films and early clinic review, and instruct the patient to return sooner if his condition deteriorates. If in doubt, admit him for observation.

- Is patient isolation required? In the setting of imported infection, this decision depends on whether the patient is deemed to be at risk of a viral haemorrhagic fever (see Key Point above), as no other major imported acute infections are easily transmissible to staff or other patients. This decision can be difficult and usually rests largely on the geographical source of the infection affecting this type of febrile patient, rather than on clinical features.

- Should the patient be given empirical therapy? Patients whom you judge to be (or at risk of becoming) seriously unwell should be given 'best guess' empirical antimicrobial therapy once specimens for culture have been obtained. Empirical therapy should be designed to cover the likely diagnoses, and those with potentially serious consequences if left untreated (see Section 1.2.1). You rarely need to treat for malaria unless the blood film is positive.

- What sort of continued evaluation? The patient will need regular review until the diagnosis and treatment are clear or the illness resolves. Consider taking advice or referring the patient to a communicable or tropical disease unit if the fever is persistent or the patient deteriorating.

1.3.17 Eosinophilia

Scenario

A 29-year-old soldier has recently returned from a 'jungle assignment'. He has fatigue and is found to have marked eosinophilia.

Introduction

Most cases of eosinophilia in patients who have been abroad are caused by infection with multicellular (metazoan) parasites, particularly tissue-invasive helminths (Table 23). Your initial assessment and investigations should be directed towards these conditions: eosinophilia is not a feature of the host response to single-celled (protozoal) parasites. A wide range of non-infectious conditions can also cause eosinophilia; the most important are allergic reactions, either atopic or drug related (Table 24). If parasitic and allergic causes are excluded, a search for rarer causes of eosinophilia is required.

History of the presenting problem

The time course of the fatigue and the relation to travel is unlikely to be illuminating: the key is to unravel the cause of the eosinophilia.

Exposure to metazoan parasites

The major risk is travel to areas of endemic parasite infections. Essentially, travel to any tropical or subtropical part of the world is a significant risk. Parasites can remain asymptomatic for years, so you should take a lifetime travel and detailed exposure history. Ask about the following exposures (this particular patient is likely to have all of these).

- Have you ever travelled to the tropics or subtropics and when?

- Which countries did you visit?

- Did you have any contact with fresh water? (Schistosomiasis.)

- Did you walk barefoot? (Strongyloidiasis.)

- Have you eaten undercooked meat? (Trichinosis.)

Clues to particular infections

Most infections with metazoan parasites are asymptomatic, making the exposure history vital. However, the history may contain some specific clues to certain parasites.

- Fever: Katayama fever in patients recently exposed to schistosomiasis.

- Cough or wheeze: pulmonary eosinophilia, eg from *Ascaris*.

- Diarrhoea.

- Blood in urine or stool.

- Rash.

- Muscle aches or pains: trichinosis.

Other relevant history

Allergy

Ask carefully about symptoms of atopy. Take a careful drug history. Drug reactions can occur even after long-term use, so potential culprits are not limited to recent changes in medication.

TABLE 23 COMMON PARASITIC CAUSES OF EOSINOPHILIA

Disease	Geographical distribution
Strongyloidiasis	Throughout the tropics and subtropics
Schistosomiasis[1]	Africa, Arabia, Caribbean, South America, Japan, China and the Philippines
Filariasis	Throughout the tropics and subtropics
Trichinosis	Worldwide
Toxocariasis	Worldwide
Ascariasis	Worldwide

1. Combined distribution of multiple species (see Section 2.14.1).

TABLE 24 NON-INFECTIOUS CAUSES OF EOSINOPHILIA

Cause	Examples
Allergic reactions	Atopy (asthma, eczema) Drug reactions
Solid neoplasms	Carcinoma of lung Renal cell carcinoma Cervical carcinoma Tumours of the large bowel Melanoma
Lymphoreticular malignancy	Hodgkin's disease B- and T-cell lymphoma T-cell leukaemia Myelomonocytic leukaemia
Vasculitic diseases	Churg–Strauss disease Wegener's granulomatosis
Idiopathic	Hypereosinophilic syndrome

Relevant past history

Pay particular attention to allergies, medication, previous autoimmune disease and cancer.

Examination

General features

Perform a full examination, but don't be disappointed if there are no external signs of disease. Specific clues to parasites include the following.

- Lymphoedema: suggests filariasis (Fig. 37).

- Rash, eg cutaneous larva migrans and dermatitis in onchocerciasis.

- Subcutaneous nodules: may be present in onchocerciasis.

- Lymphadenopathy.

- Urine dipstick for microscopic haematuria: suggests schistosomiasis in this context.

Investigation

Unless there is strong clinical suspicion of an alternative diagnosis, the first round of tests should be directed towards helminthic infection.

Blood tests

Check the FBC and film, eosinophil count, electrolytes, renal and liver function, C-reactive protein and erythrocyte sedimentation rate. If other investigations are failing to yield an answer, consider measuring total serum IgE if available: a normal level weighs against parasitic infections and allergic diseases.

Imaging

CXR (all cases) may reveal transient (if radiograph repeated) infiltrates suggestive of pulmonary eosinophilia; may be abnormal in allergic bronchopulmonary aspergillosis and Churg–Strauss disease; and may reveal calcified cysts in cysticercosis or trichinosis (see Section 2.14.3).

Parasitological investigations

Specific tests are guided by the exposure history.

- Stool microscopy for ova, cysts and parasites in all cases (see Section 3.1): this may need to be repeated several (at least three) times, and expert interpretation is required, particularly if microscopic examination for larvae of *Strongyloides stercoralis* is requested.

- Blood films at specific times of the day: to detect some forms of filariasis, eg *Loa loa* and *Wuchereria bancrofti* (see Section 2.14.4).

- Serological tests – but note that these may be difficult to interpret because there is considerable cross-reactivity between species.

- Terminal urine sample or rectal biopsy: schistosomiasis (Fig. 38) (see Section 2.14.1).

- Skin snips (see Section 3.2): to detect onchocerciasis (see Section 2.14.4).

- Duodenal biopsy or aspirate: to detect *Strongyloides stercoralis* (see Section 2.14.2).

Other tests

If there has been parasitic exposure, it is unlikely to be necessary to investigate for the diseases listed in Table 24.

Management

Appropriate investigation is the cornerstone of management. While this is progressing, stop all drugs that are not absolutely necessary. Treatment is virtually always given only when a firm diagnosis has been established. If the condition defies diagnosis, there is sometimes a role for empirical antihelminthic treatment in consultation with an expert. Treatment of specific infections is covered in Section 2.14.

▲**Fig. 37** This young woman presented with fever, swelling of the right arm and tender right axillary lymph nodes after a prolonged trip to sub-Saharan Africa. She had a marked eosinophilia with filariasis confirmed serologically.

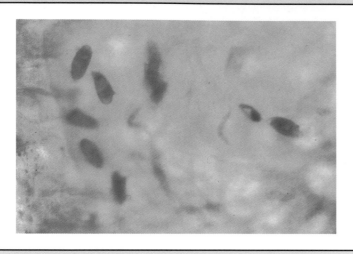

▲ **Fig. 38** *Schistosoma mansoni*, identified by the lateral spine, on a rectal biopsy (see Section 2.14.1).

1.3.18 Jaundice and fever after travelling

Scenario

A 48-year-old woman presents with fever and jaundice after a trip to the Indian subcontinent to visit her parents.

Introduction

The differential diagnosis of jaundice is extensive (see *Gastroenterology and Hepatology*, Section 1.4.5). You need to consider alcohol and toxin exposure, but the history of travel and fever makes infection likely (Table 25). A common mistake is to limit your thinking to infectious agents that primarily infect the liver, in particular the hepatitis viruses. Jaundice may be a manifestation of systemic infection that can have severe consequences if untreated. Space-occupying infections within the liver (such as bacterial or amoebic abscess) rarely present with jaundice.

History of the presenting problem

Possibility of malaria

Always consider malaria in a febrile traveller who has been exposed within the last 6 months (see Section 1.3.16).

Acute viral hepatitis

In acute viral hepatitis, systemic symptoms occur in the prodromal phase and typically resolve with the onset of jaundice. Fever rarely persists into the icteric phase. This holds true for acute hepatitis A, B and E, which cannot be distinguished reliably from each other clinically. Hepatitis C rarely presents with acute hepatitis.

A detailed history of the progression of the illness is required.

- When were you last completely well?

- When did you notice that you were looking yellow?

- What was the first thing that you noticed was wrong?

- Is your urine darker than usual and when did it change? Dark urine is caused by excretion of conjugated bilirubin in intrahepatic and posthepatic jaundice.

- Are your stools pale? Have you been itchy? Intrahepatic inflammation, such as in acute viral hepatitis, can cause cholestasis with pale stools and pruritus.

- How are you feeling now? Patients with acute viral hepatitis generally feel better once they become jaundiced.

> ⚠ **Jaundice and high fever**
>
> Do not simply accept the diagnosis of acute viral hepatitis: make sure that you consider life-threatening illnesses such as malaria, ascending cholangitis and typhoid.

TABLE 25 IMPORTANT INFECTIOUS CAUSES OF FEVER AND JAUNDICE AFTER TRAVEL TO THE TROPICS		
Tropical	Common	Acute viral hepatitis A, B and E Malaria
	Less common	Leptospirosis Typhoid
	Uncommon	Fascioliasis Relapsing fever Yellow fever
Cosmopolitan		Ascending cholangitis EBV, CMV, hepatitis A and B Toxoplasmosis

CMV, cytomegalovirus; EBV, Epstein–Barr virus.

Other relevant history

Source of infection

Remember that hepatitis A and E are spread via the faecal–oral route and hepatitis B by blood or sex. Also, keep the different incubation periods in mind (see Section 2.10.8) as you ask about the following.

- Where have you been, when and what did you do? (See Section 1.3.16.)

- Was the water safe and what did you eat (eg shellfish)?

- Have you been immunised against hepatitis? Which type and when?

- Where were you brought up? Individuals who spent their childhood in the tropics are likely to have acquired hepatitis A previously and have lifelong immunity, but hepatitis E is more sporadic and is frequently seen in such travellers returning to their country of origin.

Then concentrate on risks for the conditions listed in Table 25. Tact and care will be required to elicit this information without causing offence (see *Clinical Skills for PACES*), the key issue being to explain to the patient why you need the information: 'Jaundice can be caused by some viruses, so I need to know if you are at risk of these viruses. The things that put people at risk are . . .' Ask about the following.

- Did you have any injections, transfusions or surgical treatment while abroad?

- Did you have a tattoo or any body piercing?

- Have you had unprotected sex in the last 6 months?

- Have you ever injected yourself with drugs?

Fever and jaundice

- • Leptospirosis: this is common in 'adventure' travellers with freshwater exposure. Fever is usually low grade and the exposure history, along with associated features such as myalgia, meningism or subconjunctival haemorrhages (Fig. 39), suggest the diagnosis (see Section 2.7.4).
- Ascending cholangitis: abdominal pain, jaundice and high fever, often with rigors, raises the possibility of ascending cholangitis. This may result in severe sepsis, which can be rapidly fatal.

Drugs and alcohol

- Ask about prescription and over-the-counter medication: could the patient have glucose-6-phosphate dehydrogenase deficiency?
- Some recreational drugs, eg ecstasy, can cause acute hepatitis.
- Increased alcohol consumption on holiday may induce alcoholic hepatitis.

Other relevant history

Ask specifically about a previous history of jaundice or biliary disease

and risk factors such as alcohol intake. Acute viral hepatitis is much more severe where there is pre-existing liver disease. This woman is 48 years old but, if a younger woman, could she be pregnant? Hepatitis E is generally benign but has a high mortality in pregnancy.

Examination

Is she well, ill or very ill? Check her vital signs. Take careful note of the following:

- fever;

- jaundice;

- lymphadenopathy;

- conjunctival haemorrhage in viral haemorrhagic fever or leptospirosis.

Look for signs of hepatic failure:

- confusion;

- spontaneous bruising or bleeding at venepuncture sites;

- liver flap.

Look for signs of chronic liver disease (see *Gastroenterology and Hepatology*, Section 1.2.2). Check for

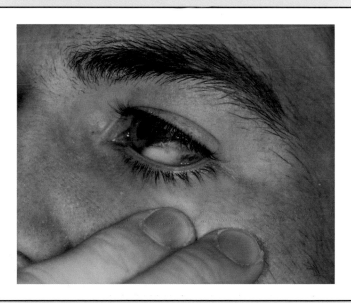

▲**Fig. 39** Subconjunctival haemorrhage.

enlargement and tenderness of the liver, and for splenomegaly.

Investigation

> **Initial investigation of jaundice**
>
> If you were allowed only two tests, which would you choose? The correct answer is as follows.
>
> - Urine dipstick for bilirubin: conjugated bilirubin is water soluble and excreted in urine, so the absence of urine bilirubin in the presence of jaundice implies a prehepatic cause such as haemolysis. If urine bilirubin is present, the cause of jaundice is intrahepatic or posthepatic.
> - Hepatic ultrasonography: intrahepatic or posthepatic causes of jaundice can be distinguished by looking for dilated biliary ducts on ultrasonography.
>
> These simple tests therefore allow you to divide jaundice into prehepatic, intrahepatic and posthepatic types.

Blood tests
Check the following.

- FBC and film: for malaria and evidence of haemolysis (see *Haematology,* Section 2.1.7).

- Renal function: may be abnormal in any patient who is acutely ill as a manifestation of haemodynamically mediated acute renal failure, but may also be a clue to leptospirosis, haemolytic–uraemic syndrome (see *Nephrology*, Section 2.7.3) or hepatorenal syndrome.

- Clotting and serum albumin: to assess hepatic synthetic function.

- Liver function tests: in acute viral hepatitis liver transaminases are always significantly elevated. Repeat measurements are useful to follow the course of the illness:

typically there will be a shift from a hepatitic to a cholestatic pattern as the viral hepatitis begins to resolve (see Section 2.10.8).

- Monospot/Paul–Bunnell test: enables rapid diagnosis of EBV.

> **Mild elevation of transaminases is non-specific and can occur in many infections, including malaria, typhoid, dengue and bacterial sepsis.**

Cultures and serology
Blood cultures should be done in all cases. Consider serological tests for the following:

- hepatitis A, B, C and E (see Section 2.10.8);

- CMV and EBV (see Sections 2.10.3 and 2.10.4);

- toxoplasmosis (see Section 2.13.4);

- leptospirosis (see Section 2.7.4).

Always save some serum.

> ⚠ **Consider paracetamol overdose in any patient presenting acutely with jaundice.**

Management
It is essential to recognise life-threatening infections such as cholangitis, bacterial sepsis, malaria, leptospirosis and haemolytic–uraemic syndrome, and treat them urgently (see Sections 1.3.2 and 1.3.16). In other patients you can wait for the results of tests and then institute specific management.

Viral hepatitis
There is no antiviral therapy for acute viral hepatitis, so consider the following.

- Is admission needed? In general, patients can be managed at home unless there is evidence of impaired liver synthetic function or hepatic failure. Follow liver function and the prothrombin time closely until liver function is improving.

- What if the patient goes into liver failure? Refer to a specialist unit sooner rather than later: intensive support and possibly transplantation may be needed (see *Gastroenterology and Hepatology*, Section 2.10.8).

- Is there a risk of spread? Give advice on hygiene and safe sex to limit the spread. Don't forget that hepatitis A can be transmitted by sexual activity. If the patient has hepatitis A, then household contacts should be offered immunoglobulin and/or hepatitis A vaccine; if hepatitis B, then trace, screen for chronic hepatitis B and immunise sexual contacts.

- For how long should patients come to the clinic? Hepatitis A and E need to be followed only until they are clearly improving. Hepatitis B and C need monitoring for chronic disease (see Section 2.10.8).

1.3.19 A traveller with diarrhoea

Scenario

A 35-year-old Australian woman has travelled through South-east Asia, India and Africa before arriving in the UK. On the flight from South Africa to London, she develops abdominal discomfort and severe diarrhoea.

TABLE 26 CAUSES OF INFECTIVE DIARRHOEA

Enterocolitis	Organism	Common examples
Non-invasive	Viruses	Rotavirus, Norwalk, calicivirus, adenovirus, astrovirus, SRSV
	Bacteria	EPEC, ETEC, *Vibrio* spp., *Staphylococcus aureus*, *Bacillus cereus*, *Clostridium perfringens*, *Clostridium difficile*
	Parasites	*Giardia lamblia, Cryptosporidium parvum, Isospora belli, Cyclospora* spp.
Invasive	Bacteria	EHEC, *Shigella* spp., *Salmonella* spp., *Campylobacter jejuni, Clostridium difficile*
	Parasites	*Entamoeba histolytica, Balantidium coli, Schistosoma mansoni/japonicum*
Enteric fever	Bacteria	*Salmonella typhi, Salmonella paratyphi* A and B, *Yersinia* spp.

EHEC, enterohaemorrhagic *Escherichia coli*; EPEC, enteropathogenic *Escherichia coli*; ETEC, enterotoxigenic *Escherichia coli*; SRSV, small, round, structured virus.

Introduction

This is most probably a case of infectious enterocolitis (Table 26). Try to decide if the infection is non-invasive or invasive, because this will guide therapeutic decisions. A bewildering array of tropical parasites can cause diarrhoea, but few require urgent treatment. Consideration of these can be delayed until test results become available and, if the diarrhoea persists, efforts to find parasites can be intensified. The only exception is amoebic colitis, which needs early treatment.

🔑 Do not fall into the trap of making a cursory assessment. As you approach the patient, do not limit your thinking to infectious enterocolitis. Diarrhoea can be a prominent symptom in severe systemic infections such as bacterial sepsis or toxic shock syndrome (see Section 1.3.2). In travellers, consider malaria or typhoid. Do not forget surgical causes of abdominal pain such as appendicitis.

History of the presenting problem

Type of enteric infection

The history will help you decide whether the infection is non-invasive or invasive.

- What is the diarrhoea like? Ask about frequency, volume, consistency, blood and mucus.

- Abdominal pain: is any pain continuous or colicky, and is it relieved by defecation?

- Tenesmus: an intense, painful but fruitless desire to defecate.

- Nausea or vomiting.

- Fever/shivers/chills or other systemic symptoms.

Non-invasive diarrhoea

This is caused by viruses, bacterial enterotoxins or protozoa affecting the proximal small bowel. Typically the diarrhoea is watery and associated with nausea and vomiting. Abdominal cramps may be prominent, but the pain is not relieved by defecation. There is usually minimal or no systemic upset.

Invasive diarrhoea

This is commonly bacterial, but consider amoebic colitis. Typically, bowel movements are frequent and may contain mucus or blood (dysentery). Cramping pain is relieved by defecation and tenesmus is common. Low-grade fever is common, but high fever or rigors suggest bloodstream invasion.

Other relevant history

Source of infection

Has anyone else had the same symptoms? Unless more than one person has been affected a food history rarely identifies the source of enteric infection, but a detailed travel history is required (see Section 1.3.16).

Systemic infection

Marked systemic symptoms imply invasion from bacterial colitis, infection at another site or generalised infection (eg malaria or enteric fever). Take particular note of the following:

- symptoms of infection outside the gastrointestinal tract;

- symptoms of severe sepsis (see Section 1.3.2);

- menstrual history/tampon use (see Section 1.3.2).

Relevant past history

- Underlying illness, particularly immunosuppression.

- Antacid drug use, proton pump inhibitors and histamine H_2 receptor antagonists all increase the risk of infectious enterocolitis.

- Recent antibiotic use: consider antibiotic-associated colitis (see Section 2.5.1).

> ### Immunocompromised host
>
> In such a patient, remember the following.
>
> - Increased range of pathogens, eg cytomegalovirus enterocolitis.
> - Increased disease severity with invasive pathogens.
> - Antimicrobial therapy is more likely to be required.
> - Increased incidence of *Salmonella* bacteraemia.
> - Prolonged infection/carriage may occur, eg cryptosporidia.

Examination

Is the woman well, ill, very ill or nearly dead? Check temperature, peripheral perfusion, pulse, BP (lying and standing/sitting), respiratory rate and pulse oximetry. Begin resuscitation immediately if required (see Section 1.3.2 and *Acute Medicine*, Section 1.2.2).

Attention will then obviously focus on the abdomen. Are there signs of peritonism? This should not occur in uncomplicated infectious enterocolitis. Splenomegaly implies systemic infection such as malaria or typhoid.

Look for focal signs of infection outside the gastrointestinal tract.

Investigation

Blood tests

- FBC, eosinophil count (see Section 1.3.17), electrolytes, renal and liver function, and C-reactive protein.

- Malaria films are mandatory if the patient is febrile and has visited a malarious area (see Section 1.3.16).

Cultures and serology

- Blood and stool cultures: if stool is not available, take a rectal swab for culture.

- Stool microscopy for ova, cysts and parasites, even if the illness does not suggest parasitic infection, because gastrointestinal infection with multiple pathogens is common as a result of a shared route of transmission.

- Hot stool: microscopic examination of a fresh stool specimen is useful if amoebic dysentery is suspected. Neutrophils within the specimen imply invasive or inflammatory diarrhoea, but may be absent in amoebic colitis because they are destroyed by the amoebae.

- Amoebic serology: if the patient has dysentery, but note that this may be negative early in the disease.

Searching for a viral cause is most rewarding in young children (rotavirus) and where there has been an outbreak of acute self-limiting gastroenteritis suggesting norovirus infection.

Imaging

A plain abdominal film should be performed in any patient who requires hospital admission for diarrhoea, but is rarely helpful unless marked tenderness suggests the possibility of toxic megacolon (Fig. 40).

Management

General

Fluid replacement is the mainstay of management, by drinking if possible. Intravenous replacement is needed if the patient is shocked or vomiting. Antidiarrhoeal agents should be avoided if there are signs of invasive disease.

Antibiotic therapy

Most cases of diarrhoea do not require specific antimicrobial therapy and will settle with rehydration and time. In traveller's diarrhoea antibiotics such as ciprofloxacin lead to a slight shortening of the time for which

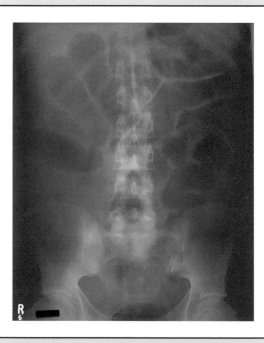

▲**Fig. 40** Toxic megacolon in a case of *Clostridium difficile* colitis.

the diarrhoea persists, but they are rarely recommended. In uncomplicated *Salmonella* infection, antibiotics are of no benefit and prolong stool carriage. Drug susceptibility data may help when therapy is indicated, but empirical treatment is required while awaiting culture results. Indications for this include the following.

- Marked systemic symptoms, particularly severe sepsis or shock, extraintestinal manifestations or a very marked inflammatory response: ciprofloxacin is widely used to treat these symptoms, but note increasing ciprofloxacin resistance.

- Moderate-to-severe bloody diarrhoea: ciprofloxacin for presumed bacterial dysentery; add metronidazole if the patient is at risk of amoebic dysentery.

- Very profuse non-inflammatory diarrhoea, which suggests cholera: consider tetracycline or ciprofloxacin.

Specific antibiotics are indicated for positive blood cultures, typhoid/paratyphoid and parasitic infections (including amoebiasis).

Public health

Note the following.

- Nurse the patient in a side room if admitted.

- Give advice on hygiene if patient is discharged.

- Food poisoning, suspected or proven, and typhoid are notifiable diseases.

- *Salmonella* infections require repeat stool cultures to detect chronic carriage, particularly if the patient is a food handler.

1.3.20 Malaise, mouth ulcers and fever

Scenario

You are asked to review a 54-year-old gay man complaining of malaise, rash, mouth ulcers and pyrexia.

Introduction

Is this primary HIV infection (seroconversion illness)? A seroconversion illness occurs in 10–90% of patients acquiring HIV, but is often mild. Primary HIV

infection has an incubation period of 2–4 weeks (range 1–6) and typically resolves within 14 days. The differential diagnosis is wide (Table 27) and you must assess the HIV risk and exclude other conditions.

History of the presenting problem

Risk of HIV infection

- A full sexual history is needed: what sexual exposure has occurred both recently and in the past, how many partners and what type of sex? There is no 100% safe sex: unprotected receptive anal sex carries the highest risk, but oral sex still confers a risk.

- Does the man use recreational drugs? Drugs and alcohol increase high-risk behaviour. Intravenous drug use may directly transmit HIV.

- Is there a travel history? Sex abroad often carries a higher risk.

Symptoms of seroconversion illness

Symptoms associated with HIV seroconversion are shown in Table 28. Similar symptoms are seen in many other conditions and linking them with the exposure risk is required to make the correct diagnosis.

> ⚠ Primary HIV mimics other illnesses. HIV risk should be assessed in all cases of unexplained fever, fever plus rash, meningoencephalitis, hepatitis and oesophageal/rectal ulceration.

Examination

In someone with suspected seroconversion illness a full physical examination is required, noting the following in particular.

TABLE 27 DIFFERENTIAL DIAGNOSIS OF MALAISE, RASH, MOUTH ULCERS AND FEVER IN A GAY MAN

Cause	Example
Viral	Primary HIV infection Infectious mononucleosis (CMV, EBV, toxoplasmosis) Primary HSV Enteroviruses Rubella and parvovirus infection
Bacterial	Secondary syphilis Disseminated gonorrhoea β-Haemolytic *Streptococcus* Meningococcal infection
Non-infective	Crohn's disease Behçet's syndrome Leukaemia

CMV, cytomegalovirus; EBV, Epstein–Barr virus; HSV, herpes simplex virus.

TABLE 28 PRESENTING SYMPTOMS IN PRIMARY HIV

System	Comments
General	Fever, sweats, malaise, myalgia, arthralgia
Mouth	Sore throat, mouth ulcers
Gastrointestinal	Odynophagia resulting from oesophageal ulcers (Fig. 41) Nausea, vomiting, diarrhoea, rectal ulcers
Skin	Rashes: macular, papular or erythema multiforme-like (Fig. 42)
Genitourinary	Ulceration
Neurological	Headache, photophobia, confusion, neuropathic pain

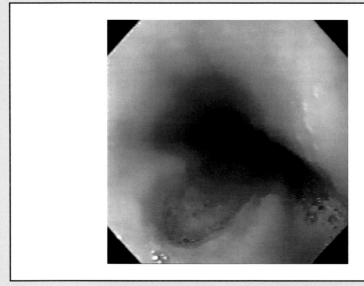

▲ **Fig. 41** Oesophageal ulcer during HIV seroconversion.

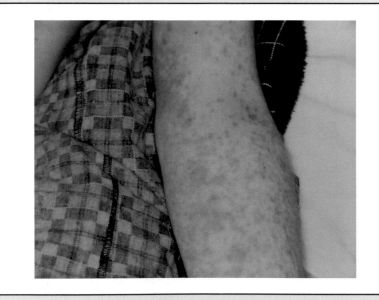

▲ **Fig. 42** Macular rash of HIV seroconversion.

- Pyrexia: invariable in primary HIV.

- Mouth ulcers: common in HIV seroconversion, but in contrast to EBV disease tonsillar enlargement is rare.

- Rashes: frequent and most often macular or maculopapular (Fig. 42), although nodular and vesicular forms may be seen. Alopecia and desquamation may follow.

- Lymphadenopathy: typically generalised, with smooth non-tender nodes appearing in 70% of cases in the second week.

- Hepatosplenomegaly in some cases.

- Neurological signs and aseptic (lymphocytic) meningitis in some cases.

Investigation

'Routine' blood tests

- FBC: may see reactive (atypical) lymphocytes, low platelets and anaemia (rarely).

- Liver function: abnormal aminotransferase (aspartate aminotransferase and alanine aminotransferase) levels.

- Creatine kinase: mild myositis.

- Inflammatory markers: raised C-reactive protein and erythrocyte sedimentation rate are common.

Blood tests to confirm the diagnosis

Tests that depend on antibodies alone are of little value in diagnosing seroconversion illness because anti-HIV antibodies only appear 2–6 weeks after the onset of symptoms. The HIV p24 antigen appears within 2–3 days of the onset of illness: many modern serological test kits detect the p24 antigen as well as HIV antibodies and thus can be positive during the seroconversion illness, but not reliably. A nucleic acid amplification test can detect HIV plasma RNA or whole-blood DNA from 1–2 days before the onset of symptoms, so to diagnose seroconversion request tests for p24 antigen and HIV RNA or proviral DNA.

> To diagnose HIV seroconversion illness reliably requires tests for p24 antigen and HIV RNA or proviral DNA.

Lymphocyte subsets are sometimes measured, looking for raised CD8$^+$ and falling CD4$^+$ lymphocytes; occasionally, the CD4$^+$ cell count falls below 200×10^6/L, predisposing to AIDS-defining illness.

Tests to exclude other infections

- Blood cultures and throat swab for bacterial culture (streptococci).

- Viral culture from stool and throat for enteroviruses; viral throat swab for HSV.

- Syphilis serology: always positive if there is secondary disease.

- Positive monospot test: suggests EBV, but false positives may occur.

- Specific serology for CMV, EBV and toxoplasmosis.

> **Serological diagnosis of HIV infection**
>
> - Enzyme-linked immunosorbent assay (ELISA) tests are used to screen for anti-HIV-1 and anti-HIV-2 antibodies.
> - There is an approximately 1% equivocal or false-positive rate.
> - Confirm positive tests by further ELISA or Western blot.
> - Window period from exposure to seroconversion of up to 3 months.

Management

Consideration must be given to antiretroviral therapy (ART) when primary HIV is confirmed, there being a theoretical argument to commence treatment immediately while the virus is still genetically homogeneous and before extensive spread has occurred. However, this must be weighed against committing patients with early disease to long-term, potentially toxic therapy and the risk of them developing antiretroviral resistance.

The outcomes of long-term clinical studies are awaited to define the role of short courses (3–12 months) of ART in primary HIV infection. If ART is not started, treatment is essentially symptomatic and the patient should be monitored closely. Patients who appear to be rapidly progressing, with a CD4 cell count persistently below 250×10^6/L, can then be considered for early ART.

> **Factors associated with rapid HIV progression**
>
> - Age over 40 years at seroconversion.
> - Severe or prolonged seroconversion illness.
> - CD4 cell count falls to $<200 \times 10^6$/L during seroconversion.
> - Failure of CD4 cell count to rise above 500×10^6/L after seroconversion.
> - High HIV viral load after seroconversion.

1.3.21 Breathlessness in a HIV-positive patient

Scenario

An HIV-positive patient presents with a dry non-productive cough and breathlessness.

Introduction

There are many causes of breathlessness in HIV-positive patients (Table 29). A key priority is to determine whether this is *Pneumocystis carinii* pneumonia (PCP), also called *Pneumocystis jiroveci* pneumonia.

> The breathless HIV-positive patient has *Pneumocystis* until proved otherwise.

History of the presenting problem

HIV disease

The level of immunosuppression relates well to the risk of infection (see Section 2.11).

- Does he know his most recent CD4 cell count and HIV viral load?

- Has he had any HIV-related problems? There are certain severe problems that are AIDS-defining and which only occur when the immune system is severely compromised (Table 30).

- Is he on anti-HIV therapy? If so, what are the drugs and have they been working? Most clinics will have these data to hand.

- Is he taking prophylactic therapy for PCP?

Breathlessness

Aside from assessing the degree of breathlessness, ask about the following, which may help in the differential diagnosis.

- How long has he been breathless? PCP is generally indolent or subacute.

- Cough and sputum: PCP is usually non-productive; purulent sputum suggests bacterial infection;

TABLE 29 BREATHLESSNESS IN HIV INFECTION

Category	CD4 cell count (×10⁶/L)	More common conditions
Pulmonary infection	Any <200	Bacterial pneumonia, tuberculosis (TB) PCP Viral: RSV and CMV (uncommon) Fungal: *Cryptococcus* and *Histoplasma* spp.
Malignancy	Very low Any	Kaposi's sarcoma Lymphoma
Anaemia	Not relevant	HIV related Caused by infection or malignancy Drug induced
Pulmonary: non-infective	<200 Any Any Any <300 <200	Pneumothorax: may complicate PCP Primary pulmonary hypertension Thromboembolic disease Non-infective pulmonary effusion Lymphoid interstitial pneumonitis Interstitial lung disease
Cardiac	Not relevant <200	HIV-related cardiomyopathy Pericardial effusion
Metabolic	Not relevant Any Any	Bacterial sepsis Drug-induced lactic acidosis Renal failure

CMV, cytomegalovirus; RSV, respiratory syncytial virus.

TABLE 30 SOME MORE COMMON AIDS-DEFINING CONDITIONS SEEN IN THE UK

Category	Examples
Malignancy	Kaposi's sarcoma Lymphoma (non-Hodgkin's, Hodgkin's and other) Anal carcinoma
Infection	PCP Oesophageal *Candida* Toxoplasmosis TB Atypical mycobacterial infection CMV retinitis
Others	HIV-wasting syndrome HIV encephalopathy

bacteria and TB) and specific contacts with TB. Has there been a local influenza or mycoplasma outbreak?

Examination

Is the patient well, ill, very ill or nearly dead? Immediately assess the airway, breathing and circulation.

- Can the patient speak?

- Is he using accessory muscles?

- Is he cyanosed?

- Is there a pneumothorax?

- Are there focal lung signs? Often there are few chest signs in PCP, although there may be fine or coarse crackles. Focal consolidation suggests bacterial pneumonia.

- Does he look exhausted?

- Check pulse oximetry.

Have a low threshold for asking for help from the intensive care unit if the patient has, or is developing, respiratory failure (see *Acute Medicine*, Section 1.2.5).

Look for signs of the other conditions listed in Table 29, including bacterial sepsis, heart failure and anaemia. Fundoscopy may show focal lesions from extrapulmonary PCP or signs of CMV retinitis (see Section 1.3.22).

Investigation

> The baseline CD4 cell count is critical. PCP and viral and fungal pneumonia are unlikely if this is significantly above 200 × 10⁶/L.

haemoptysis means that TB must be excluded.

- Chest pain: PCP is generally painless.

- Fever and sweats: if these have been totally absent, consider non-infective causes. Abrupt onset of high fever suggests bacterial infection.

Exposure to possible infections

Ask about travel, ethnic origin (TB and histoplasmosis), birds (cryptococci and *Chlamydia psittaci*), hospital admissions (resistant

Immediate blood tests

- FBC, electrolytes, glucose, renal and liver function tests to exclude anaemia and hepatic or renal failure.

- CD4 cell count: unless a recent clinic result is available, although it may take several days to obtain and can fall in any acute illness.

- Lactate dehydrogenase: typically raised in PCP.

Arterial blood gases

Arterial blood gas analysis is needed to assess respiratory failure and exclude acidosis. If the patient is acidotic, measure blood lactate levels (see below). Exercise oximetry can be helpful in early PCP: arterial oxygen saturation is normal at rest but will fall on exercise.

Imaging of the chest

- CXR: typically reveals a fine interstitial and/or nodular infiltrate in PCP, with relative sparing of the bases and apices (Fig. 43). However, 5–10% of patients will have a normal CXR at presentation. Occasionally, PCP may present with focal infiltrates or thin-walled cavities (pneumatoceles), but cavitation is more suggestive of a

tuberculous, bacterial or fungal (histoplasmosis) aetiology.

- High-resolution CT: reveals a 'ground-glass' pattern of alveolar consolidation in PCP.

Pulmonary function tests

In PCP the key abnormality is impaired diffusing capacity (Kco; see *Respiratory Medicine*, Section 3.6.2). Lung volumes may be reduced with a restrictive pattern.

Microbiological tests

Imaging is not diagnostic and you should strive to obtain a microbiological diagnosis. Alveolar specimens are needed to diagnose PCP, whereas other pathogens may be identified in ordinary sputum. Inducing sputum with nebulised saline produces specimens suitable for PCP, TB and bacterial studies (see Section 3.1) but is of low sensitivity and is not performed often nowadays. Bronchoalveolar lavage is the test of choice. Lung biopsy (transbronchial, CT-guided or thoracoscopic) may rarely be needed to establish the diagnosis.

Breathlessness in an HIV patient with a normal CXR

- PCP is suggested by exercise desaturation.
- Lactic acidosis is an increasingly recognised and serious complication of anti-HIV therapy: the patient will usually have abdominal pain, abnormal liver function and hepatic steatosis.
- Consider bacterial sepsis.
- Consider cardiac failure/thromboembolism/pulmonary hypertension.
- Do not delay bronchoscopy in immunocompromised patients with unexplained respiratory symptoms: pneumonia may progress rapidly and the patient become too hypoxic to bronchoscope safely.

Management

Respiratory support

- Monitor respiratory rate, pulse oximetry and for signs of exhaustion.

- Give supplemental oxygen as needed to keep Sao_2 >92%.

- Consider non-invasive ventilation if hypoxia is not corrected (see *Respiratory Medicine*, Section 2.12.3).

- Consider the need for endotracheal intubation and ventilation early and notify intensive care if this is likely. The indications for mechanical ventilation are the same as for any respiratory condition.

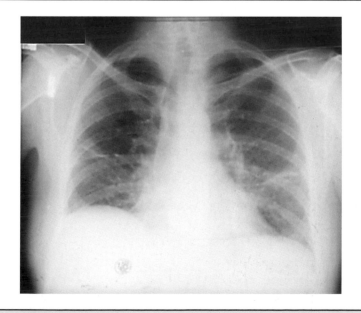

▲**Fig. 43** CXR of a patient with severe PCP.

The fact that a patient is HIV positive should not prevent transfer to intensive care if appropriate to the clinical situation. HIV is a treatable disease with excellent long-term prognosis.

Antimicrobial therapy

Empirical therapy for bacterial infection (see Section 1.3.4) and PCP (if the patient has a low CD4 count) is needed for those who are very ill. Treatment options for the therapy of PCP are given in Table 31. In moderate-to-severe hypoxia (Pao_2 <8 kPa on air), adjunctive corticosteroids (oral prednisolone 40–60 mg/day or equivalent) significantly reduce morbidity and mortality.

Further comments

Prophylaxis of PCP

Primary prophylaxis (Table 31) should be instituted in all patients with a CD4 cell count below 200×10^6/L or a diagnosis of AIDS. Secondary prophylaxis should be given to patients who have recovered from an episode of PCP. Prophylaxis can be discontinued if the CD4 cell count stabilises above 200×10^6/L on antiretroviral therapy.

1.3.22 HIV positive and blurred vision

Scenario

A patient with AIDS phones the HIV unit complaining of altered vision.

Introduction

This is an emergency and the patient must be assessed promptly. Rapid visual loss can occur directly from opportunistic infection (Table 32) or as a result of retinal detachment. Cytomegalovirus (CMV) is responsible for 80–90% of retinal infection in patients with AIDS.

History of the presenting problem

Assess immune function using the same initial approach as that described in Section 1.3.21. CMV retinitis is rarely seen in patients with a CD4 cell count above 75×10^6/L.

Ocular symptoms

- Does the problem affect one or both eyes? Most retinal infections will start in one eye and a problem affecting vision in both eyes may have an extraocular cause.

- How much is the vision affected? Can he still read?

- Is there pain and is the eye bloodshot? A painful red eye is unusual in retinal infections in AIDS unless the patient has recently been started on ART and developed an immune-reconstitution syndrome.

TABLE 31 OPTIONS FOR THE THERAPY OF PCP

Scenario	When to use	Medication
Acute disease	First line	High-dose co-trimoxazole (120 mg/kg in two to four divided doses daily) Usually given intravenously but orally is sufficient in mild illness; increased adverse reactions in HIV
	Second line	Dapsone + trimethoprim (check G6PD) Clindamycin + primaquine (check G6PD) Pentamidine 4 mg/kg iv daily (nebulised insufficient) Atovaquone
Prophylaxis	First line	Co-trimoxazole 960 mg three times a week or 480 mg/day
	Second line	Dapsone 100 mg/day alone Dapsone 100 mg + pyrimethamine 25 mg three times a week Pentamidine 300 mg via nebuliser every 4 weeks Atovaquone 750 mg once daily

G6PD, glucose-6-phosphate dehydrogenase.

TABLE 32 OCULAR COMPLICATIONS IN HIV

Site	Causes/comments
Conjunctiva	Bacterial conjunctivitis Kaposi's sarcoma
Cornea	Keratitis from HSV or VZV
Anterior chamber, uveitis	HIV, CMV if recently started on ART, TB, syphilis, drug reactions
Posterior chamber and retina	HIV retinopathy (Fig. 44) CMV retinitis (Fig. 45) Progressive outer retinal necrosis, caused by VZV/HSV (Fig. 46) *Candida* spp. rare unless neutropenic Retinal detachment after infection
Choroidoretinitis	Toxoplasmosis, TB, syphilis

ART, antiretroviral therapy; HSV, herpes simplex virus; TB, tuberculosis; VZV, varicella-zoster virus.

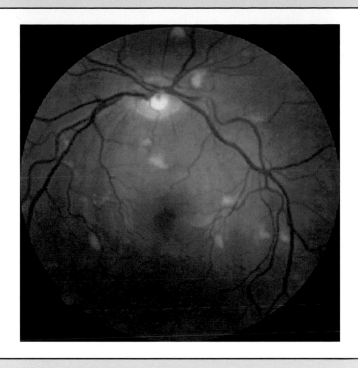

▲ **Fig. 44** Changes of HIV retinopathy. There are numerous 'cotton-wool' spots on the retina. These are generally asymptomatic and disappear when ART is commenced.

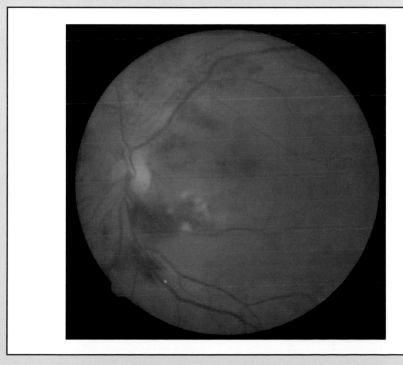

▲ **Fig. 45** CMV retinitis. Typical mixture of haemorrhage and exudate often referred to as a 'pizza pie' appearance.

- Are there 'holes' in the vision, flashing lights or floaters? These features suggest retinal disease.

- Was it like a 'curtain' coming down? If so, refer the patient urgently to exclude retinal detachment.

Other relevant history

Note in particular the following.

- Previous ocular disease: inflammatory disease can lead to cataracts, and retinal disease to detachment.

- Previous infections in the eye or elsewhere, eg CMV, TB, toxoplasmosis and syphilis: CMV in particular may reactivate if the CD4 cell count falls when HIV therapy is failing.

If a general enquiry reveals other problems, then is he on treatment for something else? If so, what medication is being taken? Ethambutol may cause visual loss, and rifabutin and fluconazole can interact leading to pseudo-jaundice and uveitis.

Examination

Perform a full general examination, looking for signs of infection elsewhere.

Ocular examination

Consult *Ophthalmology*, Section 3.1 for a description of how to examine the eye, and check carefully for the eye: note features listed in Table 33 and consider diagnoses listed in Table 32'.

⚠️ **HIV and a visual problem**

If in doubt seek an urgent expert ophthalmological opinion. Retinal infection or detachment can rapidly lead to permanent visual loss unless managed correctly.

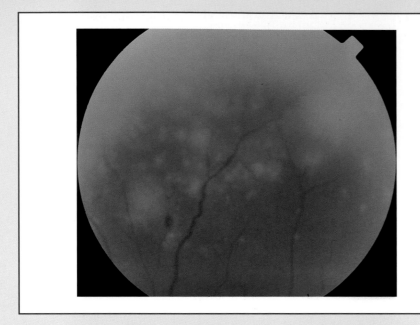

▲**Fig. 46** Progressive outer retinal necrosis (PORN): pale necrotic retina with an advancing edge. This is most commonly the result of VZV; untreated it rapidly leads to blindness. Treating PORN requires a combination of high-dose systemic and intraocular therapy. (Courtesy of Professor S. Lightman.)

TABLE 33 EYE EXAMINATION IN **HIV**

Examination	Abnormalities to look for
Conjunctiva	Inflammation, ulceration, pus and lesions of Kaposi's sarcoma
Red eye	Slit-lamp examination required to identify depth of inflammation
Visual acuity	Visual loss requires urgent ophthalmological opinion
Pupilary reflexes	
Visual field defects	Unilateral disease suggests retinal disease; consider intracerebral pathology if there is a homonymous defect
Fundoscopy (dilated)	Look for debris/abscess in the anterior and posterior chambers. Retinal changes in zone 1 (macula and optic disc area) disease can be sight-threatening and need immediate attention

Investigation

The aim must be to exclude sight-threatening disease as rapidly as possible. Most infections can be recognised clinically. The opinion of an HIV-experienced ophthalmologist is invaluable. Check the following.

- FBC: neutropenia is a risk factor for fungal infection.

- CD4 cell count: unless a recent clinic result is available (CMV retinitis is unlikely with a CD4 cell count $>75 \times 10^6$/L).

- Infection screen: serology can be used to assess the risk of latent infection for toxoplasmosis, CMV and syphilis, but the results cannot establish a definitive diagnosis. CMV may be cultured from blood, but polymerase chain reaction (PCR) or antigen detection is more sensitive. However, patients can have CMV retinitis without detectable CMV in the blood, when the diagnosis is made on the basis of the characteristic clinical picture.

Vitreal or retinal samples can be sent, where indicated, for microscopy, culture and PCR. Examination of the cerebrospinal fluid is occasionally helpful.

- Imaging: cranial CT/MRI is appropriate if optic nerve or cortical involvement is suspected.

Management

This depends entirely on the cause. Management of a serious infection should involve an ophthalmologist. Many drugs penetrate the eye poorly so that a combination of systemic and intraocular therapy is often needed for viral or fungal retinitis. Antimicrobial therapy cannot eradicate some infections such as CMV and toxoplasmosis until immune function has been restored, necessitating continuous suppressive therapy. Prolonged remission requires restoration of immune function with effective ART leading to a CD4 cell count consistently above 100×10^6/L.

1.3.23 Abdominal pain and vaginal discharge

Scenario

A 20-year-old woman presents with fever, lower abdominal pain and vaginal discharge.

Introduction

Is this pelvic inflammatory disease (PID)? You must first exclude life-threatening surgical conditions and then decide on the relationship of the vaginal discharge to her abdominal pain.

History of the presenting problem

Abdominal pain

The most likely diagnosis from the brief details given above is PID, but

TABLE 34 VAGINAL DISCHARGE

Cause	Examples	Features
Physiological		Thin, watery and non-offensive May vary with menstrual cycle
Vaginal origin	Bacterial vaginosis	Malodorous; clue cells on wet preparation; risk of preterm labour
	Candidiasis	Moderate and white (cream or 'curdy'); pruritis
	Trichomonas spp.	Profuse, yellow, frothy and offensive; soreness and dyspareunia
Cervicitis	*Neisseria gonorrhoeae*	Often asymptomatic and detected at examination for other genital symptoms; may be purulent
	Chlamydia trachomatis	As *Neisseria gonorrhoeae*
	Herpes simplex virus	Rarely see acute cervicitis in the primary attack
Non-infectious	Foreign body or allergy	Profuse and offensive; pruritis

could the pain be the result of anything else? Ask about the following if the details are not forthcoming.

- What is the site, severity and radiation of the pain? Does it fit the pattern of any well-recognised cause of abdominal pain, eg appendicitis? (See *Acute Medicine*, Section 1.2.17.)

- Has there been diarrhoea, alteration in bowel habit or rectal bleeding? These would suggest an intestinal cause of abdominal pain, with the vaginal discharge unrelated to it.

- Have there been symptoms to suggest a urinary tract infection, eg frequency, dysuria, strong urinary smell and fever? Has she had a urinary infection before?

- When was her last period? Is there any risk of pregnancy? If she is pregnant, exclude an ectopic pregnancy urgently.

- Has there been bleeding after sex or between periods? Vaginal bleeding can occur in spontaneous abortion or ectopic pregnancy

and, in an older woman, may signify underlying malignancy. Irregular bleeding may also be a symptom of endometritis that accompanies PID.

Vaginal discharge

- What is the discharge like? Enquire about quantity, consistency, colour and odour (Table 34). Creamy white discharge suggests candidal infection, and malodorous discharge may occur with PID or *Trichomonas vaginalis* infection or bacterial vaginosis.

- Have there been other genital symptoms? Vaginal itching and dyspareunia occur with vaginitis due to *Candida* or trichomoniasis.

Other relevant history

- Contraceptive use: ask specifically about intrauterine contraceptive devices that may be associated with PID, expecially if fitted in the past 6 weeks. Ask whether she uses tampons and if there is a possibility of a retained tampon, which can cause discharge but

also predispose to toxic shock syndrome (see Section 1.3.2).

- Full sexual history (see Section 1.1.5): PID occurs in sexually active women, especially those <20 years, and is increased in relation to the number of sexual partners and the frequency of sexual intercourse.

What if this patient reports a sexual assault?

- Believe her and take immediate action.
- This requires privacy, care and sensitivity.
- Refer the case to the appropriate authorities only with her consent.
- Do not examine or take samples until you have received expert advice from a genitourinary or forensic specialist.
- Consider postexposure prophylaxis against sexually transmitted infections (STIs), including HIV, and emergency contraception.
- Refer her to a specialist rape counselling service.

Issues with 'children'

When dealing with those <16 years old (or <18 years in care), consider the following.

- Confidentiality: refer to General Medical Council (GMC) guidance.
- Children's Act.
- Child protection issues.

The issues can be complex in individual cases. If in doubt about medico-legal aspects, consult senior clinicians and/or contact the Medical Protection Society (MPS)/Medical Defence Union (MDU) and GMC before breaching confidentiality.

Examination

Is the woman well, ill, very ill or nearly dead? The situation may be life-threatening, for instance in ruptured ectopic pregnancy.

- Check vital signs: temperature, pulse, BP, respiratory rate and pulse oximetry.

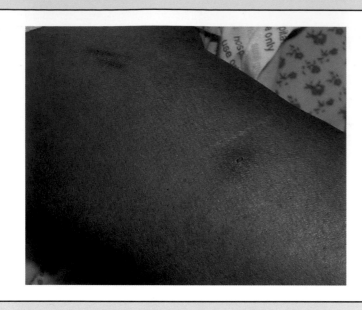

▲ **Fig. 47** Typical lesion of disseminated gonococcal infection on the upper arm.

• Is there any evidence of bleeding or sepsis?

General examination
Look in particular for evidence of immunodeficiency (see Section 1.3.20) in case of HIV. Arthritis or rash suggests Reiter's syndrome or disseminated gonococcal infection (Fig. 47).

Abdominal examination
Check for masses and local or generalised peritonitis. Bilateral suprapubic tenderness suggests pelvic pathology such as PID or endometriosis. Unilateral tenderness could be a sign of ectopic pregnancy, appendicitis or ruptured ovarian cyst.

Genital examination
Bimanual vaginal examination is essential: feel for swelling or tenderness of the cervix and adnexa. Pain on cervical excitation is typical of PID, but will also be present in ectopic pregnancy. Perform a vaginal speculum examination to look for fluid in the vaginal vault, and check for cervicitis/cervical discharge.

Rectal examination
Tenderness on the right side may indicate appendicitis.

Investigation

Microbiological tests

• Blood cultures: may detect gonorrhoea in disseminated disease. Perform gonococcal polymerase chain reaction if available.

• Urine microscopy and culture: if urinary dipstick is abnormal.

• Urethral and endocervical swabs as well as a full genitourinary screen (see Section 1.1.7) to test for chlamydia, gonorrhoea, trichomoniasis, bacterial vaginosis and vaginal candidiasis.

> **Detection of *Chlamydia trachomatis***
>
> • Patients are frequently asymptomatic.
> • Screen all STI clinic attendees.
> • Immunoassays superseded by DNA-based tests.
> • Screening is now possible on urine samples or self-taken vaginal swab.

Blood tests

• FBC: raised white cell count suggests bacterial infection; anaemia may be due to slow haemorrhage in ectopic pregnancy.

• Electrolytes and renal function: renal impairment may be due to severe sepsis or pre-existing chronic renal disease.

• Liver function tests: may be impaired in severe sepsis.

• Inflammatory markers: high C-reactive protein suggests bacterial infection or other severe inflammatory disease.

• Amylase: to exclude pancreatitis in cases where pain is not confined to the lower abdomen.

Imaging
The following may be needed.

• Abdominal ultrasonography: this may show tubal swelling in PID and detect ectopic pregnancy, tubo-ovarian abscess or appendicitis.

• CT scan: if pelvic abscess is suspected (Fig. 48).

• Abdominal radiograph (of kidneys, ureter and bladder): if renal stones or bowel disease suspected.

> • Pregnancy test: in all potentially fertile women. If the result is positive then suspect ectopic pregnancy, but note that in some women with ectopic pregnancy this test may be negative or only weakly positive.
> • Laparoscopy: the definitive method for diagnosing PID and ectopic pregnancy; it can also be used to drain an abscess or to treat less severe forms of ectopic pregnancy. Consider when there is diagnostic uncertainty or the patient is failing to respond to therapy.

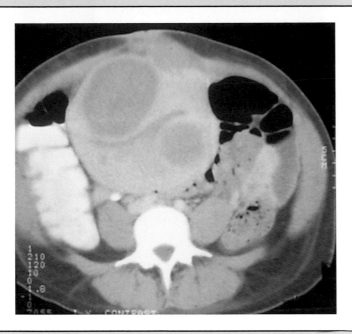

▲ Fig. 48 Pelvic CT scan showing deep-seated abscess formation as a result of infection after premature labour.

 Do not perform a cervical smear when there is obvious cervical infection because inflammatory cells make interpretation difficult.

Management

If the woman is seriously ill, obtain intravenous access immediately and begin resuscitation while completing the history and examination (see Section 1.3.2).

 Abdominal pain and vaginal discharge

If there is evidence of an 'acute abdomen' or ectopic pregnancy, you should organise urgent surgical referral.

Pelvic inflammatory disease

Microbiology of PID

- *Chlamydia trachomatis.*
- *Neisseria gonorrhoeae.*
- *Escherichia coli* and other enteric bacteria.
- Streptococci and anaerobes.
- Genital mycoplasmas (less common).

- If the patient is systemically well, consider outpatient therapy with oral antibiotics (see Sections 2.5.2 and 2.8.4).

- If the patient is in severe pain, has a high fever, shows signs of severe sepsis or is pregnant, admit them for intravenous antimicrobials. Commence empirical therapy based on the likely microbiology and local antibiotic policy (eg ceftriaxone plus doxycycline plus metronidazole). If this fails to produce improvement, you must reconsider the underlying diagnosis and investigate for other causes or abscess formation. Consider genitourinary tuberculosis in chronic cases.

Disseminated gonorrhoea

See Fig. 47 and remember the following.

- Generally follows asymptomatic local gonococcal infection.
- Skin: sparse (<30) pustular, papular or petechial lesions.

- Joints: tenosynovitis or asymmetrical polyarthritis.
- Blood/joint fluid culture: positive in 50%.
- Genital/pharyngeal cultures: may be positive.

1.3.24 Penicillin allergy

Scenario

A 38-year-old man is admitted to hospital following 3 days of fever and breathlessness. He is dull to percussion at his right base, where bronchial breathing can be heard. A CXR shows consolidation of his right lower lobe. A diagnosis of pneumonia, probably due to *Streptococcus pneumoniae*, is made and you are asked to prescribe antibiotics. He tells you that he is allergic to penicillin.

Introduction

The clinician is faced with a dilemma if a patient presents with a serious infection and reports an allergy to an antibiotic you might wish to prescribe. You do not want to risk a serious drug reaction, but you need to ensure that the patient receives adequate treatment for the infection.

See Section 1.3.4 for details of other aspects of history-taking, examination, investigation and management of the patient with pneumonia, but enquire about the points below with regard to penicillin allergy.

 Suspected drug allergy

- What is the allergy?
- How severe is it?
- Was it documented?
- What disease is being treated?
- Is there an acceptable alternative treatment?

History of the 'allergic reaction'

When, what and how bad?

Always clarify what is meant by 'allergy' (Table 35). Many patients are unable to give any further information other than the belief that they have an allergy ('my mother told me that I was allergic') or report side effects of the drug that are not related to an allergic phenomenon, eg nausea, diarrhoea and headache. The most important history to obtain is of anaphylaxis, severe skin disorders such as Stevens–Johnson syndrome (see *Dermatology*, Section 2.10), or other life-threatening reactions. You do not want to give an individual who has had one of these reactions another dose of the same antibiotic or a closely related one.

Penicillin allergy

- The most common antibiotic allergy, reported to occur in 7–40 per 1,000 penicillin treatment courses.
- Anaphylaxis occurs in 1 in 32,000–100,000 treatment courses.

Risk factors for β-lactam allergy

- Prior history of reaction to penicillins/β-lactam drugs: patient is four to six times more at risk of subsequent reaction, especially if the previous reaction was anaphylaxis or urticaria.
- Risk is greater with parenteral than with oral therapy.
- Children and elderly people appear to have fewer reactions.
- Atopy is not an independent risk factor.

Investigation

IgE-mediated allergy to penicillin (severe immediate reactions) can be confirmed in some cases by skin-prick testing. This may be of help in

TABLE 35	MANIFESTATIONS OF ANTIBIOTIC ALLERGY	
Clinical manifestation	**Type of reaction (Gell and Coombs)**	**Onset**
Anaphylaxis and urticaria	I (IgE)	0–24 hours
Haemolytic anaemia, neutropenia and thrombocytopenia	II	>72 hours
Drug fever and serum sickness	III	7–14 days
Contact dermatitis	IV	Variable
Rash (Fig. 49), fixed drug reactions and exfoliative dermatitis	V (idiopathic)	7–14 days

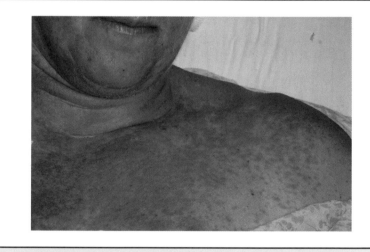

▲**Fig. 49** Typical maculopapular rash of penicillin allergy.

individual cases, but not as a general screening test, and as such it is not helpful in this scenario.

Management

Need for penicillin

The choice of antibiotic should always be guided by suspected pathogens and the severity of disease. Consider the most likely pathogens implicated in the clinical presentation (eg *Streptococcus pneumoniae* in this case), but other pathogens also need to be considered. Published treatment guidelines may be helpful and may suggest alternatives to a penicillin-based antibiotic (eg the pneumonia guidelines published by the British Thoracic Society or the meningitis management algorithm published by the British Infection Society).

Alternatives to a penicillin-based antibiotic

Mild infection For pneumonia that is not severe the appropriate alternative to the standard regimen of an extended-spectrum penicillin (amoxicillin) alone or plus a macrolide (erythromycin) would be to use a macrolide alone and omit the amoxicillin. For other infections that are not life-threatening, eg bacterial tonsillitis, a macrolide may also be substituted for the amoxicillin and used alone.

Moderate/severe infection Patients with penicillin allergy often tolerate a cephalosporin, but these are also β-lactam drugs and they have a 5–10% cross-reactivity with penicillin allergies. If the previous reaction to penicillin was simply a rash, you should not be dissuaded from using a cephalosporin in this situation. It is more difficult to know what to do if the penicillin allergy were severe. In patients with moderate or severe pneumonia the options most commonly taken would be:

- to use an intravenous macrolide alone or a newer quinolone such as levofloxacin, observing clinical progress very closely;

- to give a cephalosporin, but monitoring carefully for side effects and treating these promptly should they arise.

Antibiotic allergy

There is usually an acceptable alternative antibiotic that you can prescribe, so you must judge how likely a severe reaction is. If the history is not suggestive of allergy and you choose to give the drug in question or a related compound, advise the patient to report any adverse effects immediately. The first dose, particularly if intravenous, should be administered under supervision with an initial test dose.

2.1 Antimicrobial prophylaxis

Principle

In addition to treating established infection, antibiotics can, on occasion, be used to prevent infectious disease.

- Primary prophylaxis is used when infection is not present, but there is a high risk of developing infection, eg co-trimoxazole prophylaxis to prevent *Pneumocystis carinii* pneumonia (PCP) in patients with HIV or other significantly immunocompromised patients, antibiotic prophylaxis for dental treatment in patients with heart murmurs, and antibiotic prophylaxis before surgery.

- Pre-emptive treatment is used when there is evidence of the organism but no clinical disease.

If the patient is at high risk of developing symptomatic infection it may be appropriate to treat the organism, eg taking surveillance samples for cytomegalovirus (CMV) in patients following bone marrow transplantation enables pre-emptive treatment if the samples are positive for CMV antigen or by polymerase chain reaction prior to the development of clinical disease; and chemoprophylaxis of latent tuberculosis.

- Secondary prophylaxis is used after an infection to prevent relapse or recurrence, eg co-trimoxazole prophylaxis following PCP.

Because of the risk of encouraging the emergence of antibiotic resistance, prophylaxis should be reserved for infections with a risk of mortality or serious morbidity and where there is clear evidence of effectiveness.

Preventing infection

Preventing infection is not limited to antibiotic prophylaxis but includes the following:

- infection control (see Section 2.3);
- immunisation or immunoprophylaxis (see Section 2.2);
- lifestyle advice.

Practical details

When

Situations where prophylaxis is of proven benefit are shown in Table 36. The aim of therapy is to achieve therapeutic levels of the correct antibiotic for the period of risk. For surgical procedures, this means having high levels of antibiotic during the period from the initial incision until skin closure. However, an immunocompromised patient may require prolonged prophylaxis until the period of immunosuppression is over.

TABLE 36 USES OF ANTIMICROBIAL PROPHYLAXIS

Situations	Examples
Immunocompetent at high risk	Malaria prophylaxis
Procedures in a normal host	Perioperative antibiotic prophylaxis
Procedures with an underlying cardiac defect	Infective endocarditis prophylaxis
After exposure to specific pathogens	PEP following needlestick injury (see Section 2.11)
	Antituberculous prophylaxis (see Section 2.6.1)
Block transmission from colonised hosts	*Neisseria meningitidis* (see Section 1.3.11)
	Selected cases of *Staphylococcus aureus*
Recurrent infections	Urinary tract and rheumatic fever
Prevent infection in immunocompromised patients	PCP prophylaxis in HIV (see Section 2.11)

PEP, postexposure prophylaxis.

TABLE 37 PROPHYLACTIC REGIMENS IN IMMUNODEFICIENCY

Host defect	Infecting organisms	Consider prophylaxis with:
Post splenectomy or complement deficiency	Encapsulated bacteria, eg pneumococci and meningococci	Penicillin Immunise against pneumococci, *Haemophilus* spp. and meningococci
Antibody deficiency	Bacteria including pneumococci	Penicillin Consider intravenous immunoglobulin
Neutropenia	Bacteria including *Pseudomonas* spp. *Candida* spp. Herpes simplex virus	Quinolone Fluconazole Aciclovir
HIV/AIDS, CD4 $>200 \times 10^6$/L	Pneumococcal pneumonia Herpes simplex and shingles	Pneumococcal immunisations Aciclovir for recurrent disease
HIV/AIDS, CD4 $<200 \times 10^6$/L	PCP and toxoplasmosis	Co-trimoxazole
HIV/AIDS, CD4 $<75 \times 10^6$/L	Cytomegalovirus *Mycobacterium avium-intracellulare*	Ganciclovir/valganciclovir Azithromycin or rifabutin

What

The choice of an individual prophylactic regimen is made using similar principles to those employed in selecting empirical therapy for established infection (see Sections 1.3.2 and 1.3.11). One needs to consider the likely infecting organisms, the site of infection and host factors, eg in immunodeficiency the need for prophylaxis varies according to the host defect (Table 37).

Factors in choosing antimicrobial prophylaxis

- Likely infecting organisms.
- Site at risk of infection.
- Exposure, eg tropical travel.
- Patterns of local antimicrobial resistance.
- Host factors, eg immunodeficiency, allergy and organ impairment.
- Route of administration.
- Cost-effectiveness.

Outcome

Antimicrobial prophylaxis can substantially reduce the morbidity and mortality associated with infection in high-risk situations. This has to be balanced against the risks of encouraging antimicrobial resistance, and resistance should always be considered where prophylaxis fails.

Lifestyle advice

- Using boiled water reduces *Mycobacterium avium-intracellulare* and cryptosporidiosis in AIDS.
- Avoid mosquito bites by using impregnated bednets and insect repellants containing DEET.
- Marijuana may contain viable *Aspergillus* spores.
- Reptiles often carry *Salmonella*.
- Immunisation will prevent many infections.

2.2 Immunisation

Principle

Immunisation (synonym: vaccination) aims to induce long-term protective immunological memory (active immunisation). This is done using a variety of strategies to present foreign antigens to the immune system. In this context, an antigen is any portion of the pathogen or its products that can be recognised by the immune system, eg a viral coat protein or bacterial toxin. Rarely, it is appropriate to give temporary immunisation by passive transfer of preformed antibody.

Active immunisation

Protective immunity involves humoral and cellular elements (Fig. 50).

Humoral or B-cell memory

- Common type of immunity generated by antiviral vaccines (eg hepatitis B and influenza).

- Wanes over time against non-replicating pathogens, and may therefore require boosting.

- Induces sterilising immunity, ie a circulating antibody prevents initial infection (the neutralising antibody).

- Protective only if directed against conserved surface antigens. Mutation of surface proteins within populations (influenza) or within individuals (HIV) may enable escape from these antibodies.

Cellular or T-cell memory

- CD8 or cytotoxic T lymphocytes and CD4 or helper T lymphocytes.

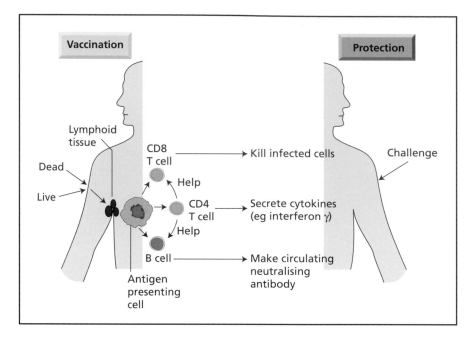

▲**Fig. 50** Events following immunisation.

- Evoked by presentation of small viral peptides (epitopes) derived from any viral protein to human leucocyte antigen (HLA) molecules on specialised antigen-presenting cells.

- CD4 cells help to sustain antibody responses or provide direct protection against certain pathogens (eg BCG and TB).

- Epitopes recognised depend on the HLA type of the individual.

- T cells recognise only cells that are already infected and cannot provide sterilising immunity.

- CD8 cells are active against persistent or non-cytopathic organisms, the intracellular position of which is protected against antibodies.

Passive immunisation

This involves the transfer of preformed antibody. The antibody confers immediate protection, but only for a limited time period, and is often combined with or followed by active immunisation.

Chickenpox (herpes/varicella zoster)

This is given in cases where there has been significant exposure to a non-immune individual at high risk of life-threatening disease (newborn, pregnant or immunosuppressed). Non-immune status is confirmed by measuring a specific anti-zoster antibody (laboratory report will indicate 'varicella-zoster virus IgG negative').

Hepatitis B

This is given where there has been exposure to infected blood from a known carrier (eg a needlestick injury) (see Section 2.11) and there is no pre-existing antibody. This is usually combined with an accelerated hepatitis B vaccine schedule to stimulate long-term immunity.

Hepatitis A

Human immunoglobulin protects against this for 3 months and was routinely given to travellers to an endemic area. It has largely been replaced by active immunisation, but it may still be needed where

there is insufficient time for active immunisation to work or for close contacts of a hepatitis A case.

Respiratory syncytial virus

There is evidence that specific anti-respiratory syncytial virus antibodies improve morbidity and mortality when combined with ribavirin for the treatment of severe disease in young children.

Others

Specific immunoglobulin protects after rabies exposure and against tick-borne encephalitis (mainly in eastern Europe and Austria; a killed vaccine is also available).

Inducing immunity

There are several methods of inducing protective immunity (Table 38).

Live attenuated vaccines

As these replicate they will induce cellular and humoral immunity, of appropriate specificity, at a high level which is maintained lifelong. In general, avoid in an immunocompromised host.

Antigen-only (dead) vaccines

These induce high antibody levels, although they may be short-lived and require boosting.

- Killed, eg polio-inactivated vaccine.

- Subunit vaccines, eg influenza vaccines.

- Recombinant vaccines (eg HBV vaccine): use antigens made by artificial expression *in vitro*, rather than by growth of a whole virus.

Novel approaches

Vaccines that are simply strips of DNA encoding the relevant viral genes induce very effective

TABLE 38 METHODS OF IMMUNISATION AND EXAMPLES

Vaccine	Examples	Advantages	Disadvantages
Live attenuated organism	Oral polio Measles Mumps Rubella BCG Yellow fever	Sustained broad immunological response	Must be kept cold Risk of reversion to pathogenicity Avoid in immunosuppression
Killed	Inactivated polio HAV	Safe Good antibody response Long shelf-life	Booster often needed
Subunit	Tetanus	Very effective	Booster needed
Conjugate	Meningococcus *Haemophilus* B Pneumococcus	Very effective More immunogenic than unconjugated vaccines	Not all clinically important strains covered
Recombinant	HBV	Very effective and safe	
Passive	IVIG VZV Rabies HBV	Immediate action	Limited supply and potential risk of transmissible infection

BCG, bacille Calmette–Guérin; HAV, hepatitis A virus; HBV, hepatitis B virus; IVIG, intravenous immunoglobulin; VZV, varicella-zoster virus.

antibodies and cellular immunity. They are effective in animal models and are entering human trials.

Future vaccine possibilities

- Recombinant vectors, eg vaccinia based, such as modified vaccinia ankara-based vectors for tuberculosis.
- DNA vectors.
- Monoclonal antibodies.

Vaccine policy

The key document here is Salisbury D, Ramsay M and Noakes K, eds. *Immunisation Against Infectious Disease*, 3rd ed. London: The Stationery Office, 2006 ('The Green Book'). This is available from http://www.dh.gov.uk. This describes the rationale and practice of current immunisation strategies.

Contraindications

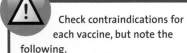

Check contraindications for each vaccine, but note the following.

- Most live vaccines are contraindicated in immunosuppressed patients.
- Influenza immunisation should be avoided if the patient has a history of egg allergy.
- MMR (mumps, measles and rubella) vaccine has been the subject of some controversy regarding a potential link with autism, but most investigators have found no evidence for this association.

Do not forget patients going for splenectomy! They should receive vaccines against the capsulated organisms (pneumococci, *Haemophilus influenzae* and meningococci).

2.3 Infection control

Principle

In the UK, about 10% of hospital admissions are the result of infection, with a further 10% of patients acquiring infection in hospital. Recent Audit Commission reports have revealed that, in England and Wales, 5,000 people die yearly as a direct result of hospital-acquired infection (HAI) costing £1 billion per annum. Both *Winning Ways* and *Getting Ahead of the Curve* have identified HAI as major areas for healthcare improvement. Reasons underlying HAI are complex, as illustrated in Fig. 51. Infection control tries to reduce infection rates in the following ways.

Universal precautions

This refers to the application of general measures to all patients irrespective of their infection status, and should protect patients and staff from contact and blood-borne infections.

Universal precautions

- Handwashing/alcohol gel: between all contacts with the patient.
- Wear protective clothing where indicated to prevent contamination with body fluids.
- Wear gloves when possibility of contamination with body fluids.

Specific precautions

The second mechanism of control is through the isolation of patients with infections that pose particular problems. Recognising who needs additional precautions depends on an understanding of the mechanisms involved in transmission of HAI.

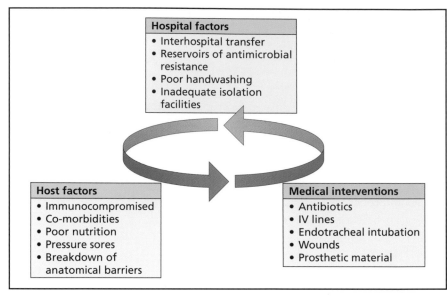

Hospital factors
- Interhospital transfer
- Reservoirs of antimicrobial resistance
- Poor handwashing
- Inadequate isolation facilities

Host factors
- Immunocompromised
- Co-morbidities
- Poor nutrition
- Pressure sores
- Breakdown of anatomical barriers

Medical interventions
- Antibiotics
- IV lines
- Endotracheal intubation
- Wounds
- Prosthetic material

▲ **Fig. 51** Interrelationships in hospital-acquired infection.

- If the diagnosis is known, then consider the following.

  (a) Nature of the organism, eg potential route of spread, pathogenicity of the organism and potential for outbreaks.

  (b) Host factors, eg immune status, sputum production, diarrhoea and confusion.

  (c) Population at risk, eg immunocompromised or vulnerable patients.

  (d) Surroundings: are isolation rooms available, and can the patient be safely nursed in isolation?

Routes of dissemination are predominantly by contact, droplet, airborne or blood (Table 39).

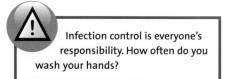

Infection control is everyone's responsibility. How often do you wash your hands?

Protective isolation

In some circumstances, an immunocompromised patient may be isolated to protect him or her from HAI. Handwashing still remains the most important means of reducing cross-infection. Nursing neutropenic patients in a filtered positive-pressure room reduces the risk of aspergillosis.

Practical details

Risk assessment

When assessing whether to take precautions, such as protective isolation, a risk assessment is made of the situation, taking the following factors into consideration.

- Is the diagnosis clear? If not, could it be infectious?

TABLE 39 ROUTES OF TRANSMISSION OF INFECTION WITHIN HOSPITAL

Route	Organisms	Response to prevent spread
Airborne	TB Varicella-zoster virus RSV Smallpox SARS Norovirus	Isolation in an appropriately ventilated room Negative-pressure room recommended for TB Patient to wear mask outside room
Droplet	*Neisseria meningitidis* *Haemophilus influenzae* Whooping cough Respiratory viruses (influenza) Mumps Rubella	Cover mouth when sneezing Handwashing/alcohol gel
Contact	*Staphylococcus aureus*, including MRSA Most other bacteria Enteric pathogens, including *Clostridium difficile* and *Escherichia coli* 0157 RSV, HSV and scabies	Handwashing/alcohol gel, gloves, gowns and protective clothing where contamination likely Note that alcohol gel is not effective against *Clostridium difficile* spores
Blood: via needlestick	Hepatitis B Hepatitis C HIV Ebola virus Malaria Trypanosomiasis	Universal precautions Postexposure prophylaxis
Unknown	New-variant CJD	Risk unknown: probably transmitted by ingestion of contaminated meat or iatrogenic transmission. Incubation period may be many years

CJD, Creutzfeldt–Jakob disease; HSV, herpes simplex virus; MRSA, meticillin-resistant *Staphylococcus aureus*; RSV, respiratory syncytial virus; SARS, severe acute respiratory syndrome; TB, tuberculosis.

Elements of effective infection control

- Surveillance/audit of indicator infections such as wound or central line infections.
- Infection control policy, including outbreak plan.
- Training of staff, eg handwashing techniques and management of lines, catheters and other devices.
- Audit of infection control practices.
- Support/resources.

Control of HAI

Infection control plays a central role in reducing the transmission of infection, but a sustained reduction in HAI needs a coordinated approach using:

- infection control policies;
- staff education;
- antibiotic protocols and control;
- surveillance at local, regional, national and international levels.

FURTHER READING

Chief Medical Officer. *Winning Ways: Working Together to Reduce Healthcare Associated Infection in England.* London: Department of Health, 2003. Available from http://www.dh.gov.uk

- - - - - - - - - - - - - - - - - -

Chief Medical Officer. *Getting Ahead of the Curve: a Strategy for Combating Infectious Diseases (Including Other Aspects of Health Promotion).* London: Department of Health, 2002. Available from http://www.dh.gov.uk

2.4 Travel advice

Principle

Most travellers experience no serious health problems. Simple steps can be taken to minimise the risk of travel-related illness. Travellers can be educated how to treat simple conditions and to recognise the features of serious illness. You should tailor your advice taking account of the following.

- Geographical area to be visited: where, when and for how long?
- Special risks of the journey or visit.
- General health of the traveller.

Practical details

Below is a brief list of subjects that you should consider when dispensing travel advice. Some advice requires specialised knowledge and up-to-date information. Seek help from an appropriate specialist if you are unsure.

Travel-related mortality

- Cardiovascular disease is the most common cause of mortality.
- Accidents are more common whilst on holiday abroad, including road traffic accidents, drowning incidents and falls.
- Altitude sickness: if ascending rapidly into mountainous areas (usually >2,500 m).
- Ensure that travellers at risk of cardiovascular disease are well controlled, have an ample supply of medication and take steps to avoid dehydration.

General advice

- Water and food: 'boil it, peel it or forget it'. Use treated water even for toothbrushing; avoid ice in drinks and salads unless washed in treated water.
- Climate: be aware of the dangers of dehydration and sunburn.
- Sex with new partners: this is an increased risk when travelling; advise on safe sex and condom use.
- Avoid insects and other nasty beasts. Use insect repellents and examine daily for ticks in an endemic area.
- Recommend taking out appropriate travel insurance.

First-aid kit The contents will need to reflect the purpose of the trip, eg a remote trek will have different requirements to a hotel-based tour. As a minimum consider the following.

- Digital thermometer.
- Antiseptic solution, bandages and plasters.
- Scissors and tweezers.
- Proprietary analgesic, antipyretic, antidiarrhoeal, antihistamine and a drug for motion sickness.
- Needles and syringes (official letter of explanation for customs). Medical packs may be purchased prior to travel.

⚠ Aid workers and medical or nursing personnel may be at risk of needlestick injury far from help. Consider providing a supply of HIV postexposure prophylaxis, with specific advice on how to take it, and recommend review by an experienced physician as soon as possible after the event (see Section 2.11.1).

Specific advice: prevention of malaria

Antimosquito measures The mosquito that transmits malaria bites at dusk and during the night. Wear long-sleeved shirts, long trousers and socks in the evening. Use a bed net, preferably impregnated with permethrin. Use a DEET-based insect repellent.

Chemoprophylaxis Although no regimen is completely effective, correctly used prophylaxis can reduce the risks of malaria. If you are not familiar with the area of travel, obtain up-to-date advice on recommended prophylaxis.

Recognition of symptoms and signs Warn the patient that prophylaxis does not completely prevent malaria. Discuss the symptoms (see Section 1.3.16) of disease so that the traveller can seek appropriate help when abroad. Stress that malaria can kill and not to delay seeking treatment until returning home.

> Fever is due to malaria in any patient from a high-risk area until proved otherwise (see Section 1.3.16).

Specific advice: travellers' diarrhoea

Travellers' diarrhoea is the most common travel-related infection, affecting up to 50% of travellers to certain destinations. Although mortality is very low, there is significant associated morbidity and holiday upset. Symptoms are generally mild and resolve within 3–5 days. Oral hydration and symptomatic management are the mainstays of treatment, but occasionally severe disease requires antimicrobial therapy, particularly if a long way from medical help (Table 40). Advise to seek help if diarrhoea lasts more than 2 weeks or is associated with bloody stools, fever or abdominal pain.

> ⚠ Patients with significant immunocompromise are at increased risk of severe *Salmonella* and other bacterial infections. If travel is essential, warn them of the risks and consider supplying a course of antibiotics for them to take if severe symptoms develop and medical help cannot be readily accessed.

Immunisations

Yellow fever is the only vaccine for which there is an international requirement before entering some countries. Yellow fever vaccine is contraindicated in pregnancy and those who are immunocompromised (you can issue an exemption certificate).

Other vaccines should be given as appropriate to the expected risk. Consider hepatitis A, hepatitis B, typhoid, meningococcal, Japanese B encephalitis, tick-borne encephalitis and rabies where necessary. Ensure travellers are aware that urgent post-bite (or other potential exposure) rabies vaccination is essential (with immunoglobulin if indicated) and that the pre-exposure vaccination alone is not adequate prevention. Take the opportunity also to update routine immunisations such as polio and tetanus.

Up-to-date advice on vaccines may be obtained from a number of sources including The Yellow Book (www.cdc.gov/travel/index.htm) or the Health Protection Agency (www.hpa.org.uk).

Post-travel review

This is of limited benefit in asymptomatic travellers. Warn travellers to report any unusual symptoms, particularly fever, after their return and to ensure that their treating physician is aware of their travel history.

2.5 Bacteria

Description of the organism

In the usual laboratory system of bacterial classification, the main groups of bacteria are distinguished by their morphology, staining reactions and growth requirements.

Morphology

Most bacteria can be classified as either:

- coccoid/spherical, or
- bacilli/rod like.

Staining characteristics

Differences on Gram stain reflect fundamental differences in cell wall structure and separate most bacteria into two main groups:

- Gram-positive bacteria.
- Gram-negative bacteria.

Growth requirements

Strict aerobes require oxygen and strict anaerobes the absence of oxygen for optimal growth. However, there are many bacteria that can tolerate various environments.

Others

There are some groups of bacteria that do not fit neatly into the above scheme.

- Mycobacteria (see Section 2.6) have a cell wall rich in mycolic acid and do not stain well by the Gram method, although if they do they are Gram-positive.

- Spirochaetes (see Section 2.7) stain as Gram-negative but differ in morphology, being slender, spiral and motile.

- Rickettsiae and chlamydiae (see Section 2.8) are obligate intracellular parasites that lack an outer cell wall.

TABLE 40 EMPIRICAL THERAPY OF SEVERE DIARRHOEA IN REMOTE AREAS

Syndrome	Therapy
Diarrhoea without fever or blood	Rehydration and antimotility agents
Diarrhoea with fever but no blood	Quinolone
Bloody diarrhoea with or without fever	Quinolone + metronidazole

2.5.1 Gram-positive bacteria

Description of the organism

Using the scheme outlined above, medically important Gram-positive bacteria can be rapidly grouped as shown in Table 41.

Disease syndromes and therapy

Aerobic Gram-positive cocci

Staphylococci *Staphylococcus aureus* (Fig. 52) is a high-grade pathogen and may cause both community- and hospital-acquired infection (Table 42). Other staphylococcal species are less pathogenic and are mainly encountered as opportunistic infections in the hospital setting.

TABLE 41 MEDICALLY IMPORTANT GRAM-POSITIVE BACTERIA

Morphology	Aerobic	Anaerobic
Cocci	Staphylococci Streptococci Enterococci	Anaerobic streptococci
Bacilli	*Corynebacterium* spp. *Bacillus* spp. *Listeria monocytogenes* *Nocardia asteroides*	*Clostridium* spp. *Lactobacillus* spp. *Actinomyces* spp.

Staphylococcus aureus bacteraemia
Staphylococcus aureus bacteraemia may seed to distant sites:

- bone/joints;
- heart valves;
- prosthetic material.

Streptococci Streptococci (Fig. 53) are traditionally classified by the type of haemolysis seen on blood agar (Table 43).

- Some produce a clear zone of haemolysis (β-haemolysis) and these can be further subdivided on the basis of cell wall antigens (Lancefield groups).

TABLE 42 STAPHYLOCOCCI AND THEIR DISEASE SYNDROMES

Organism	Epidemiology	Disease syndromes	Therapy
Staphylococcus aureus (meticillin sensitive)	Asymptomatic carriage in the nasopharynx of up to 30% of the population May cause severe disease, particularly in diabetic and immunocompromised patients	Boils Wound infections Cellulitis Abscesses Bacteraemia Endocarditis (see Section 1.3.6) Septic arthritis Osteomyelitis (see Section 1.3.5) Pneumonia (uncommon, post influenza)	Mainstay of therapy is flucloxacillin High-dose intravenous therapy needed for bacteraemia, endocarditis (see Section 1.3.6) and osteomyelitis Consider adding a second agent such as fusidic acid, rifampicin or gentamicin in serious infection Surgery for deep-seated abscess, osteomyelitis or prosthetic material
MRSA distinguished by resistance to meticillin	Increasing in the UK Outbreaks in high-risk areas, such as intensive care units	Nosocomial infection at any site but commonly infection of wounds, intravenous lines and prosthetic devices. Community-acquired strains are emerging	Vancomycin: monitor levels Oral therapy may be appropriate, according to susceptibility (eg doxycycline/rifampicin)
Toxin-producing *Staphylococcus aureus*	Sporadic cases with occasional clusters Outbreaks of tampon-associated toxic shock syndrome	Food poisoning Toxic shock syndrome Scalded skin syndrome	Anti-staphylococcal antibiotics when appropriate plus supportive care. Clindamycin may be helpful to suppress toxin production Consider IVIG in toxic shock
Coagulase-negative staphylococci, eg *Staphylococcus epidermidis*	Majority are normal skin commensals	Prosthetic valve endocarditis Long line infections Prosthetic joint infections Cerebrospinal shunt infections Peritoneal dialysis catheter infection	Removal of prosthetic material and/or prolonged intravenous therapy, commonly with glycopeptides (vancomycin/teicoplanin)
Staphylococcus saprophyticus	Tends to occur in young women	Urinary tract infection	Guided by sensitivities Usually trimethoprim sensitive

IVIG, intravenous immunoglobulin; MRSA, meticillin-resistant *Staphylococcus aureus*.

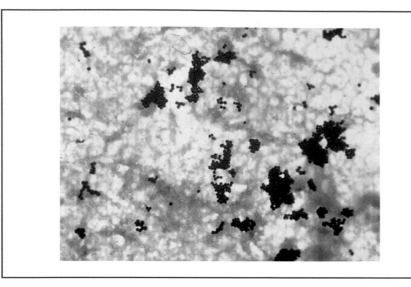

▲ **Fig. 52** *Staphylococcus aureus.*

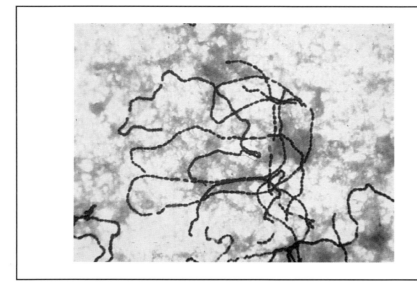

▲ **Fig. 53** Streptococci.

• Others produce a partial clearing of the agar and green coloration (α-haemolysis) or no obvious change in the agar around the colony.

> **Pneumococcal immunisation**
>
> Polysaccharide vaccine is now being replaced by highly immunogenic conjugate vaccine for the following:
>
> • elderly people;
> • chronic respiratory/cardiovascular disease;
> • diabetes or renal failure;
> • immunocompromised individuals;
> • hyposplenism;
> • infants <2 years of age.

Aerobic Gram-positive bacilli

Gram-positive bacilli (Table 44) tend to be normal skin commensals or spore-forming, environmental organisms. They seldom cause disease, but there are some very important pathogens.

Anaerobic Gram-positive bacilli

These spore-forming organisms (Table 45) are generally found in soil. Improvements in immunisation and public health have dramatically reduced the incidence of tetanus and botulism in the developed world, but they are still a major cause of disease in other countries.

TABLE 43 STREPTOCOCCI AND ENTEROCOCCI AND THEIR DISEASE SYNDROMES

Haemolysis	Organism	Epidemiology/public health	Disease syndromes	Therapy
β-Haemolytic	Lancefield GAS (*Streptococcus pyogenes*)	May cause institutional outbreaks Long-term pharyngeal carriage can occur	Pharyngitis	Penicillin
			Cellulitis and impetigo Scarlet fever	Erythromycin or clindamycin in penicillin allergy
			Necrotising fasciitis Septic arthritis	Antibiotics as above Fasciitis requires aggressive débridement
			Rheumatic fever Glomerulonephritis	Antibiotics to prevent recurrence
	Lancefield GBS (*Streptococcus agalactiae*)	Normal vaginal flora in 30% of women	Neonatal and peripartum infections Skin, soft tissue, bone and joint infections	Penicillin Neonatal meningitis requires 2–3 weeks' intravenous therapy

Table 43 (Cont'd)

Haemolysis	Organism	Epidemiology/public health	Disease syndromes	Therapy
α-Haemolytic	Streptococcus pneumoniae	Colonises the respiratory tract Invasive disease common in smokers, respiratory illness and immunodeficiency	Pneumonia Sinusitis and otitis media Empyema Bacteraemia Meningitis Septic arthritis Spontaneous peritonitis	Penicillin, if sensitive; second- or third-generation cephalosporin or a macrolide if sensitive Penicillin resistance is increasing and is now 5–15% in the UK, and 50% in parts of southern Europe
	Viridans streptococci	Mouth commensals	Endocarditis Line infection in neutropenic host	Benzylpenicillin Add gentamicin in endocarditis (see Section 1.3.6)
	Streptococcus milleri	Colonises gastrointestinal tract	Abscess formation in brain, lung and abdomen	Penicillin sensitive, but infections are often polymicrobial requiring broad-spectrum antibiotics
	Enterococcus faecalis	Colonises gastrointestinal tract Occasional cause of community-acquired infection	UTIs Endocarditis	Ampicillin or vancomycin Add gentamicin in endocarditis (see Section 1.3.6)
	Enterococcus faecium	Hospital-acquired pathogen VRE are an increasing infection control concern	Intra-abdominal infection Septicaemia UTIs Wound infection Line infection Endocarditis	As above unless VRE If VRE, seek expert advice

GAS, group A *Streptococcus*; GBS, group B *Streptococcus*; VRE, vancomycin-resistant enterococci; UTI, urinary tract infection.

Table 44 Aerobic Gram-positive bacilli and their disease syndromes

Organism	Epidemiology/public health	Disease syndromes	Therapy
Corynebacterium spp.	Most corynebacteria (diphtheroids) are normal skin commensals	Occasional cause of central line infection in neutropenia	Penicillin or vancomycin
Corynebacterium diphtheriae	Diphtheria is rare in most developed countries because of mass immunisation Still common in developing countries	Diphtheria Pharyngitis Toxin (cardiotoxic and neurotoxic) Skin ulcers (less common)	Penicillin, erythromycin or tetracyclines Supportive care for the effects of the toxin Immunisation of contacts
Bacillus spp.	Frequent skin commensals	Occasional cause of central line infection in neutropenia	Penicillin or vancomycin
Bacillus anthracis	Zoonosis reported in Africa and Asia Human infection arises from inoculation injury Inhalation of spores can lead to rapidly fatal disease Potential use in bacterial warfare	Anthrax Malignant pustule Septicaemia Haemorrhagic pneumonia High case fatality in invasive disease	Penicillin Immunisation requires annual boosters and hence is only of use if there is serious risk of infection
Bacillus cereus	Outbreaks related to poor reheating of cooked food	Food poisoning caused by preformed toxin	Supportive
Listeria monocytogenes	Found in various foodstuffs, eg pâté and soft cheeses Invasive disease in immunocompromised people, including pregnant women	Septicaemia Neonatal disease Meningitis Endocarditis	Ampicillin + gentamicin
Nocardia spp.	Found in soil Inoculation infections in Africa and Asia Invasive disease in immunocompromised people	Skin and soft tissue, eg Madura foot Invasive, pulmonary, CNS and disseminated infection	Co-trimoxazole, amikacin or imipenem all have useful activity

CNS, central nervous system.

TABLE 45 IMPORTANT ANAEROBIC GRAM-POSITIVE BACILLI AND THEIR DISEASE SYNDROMES

Organism	Epidemiology/public health	Disease syndromes	Therapy
Clostridium perfringens	Ubiquitous in soil; may colonise gastrointestinal tract	Gas gangrene Food poisoning	Penicillin or metronidazole + aggressive débridement
Clostridium tetani	Ubiquitous in soil worldwide, infection following inoculation	Tetanus	Penicillin + antitoxin Débridement of wound Ventilatory support
Clostridium botulinum	May contaminate food processing, particularly in tins where anaerobic conditions may exist	Botulism	Antitoxin Supportive care
Clostridium difficile	Colonises gastrointestinal tract Nosocomial pathogen particularly in elderly and debilitated patients	Antibiotic-associated and pseudomembranous colitis	Cessation of causative antibiotic Oral metronidazole or oral vancomycin
Actinomyces spp.	Found as part of oral flora Increased in poor dental hygiene May complicate intrauterine contraceptive device	Actinomycosis is a chronic suppurative infection with sinus formation Maxillofacial infections Pelvic Hand infection acquired from an adversary's teeth	Penicillin is the treatment of choice

2.5.2 Gram-negative bacteria

Description of the organism

Gram-negative bacteria (Table 46) are characterised by the presence of endotoxin (lipopolysaccharide) in the outer leaflet of the bacterial cell wall. Endotoxin is a potent immune activator and has been strongly implicated in cases of severe sepsis and shock associated with Gram-negative bacterial infection.

Meningococcal immunisation

- Type A polysaccharide vaccine for travellers to at-risk areas.
- No vaccine for type B.
- Meningo-C conjugate vaccine introduced in 2000.

Disease syndromes and therapy

Gram-negative cocci

Meningococci and gonococci are of clinical importance (Table 47). The majority of other *Neisseria* spp. are commensals of the upper respiratory tract and do not cause serious disease apart from rare cases of endocarditis.

Gram-negative bacilli

Enterobacteriaceae The taxonomy of Gram-negative bacilli is very complicated. Enterobacteriaceae is the name given to a group of Gram-negative bacilli that fulfil certain laboratory-based criteria, based on

biochemical testing (Table 48). It includes organisms often found in the gastrointestinal tract, many of which are associated with similar diseases.

Antibacterial resistance in the Enterobacteriaceae

- Emergence of multiresistant strains as nosocomial pathogens.
- Public health and infection control concern.
- Resistance is usually the result of β-lactamase production.
- Often transferable on plasmids.
- Requires isolation and infection control precautions.

TABLE 46 MEDICALLY IMPORTANT GRAM-NEGATIVE BACTERIA

Morphology	Aerobic	Anaerobic
Cocci	*Neisseria* spp.	–
Bacilli	Enterobacteriaceae Pseudomonads Coccobacilli Curved Gram-negative rods	*Bacteroides* spp. *Fusobacterium* spp.

TABLE 47 MEDICALLY IMPORTANT GRAM-NEGATIVE COCCI

Organism	Epidemiology/public health	Disease	Treatment
Neisseria meningitidis (meningococcus)	Subtyped by capsular polysaccharides, most common being A, B and C Types B and C are prevalent in Europe and the USA Type A is associated with epidemics in the meningitis belt of sub-Saharan Africa	Septicaemia Meningitis Septic arthritis Pneumonia or pericarditis is uncommon	Penicillin or third-generation cephalosporin (see Sections 1.3.2 and 1.3.11) Penicillin resistance emerging abroad Chemoprophylaxis for contacts (see Section 1.3.11)
Neisseria gonorrhoeae (gonococcus)	Sexually transmitted disease Occasional mother–child transmission at delivery (ophthalmia neonatorum)	Urethritis, cervicitis Epididymo-orchitis, proctitis, PID Disseminated infection (arthritis–dermatitis syndrome) Perihepatitis (FitzHugh–Curtis syndrome)	Options include: penicillin + probenicid, im ceftriaxone, azithromycin and fluoroquinolones Antibiotic resistance patterns vary from region to region and resistance is a worldwide problem Resistance to penicillin is as high as 30–40% in South-east Asia

PID, pelvic inflammatory disease.

TABLE 48 MEDICALLY IMPORTANT ENTEROBACTERIACEAE

Organism	Epidemiology/public health	Diseases	Treatment
Escherichia coli	Colonise the GI tract Important nosocomial pathogen	UTI at all ages Septicaemia Intra-abdominal/biliary tract infection Pneumonia in debilitated or hospital-acquired Meningitis in neonates or elderly patients	Guided by antimicrobial susceptibilities and local empirical guidelines
EPEC/ETEC *E. coli* 0157	Contaminated food or water	Diarrhoea (see Section 1.3.19) HUS complicating *E. coli* 0157	Rehydration; no evidence for role of antimicrobials, even in HUS
Klebsiella spp.	Occasional cause of community-acquired infection Nosocomial pathogen	Biliary and GI tract septicaemia Cavitating pneumonia Nosocomial infections	Typically amoxicillin resistant Multiresistant strains in hospital Specific therapy is guided by susceptibilities
Proteus spp.	Colonise GI tract	UTI: association with renal stones	Specific therapy is guided by susceptibilities (see Section 1.3.9)
Salmonella typhi	Tropical and subtropical distribution	Typhoid/enteric fever	Oral fluoroquinolones or intravenous ceftriaxone
Salmonella paratyphi	Human-only pathogen Acquired via contaminated food or drink		Complicated by the emergence of resistant strains
Non-typhoidal Salmonella spp.	Sporadic cases and outbreaks related to poor hygiene	Food poisoning Rare cause of osteomyelitis or infected aneurysm	Normally self-limiting and does not require antibiotics Quinolones for invasive disease or immunocompromised patients
Shigella spp.	Faecal–oral spread More common in developing world	Common Diarrhoea/food poisoning	Normally self-limiting and does not require specific antimicrobial treatment
Yersinia pestis	Zoonotic infection Still found in many parts of the world, such as South-east Asia and Central/Southern Africa	Plague: bubonic form involves regional lymph nodes; pneumonic forms may occur	First line: streptomycin or gentamicin Alternatives: chloramphenicol or tetracyclines
Yersinia enterocolitica and other *Yersinia* spp.	Worldwide distribution	GI infection Mesenteric adenitis Reactive arthritis	Usually no specific antimicrobial treatment required
	Iron overload states	Severe sepsis	Co-trimoxazole

EPEC, enteropathogenic *Escherichia coli*; ETEC, enterotoxigenic *Escherichia coli*; GI, gastrointestinal; HUS, haemolytic–uraemic syndrome; UTI, urinary tract infection.

TABLE 49 MEDICALLY IMPORTANT PSEUDOMONADS

Organism	Epidemiology/public health	Diseases	Treatment

Pseudomonas aeruginosa	Hospital-acquired infection
	Risk factors include:
	  Burns
	  Prolonged hospital stay
	  Antibiotic usage
	  Neutropenia
	  Chronic suppurative lung disease
	  Diabetes
		Septicaemia
		Nosocomial pneumonia
		Nosocomial UTI
		Line infections
		Wound infections
		Malignant otitis externa
		Keratitis
		Pneumonia complicating CF
			Aminoglycosides
			Ceftazidime
			Carbapenems
			Fluoroquinolones
			Penicillins, eg piperacillin
			Dual therapy used in the neutropenic population
			Often resistant to disinfectants

Burkholderia cepacia	Nosocomial pathogen Colonises respiratory tract in CF	Pneumonia, particularly CF	Difficult to eradicate and often multidrug resistant
Burkholderia pseudomallei	Ubiquitous in soil and waterlogged areas in parts of Asia, northern Australia, Africa and South America	Melioidosis Septicaemia Pneumonia Suppurative disease	Ceftazidime iv for a prolonged course followed by long-term oral therapy

CF, cystic fibrosis.

Pseudomonads The pseudomonads include a mixture of aerobic Gram-negative rods (Table 49). The majority are environmental organisms often found in water and soil. Many are recognised as opportunistic pathogens, being responsible for severe nosocomial infections.

Gram-negative coccobacilli
These are short rods most commonly responsible for respiratory tract disease (Table 50).

Invasive *Haemophilus influenzae* type b

- Uncommon now that immunisation available.
- Remains an important pathogen in the developing world.
- Prophylaxis is given to non-immunised household contacts of cases with invasive *Haemophilus influenzae* type b infection.

TABLE 50 MEDICALLY IMPORTANT GRAM-NEGATIVE COCCOBACILLI

Organism	Epidemiology/public health	Diseases	Treatment
Haemophilus influenzae type b	Colonises nasopharynx of 25–75% of the population Invasive disease predominantly <2 years of age	Sinusitis Otitis media Meningitis Epiglottitis Cellulitis Septic arthritis Osteomyelitis	Third-generation cephalosporin for serious disease Erythromycin or co-amoxiclav for localised respiratory disease β-Lactamase production in about 25% of strains leads to ampicillin resistance
Non-type B *Haemophilus* spp.	Colonises nasopharynx of 25–75% of the population Increased disease in smokers	Sinusitis Otitis media Acute exacerbation of COPD Pneumonia Endocarditis (rare)	Erythromycin or co-amoxiclav for localised respiratory disease Seek advice in endocarditis
Haemophilus ducreyi	Sexually transmitted, endemic in tropical areas	Chancroid	Azithromycin
Bordetella pertussis	Of worldwide importance, but incidence in countries with active immunisation programmes is low	Whooping cough	Erythromycin is the antibiotic of choice but often has little or no effect with established infection
Legionella pneumophila	Infection from inhalation of infected droplets Outbreaks linked to aerosols from hot water, cooling towers, air-conditioning, spa baths and showers	Legionnaire's disease (atypical pneumonia) (see Section 1.3.4) Pontiac fever (self-limiting 'flu-like illness)	Erythromycin/clarithromycin for 10–14 days. Consider adding rifampicin in severe disease

TABLE 50 (*Cont'd*)

Organism	Epidemiology/public health	Diseases	Treatment
Brucella spp.	Zoonotic infection (*Brucella abortus* from cattle and *Brucella melitensis* from goats) Transmitted to humans by contact with infected animals or ingestion of unpasteurised dairy products Endemic to Mediterranean basin, North Africa, Central and South America and the Middle East Farmers and vets at increased risk	Acute disease: self-limiting 'flu-like illness Bacteraemia, septic arthritis, granulomatous hepatitis or endocarditis may occur Chronic disease: osteoarticular in 30–40% of cases Sacroilitis, vertebral osteomyelitis and monoarthritis Epididymo-orchitis or meningitis are less common	Combination therapy with doxycycline and rifampicin or streptomycin is better than monotherapy Co-trimoxazole as second line Osteoarthritis requires 6–12 weeks' therapy

COPD, chronic obstructive pulmonary disease.

TABLE 51 MEDICALLY IMPORTANT CURVED GRAM-NEGATIVE RODS

Organism	Epidemiology/public health	Diseases	Treatment
Campylobacter jejuni	Most common cause of acute infective diarrhoea in developed countries	Diarrhoea/food poisoning	Self-limiting and does not require antimicrobial treatment
Helicobacter pylori	Worldwide; higher prevalence in developing world	Acute and chronic gastritis Duodenal ulceration Possible link to gastric carcinoma and lymphoma	Eradication therapy requires multiple drug therapy for 7–10 days Typically two antibiotics plus an acid inhibitor
Vibrio cholerae	Epidemics and pandemics, spread through contaminated water Increased after natural disasters	Profuse watery diarrhoea: rice water stool (toxin-related disease)	Rehydration is of paramount importance Tetracycline reduces excretion period
Vibrio parahaemolyticus	Associated with shellfish	Diarrhoea	Supportive therapy
Vibrio vulnificus	Warm saltwater exposure	Cellulitis and sepsis	Tetracycline

Curved Gram-negative bacilli

The importance of *Campylobacter* spp. and *Helicobacter* spp. in gastrointestinal disease has been recognised since the 1970s and 1980s (Table 51). *Vibrio* spp. are commonly found in aquatic environments, and their historical importance has been almost exclusively related to pandemics and epidemics of cholera.

Anaerobes

Anaerobes are the predominant component of the gastrointestinal bacterial flora. As a result of their fastidious nature, they are difficult to isolate and are often overlooked (Table 52).

TABLE 52 MEDICALLY IMPORTANT GRAM-NEGATIVE ANAEROBES

Organism	Epidemiology/public health	Diseases	Treatment
Bacteroides spp.	Gut commensal Most common cause of non-clostridial anaerobic infections in humans	Intra-abdominal infections Decubitus ulcers Lung abscess	Metronidazole Co-amoxiclav and clindamycin are suitable alternatives
Fusobacterium spp.	Part of the normal oral flora	Head and neck infections (Lemierre's syndrome associated with local jugular thrombosis and distal septic emboli)	Drainage of pus Sensitive to penicillin and metronidazole

2.6 Mycobacteria

Description of the organism

The genus *Mycobacterium* includes a large number of bacteria with widely differing pathogenicity. They are described as acid- and alcohol-fast bacilli, and all appear red when stained using the Ziehl–Neelsen stain (Fig. 54). This group of bacteria can be divided broadly into three groups.

- *Mycobacterium tuberculosis* complex which causes tuberculosis (TB).

- *Mycobacterium leprae*, the causative agent of leprosy.

- Opportunistic (environmental or atypical) mycobacteria.

2.6.1 Mycobacterium tuberculosis

Most cases of TB result from *Mycobacterium tuberculosis*, although less commonly TB may be caused by other bacteria from the *M. tuberculosis*

complex such as *M. bovis* and *M. africanum*.

Epidemiology

Approximately one-third of the world's population is infected with *M. tuberculosis*, with humans as the only reservoir (cattle are a reservoir for *M. bovis*). Poverty and social deprivation are the most common factors associated with a high prevalence of TB due to overcrowding and undernutrition. The incidence of TB in developed countries was decreasing steadily until the mid-1980s, when there was an upturn in notifications related in part to the HIV epidemic. The lifetime risk of developing clinical TB disease in HIV-uninfected individuals is approximately 10%. In HIV infection the risk can exceed 10% per year. Transmission is by inhalation of tubercle bacilli and patients with smear-positive pulmonary TB are highly infectious. In the past *M. bovis* infection was commonly acquired through ingestion of contaminated milk, but this is now very rare.

Tuberculosis and public health

- TB is a notifiable disease under the public health regulations of 1988.
- TB is a disease of public health importance and has been highlighted by the Department of Health as an area of concern for prevention and control.
- Treatment, except in exceptional circumstances, is compulsory not optional.
- Treatment of all cases of TB should be supervised by a consultant with appropriate experience (usually the respiratory or infectious diseases consultant).
- Checks on patient compliance should be routine.
- Arrangements should be in place to follow up those who default from clinic attendance.
- Contact tracing is an integral part of management of patients with TB (Fig. 55).

Diagnostic tests

Imaging

- The most common finding on the CXR in patients with pulmonary TB is upper-lobe shadowing with or without cavitation (Fig. 56). In miliary TB, fine nodular shadows are seen throughout both lung fields (Fig. 57). Pleural TB in the absence of parenchymal lung disease may occur (Fig. 58).

- Ultrasonography, CT or MRI may be used to localise extrapulmonary disease and guide diagnostic procedures.

Cultures

- Sputum: three samples on consecutive days should be sent for acid-fast smear and TB culture. A minimum of 5,000–10,000 mycobacteria/mL of sputum must be present to be detected on sputum smear.

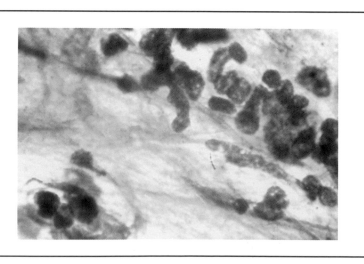

▲**Fig. 54** Ziehl–Neelsen stain for mycobacteria. A red beaded bacterium, *Mycobacterium tuberculosis*, can be seen against a blue background.

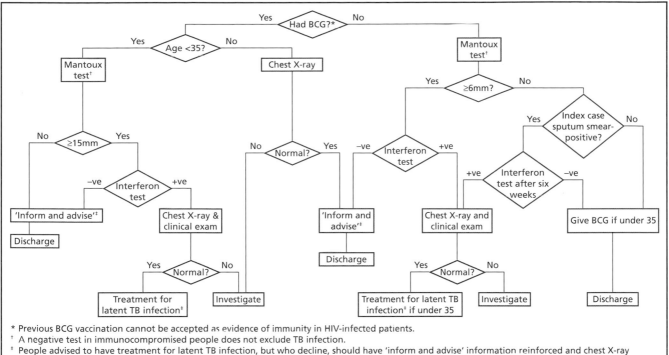

Flowchart content (Fig. 55):

Had BCG?* — Yes / No

Yes branch (Had BCG):
Age <35? — Yes / No

Yes → Mantoux test† → ≥15mm? — No / Yes
- No → 'Inform and advise'‡ → Discharge
- Yes → Interferon test → −ve / +ve
  - −ve → (to 'Inform and advise')
  - +ve → Chest X-ray & clinical exam → Normal? — Yes / No
    - Yes → Treatment for latent TB infection‡
    - No → Investigate

No (Age ≥35) → Chest X-ray → Normal? — No / Yes
- Yes → 'Inform and advise'‡ → Discharge
- No → Interferon test → −ve / +ve
  - +ve → Chest X-ray and clinical exam → Normal? — Yes / No
    - Yes → Treatment for latent TB infection‡ if under 35
    - No → Investigate

No branch (Had BCG = No):
Mantoux test† → ≥6mm? — Yes / No
- Yes → (to Interferon test)
- No → Index case sputum smear-positive? — Yes / No
  - Yes → Interferon test after six weeks → +ve / −ve
    - +ve → Chest X-ray and clinical exam
    - −ve → Give BCG if under 35
  - No → Give BCG if under 35 → Discharge

* Previous BCG vaccination cannot be accepted as evidence of immunity in HIV-infected patients.
† A negative test in immunocompromised people does not exclude TB infection.
‡ People advised to have treatment for latent TB infection, but who decline, should have 'inform and advise' information reinforced and chest X-ray follow-up at three and 12 months.

▲ **Fig. 55** Examination of contacts with pulmonary TB. BCG, bacillus Calmette–Guérin. Reproduced with permission from the National Institute for Health and Clinical Excellence (NICE).

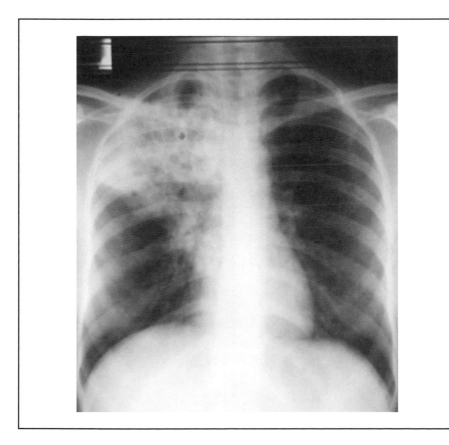

▲ **Fig. 56** Right upper-lobe cavitating pneumonia caused by *M. tuberculosis*.

Culture and sensitivity testing may take 6–8 weeks on standard solid media, but this may be reduced to 2–3 weeks using liquid media such as the BACTEC system.

- The World Health Organisation global DOTS strategy for TB control relies on sputum smear microscopy alone (because it is cheap and relatively easy), although only 50% of culture-positive patients are smear positive.

- Bronchoscopy: if sputum is not available, refer the patient for bronchoscopy and send washings from affected individuals for microscopy and culture.

- Gastric washings: an alternative to bronchoscopy in patients in whom sputum collection is not possible.

- Early-morning urine: this is rarely positive on direct smear, but may culture TB if sterile pyuria is present.

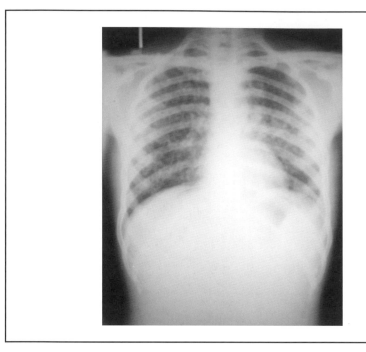

▲**Fig. 57** Miliary tuberculosis.

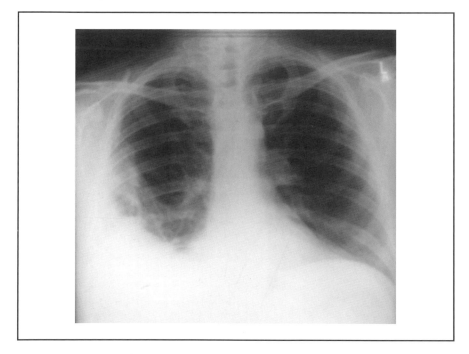

▲**Fig. 58** Right-sided pleural effusion diagnosed as tuberculous on pleural biopsy.

- Blood: blood cultures on specific media may be positive in patients with AIDS.

- Bone marrow: smear and culture should be considered in patients with suspected miliary disease.

- Polymerase chain reaction (PCR): TB differs from many infectious diseases in that PCR (at least in its current form) is not a particularly sensitive test for diagnosis from clinical specimens; its sensitivity is only marginally better than smear and much lower than culture. PCR is a rapid test and a positive PCR may sometimes be helpful on clinical samples (eg cerebrospinal fluid) that are negative for acid-fast bacilli by microscopy, pending the results of culture.

- Use of PCR on cultured isolates for the identification of a mutation in the *rpoB* gene, which is responsible for 95% of rifampicin resistance, is gaining acceptance in the developed world.

Tuberculin testing

A Mantoux or Heaf test (see Section 3.2) is often used in patients with suspected TB. The size of the tuberculin reaction relates to antituberculous cell-mediated immunity and is a marker of disease exposure. A strongly positive reaction gives additional weight to the diagnosis of TB. However, 20% of patients with TB may be negative on these tests and the test is often negative in severely immunocompromised individuals. Moreover, the usefulness of tuberculin skin testing is diminished in BCG-vaccinated subjects and in settings where exposure to environmental mycobacteria is common, as both of these can give rise to positive reactions.

Interferon-γ testing

Interferon-γ tests (including T spot-TB and QuantiFERON-TB Gold; see Section 3.2) measure *in vitro* interferon-γ production in response to *M. tuberculosis*-specific antigens. The tests detect latent or active TB and have high sensitivity (with good results but limited experience in immunocompromised individuals) and increased specificity compared with tuberculin skin testing.

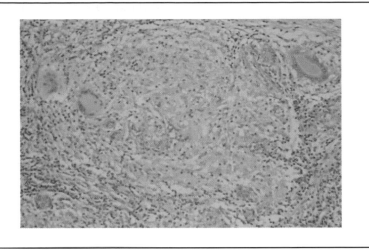

▲ **Fig. 59** Granuloma with multinucleate giant cells and central necrosis consistent with TB.

Histology

In the absence of any abnormal findings on CXR, the diagnosis of extrapulmonary TB often depends on obtaining a sample of tissue. It is very important that, when this tissue is taken, it is split in two: one sample is sent in formalin for histology and the other in a sterile pot for TB culture. On histology, caseating or non-caseating epithelioid cell granulomas may be seen (Fig. 59).

> ⚠ Remember that negative microscopy and culture does not exclude a diagnosis of TB infection.

Disease syndromes

Pulmonary tuberculosis

This accounts for about 75% of cases of TB (see Figs 56–58).

Extrapulmonary disease

After primary infection, TB disseminates haematogenously. This may lead to miliary disease or to late reactivation at one or more body sites. Diagnosis is often delayed in extrapulmonary TB and there is a higher morbidity and mortality. Extrapulmonary disease is more common in the immunocompromised host, including AIDS. Typical sites include the following:

- lymph nodes (Fig. 60);
- abscesses (Fig. 61);
- bone, particularly the spine (Pott's disease);
- central nervous system (CNS) tuberculous meningitis (see Section 1.3.11) and tuberculomas (Fig. 62);

- pericardial;
- genitourinary;
- gastrointestinal tract, typically affecting terminal ileum and peritoneum;
- skin (lupus vulgaris).

Complications

Pulmonary disease

- Erythema nodosum is seen in some cases of primary TB.
- Fibrosis and respiratory failure.
- Pneumothorax.
- Massive haemoptysis.
- Aspergilloma in a healed TB cavity (see Section 2.9.2).
- Paradoxical reactions, eg enlargement of lymph nodes or cerebral tuberculomas while on effective treatment, which is thought to be due to immune activation. This may be particularly pronounced in HIV-infected patients commenced on antiretroviral therapy, where it is termed 'immune restoration syndrome'.

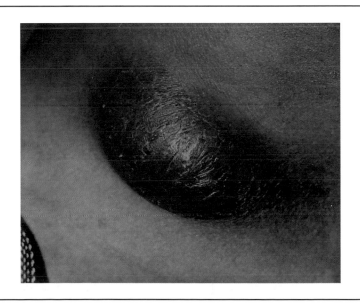

▲ **Fig. 60** Suppurative supraclavicular lymphadenopathy, in this case caused by *M. tuberculosis*.

111

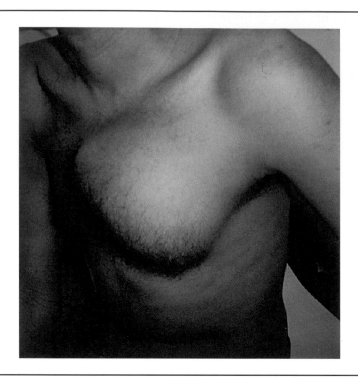

▲ **Fig. 61** Large tuberculous cold abscess on the chest wall.

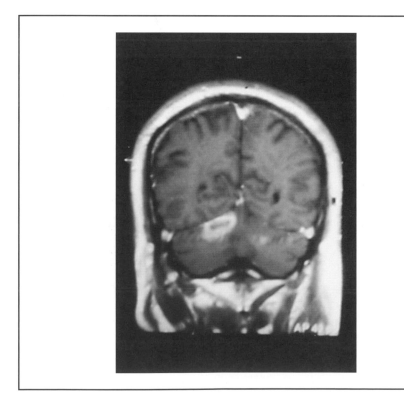

▲ **Fig. 62** MRI scan of a tuberculoma. A ring-enhancing lesion is present in the right cerebellum. This lesion enlarged during antituberculous treatment, necessitating corticosteroid use.

Extrapulmonary disease

- Cranial nerve palsy and other neurological sequelae.

- Spinal cord damage.

- Constrictive pericarditis.

- Infertility as a result of fallopian tube blockage.

- Interstitial nephritis.

- Uveitis and other ophthalmic disease.

Therapy

Drugs

All tuberculosis except CNS disease Treatment is with rifampicin, isoniazid, pyrazinamide and ethambutol for 2 months, followed by rifampicin and isoniazid for a further 4 months.

CNS tuberculosis Treatment is with rifampicin, isoniazid, pyrazinamide and ethambutol for 2 months, followed by rifampicin and isoniazid for a further 10 months, making a total of 12 months' therapy.

Corticosteroids There is good evidence that these should be given in addition to antituberculous treatment for pericarditis and TB meningitis (all stages). They may be beneficial in patients with TB lymphadenitis whose lymph nodes enlarge during treatment, in pleural effusions and in TB involving the ureter.

Advice

- Compliance is essential. Explain why and give practical help such as dosette boxes where needed.

- Rifampicin may render all bodily fluids (including urine, saliva and tears) orange.

- Rifampicin may render the oral contraceptive ineffective.

- Drug-induced hepatitis (rifampicin, isoniazid and pyrazinamide) may complicate therapy. Warn patients to contact the clinic immediately if they become jaundiced. This complication is more likely in elderly people or those with underlying chronic liver disease. Liver function tests should be checked regularly in these patients, and before commencement of therapy in all patients.

- Ethambutol may occasionally cause visual impairment.

- Isoniazid may cause peripheral neuropathy. Prophylactic pyridoxine is often given.

Ethambutol and the eye

- Check visual acuity using a Snellen chart.
- Check colour vision using an Ishihara chart.

Document the results in the case notes. Tell the patient to stop ethambutol and to contact you if he or she notices any change in vision.

Monitoring therapy
Monitor the following for clinical improvement:

- symptoms, eg fever/cough;

- weight;

- inflammatory or other laboratory markers;

- CXR.

Treatment failure There are several possible reasons for apparent treatment failure. It may be helpful to check drug levels. Rifampicin ingestion and absorption can be simply monitored at the bedside by observing urine colour. Check for the following.

- Non-compliance: check urine for the orange colour and check rifampicin levels.

- Multidrug resistance: chase sensitivity results, and consider PCR for rifampicin resistance. Seek specialist advice regarding the next regimen.

- Wrong diagnosis, eg sarcoidosis. Was an organism cultured?

- Malabsorption: the patient may have unsuspected small bowel TB. Drug interactions (eg with HIV drugs) may be important. Rifampicin and isoniazid drug levels may help.

- Drug fever: the TB may be responding well and new symptoms are the result of a drug reaction (particularly common with rifampicin) or a paradoxical reaction.

The law

An infectious patient who presents a risk to others can be compulsorily admitted to hospital on a magistrate's order, but cannot be compulsorily treated.

Directly observed therapy

- Treatment of choice in suspected non-compliance.
- Use a dosing regimen of three times a week.
- Each dose to be given by a nurse at the clinic or at home.

Patient isolation
Risk assessment algorithms have been drawn up for the UK to assist in placing TB patients and those with suspected drug-resistant disease. Patients in hospital with smear-positive pulmonary TB should be isolated in a negative-pressure room. Smear-positive cases of

pulmonary TB who reside within an institution (eg nursing home) should be admitted for isolation until they have received 2 weeks of antituberculous therapy and sputum bacterial levels have declined.

If the patient is moved around the hospital, he or she should wear a well-fitting high-filter face mask.

Confirmed or suspected multidrug-resistant pulmonary TB cases should be admitted to hospital and isolated in a negative-pressure room.

FURTHER READING

Joint Tuberculosis Committee of the British Thoracic Society. Chemotherapy and management of tuberculosis in the United Kingdom: recommendations 1998. *Thorax* 1998; 53: 536–48. Full text available at: http://www.brit-thoracic.org.uk/

Joint Tuberculosis Committee of the British Thoracic Society. Control and prevention of tuberculosis in the United Kingdom: Code of Practice 2000. *Thorax* 2000; 55: 887–901. Full text available at: http://www. brit-thoracic.org.uk/

National Collaborating Centre for Chronic Conditions. *Tuberculosis: Clinical Diagnosis and Management of Tuberculosis, and Measures for its Prevention and Control.* London: Royal College of Physicians of London, 2006. Full text available at: http://www.nice.org.uk/

Yee D, Valiquette C, Pelletier M, *et al.* Incidence of serious side effects from first-line antituberculosis drugs among patients treated for active tuberculosis. *Am J Respir Crit Care Med* 2003; 167: 1472–7.

2.6.2 Mycobacterium leprae
This is the agent of leprosy or Hansen's disease.

Epidemiology
There are an estimated 6 million people with leprosy worldwide. It is

endemic in Africa, Asia and South America. Its spread is thought to be person to person through infected nasal droplets, but less than 10% of those exposed develop the disease.

Diagnostic tests

The organism cannot be grown *in vitro*. Diagnosis is clinical and confirmed by biopsy of a skin lesion or thickened nerve.

Disease syndromes

The majority of people exposed to *M. leprae* develop no clinical symptoms. In patients who develop the disease, the clinical manifestations depend on the level of cell-mediated immunity (CMI) against the organism.

- Strong CMI response (Th1) (see *Scientific Background to Medicine 1*, Immunology and Immunosuppression – T cells) is associated with tuberculoid leprosy.

- Weak CMI response (Th2) is associated with lepromatous leprosy.

- Intermediate response leads to borderline disease.

Tuberculoid leprosy

This presents with one to a few macules (pale on dark skin, red on white skin), with loss of sensation and sweating over them. A few nerves may be affected and thickened, with associated sensory or motor impairment. Few or no bacilli are seen on histology in these patients.

Lepromatous leprosy

Numerous skin lesions occur, mainly macules, infiltrating lesions and nodules. These are not anaesthetic or anhidrotic. As the disease progresses, the skin becomes thickened and the ears, lips and nose swell. Nerve thickening tends to be symmetrical and leads to peripheral neuropathy, neuropathic ulcers and

deformity. Many bacilli are seen on biopsy.

Indeterminate leprosy

This is often the initial clinical manifestation and is characterised by a small macule without sensory loss. At this stage, the disease may progress to either of the types described above.

Complications

Tissue damage

Severe sensory neuropathy leads to deformity and loss of digits, tip of the nose and ears in lepromatous disease.

Erythema nodosum leprosum

This usually occurs in lepromatous or, less commonly, borderline leprosy after treatment has been commenced. Symptoms include fever and crops of painful red nodules that last for a few days. Other affected organs include the eyes (iridocyclitis), testes (orchitis), swollen joints and rarely an immune complex nephritis. Thalidomide is an effective treatment.

Reversal reaction

This occurs in borderline leprosy as the bacterial load is reduced with treatment. Skin lesions and affected nerves swell and may lead to severe nerve compression and damage within days. Treatment is with steroids, which may need to be continued for several months.

Therapy

- Tuberculoid leprosy (paucibacillary): rifampicin and dapsone for 6 months.

- Lepromatous and borderline leprosy (multibacillary): rifampicin, dapsone and clofazimine for a minimum of 2 years or until skin-smear negativity occurs.

FURTHER READING

Levis WR and Ernst JD. *Mycobacterium leprae*. In: Mandell GL, Bennett JE and Dolin R, eds. *Principles and Practice of Infectious Disease*, 6th edn. Philadelphia: Churchill Livingstone, 2005: 2886–96.

– – – – – – – – – – – – – – – – – –

Lockwood DNJ. Leprosy (Hansen's disease). In: Warrell DA, Cox TM and Firth JD, eds. *Oxford Textbook of Medicine*, 4th edn. Oxford: Oxford University Press, 2003: 575–83.

2.6.3 Opportunistic mycobacteria

Epidemiology

These species of mycobacteria are widespread in the environment (soil, water, birds and animals) and person-to-person spread is very unusual. The prevalence of infection by individual species varies from country to country.

Diagnostic tests

Isolation of atypical mycobacteria may represent true infection or simply contamination, so always interpret culture results within the clinical context. Atypical mycobacteria often grow more quickly in culture than *M. tuberculosis*. Polymerase chain reaction or DNA-based tests can rapidly distinguish between the *M. tuberculosis* group and other species.

Disease syndromes

There is a variety of disease syndromes caused by these mycobacteria, depending on age, level of immunocompromise and underlying lung disease (Table 53). *Mycobacterium avium-intracellulare* tends to be the predominant species causing disseminated disease in patients with AIDS.

Therapy

In general, atypical mycobacteria are inherently more drug resistant

TABLE 53 PRINCIPAL DISEASE SITE(S) OF MORE COMMON OPPORTUNISTIC MYCOBACTERIA

Mycobacterial species	Site(s) of infection
Mycobacterium kansasii	Pulmonary
Mycobacterium malmoense	Pulmonary
Mycobacterium xenopi	Pulmonary
Mycobacterium avium-intracellulare	Pulmonary
	Lymph nodes: predominantly in children
	Disseminated infection in HIV-infected patients
Mycobacterium fortuitum	Skin and soft tissue
Mycobacterium chelonae	Skin and soft tissue
Mycobacterium abscessus	Skin and soft tissue
	Pulmonary
Mycobacterium marinum	Skin and soft tissue
Mycobacterium ulcerans	Skin and soft tissue

than *M. tuberculosis*. Recommended therapy varies according to site of infection, species of *Mycobacterium* and the presence or absence of immunocompromise. See the British Thoracic Society guidelines for detailed information on therapy. In severely immunocompromised patients, the response to therapy is often poor unless the immune response can be improved.

FURTHER READING

Subcommittee of the Joint Tuberculosis Committee of the British Thoracic Society. Management of opportunist mycobacterial infections: Joint Tuberculosis Committee guidelines 1999. *Thorax* 2000; 55: 210–18.

2.7 Spirochaetes

Description of the organism
Spirochaetes are thin, helical, Gram-negative bacteria. They include *Treponema*, *Borrelia* and *Leptospira* spp. (Table 54).

2.7.1 Syphilis

Epidemiology
The majority of cases are sexually transmitted, with increased incidence in gay men, commercial sex workers and people from/visiting the developing world. Syphilis can be transmitted transplacentally and via blood transfusion or needlestick injury.

Clinical presentation
See Table 55.

Diagnostic tests

- Serology, as shown in Table 56.

- Identification can be made from primary lesions by dark-field microscopy.

Disease syndromes
Local infection at the site of inoculation is followed by dissemination (secondary syphilis). There follows a long period of clinical latency before late-stage end-organ disease.

Features of secondary syphilis

- Signs start 6–8 weeks after infection.
- Fever, headache and musculoskeletal pains.
- Rash: macular, and becoming papular on trunk, palms and soles (Fig. 63).
- Alopecia: moth-eaten.
- Oral: mucous patches and snail-track ulcers.
- Anogenital: condylomata lata.
- Generalised lymphadenopathy.

TABLE 54 IMPORTANT SPIROCHAETES, THEIR VECTORS AND DISEASES

Genus	Species	Vector	Human disease
Treponema	*T. pallidum* subsp. *pallidum*	None	Syphilis
	T. pallidum subsp. *endemicum*	None	Bejel
	T. pallidum subsp. *pertenue*	None	Yaws
	T. pallidum subsp. *carateum*	None	Pinta
Borrelia	*B. burgdorferi*	*Ixodes* tick	Lyme disease
	B. recurrentis	Human louse	Louse-borne relapsing fever
	B. duttoni and other species	Soft tick	Tick-borne relapsing fever
Leptospira	*L. interrogans* serovars	Rodent urine	Leptospirosis
	L. interrogans var. *icterohaemorrhagiae*	Rodent urine	Weil's disease

TABLE 55 CLINICAL FEATURES OF SYPHILIS

Stage of disease	Timing	Site	Clinical features
Primary	3 days to 3 months (average 3 weeks)	Site of inoculation	Painless chancre (indurated ulcer) Regional lymphadenopathy
Secondary ('the great imitator')	2–8 weeks after appearance of chancre	General	Diffuse lymphadenopathy, fever, malaise, arthralgia
		Skin	Maculopapular rash, involving palms and soles
		Skin folds	Condylomata lata
		Mouth	Snail-track ulcers, mucous patches
		CNS	Headache, meningism
		Eyes	Uveitis, retinitis
Latent	Early: immediate to 2 years Late: 3 years or more	–	Asymptomatic
Tertiary	Years	Skin, mucosa and skeletal system	Gumma: 15% untreated cases
		Cardiac	Aortitis/aneurysm formation and aortic valve incompetence
		CNS	Argyll Robertson pupil Tabes dorsalis Charcot's joints Psychiatric manifestations
Congenital	Early	General	Osteochondritis Rash Anaemia Hepatosplenomegaly
	Late	General	Saddle nose Frontal bossing Hutchinson's teeth

CNS, central nervous system.

TABLE 56 COMMONLY ENCOUNTERED PATTERNS OF SYPHILIS SEROLOGY

Test results	Interpretation
VDRL/RPR positive TPHA/FTA/EIA negative	Biological false positive, eg pregnancy, connective tissue disease and HIV
VDRL/RPR positive TPHA/FTA/EIA positive	If VDRL/RPR titre is high, infection with syphilis is more likely to be active In latent syphilis the RPR/VDRL will be of low titre
VDRL/RPR negative or low titre TPHA/FTA/EIA positive	Either latent untreated syphilis, fully treated syphilis or a different treponemal infection such as yaws, pinta or bejel Can have TPHA false positive, but this is uncommon

EIA, enzyme immunoassay; FTA, fluorescent treponemal antigen; RPR, rapid plasma reagin; TPHA, *Treponema pallidum* haemagglutinin assay; VDRL, Venereal Disease Research Laboratory.

Possible features of congenital syphilis

- Systemic illness with bullous rash, anaemia, jaundice and hepatosplenomegaly in severe cases.
- Intrauterine growth retardation (small for dates).
- A baby may appear initially normal, but fail to thrive over the first few months of life.
- Rash similar to secondary syphilis.
- Periostitis.
- Subsequent late features: skull bossing, Hutchinson's teeth, interstitial keratitis and Clutton's joints.
- Nerve deafnesss.
- Generalised CNS disease.

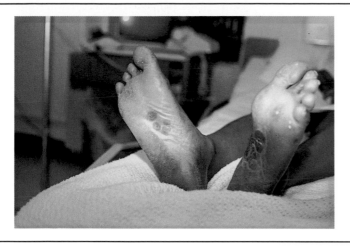

▲ **Fig. 63** Soles of a patient who had no antenatal care presenting to the Emergency Department in labour, showing lesions of secondary syphilis.

Therapy

Parenteral long-acting penicillins are preferred at all stages of syphilis. The dosage and duration of therapy depend on the clinical stage (Table 57).

Jarisch–Herxheimer reaction

- Acute reaction to antitreponemal therapy mediated by inflammatory cytokines.
- Occurs within 24 hours of therapy and is most common with the first treatment dose.
- Fever, myalgia, headache and hypotension.
- Can (rarely) be fatal.
- In pregnancy, may trigger labour.

Contacts

Contact tracing in syphilis

- Trace contacts in the time before disease onset: in primary syphilis, trace back 3 months; in secondary syphilis, trace back 6 months; and in latent syphilis, trace back up to 1 year.
- Offer testing to all partners of patients with late syphilis.
- Offer to anonymously trace and offer therapy to all sexual contacts on patient's behalf if necessary.

Stage	Drug	Duration
Early (<2 years)	Benzathine benzylpenicillin 1.8 g (2.4 MU) im	One or two doses
	Procaine penicillin 750 mg daily[1]	10 days
	Doxycycline 100 mg twice daily	10 days
	Erythromycin 500 mg four times daily	14 days
Late (>2 years, including cardiovascular)	Procaine penicillin 750 mg im daily[1]	17 days
	Doxycycline 100–200 mg twice daily	28 days
Neurosyphilis	Procaine penicillin 1.8 g–2.4 g im od[1] + probenecid 500 mg po qds	17 days
	Benzylpenicillin 13.5–18 g (18–24 MU) daily, given as 2.4–3 g (3–4 MU) iv every 4 hours	17 days

TABLE 57 THERAPY OF SYPHILIS

1. Procaine penicillin is available in the UK as a mixture with benzylpenicillin.

2.7.2 Lyme disease

Epidemiology

Lyme disease occurs throughout the USA, Europe and the former Soviet Union. There are small foci of disease in the New Forest, Exmoor and other areas of the UK. Deer and rodents serve as the most common hosts for the ticks. Campers and hikers are at particular risk. Infection can be prevented by removing ticks within 24 hours.

Diagnostic tests

The diagnosis is usually made on serology in association with a suitable clinical picture, although only 50% of people with early disease have a positive antibody test. Serology may be difficult to interpret in people from an endemic area. In central nervous system (CNS) disease, polymerase chain reaction for *Borrelia burgdorferi* can be performed on the cerebrospinal fluid.

Disease syndromes

The illness is characterised by three stages.

Localised early

Onset is from 3 days to 1 month after tick bite. In 50–90% of cases there is a spreading rash with central clearing, erythema chronicum migrans, at the site of the bite. This clears after 2–6 weeks.

Early disseminated

Secondary skin lesions, malaise, arthralgia and lymphadenopathy are common and may start within a few days of the initial lesion. Aseptic meningitis may occur.

Late persistent infection

Late manifestations (months to years after initial infection) occur in 20–50% of untreated patients.

- Arthritis: large-joint monoarthopathy or oligoarthopathy, often as recurrent attacks over months to years. Polyarthritis is unusual.

- Carditis: occurs in 10% of cases; is more commonly seen in the USA and manifests as dysrhythmias or heart block.

- CNS manifestations: in 10–15% of cases, including lymphocytic meningitis, cranial nerve palsies (especially VII), encephalopathy, neuropathy and radiculopathy, and chronic fatigue-type syndrome.

- Skin: acrodermatitis chronicum atrophicans (skin discoloration and swelling at original erythema chronicum migrans site).

Therapy

Stage 1 and mild cases at stage 2 can be treated with 2–3 weeks of doxycycline or amoxicillin. Serious complications usually require intravenous ceftriaxone.

2.7.3 Relapsing fever

Epidemiology

Louse-borne relapsing fever

This is highly endemic in the highlands of Ethiopia and Burundi, but is found throughout Asia, North-west and East Africa, India, China, Peru and Bolivia. The disease thrives where people live in crowded conditions.

Tick-borne relapsing fever

This has a worldwide distribution. *Borrelia duttoni* and other *Borrelia* spp. are prevalent in parts of East, Central and South Africa.

Diagnostic tests

The spirochaetes can be seen on blood films taken as for malaria (see Section 3.2). They are less easily detected in tick-borne disease. Serology is helpful: there is cross-reactivity with *Borrelia burgdorferi*.

Disease syndromes

Louse-borne relapsing fever

- Severe febrile illness for 5–7 days, with one to three relapses about a week apart.

- Haemorrhagic complications in 50% of cases, including hepatitis and myocarditis.

- Mortality rate of 9–50% in epidemics.

Tick-borne relapsing fever

- Mild: severe febrile illness is followed by multiple relapses separated by 1–21 days.

- Mortality is <10%, but neurological complications in 5–10% of cases.

Therapy

Treatment with tetracycline (with or without penicillin) or erythromycin to eliminate spirochaetes may be complicated by a Jarisch–Herxheimer (hypersensitivity) reaction in 30–100%. This is characterised by rigors, delirium and shock a few hours after antimicrobial administration, and is thought to be principally related to release of tumour necrosis factor. Monitoring and support through a Jarisch–Herxheimer reaction are essential.

2.7.4 Leptospirosis

Epidemiology

Leptospirosis has a worldwide distribution. *Leptospira* spp. are excreted in rodent urine, the rat being the most common vector, and humans are infected from environmental contact through skin abrasions or the mucosa. Risk factors include farming, sewage work, veterinary medicine and recreational freshwater exposure.

Diagnostic tests

Diagnosis relies on suspicion from the clinical picture and relevant exposure history (see Section 1.3.16). The organism can sometimes be cultured from blood or urine in acute disease, but this is beyond the capability of routine microbiology laboratories. The diagnosis is usually confirmed retrospectively by serology.

Disease syndromes and complications

There is a range of presentations, from asymptomatic infection, to a 'flu-like illness 7–14 days after infection, to severe illness in about 10% of those with clinical disease. There are two phases to the illness, an early non-specific bacteraemic illness and a week or so later a second phase that is immune-mediated and in which the major complications occur. Severe disease (Weil's disease) is characterised by severe hepatitis, conjunctival suffusion, renal failure, haemorrhages, impaired consciousness, myocarditis and shock, and has a mortality rate approaching 10%. *Leptospira* spp. can also cause aseptic meningitis without hepatic or renal involvement.

Therapy

Penicillin is active against *Leptospira* spp. and should be administered, if possible, early in disease, although there are conflicting data on whether antibiotics improve outcome. Tetracycline is suitable in penicillin allergy. Supportive care in serious illness is the most important factor in determining outcome.

2.8 Miscellaneous bacteria

2.8.1 *Mycoplasma* and *Ureaplasma*

Description of the organism

Mycoplasmas and ureaplasmas lack a cell wall and are the smallest free-living organisms known. They require special media for culture and do not stain using Gram stain. Many species have been described, with a few of clinical importance, the most significant of these being *Mycoplasma pneumoniae*.

Mycoplasmas and ureaplasmas of clinical importance

- *Mycoplasma pneumoniae.*
- Genital mycoplasmas, eg *Mycoplasma hominis* and *Mycoplasma genitalum.*
- *Ureaplasma urealyticum.*

Epidemiology

Mycoplasma pneumoniae

Worldwide distribution, transmitted by respiratory droplets from an infected case. There are sporadic cases continuously, and epidemic outbreaks every 3–5 years. Children and adolescents are particularly likely to acquire infection.

Genital mycoplasmas and ureaplasmas

These are found worldwide as common colonising organisms in the female genital tract. There is an epidemiological association with genital and pelvic disease.

Diagnostic tests

Mycoplasma pneumoniae

- Blood tests: white cell count is usually normal or slightly raised

($<15 \times 10^9$/L). Cold agglutinins are present in about 50% of patients with *Mycoplasma pneumoniae* infection. Although not specific (the same results may occur in Epstein–Barr virus, cytomegalovirus and some lymphomas), their detection is highly suggestive of the diagnosis in the correct clinical setting. Serology confirms the diagnosis, based on the demonstration of a fourfold rise in antibody titre between acute and convalescent (10–14 days) samples.

- Imaging: CXR may reveal consolidation at lung bases, but is not diagnostic; pleural effusion is uncommon.

Genital mycoplasmas and ureaplasmas

Culture from relevant genital specimens requires specific techniques and is not routinely practised. *Mycoplasma hominis* can occasionally be isolated from blood in severe infection.

Disease syndromes

Mycoplasma pneumoniae

The most common site of infection with *M. pneumoniae* is the respiratory tract (see Section 1.3.4). The majority of cases are limited to the upper respiratory tract but pneumonia develops in 5–10% of patients. *Mycoplasma pneumoniae* is the second most common cause of community-acquired pneumonia in young adults. There is an insidious onset with fever, headache and malaise, and there may be prominent abdominal symptoms including diarrhoea. The cough is initially dry, but may become productive. Pleuritic chest pain or pleural effusion is rare in *Mycoplasma* pneumonia. As with the other atypical organisms,

auscultation of the chest may reveal no or only minimal abnormality.

Genital mycoplasmas and ureaplasmas

Females *Mycoplasma hominis* and *Ureaplasma urealyticum* are common genital tract commensals, but are implicated in some cases of salpingitis, endometritis and pelvic inflammatory disease. Both may cause chorioamnionitis and can be isolated in septic abortion, postpartum sepsis and some cases of neonatal meningitis. Systemic spread with septic arthritis has rarely been reported for both organisms.

Males The role of genital mycoplasmas in non-gonococcal urethritis is controversial. *Ureaplasma urealyticum* can cause urethritis, epididymo-orchitis and prostatitis.

Complications

Mycoplasma pneumoniae

- Rashes: often macular but erythema multiforme and erythema nodosum described.
- Bullous myringitis.
- Arthralgia and, rarely, arthritis.
- Myocarditis and pericarditis.
- Meningitis and encephalitis.
- Raynaud's phenomenon related to cold agglutinins.
- Haemolytic anaemia.

Therapy

Mycoplasma pneumoniae

Upper respiratory tract infections with *M. pneumoniae* do not require antibiotics. Pneumonia is usually self-limiting but 10–14 days with a macrolide antibiotic can shorten the duration of the illness. Tetracyclines are also effective.

Genital mycoplasmas and ureaplasmas

Doxycycline 100 mg twice daily is the drug of choice for *Ureaplasma*. Clindamycin is the choice for *M. hominis*, and for children. *Mycoplasma hominis* is resistant to macrolides.

2.8.2 Rickettsiae

Description of the organism

Rickettsiae are small, aerobic, Gram-negative and obligate intracellular parasites.

Epidemiology

Rickettsiae are zoonoses and are transmitted to humans by a number of arthropods (Table 58). Rickettsial infections are distributed throughout the world.

Diagnostic tests

The diagnosis is initially made on clinical grounds and confirmed by serological tests. Significant cross-reactivity is encountered. Polymerase chain reaction of blood and cell culture may be available.

Disease syndromes

General features include fever, headache and rash. Many are associated with an eschar at the site of the bite with associated regional lymphadenopathy. The severity varies from epidemic louse-borne typhus, which has a mortality rate reported as high as 40%, to rickettsialpox, which is usually a self-limiting illness.

The tetracyclines are the drugs of choice.

2.8.3 *Coxiella burnetii* (Q fever)

Epidemiology

Coxiella burnetii is a zoonotic rickettsiosis reported throughout the world. Cattle, sheep and goats are the main animal reservoirs. Spread is by inhalation of aerosolised particles from infected animals or their contaminated environment. Farmers, veterinarians and abattoir workers are particularly at risk. The organism could potentially be used as a bioterrorism agent.

Diagnostic tests

- Serology is the usual method of confirming diagnosis. Acute infection can be distinguished from chronic infection based on antibody responses to phase I and phase II antigens, but significant titres may take 4 weeks to develop.

- Polymerase chain reaction has poor sensitivity and specificity.

- White cell count is usually normal or slightly raised.

- Liver function tests: slight elevation of the transaminases occurs in most patients.

Disease syndromes

Acute Q fever

The disease has an incubation period of 7–30 days. About 50% of people infected develop acute symptoms, often an influenza-like illness, but also pneumonia and hepatitis.

Chronic Q fever

Chronic infection generally develops 1–18 months after acute infection.

- Endocarditis, usually with a prosthetic, or previously abnormal, heart valve.

- Meningoencephalitis.

- Hepatitis.

- Osteomyelitis.

Therapy

- Acute Q fever: doxycycline 200 mg daily for 14 days. A quinolone may be used as an alternative.

- Q fever endocarditis: the optimal drugs are uncertain but some authors recommend doxycycline combined with chloroquine for at least 18 months. Doxycycline combined with rifampicin or ciprofloxacin has also been successful. Relapse rates of over 50% are seen despite therapy.

TABLE 58 DISEASE SYNDROMES AND EPIDEMIOLOGY OF THE MORE COMMON RICKETTSIOSES

Group	Disease syndrome	Organism	Vector	Geographical distribution
Typhus	Epidemic typhus	*Rickettsia prowazekii*	Body louse	South America, Africa, Asia
	Endemic murine typhus	*Rickettsia typhi*	Flea	Worldwide
	Scrub typhus	*Rickettsia tsutsugamushi*	Larval trombiculid mite	South-east Asia, South Pacific
Spotted fever	American (Rocky Mountain) spotted fever	*Rickettsia rickettsii*	Tick	USA
	Old world (Boutonneuse) fever	*Rickettsia conorii*	Tick	Africa, Mediterranean
	Rickettsialpox	*Rickettsia akari*	Mite	USA, Africa, Asia

2.8.4 Chlamydiae

Description of the organism
Chlamydiae are small obligate intracellular parasites. There are three species causing human disease:

- *Chlamydia trachomatis*;
- *Chlamydia pneumoniae*;
- *Chlamydia psittaci*.

Epidemiology

Chlamydia trachomatis

Trachoma Widespread in the developing world, *C. trachomatis* can spread from eye to eye by direct contact, fomites or fly inoculation.

Genital Chlamydia The prevalence of genital chlamydial infection is high in young sexually active women (up to 10–25%) making *C. trachomatis*, spread by sexual intercourse, the most common sexually transmitted disease and probably the single most common cause of tubal infertility.

Chlamydia pneumoniae
This is a common respiratory pathogen worldwide. Its spread is by the respiratory route and infections occur particularly in children and young adults. Epidemiological links to heart disease have not been proven.

Chlamydia psittaci
A zoonosis; avian infection is transmitted to humans from infected birds by the respiratory route.

Diagnostic tests
The main diagnostic methods are serology, antigen detection, polymerase chain reaction and culture.

- Genital *Chlamydia*: nucleic acid amplification tests on urine and

TABLE 59 CLINICAL SYNDROMES CAUSED BY *CHLAMYDIA* SPECIES

Species	Affected group	Disease syndrome
C. trachomatis	Young children	Trachoma in developing world
	Men and women	Inclusion body conjunctivitis
		Reactive arthritis
	Genital infection in men	Urethritis
		Epididymo-orchitis
		Prostatitis
	Genital infection in women	Cervicitis and urethritis
		Endometritis
		Pelvic inflammatory disease
		Perihepatitis (FitzHugh–Curtis syndrome)
	Perinatal infection	Ophthalmia neonatorum
		Pneumonia
C. trachomatis	Sexually active men and women	Lymphogranuloma venereum (LGV). Recently associated with outbreaks of proctitis in gay men, often with HIV
C. pneumoniae	Children and young adults	Upper respiratory tract infection
		Atypical pneumonia
C. psittaci	Contact with birds	Psittacosis

cervical swabs, and DNA probes, are more sensitive and specific than cell culture or antigen detection.

- *Chlamydia pneumoniae*: serum antibody detection is diagnostic.

Clinical syndromes
A wide range of clinical manifestations may occur (Table 59).

Complications
Chlamydiae may cause tissue damage and subsequent scarring. It can also cause:

- blindness in trachoma;
- fallopian tube scarring and infertility;
- lymphoedema and rectal strictures in LGV.

Therapy
- Trachoma or conjunctivitis caused by *C. trachomatis* may be treated with topical tetracycline eye ointment and/or oral tetracycline or azithromycin.

- Genital infections caused by *C. trachomatis* may be treated with doxycycline or azithromycin.

- *C. psittaci* and *C. pneumoniae* pneumonia require a tetracycline or macrolide for 2–3 weeks.

2.9 Fungi

Fungi are an important cause of disease in both immunocompetent and immunocompromised hosts. However, the more serious consequences of fungal infection are most often encountered in patients with significant immune defects.

2.9.1 *Candida* spp.

Description of the organism
Candida spp. are budding yeasts that may form pseudohyphae during tissue invasion. They are ubiquitous and common commensals of mucosal surfaces and the gastrointestinal tract.

Epidemiology

Candida spp. are opportunistic pathogens that take advantage of breakdown in local or systemic defences to cause disease. Mucosal protection may be impaired by trauma or by antibiotics altering normal bacterial flora. Impaired cell-mediated immunity predisposes to mucocutaneous infection and neutropenia to disseminated candidiasis. Most infections are endogenous but nosocomial spread has been described.

Diagnostic tests

Candida spp. grow readily on simple laboratory media and can be isolated from blood cultures. The germ tube test rapidly distinguishes *Candida albicans* (produces germ tubes) from other *Candida* spp. Culture cannot always distinguish colonisation from invasive disease and tissue biopsies may be required where budding yeasts and pseudohyphae are seen. There is no reliable serological test for invasive candidiasis.

Disease syndromes and complications

Mucocutaneous disease

Mucosal disease, either oral or vaginal, is the most common manifestation of candidiasis; it is seen in immunocompetent individuals and with greater frequency in those with immunodeficiency. Cutaneous candidal infection occurs in moist skin creases and is a common cause of nappy rash. More serious mucocutaneous diseases, including chronic nail infection (onychomycosis) and oesophageal disease (Fig. 64), may complicate cell-mediated immunodeficiency. Urinary infection with *Candida* is seen in people with diabetes and patients with indwelling urinary catheters.

Disseminated disease

Invasive candidiasis is seen in patients with neutropenia, intravenous drug users and those with long-term central venous cannulation, particularly in intensive care. Manifestations include candidaemia, endocarditis, and invasion of liver/spleen, skin (Fig. 65), eyes or lungs.

Candidaemia

- May be complicated by endophthalmitis or endocarditis.
- Patients with candidaemia should have a full ophthalmic evaluation. Candidal infection appears as white patches on the retina (Fig. 66).
- Consider endocarditis in intravenous drug users and persistent fungaemia.

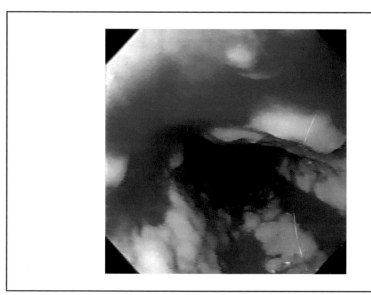

▲ **Fig. 64** Severe oesophageal candidiasis in a patient with AIDS and a CD4 cell count of 50×10^6/L.

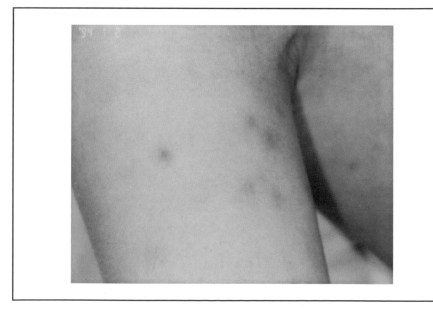

▲ **Fig. 65** Disseminated cutaneous candidiasis in a neutropenic patient.

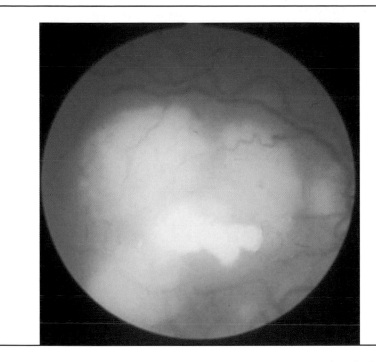

▲ **Fig. 66** *Candida* retinitis with white exudate extending into the vitreous. Intravitreal satellite lesions can be seen on slit-lamp examination. (Courtesy of Professor S. Lightman.)

Therapy

Antifungal therapy (Table 60) should be complemented by management of the underlying predisposing factors, eg diabetes, neutropenia or poor dental hygiene.

Amphotericin

- May cause fever, rigors and hypotension, which can be prevented with hydrocortisone.
- Dose-related renal toxicity, with increased creatinine, hypokalaemia and hypomagnesaemia.
- Encapsulating amphotericin in lipid vesicles reduces toxicity, but there are no data that lipid preparations are more effective than the conventional agent.

2.9.2 *Aspergillus*

Description of the organism

Most human infections are caused by *Aspergillus fumigatus* which is a spore-forming mould (Fig. 67). *Aspergillus* spp. are ubiquitous and predominantly transmitted by inhalation of spores.

Epidemiology

Aspergillus sp. causes invasive disease in severely immunocompromised patients, particularly those with prolonged neutropenia. Outbreaks resulting from aerosolisation of *Aspergillus* spores have been described in association with building works in hospitals. Air filters can reduce the incidence of invasive disease in neutropenic patients.

Diagnostic tests

- Invasive aspergillosis is confirmed by identifying typical fungal hyphae in tissue specimens.

- Positive culture of respiratory material may only indicate colonisation, but is strongly associated with invasive disease in severely immunocompromised hosts.

- Detection of galactomannan in serum may be a useful screening test for early invasive aspergillosis.

Organism	Disease syndrome	Therapy
Candida albicans (most common cause of candidiasis)	Uncomplicated mucosal disease, eg oral/vaginal	Topical therapy with nystatin, amphotericin and azole. Systemic therapy if this fails
	Mucosal disease in immunocompromised host	Systemic therapy: azole first line (eg fluconazole). Amphotericin for resistant disease
	Urinary tract infection[1]	Fluconazole
	Disseminated infection[1]	Intravenous fluconazole, amphotcricin or caspofungin
	Endocarditis/meningitis[1]	Amphotericin + 5-flucytosine
	Endophthalmitis	Fluconazole penetrates eye well. Intraocular/intravenous amphotericin
Non-*albicans* *Candida* spp.	May cause all of the above but less frequently than *Candida albicans*	Increased azole resistance Use azoles for mucosal disease, but amphotericin or voriconazole for initial therapy of systemic infections, eg *C. glabrata*, *C. kruseii*, *C. parapsilosis*

TABLE 60 THERAPY OF CANDIDIASIS

1. Remove synthetic material, eg lines and catheters.

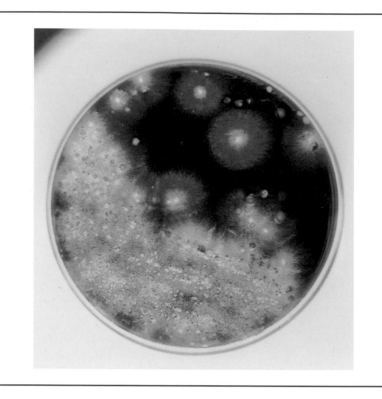

▲ **Fig. 67** *Aspergillus fumigatus* growing on chocolate agar. The mould produces numerous spores that easily aerosolise.

- Cutaneous hypersensitivity reactions to *Aspergillus* preparations and the detection of serum *Aspergillus* precipitins help to establish the diagnoses of allergic disease and aspergilloma.

Disease syndromes and therapy

Disease may occur as a result of tissue invasion or a hypersensitivity reaction to *Aspergillus* colonisation of the respiratory tract (Table 61).

2.9.3 *Cryptococcus neoformans*

Description of the organism
This is an encapsulated yeast carried by avian species and acquired by inhalation.

Epidemiology
Distribution is worldwide, with the most serious disease being seen in cell-mediated immune deficiency. *Cryptococcus neoformans* var. *gatti* has a subtropical distribution and may be more pathogenic to immunocompetent hosts.

Diagnostic tests
Diagnosis is by microscopy (using India ink to outline the capsule) and culture of the organism. The capsular polysaccharide can be detected by enzyme-linked immunosorbent assay in cerebrospinal fluid (CSF)/blood (cryptococcal antigen).

Disease syndromes
Manifestations are rare in the immunocompetent host; in immunocompromised individuals the following disease patterns are seen.

Pneumonia
After inhalation pulmonary invasion is often asymptomatic, but a diffuse pneumonitis may be seen. Chronic pulmonary disease with nodules and effusions may be seen.

Meningitis
Haematogenous dissemination leads to meningitis, which is the most common presentation. Meningitis is accompanied by CSF lymphocytosis and low CSF glucose, but in severely immunocompromised patients the CSF may have no inflammatory cells. Meningitis may be complicated by cryptococcal abscess (cryptococcoma), cranial

TABLE 61 TYPES OF ASPERGILLOSIS AND THERAPY		
Disease syndrome	**Clinical presentation**	**Therapy**
Aspergilloma (colonisation of a pre-existing lung cavity)	Haemoptysis, fever and malaise, and a fungal ball inside the cavity on CXR	Surgery is the only definitive treatment
Allergic bronchopulmonary aspergillosis	Airflow obstruction, eosinophilia, pulmonary infiltrates, proximal bronchiectasis and positive *Aspergillus* precipitins	Corticosteroids
Invasive aspergillosis	Pulmonary: pleurisy, haemoptysis and focal infiltrate Disseminated: fungaemia, brain abscess and liver/spleen	Amphotericin, voriconazole and caspofungin (but note that these conditions have high mortality despite treatment). Itraconazole may be useful in prophylaxis

nerve palsies and markedly raised intracranial pressure resulting from impaired CSF reabsorption.

Cutaneous

Nodules or shallow ulcers may be a sign of disseminated disease. Rarely, there is isolated cutaneous disease after inoculation.

Therapy

Therapy has been best defined for patients with AIDS. Induction treatment is with amphotericin and 5-flucytosine for up to 6 weeks until the CSF has been sterilised. Blood levels of flucytosine should be checked. Repeated lumbar puncture may be necessary to reduce CSF pressure. Secondary prophylaxis is continued with fluconazole while the CD4 cell count remains below 200×10^6/L. Note that itraconazole has poor central nervous system penetration and is not used.

2.9.4 Dimorphic fungi

Description of the organism

Dimorphic fungi are not endemic to the UK. They exist in the soil as mycetes (filamentous) and are acquired through inhalation. During human infection they take on a yeast form. They all have primary infection via the respiratory tract, which is asymptomatic in many cases. Dissemination can occur in immunocompetent hosts but is more common in cell-mediated immunodeficiency states.

Diagnostic tests

Identification of typical yeast forms in tissue specimens. In disseminated disease, *Histoplasma capsulatum* may be seen in peripheral mononuclear cells (Fig. 68). Specific serological tests are available, but are difficult to interpret in endemic areas.

Epidemiology, disease syndromes and therapy

Dimorphic fungi are most prevalent in river valleys in parts of the USA and in Central and South America (Table 62). Most infections in immunocompetent individuals are subclinical but a significant minority experience clinical disease. Wide dissemination may occur in the immunocompromised host even many years after initial exposure.

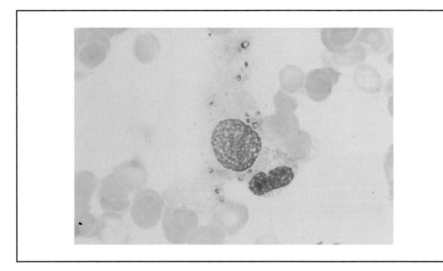

▲ **Fig. 68** Giemsa-stained peripheral blood smear from an AIDS patient with disseminated histoplasmosis. The intracellular organisms appear as small spherical inclusions within white cells. (Courtesy of B. Viner.)

TABLE 62 INFECTIONS CAUSED BY DIMORPHIC FUNGI

Disease	Organism	Epidemiology	Syndromes	Therapy
Blastomycosis	*Blastomyces dermatitidis*	Central/southern USA	Chronic cutaneous disease Disseminates to lung, skin, bones	Azole or amphotericin
Coccidioidomycosis	*Coccidioides immitis*	South-western USA and Mexico	'Flu-like illness, pulmonary nodules, meningitis, osteomyelitis	Azole or amphotericin
Histoplasmosis	*Histoplasma capsulatum*	Central/south USA, Central and South America, Caribbean	Fever, erythema nodosum, hilar lymphadenopathy, pulmonary nodules (may calcify) Disseminated: skin, liver, spleen, bone marrow, lung and brain	Azole or amphotericin
	Histoplasma capsulatum var. *duboisii*	Central Africa	Disseminated disease	
Paracoccidioidomycosis	*Paracoccidioides braziliensis*	Central and South America	Cutaneous, pulmonary and disseminated forms	Sulphonamides, azoles or amphotericin

TABLE 63 FEATURES AND THERAPY OF SPECIFIC FUNGAL INFECTIONS

Disease	Organism	Disease syndromes	Therapy
Mucormycosis	*Mucor mycetales* (+ other zygomycetes)	Rhinosinusitis and intracranial spread in immunocompromised patients, particularly diabetes mellitus	Surgical débridement and high-dose amphotericin; high mortality
Fusariosis	*Fusarium* spp.	Local infection at sites of inoculation Disseminated disease in neutropenia	Responds poorly to amphotericin
Penicilliosis	*Penicillium marneffei*	Endemic to South-east Asia Cutaneous and disseminated disease in AIDS	Acute therapy with amphotericin Maintenance with itraconazole
Chromomycosis	Various pigmented fungi	Chronic subcutaneous disease with scarring	5-Flucytosine or azole therapy
Sporotrichosis	*Sporothrix schenckii*	Cutaneous, bone or joint infection at sites of inoculation Disseminated disease in immunocompromised patients	Potassium iodide or azoles Heat is effective for local lesions
Superficial skin and nail infections	*Malassezia* spp. *Trichophyton* spp. *Microsporum* spp.	Tinea (ringworm) and chronic nail infection (onychomycosis)	Topical therapy with an azole Systemic therapy with terbinafine, itraconazole or griseofulvin Treatment directed by skin scraping results

---

> Consider disseminated infection with dimorphic fungi in immunocompromised patients who have lived/travelled in an endemic area and present with pneumonia, pyrexia of unknown origin or meningitis.

2.9.5 Miscellaneous fungi

Description of the organism

A number of other fungal species are relatively common causes of minor cutaneous disease, and in rare cases life-threatening or disfiguring illness (Table 63).

2.10 Viruses

Description of the organism

Viruses are the smallest living organisms that replicate through nucleic acids. They are classified according to their genome and structure. A detailed knowledge of their classification is not required to understand them in a clinical context, but some idea of their relatedness is useful (Fig. 69). In general, DNA viruses have more stable genomes than RNA viruses and mutate less rapidly.

Diagnostic tests

Direct viral tests
Various methods are used to visualise, detect or culture viruses (Table 64).

The future is likely to see expansion of the use of rapid diagnostic tests for the detection and identification of viral infections. This will be essential to enable rational use of the next generation of antiviral agents.

Serological methods
The antibody response to viruses is often used to establish the diagnosis (Fig. 70). In general, detection of organism-specific IgM antibody or a rising IgG titre signifies recent infection.

> **Pitfalls in diagnostic serology**
>
> • Antibodies arise slowly, so early tests may be negative. Always note the date of onset/exposure when requesting serology to avoid false reassurance.
> • IgM antibodies persist for variable lengths of time. Parvovirus B19 antibodies of IgM class may be present for short periods only, while those against cytomegalovirus (CMV) persist for months.
> • IgM antibodies in particular may cross-react (especially between CMV and Epstein–Barr virus).
> • Severely immunocompromised patients may fail to mount an antibody response.
> • Serology is of little value in identifying the reactivation of a disease (such as CMV).
> • Cross-reactive antibodies limit the usefulness of diagnostic serology in some situations, eg diagnosing enterovirus infection.
> • Immunoglobulin therapy will potentially interfere with the interpretation of serology.

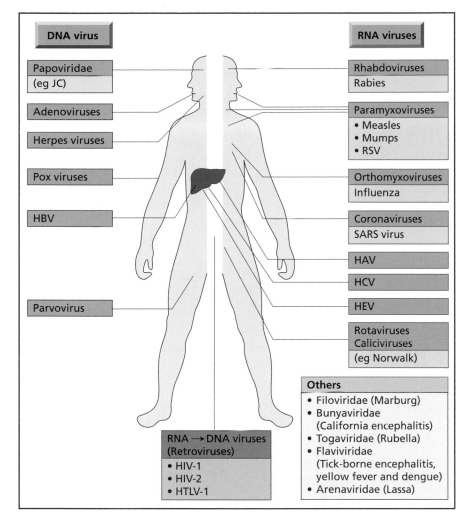

DNA virus

Papoviridae
(eg JC)

Adenoviruses

Herpes viruses

Pox viruses

HBV

Parvovirus

RNA viruses

Rhabdoviruses
Rabies

Paramyxoviruses
• Measles
• Mumps
• RSV

Orthomyxoviruses
Influenza

Coronaviruses
SARS virus

HAV

HCV

HEV

Rotaviruses
Caliciviruses
(eg Norwalk)

Others
• Filoviridae (Marburg)
• Bunyaviridae
(California encephalitis)
• Togaviridae (Rubella)
• Flaviviridae
(Tick-borne encephalitis,
yellow fever and dengue)
• Arenaviridae (Lassa)

RNA → DNA viruses
(Retroviruses)
• HIV-1
• HIV-2
• HTLV-1

▲ **Fig. 69** Medically important viruses. HAV, hepatitis A virus; HBV, hepatitis B virus; HCV, hepatitis C virus; HEV, hepatitis E virus; HTLV, human T-cell lymphotropic virus; RSV, respiratory syncytial virus; SARS, severe acute respiratory syndrome.

TABLE 64 VIRAL DETECTION METHODS

Method	Example	Advantages	Disadvantages
Electron microscopy	Herpesviruses	Rapid	Operator dependent Cannot type or speciate
Viral culture	Adenovirus Herpesviruses	Generic Can enable sensitivity testing	Slow and labour intensive Requires viable virus
Antigen detection by ELISA	HBV	Rapid	May be insensitive
Antigen detection by immunofluorescence	RSV Influenza	Rapid	Operator dependent
PCR	Herpesviruses, HIV, HBV and HCV	Sensitive May enable quantitative estimates	Expensive Contamination may lead to false positives Availability
Nucleic acid sequencing	HIV and HBV	Detect mutations associated with drug resistance	Slow Expensive

ELISA, enzyme-linked immunosorbent assay; HBV, hepatitis B virus; HCV hepatitis C virus; PCR, polymerase chain reaction; RSV, respiratory syncytial virus.

2.10.1 Herpes simplex viruses

Herpesviruses

• Large enveloped DNA viruses.

• Complex genome enabling them to evade immune responses.

• Latency leads to persistent infection.

• Over 150 are described, but only eight are of clinical importance (Fig. 71).

• Gamma herpesviruses are oncogenic in immunosuppressed patients.

Herpes simplex virus types 1 and 2

Pathogenesis

The virus enters through mucosal surfaces and breaks in the skin. HSV-1 commonly enters through the buccal mucosa and HSV-2 through genital mucosa, but they can invade either region causing local inflammation and vesicles. The virus attaches to and enters cutaneous sensory nerves followed by retrograde transport to the nucleus. Latency is established without expression of viral proteins, which means that immune responses are unable to detect these cells. Virus may then re-emerge, causing recurrent disease.

Epidemiology

HSV-1 and HSV-2 are found worldwide, affecting over 70% of the global population. Person-to-person transmission is by direct contact with no animal reservoir. HSV-2 has traditionally been considered a sexually transmitted disease, but HSV-1 may also cause genital disease.

Diagnostic tests

This is largely clinical. Herpes-like virus particles can be readily

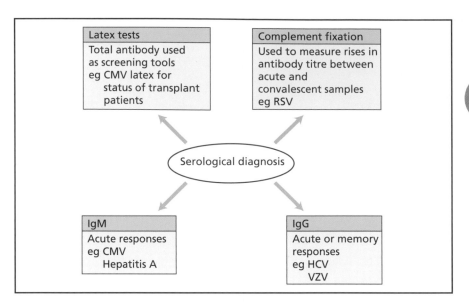

▲**Fig. 70** Different serological methods used in viral diagnosis. A fourfold or greater rise in titre determines significance. CMV, cytomegalovirus; HCV, hepatitis C virus; RSV, respiratory syncytial virus; VZV, varicella-zoster virus.

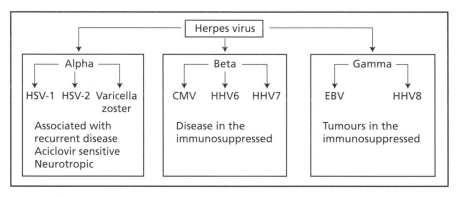

▲**Fig. 71** Medically important herpesviruses. EBV, Epstein–Barr virus; HHV, human herpesvirus; HSV, herpes simplex virus.

detected by electron microscopy of vesicle fluid. Specific immunofluorescence will detect virally infected cells, eg from a vesicle base. Polymerase chain reaction (PCR) can distinguish between HSV-1 and HSV-2. Cerebrospinal fluid PCR is both sensitive and specific in the diagnosis of HSV encephalitis (see Section 1.3.12). Serology may confirm exposure but plays little role in disease diagnosis.

Disease syndromes
Most primary infections in childhood are mild or asymptomatic. In addition,

there are a variety of clinical syndromes associated with primary or recurrent disease (Fig. 72).

Complications
The most severe of these are the following:

- acute retinal necrosis;

- herpes simplex encephalitis (see Section 1.3.12);

- neonatal encephalitis and/or disseminated infection if the mother has active genital herpes at delivery;

- postherpetic erythema multiforme;

- radiculopathy in immunocompromised patients.

⚠ Eczema herpeticum is a severe disseminated form of HSV in patients with underlying eczema. It is frequently misdiagnosed at presentation because vesicles are often not visible.

Therapy
Aciclovir and related drugs (valaciclovir and famciclovir) may be used in either acute treatment or prevention of recurrent disease. High-dose intravenous aciclovir is required for treatment of encephalitis or severe disease in the immunocompromised.

2.10.2 Varicella-zoster virus

Epidemiology
There is ubiquitous distribution, with most people acquiring primary disease (chickenpox) as a child. After primary infection the virus enters latency in the sensory dorsal root ganglion, leading to a lifelong risk of reactivation disease.

Diagnostic tests
The clinical picture enables accurate diagnosis and supportive tests are not needed in uncomplicated disease. Serology can establish past exposure and risk of primary infection (see Section 1.3.15). Viral culture, immunofluorescence and polymerase chain reaction are useful in some circumstances.

Disease syndromes and complications

Primary
Infection enters through the respiratory tract and is clinically silent for 2–3 weeks. A brief 'prodrome' (fever and headache) is

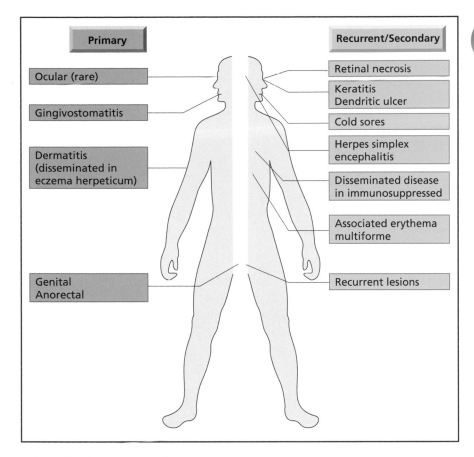

Primary

- Ocular (rare)
- Gingivostomatitis
- Dermatitis (disseminated in eczema herpeticum)
- Genital Anorectal

Recurrent/Secondary

- Retinal necrosis
- Keratitis Dendritic ulcer
- Cold sores
- Herpes simplex encephalitis
- Disseminated disease in immunosuppressed
- Associated erythema multiforme
- Recurrent lesions

▲ **Fig. 72** Clinical manifestations of HSV infection.

Postherpetic neuralgia

- More common as age increases; rare in those aged under 50.
- More frequent with facial zoster.
- May be reduced by early antiviral therapy.
- Resulting acute pain is helped by amitriptyline or gabapentin.

Therapy

Aciclovir, valaciclovir and famciclovir are all active.

Primary

Uncomplicated primary infection does not need treatment in children, but is often associated with severe systemic illness in adults and oral aciclovir (or derivatives) may hasten the resolution of symptoms. High-dose intravenous aciclovir (10 mg/kg three times daily) is indicated in varicella pneumonia, in immunocompromised individuals and in pregnant women (see Section 1.3.15). Zoster immune globulin can be used to prevent infection in vulnerable hosts, but is ineffective in treating active disease.

followed by eruption of a blistering rash starting on the face and trunk. Lesions are sparse on the limbs but may occur on the mouth and palate. Vesicles come in crops, turn into pustules and then crust. When all lesions are crusted the patient is considered non-infectious. Pneumonia, hepatitis or encephalitis may complicate primary infection, particularly in the immunocompromised.

Secondary

Herpes zoster (shingles) occurs in a dermatomal distribution (Fig. 73), heralded by pain. A few vesicles may be seen elsewhere, but an extensive spread suggests immunodeficiency. Postherpetic neuralgia, ocular involvement and facial nerve palsy (Ramsay Hunt syndrome) are the main complications in people with normal immunity. Disseminated disease, retinal necrosis and transverse myelitis may occur in immunocompromised individuals.

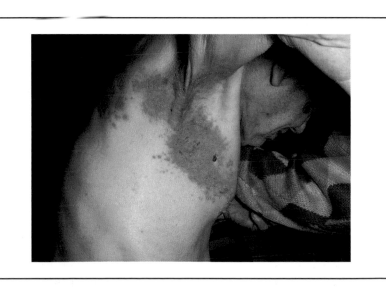

▲ **Fig. 73** Typical dermatomal distribution of herpes zoster.

Secondary

In herpes zoster, antiviral therapy should be considered within the first 72 hours if there is a high risk of postherpetic neuralgia. All patients with ocular disease and those who are immunocompromised should be treated.

2.10.3 Cytomegalovirus

Epidemiology

There is ubiquitous distribution, with most people acquiring primary disease as a child. Seroprevalence in the UK population is around 65%, and higher in at-risk groups (including gay men). The main burden of disease is in immunocompromised individuals.

Diagnostic tests

Primary disease is diagnosed serologically (IgM). Recurrence is diagnosed by a mixture of clinical suspicion and detection of the virus by polymerase chain reaction or direct antigen detection in blood, or more formally by histology of infected tissue. Fetal infection is associated with excretion of virus in the urine.

Disease syndromes and complications

Primary cytomegalovirus (CMV) infection is often silent, but may cause a 'glandular fever'-type illness, including hepatitis. The most significant consequences of infection are in severely immunosuppressed individuals, eg organ and bone-marrow transplant recipients and those with HIV infection.

Severe primary infection may result if a seropositive organ is given to a seronegative donor (see Section 1.3.14). CMV reactivation in transplant recipients may present with diffuse disease affecting the gut, lungs, liver or central nervous system.

In AIDS the virus replicates widely, with the principal syndromes of retinitis, gastrointestinal disease and encephalitis (see Section 1.3.22).

Congenital infection may complicate primary CMV during pregnancy, resulting in fetal malformations.

Therapy

Disease in immunosuppressed people is usually treated with intravenous ganciclovir or foscarnet (see Section 1.3.22). Therapy will not eradicate disease while the patient remains immunocompromised, and increasing antiviral resistance may be encountered.

Adverse reactions to foscarnet

- Hypocalcaemia and hypomagnesaemia.
- Renal failure.
- Penile ulceration.

2.10.4 Epstein–Barr virus

Epidemiology

Epstein–Barr virus (EBV) is distributed worldwide, but there are variations in the prevalence of EBV-related disease, particularly malignancy.

EBV-associated malignancy

- Burkitt's lymphoma in Africa.
- Nasopharyngeal carcinoma in the Far East.
- Non-Hodgkin's B-cell lymphoma in immunocompromised individuals.

Diagnostic tests

Serology is the mainstay of diagnosis (see Section 1.3.10). The Paul–Bunnell (or Monospot) test provides a rapid diagnosis that can be confirmed with measurement of specific EBV IgM. Cerebrospinal fluid polymerase chain reaction for EBV is often positive in AIDS-related cerebral lymphoma.

Disease syndromes and complications

Infection in childhood is usually asymptomatic, but 'glandular fever' commonly complicates infection in adolescence or adult life. Other manifestations of EBV are shown in Fig. 74.

Therapy

EBV is poorly sensitive to current antiviral agents. Specific therapy is rarely required, although corticosteroids are sometimes used in severe pharyngitis or hepatitis.

2.10.5 Human herpesviruses 6 and 7

Epidemiology

These are very widespread viruses, affecting almost the entire population. They infect T cells and establish lifelong latency.

Diagnostic tests

Specific diagnostic tests are not usually required. Polymerase chain reaction can detect the virus, and serology detects past exposure.

Disease syndromes

- Human herpesvirus 6 causes roseola infantum (exanthem subitum) in infants. It has also been linked with multiple sclerosis, although a causal relationship is not proven. Human herpesvirus 7 causes a similar disease, but less commonly.

- Reactivation of both viruses has been described in immunosuppressed people, but their role in disease is not understood.

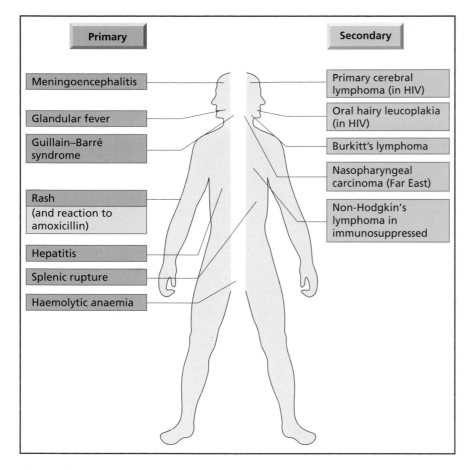

Primary

- Meningoencephalitis
- Glandular fever
- Guillain–Barré syndrome
- Rash (and reaction to amoxicillin)
- Hepatitis
- Splenic rupture
- Haemolytic anaemia

Secondary

- Primary cerebral lymphoma (in HIV)
- Oral hairy leucoplakia (in HIV)
- Burkitt's lymphoma
- Nasopharyngeal carcinoma (Far East)
- Non-Hodgkin's lymphoma in immunosuppressed

▲**Fig. 74** EBV-related disease.

Therapy

None is currently available.

2.10.6 Human herpesvirus 8

Epidemiology

Human herpesvirus 8 (HHV8) is also known as Kaposi's sarcoma-associated herpesvirus. It is found worldwide and is mainly of interest by association with certain malignancies.

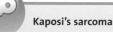

Kaposi's sarcoma

- Common in elderly Mediterranean men, usually on the lower leg.
- Frequently occurs in those with severe cell-mediated immunosuppression, eg AIDS or transplantation.
- Endemic form is found in Africa.

Diagnostic tests

HHV8-associated malignancies are suspected clinically and confirmed on histology. Serological tests and polymerase chain reaction have been used in research.

Disease syndromes

HHV8 is associated with three tumours:

- Kaposi's sarcoma, most commonly on the skin (see Section 2.11), but may involve the lung or gut;
- primary effusion lymphoma (a rare B-cell lymphoma in AIDS);
- multicentric Castleman's disease.

Therapy

There is no specific antiviral therapy, although aciclovir and ganciclovir have anti-HHV8 activity. Chemotherapy is used to control the malignancy, but long-term remission can be achieved only by improving immunological function (Fig. 75).

2.10.7 Parvovirus

Epidemiology

Parvovirus B19 is a DNA virus and the only parvovirus known to infect humans. A related DNA virus, transfusion transmitted virus (TTV), is not clearly associated with any clinical syndrome and is almost universally carried.

Diagnostic tests

Parvovirus is diagnosed clinically but may be confirmed (and distinguished from rubella) by detection of IgM. Parvovirus DNA can be directly identified by hybridisation in blood from chronically infected, immunocompromised patients.

Disease syndromes

- Infection with parvovirus B19 in childhood is usually subclinical, but may cause an acute illness characterised by a high fever and bright red face ('slapped cheek' disease). Other, less common disease syndromes are related to decreased red blood cell production as a result of the effects of parvovirus on the bone marrow.

- Arthritis: in adults pain, swelling and stiffness of the small joints often complicate parvovirus B19. There is no clear evidence that this is associated with chronic rheumatological disease.

- Red cell crises (severe anaemia) in those with compromised red cell production (eg sickle cell).

- Chronic anaemia in severely immunosuppressed patients.

- Transplacental infection can cause hydrops fetalis and fetal loss.

131

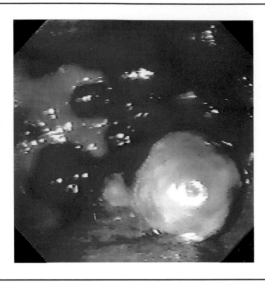

▲ **Fig. 75** Kaposi's sarcoma in the stomach of a patient with AIDS and a CD4 cell count of 10×10^6/L. Partial remission was induced with chemotherapy and antiretroviral therapy was started. Four years later, the Kaposi's sarcoma is in complete remission without chemotherapy and the patient's CD4 cell count is over 300×10^6/L.

Therapy

Treatment is supportive in most cases; intravenous immunoglobulin may benefit immunocompromised patients with chronic infection.

2.10.8 Hepatitis viruses

Description of the organism

Although linked to similar clinical syndromes, virologically these are quite distinct (Table 65).

Epidemiology

These viruses cause very common human infections.

- Faecal–oral transmission: HAV is endemic throughout the world, with prevalence closely related to standards of sanitation. HEV is mainly found in the developing world where it is responsible for both endemic and epidemic jaundice. Recently some endemic cases have been diagnosed in the UK, where the disease is carried in the pig population.

- Body fluid transmission: over one-third of the world's population has been infected with HBV, predominantly acquired through heterosexual contact or vertical transmission. The global prevalence of HCV is estimated at 200 million. Approximately 1.7% of the population of the USA are infected, as are around 0.1–0.2% of people presenting to donate blood in the UK.

TABLE 65 IMPORTANT FEATURES OF HEPATITIS VIRUSES

Virus	Genome	Diagnosis	Hepatitis	Complications	Therapy
HAV	RNA	HAV IgM	Acute	Fulminant hepatic failure (rare)	Supportive
HBV	DNA	HBsAg, HBeAg and a high viral DNA level denote active viral replication HBV core IgM is the first detectable antibody and its presence indicates acute hepatitis B infection	Acute Chronic	Fulminant hepatic failure Hepatoma, cirrhosis	Supportive Interferon alfa Lamivudine, adefovir, entecavir
HCV	RNA	Serology and PCR to detect viraemia	Chronic	Hepatoma Cirrhosis Cryoglobulinaemia Glomerulonephritis Porphyria cutanea tarda	Interferon alfa + ribavirin
HDV	RNA viroid (defective virus), co-infects with HBV	HDV IgG HDV IgM in acute infection	Chronic co-infection with HBV Acute superadded infection in patients with active HBV	Fulminant hepatic failure (rare) Cirrhosis Hepatoma	As for HBV
HEV	RNA	HEV IgM	Acute	Fulminant hepatic failure in pregnancy	Supportive

HAV, hepatitis A virus; HBV, hepatitis B virus; HBsAg, hepatitis B surface antigen; HBeAg, hepatitis B 'e' antigen; HCV, hepatitis C virus; HDV, hepatitis D virus; HEV, hepatitis E virus; PCR, polymerase chain reaction.

See Section 1.3.18 and *Gastroenterology and Hepatology*, Sections 2.10.1 and 2.10.2.

Diagnostic tests

Serology is the mainstay of making a specific diagnosis in viral hepatitis (see Table 65). PCR detection and quantification of viraemia is being increasingly used to guide management in chronic HBV and HCV.

HBV serology

In acute disease, HBsAg is present and accompanied by IgM antibodies (to core). Patients presenting with such serology should be followed to watch for the disappearance of HBsAg.

In chronic carriage, HBsAg persists (>6 months following acute infection) and may be either:

- high level, in which case it is accompanied by HBeAg; or

- low level, in which case HBeAg is absent (and HBe antibody is detected).

> **HBV precore mutants**
>
> - Fail to make HBeAg.
> - Infectivity and disease progression similar to HBeAg-positive patients.
> - Rare in the UK, but increasingly common worldwide.
> - Diagnosis requires quantification of HBV DNA. Patients will be HBeAg negative if the hepatitis B 'e' antibody is present, but high DNA level and active liver disease.

Treatment

In general, treatment of acute disease is supportive. Specific antiviral therapy for chronic hepatitis (see Table 65) may clear some, but by no means all, patients.

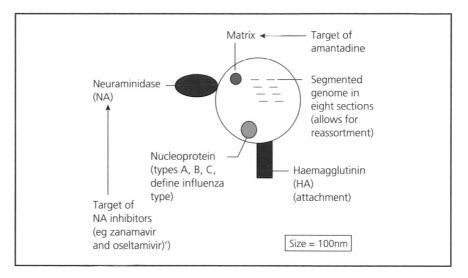

▲ **Fig. 76** Schematic representation of influenza virus.

2.10.9 Influenza virus

Description of the organism

Influenza is an RNA virus organised as shown schematically in Fig. 76. Three serogroups, A, B and C, are responsible for human disease.

Epidemiology

Influenza A and B cause disease sporadically, in epidemics or in pandemics. Influenza A appears to be the more virulent strain and is linked most closely to mortality from influenza. Influenza C causes mild endemic disease. The virus can evolve through small mutations ('drift') associated with partial loss of herd immunity and, in a more dramatic way, by reassorting its segmented genome ('shift'), leading to complete loss of herd immunity and the potential for a pandemic. This is particularly likely when the disease crosses species from its avian host. The potential for the avian H5N1 virus to cause disease in humans is very significant, but so far no clear chains of human-to-human transmission have occurred.

Diagnostic tests

Diagnosis is predominantly clinical, aided by the demonstration of a rise in antibody titres or direct immunofluorescence or culture of the virus.

Disease syndromes and complications

In most cases these infections are self-limiting, but significant morbidity and mortality occurs in elderly people, those with underlying lung disease and immunocompromised individuals. There is no systemic spread of the virus and, in most cases, severe complications are the result of secondary bacterial pneumonia, particularly *Streptococcus pneumoniae* and *Staphylococcus aureus*.

Therapy

Treatment is symptomatic. Prophylaxis and treatment with amantadine are effective but rarely used. The neuraminidase inhibitor zanamivir is the first of a new class of specific anti-influenza agents. Zanamivir and oseltamivir are highly effective, but only when started within the first 36 hours of symptoms. These reduce the duration of fever on average only by about 1 day, and so widespread use has not been recommended in normal influenza seasons. The National Institute for Health and Clinical Excellence (NICE) has issued guidance on the use of anti-influenza drugs in vulnerable groups in the UK.

2.10.10 Paramyxoviruses

Description of the organism
Paramyxoviruses are RNA viruses, including measles, mumps and respiratory syncytial virus (RSV).

Epidemiology
Measles and mumps are now much less common in the UK as a result of effective immunisation, but worldwide measles remains an important disease with high morbidity and mortality in young children. RSV is a common respiratory pathogen in children and elderly people, for which there is no effective vaccine. It also has the potential to cause severe outbreaks within paediatric units.

Diagnostic tests
Clinical diagnosis may be unreliable because the symptoms and non-specific rashes overlap those caused by other viral infections. Mumps virus can be isolated from saliva, but measles and mumps are usually confirmed serologically. RSV may be rapidly identified directly from a nasopharyngeal aspirate or bronchial lavage by immunofluorescence.

Disease syndromes

Measles
Measles classically has two phases.

- Pre-eruptive: associated with fever, coryza, conjunctivitis and Koplik's spots (grey on a red base opposite the second molar).

- Eruptive: associated with a maculopapular rash, especially over the face, that later becomes confluent.

Systemic spread involving many organs, but especially the lungs, may occur. Measles may be complicated acutely by bacterial infection and late complications include subacute sclerosing panencephalitis.

Mumps
Mumps causes parotid swelling and, rarely, meningitis or encephalitis, orchitis and pancreatitis.

Respiratory syncytial virus
RSV is associated with upper and lower respiratory tract infection. Most infections are mild. Severe and sometimes fatal disease may be seen in neonates, very young children and the immunocompromised adult.

Therapy
Therapy is supportive in most cases.

- Vitamin A supplementation is considered of benefit for malnourished children with measles.

- RSV is sensitive to ribavirin, which can be administered via a small particle nebuliser for severe disease in neonates or the immunocompromised individual. A specific anti-RSV antibody may also have a role in paediatric practice.

2.10.11 Enteroviruses

Description of the organism
This is a very large group of related RNA viruses (family Picornaviridae). Poliovirus (Fig. 77), previously the most important organism in this group, is heading towards global eradication following a WHO immunisation programme.

Enteroviruses enter the body via the gastrointestinal tract and are spread by the faecal–oral route. Despite the name, they are generally associated with mucosal, neurological, muscular or cardiac disease rather than diarrhoea.

Diagnostic tests
Enteroviruses may be cultured from stool early in an acute infection.

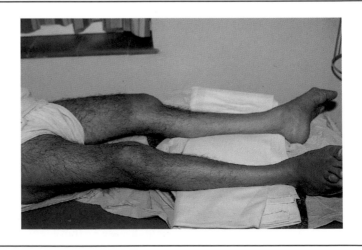

▲ **Fig. 77** Severe wasting and shortening of the legs as a result of childhood polio.

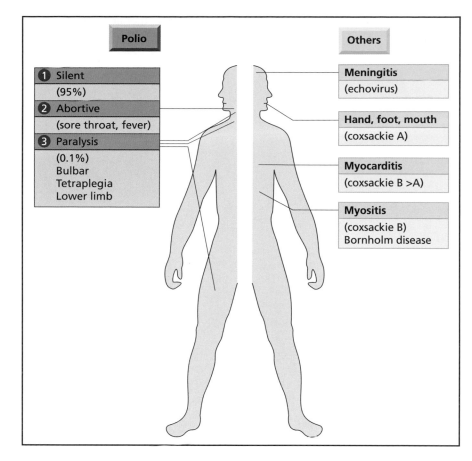

▲ **Fig. 78** Diseases associated with enteroviruses.

Diagnosis is often serological but there is much cross-reactivity in this group. Polymerase chain reaction is being increasingly used, eg of the cerebrospinal fluid in cases of meningitis.

Disease syndromes

A wide variety of illnesses has been associated with enteroviruses (Fig. 78).

Therapy

No specific antiviral therapy is available. Immunisation against polio has dramatically decreased global disease. Prevention of exposure within families relies on good hygiene and is particularly important when there is a newborn in the house, because infection may be very severe.

2.10.12 Coronaviruses and SARS

A human coronavirus associated with a severe acute respiratory syndrome (SARS) was isolated from outbreaks in Asia. It is likely that the virus was transmitted from an animal host, such as the civet cat. Spread of the virus from person to person led to epidemiological clusters of infection. The possibility remains that further such epidemics might occur.

Disease syndrome

An acute pulmonary syndrome occurred, with high mortality rates in at-risk groups such as the elderly, those with underlying lung disease or those with other comorbidities. The virus is spread by a respiratory route but may also be spread through the gastrointestinal tract. Measures to prevent hospital-acquired infection are very important.

Diagnosis

Specific antibody and polymerase chain reaction tests are available. This would only be performed at specialist centres.

Therapy

No specific antiviral therapy is available although combinations of steroids and ribavirin have been tried. Vaccines are under development, based on neutralisation of the key glycoprotein spike.

2.11 Human immunodeficiency virus

Description of the organism

HIV is a retrovirus (family of lentiviruses). Retroviruses are RNA viruses that replicate by converting RNA into DNA using the enzyme reverse transcriptase. The HIV virion contains two strands of RNA stabilised by packaging proteins and surrounded by a lipid membrane (Fig. 79).

Surface proteins

Glycoproteins Gp120 and Gp41 are important polymorphic proteins involved in attachment and entry into target cells. Gp120 binds to CD4 and Gp41 interacts with chemokine receptors (such as CCR5) to mediate fusion with the cell membrane and then cell entry (Fig. 80).

Core proteins

p24 antigen and matrix (p17) are involved in packaging HIV RNA and transporting to the nucleus.

135

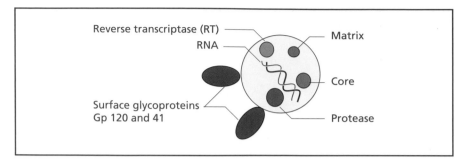

▲ **Fig. 79** Schematic representation of components of an HIV virion.

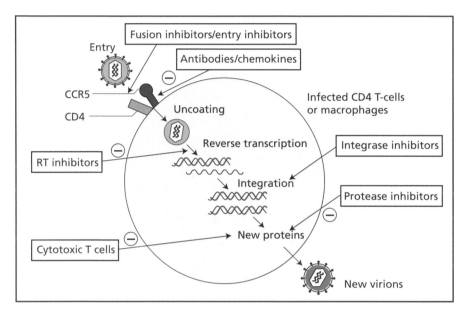

▲ **Fig. 80** HIV replication cycle showing sites where replication can be blocked by the immune system or drugs.

HIV RNA

RNA is present within the virion in two linear strands. HIV RNA is highly polymorphic as a result of its high turnover rate, accompanied by lack of 'proofreading capacity' of the viral reverse transcriptase enzyme. This degree of variation means that HIV exists as a swarm of closely related strains or 'quasi-species'.

Reverse transcriptase

This enzyme is required for the transformation of viral RNA into double-stranded DNA. The active site of reverse transcriptase is conserved between retroviruses and is a major therapeutic target.

Protease and integrase

Protease is required for maturation of the viral particle after release. Particles in which protease has not been activated are not infectious. Integrase is essential for integration of HIV DNA into the host genome.

Regulatory genes

HIV encodes genes (importantly *tat* and *nef*) for regulatory proteins that control up-regulation of transcription and virulence. *Nef*-deficient viruses are less pathogenic in animal models and human infection.

Pathogenesis of symptomatic disease

HIV causes disease through infection of CD4-positive T lymphocytes,

macrophages and other cells, leading to immunological deterioration and increased susceptibility to infections. An overview of the HIV replication cycle is shown in Fig. 80.

Cell entry

HIV attaches to the cells through specific surface receptors, including the chemokine receptors CCR5 (early/asymptomatic disease) and CXCR4 (late-stage/progressive disease). Patients with polymorphisms in CCR5 show protection against infection and also slower progression to symptomatic disease. The CD4 antigen acts as a coreceptor. Dendritic cells play a key role in transferring infectious virions from the mucosae to lymphoid organs.

Turnover

Once the virion is inside the cell, reverse transcriptase transcribes virion RNA into DNA, which is then integrated into the host nucleus and may either remain latent (if the cell is quiescent) or start to replicate. Once replicating, the turnover of virus is very fast (half-life 8 hours in the blood), and most infected cells die rapidly. A small proportion of cells may remain dormant, containing latent proviral DNA.

Host immune response

After infection, cytotoxic T lymphocytes are the most important component of the host response. These kill infected cells and secrete chemokines which block infection through CCR5. Cytotoxic T lymphocytes recognise infected cells through peptides presented by human leucocyte antigen (HLA) class I molecules, and so the HLA type of the patient affects progression of infection. Antibody responses are present, but less effective as a result of the variability in HIV Gp120.

Epidemiology

Worldwide 35–40 million people are living with HIV/AIDS infection, with the highest burden in sub-Saharan Africa. In the UK, there are thought to be approximately 73,000 people currently alive with HIV (end of 2007) and a total of over 17,000 deaths have been related to HIV infection since it was recognised in the early 1980s. The number of deaths has declined dramatically since the introduction of highly active antiretroviral therapy. HIV is spread through sex, needle sharing, blood products and from mother to child.

Diagnostic tests

HIV antibody tests

Serology forms the basis for detecting HIV infection. Following a seroconversion illness, antibody is usually detectable by enzyme-linked immunosorbent assay (ELISA) within 2–4 weeks. Modern HIV tests also detect p24 antigen and can become positive as early as 10 days after infection, although not reliably. However, serology may remain negative for up to 3 months, particularly after asymptomatic primary infection.

p24 antigen

This antigen is detectable in high levels by ELISA during HIV seroconversion. In stable disease, p24 assays were used to monitor disease but have been supplanted by nucleic acid amplification techniques.

Nucleic acid amplification techniques

Several methods are available to amplify and quantify plasma and cell-associated HIV nucleic acid. Current generation tests can detect as few as 20–50 copies of HIV RNA per millilitre. The level of the HIV circulating viral load can predict the rate of disease progression and is used to monitor therapy.

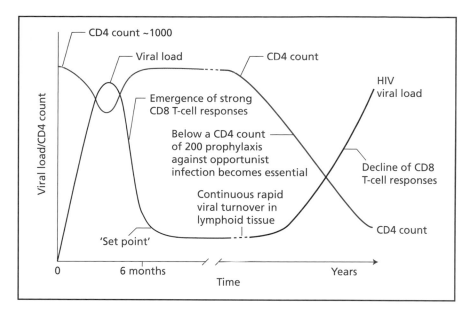

▲ **Fig. 81** Host immune response and progression of HIV disease. CD4 cell counts are $\times 10^6$/L.

HIV resistance testing

By amplifying and sequencing the reverse transcriptase and protease genes, it is possible to detect mutations associated with resistance to antiretroviral drugs.

Immunological function

The CD4 T-lymphocyte count is assayed by flow cytometry.

Disease syndromes

Primary HIV infection is accompanied by a clinical 'seroconversion illness' or 'acute retroviral syndrome' (fever, lymphadenopathy and rash with or without meningism) in 30–70% of cases. After acute infection the HIV viral load is controlled to a set point, which determines the subsequent rate of disease progression (Fig. 81). A minority of patients control HIV to below detectable levels and remain stable for many years without a decline in their CD4 count. Most patients suffer a steady decline in CD4 count and a rise in viral load. Why the immune response ultimately fails to control the virus is not fully understood. Table 66 shows the methods of staging HIV.

TABLE 66 STAGING OF HIV	
Staging parameter	**Examples**
Clinical	CDC stage I: asymptomatic CDC stage II: asymptomatic non-AIDS, eg oral *Candida* and shingles CDC stage III: symptomatic AIDS-defining (see Section 1.3.21)
Immunological	CD4 count >350 × 10⁶/L: very low likelihood of illness CD4 count 200–350 × 10⁶/L: can get symptoms which are mostly non-AIDS CD4 count <200 × 10⁶/L: high risk of AIDS-defining illness
Virological	Viral load measured by nucleic acid amplification technique, eg PCR is used mainly to monitor treatment success The higher the viral load off treatment, the higher the risk of progressive illness

CDC, Centers for Disease Control; PCR, polymerase chain reaction.

Complications of HIV

Complications may be the result of opportunistic infection, malignancy or the direct effect of HIV on organ function (Fig. 82). Opportunistic infections relate to the degree of immunosuppression and environmental exposure (eg *Penicillium marneffei* in South-east Asia). Effective combination antiretroviral therapy (ART) leads to 'immune reconstitution', a rise in CD4-positive lymphocyte count and a reduction in the risk of AIDS and death.

Therapy

Antiretroviral therapy

There are five currently licensed drug classes (Fig. 83) targeting reverse transcriptase, protease and viral/cell fusion. Most protease inhibitors are used in a combination with low-dose ritonavir, which increases their serum levels. In the near future, additional drugs may become available that inhibit HIV integrase or are targeted at viral entry into cells (chemokine receptor blockers).

Indications for starting ART are shown in Table 67. Standard treatment is with three drugs. A typical combination would be two nucleoside analogues, such as abacavir and lamivudine (Kivexa) or tenofovir and entricitabine (Truvada), and either a non-nucleoside reverse transcriptase inhibitor such as efavirenz or a protease inhibitor such as Kaletra (lopinavir plus ritonavir). These should be taken indefinitely, with routine monitoring as shown in Table 68. Combination pills are now

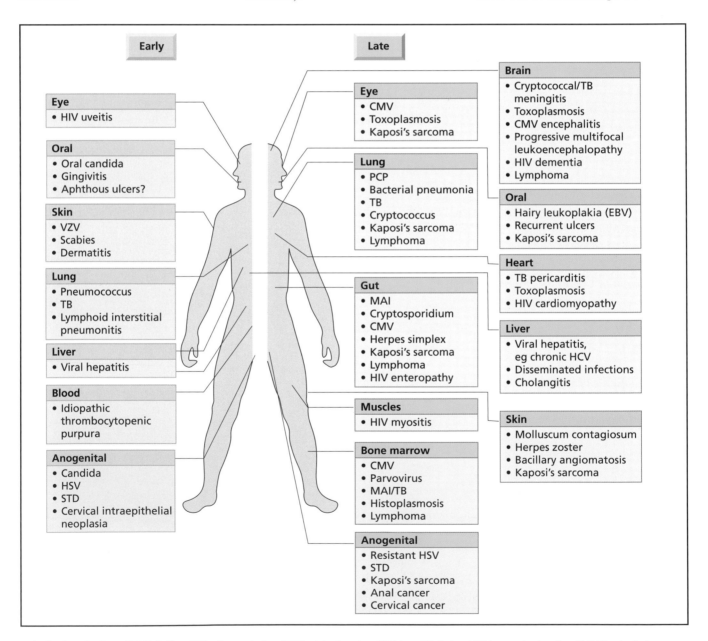

Early

Eye
- HIV uveitis

Oral
- Oral candida
- Gingivitis
- Aphthous ulcers?

Skin
- VZV
- Scabies
- Dermatitis

Lung
- Pneumococcus
- TB
- Lymphoid interstitial pneumonitis

Liver
- Viral hepatitis

Blood
- Idiopathic thrombocytopenic purpura

Anogenital
- Candida
- HSV
- STD
- Cervical intraepithelial neoplasia

Late

Eye
- CMV
- Toxoplasmosis
- Kaposi's sarcoma

Lung
- PCP
- Bacterial pneumonia
- TB
- Cryptococcus
- Kaposi's sarcoma
- Lymphoma

Gut
- MAI
- Cryptosporidium
- CMV
- Herpes simplex
- Kaposi's sarcoma
- Lymphoma
- HIV enteropathy

Muscles
- HIV myositis

Bone marrow
- CMV
- Parvovirus
- MAI/TB
- Histoplasmosis
- Lymphoma

Anogenital
- Resistant HSV
- STD
- Kaposi's sarcoma
- Anal cancer
- Cervical cancer

Brain
- Cryptococcal/TB meningitis
- Toxoplasmosis
- CMV encephalitis
- Progressive multifocal leukoencephalopathy
- HIV dementia
- Lymphoma

Oral
- Hairy leukoplakia (EBV)
- Recurrent ulcers
- Kaposi's sarcoma

Heart
- TB pericarditis
- Toxoplasmosis
- HIV cardiomyopathy

Liver
- Viral hepatitis, eg chronic HCV
- Disseminated infections
- Cholangitis

Skin
- Molluscum contagiosum
- Herpes zoster
- Bacillary angiomatosis
- Kaposi's sarcoma

▲ **Fig. 82** Complications of HIV infection. CMV, cytomegalovirus; EBV, Epstein–Barr virus; HCV, hepatitis C virus; HSV, herpes simplex virus; MAI, *Mycobacterium avium-intracellulare*; PCP, *Pneumocystis carinii* pneumonia; STD, sexually transmitted disease; TB, tuberculosis; VZV, varicella-zoster virus.

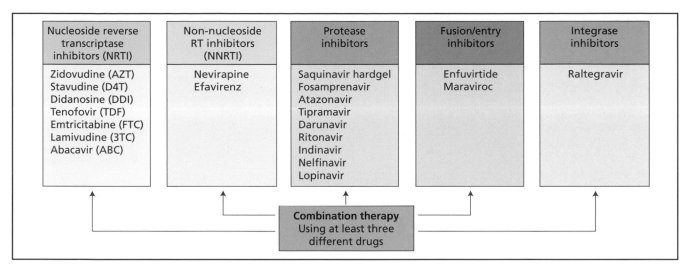

Nucleoside reverse transcriptase inhibitors (NRTI)	Non-nucleoside RT inhibitors (NNRTI)	Protease inhibitors	Fusion/entry inhibitors	Integrase inhibitors
Zidovudine (AZT) Stavudine (D4T) Didanosine (DDI) Tenofovir (TDF) Emtricitabine (FTC) Lamivudine (3TC) Abacavir (ABC)	Nevirapine Efavirenz	Saquinavir hardgel Fosamprenavir Atazonavir Tipramavir Darunavir Ritonavir Indinavir Nelfinavir Lopinavir	Enfuvirtide Maraviroc	Raltegravir

Combination therapy
Using at least three different drugs

▲ **Fig. 83** Drugs currently available in the UK for the treatment of HIV. The following should not be combined: zidovudine (AZT) and stavudine (D4T) because of antagonism, and tenofovir and didanosine (ddI) because of variable drug levels. RT, reverse transcriptase.

TABLE 67 INDICATIONS FOR STARTING ART

Indication	Comment
AIDS-defining illness	Start ART. A possible exception is tuberculosis with a high CD4 count
Non-AIDS illness	Systemic illness, eg wasting, weight loss and HIV-related marrow suppression, will improve on ART. Some illnesses are not an absolute indication, eg shingles
CD4 count $250-350 \times 10^6$/L	Start ART if the individual's CD4 count is falling rapidly
CD4 count $200-250 \times 10^6$/L	Start ART before count enters the high risk range ($<200 \times 10^6$/L)
CD4 count $<200 \times 10^6$/L	Imperative to start ART immediately: high risk of severe illness
Pregnancy	Start ART in all women at 28 weeks' gestation if asymptomatic with a high CD4 count; start earlier if patient meets one of the above criteria

 Hypersensitivity to abacavir (approximately 3% of people)

- Resulting rash is uncommon.
- Causes fever, myalgia and abdominal pain.
- May be fatal on rechallenge.
- Related to HLA B*5701 haplotype (genetic testing is now available prior to drug use).
- Make sure you warn patients of these dangers.

frequently used to aid adherence to treatment and to simplify drug regimens.

Anti-HIV drugs are toxic (Table 69), but some side effects can be avoided (Table 70).

Some HIV medications have potentially fatal side effects, including lactic acidosis (NRTIs), hepatitis (most classes), pancreatitis (didanosine) and allergy (NNRTIs and abacavir). Patients must be warned of this and followed closely.

Immunotherapy

Following successful anti-HIV therapy, a patient's CD4 cell count may rise, but in some patients it remains below 200×10^6/L placing them at risk of opportunistic infections. The role of interleukin-2 in raising the CD4 cell count is being investigated.

TABLE 68 MONITORING BLOOD TESTS DURING ART

Test	Reason
Viral load	Should become undetectable if treatment works
CD4 count	Rises when viral load is undetectable
FBC	Some ART drugs can cause cytopenias, eg anaemia
Urea and electrolytes	Rarely, drugs can cause renal dysfunction
Liver function test	Some drugs, eg nevirapine, can be hepatotoxic in some people
Blood glucose	Protease inhibitors and stavudine can cause diabetes
Blood lipids	Protease inhibitors and efavirenz can cause raised cholesterol and/or triglycerides

HIV in pregnancy

- Untreated vertical transmission rate is 16–25% in Europe.
- Risk of transmission is related to maternal HIV viral load.
- Zidovudine monotherapy for the last 12 weeks of pregnancy, intravenously during labour and then orally for the baby can reduce the rate of transmission to 8%.
- Combination triple ART reduces the rate to <2% and is now the usual choice.
- Caesarian section recommended unless the delivery is low-risk.
- Breast feeding is associated with HIV transmission.

Prophylaxis

To prevent the predictable emergence of opportunistic infections as disease progresses, there are various strategies for prophylaxis, although Septrin (co-trimoxazole) is the only one routinely used in people on ART (Fig. 84). After a robust response to antiviral therapy, discontinue prophylaxis after the CD4 cell count has been above 200×10^6/L for 6 months.

Vigilance is required to detect and treat infectious and non-infectious complications of HIV (Fig. 85).

2.11.1 Prevention following sharps injury

This is a common issue, particularly for healthcare workers. You must act quickly if postexposure prophylaxis (PEP) is to be effective. Assess the level of risk, decide on a therapeutic plan and counsel/support the member of staff. The risk of HIV transmission will depend on the HIV inoculum, which is the product of the concentration of virus in the blood and the volume transmitted (Table 71). The mean risk of HIV seroconversion after a high-risk

needlestick is 0.32%. HIV risk from blood splashing onto intact skin is minimal and that from mucous membrane exposure is estimated at 0.03%. A retrospective case–control study indicated that PEP with zidovudine monotherapy was associated with a 79% fall in transmission. Subsequent retrospective studies suggest that triple-drug ART is even more effective.

The HIV positive 'donor'

- Is the patient on ART? If so, what drugs are being taken and are they working?

- ART history? You may need to consider drug resistance when choosing PEP.

- Is the patient's syphilis, hepatitis B and hepatitis C status known?

TABLE 69 ADVERSE EFFECTS OF ANTIRETROVIRAL DRUGS

Class	Side effects	Drugs
NRTI	Bone-marrow suppression	AZT and 3TC
	Nail discoloration	AZT
	Peripheral neuropathy	D4T
		DDI (less commonly)
	Pancreatitis	DDI
	Lactic acidosis and hepatic steatosis	D4T, and others less commonly
	Lipodystrophy	D4T, and possibly AZT
	Hypersensitivity	ABC
	Renal tubular dysfunction	Tenofovir
NNRTI	Hypersensitivity	Nevirapine in those with high CD4 count ($>250 \times 10^6$/L in women, $>350 \times 10^6$/L in men)
	Hepatic failure	Nevirapine
	Vivid dreams and psychological disturbances	Efavirenz
PI	Renal stones and nephropathy	Indinavir
	Gastrointestinal	All agents
	Lipodystrophy	All except atazanavir
	Diabetes mellitus	All except atazanavir
	Lipid abnormalities	All except atazanavir

3TC, lamivudine; ABC, abacavir; AZT, zidovudine; D4T, stavudine; DDI, didanosine; NNRTI, non-nucleoside reverse transcriptase inhibitors; NRTI, nucleoside reverse transcriptase inhibitors; PI, protease inhibitors.

TABLE 70 ABACAVIR AND NEVIRAPINE REACTIONS AND HOW TO AVOID THEM

Drug and the reaction	How to reduce the risk of a reaction
Abacavir: hypersensitivity reaction with fever, rash and occasional death	Mostly in white populations with HLA B*5701 haplotype: testing for this before prescribing will reduce the incidence
Nevirapine: severe rash and/or hepatitis	Do not prescribe to men with CD4 count >350 $\times 10^6$/L or women with CD4 count >250 $\times 10^6$/L

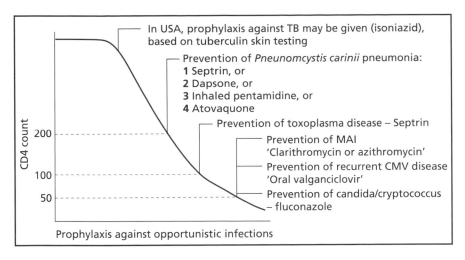

In USA, prophylaxis against TB may be given (isoniazid), based on tuberculin skin testing

Prevention of *Pneunomcystis carinii* pneumonia:
1 Septrin, or
2 Dapsone, or
3 Inhaled pentamidine, or
4 Atovaquone

Prevention of toxoplasma disease – Septrin

Prevention of MAI 'Clarithromycin or azithromycin'

Prevention of recurrent CMV disease 'Oral valganciclovir'

Prevention of candida/cryptococcus – fluconazole

CD4 count

200

100

50

Prophylaxis against opportunistic infections

▲ **Fig. 84** Prophylaxis and immune function in HIV.

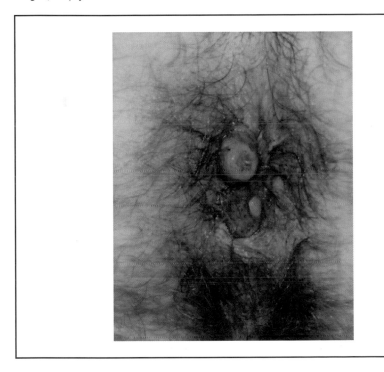

▲ **Fig. 85** Early anal carcinoma complicating HIV infection.

The 'donor' of unknown infection status

If the source is known but infection status is unclear, you can request that the patient is tested for transmissible infections. This must be done with consent. A senior member of staff should approach the patient and not the surgeon who suffered the needlestick, but treatment of the needlestick recipient should not be delayed by waiting for the results of these tests.

Personal history of the injured

Has the person been previously tested for HIV, hepatitis B and hepatitis C and has he or she been successfully vaccinated against hepatitis B? A risk assessment should be made for risks prior to the needlestick incident. This is delicate and should be discussed in a confidential setting. Enquire about other risk factors for HIV as part of pretest counselling. You should discuss sexual partners who may be at risk should the surgeon seroconvert to HIV.

Testing the healthcare worker

Check immunity to hepatitis B. Store serum for retrospective testing to HIV and hepatitis C if necessary.

Sharps injury

The event should be reported immediately and an incident form completed. Expert evaluation of the need for PEP should occur quickly and with preserved confidentiality. Involve occupational health at the first available opportunity. They will check the hepatitis B status of the healthcare worker and arrange follow-up and testing as required.

Postexposure prophylaxis

Current guidelines for HIV PEP (Table 72) recommend a 28-day course, although less than 50% of

TABLE 71 ASSESSING HIV RISKS AFTER A SHARPS INJURY

Nature of exposure	Risk
Inoculating instrument	Sharp>blunt and hollow needle>solid
Contaminating fluid	Blood>cerebrospinal fluid/genital fluid>saliva
Inoculation	Blood transfusion/tissue transplant>penetrating injury>scratch>splash
Age of inoculating fluid	Fresh blood/fluid straight from the patient>old/dried blood/fluid on the sharp
HIV risk in 'donor' of unknown HIV status	Rest of world>western Europe and Australasia Homosexual man>heterosexual man Intravenous drug user>non-injecting drug user
HIV-positive donor	Fully suppressed viral load>high viral load

TABLE 72 RECOMMENDATIONS FOR PEP IN THE UK

Regimen	Comment
Combivir (one tablet twice daily) plus Kaletra (two tablets twice daily)	Nelfinavir was previously recommended by the Department of Health, but was withdrawn in May 2007 Prescribe prophylactic antiemetic and antidiarrhoeal agents
Alternative regimen Combivir (one tablet twice daily), ritonavir (100 mg twice daily) and saquinavir (1000 mg twice daily)	Prescribe prophylactic antiemetic and antidiarrhoeal agents Ritonavir should be stored in a refrigerator
Nevirapine should never be used	Several reported deaths due to drug hypersensitivity in this situation

patients complete the course and follow-up. PEP should be started as soon as possible after the incident, ideally within 1 hour (but can also be given if there is a delay between the incident and seeking advice). Different medication must be considered if drug-resistant HIV is suspected. If the donor is HIV-positive, PEP should always be taken. The same applies to penetrating injuries if the sharp is contaminated with blood, cerebrospinal fluid or other body fluids other than sputum and the HIV status of the source patient is unknown. If the source patient is considered low risk, it may be appropriate to await the result of an urgent HIV test if the patient agrees to it.

If PEP for HIV is started, check FBC, electrolytes, and renal and liver function at 2 and 4 weeks. PEP may delay rather than prevent seroconversion and HIV antibody or HIV RNA (as well as hepatitis B and hepatitis C if relevant) should be checked at 6, 12 and 26 weeks after the event. Any febrile illness in this period should be reported and investigated as possible HIV seroconversion (see Section 1.3.20). Safe sex should be practised until these tests are clear, and women should be advised not to become pregnant. Surgeons may be allowed to continue to operate during the period of surveillance, but this depends on the local occupational health policy.

Other infective risks from sharps injury

The risk of acquiring other blood-borne viruses from a needlestick injury if the donor is also infected with these agents are 3–5% for hepatitis C and 30–50% for hepatitis B if the patient is 'e' antigen positive and the injured person is non-immune. In the latter case treatment with hepatitis B hyperimmune globulin and a rapid course of hepatitis B vaccination should be offered, which will reduce the risk of infection to about 5%.

> ⚠ Failure of HIV PEP can occur and there is no proven prophylaxis after hepatitis C exposure. Avoiding blood exposure is the best way to minimise risk.

2.12 Travel-related viruses

2.12.1 Rabies

Description of the organism
Rabies is an RNA virus belonging to the family Rhabdoviridae. Most human infections are from dog bites. The virus travels retrogradely along peripheral nerves to the central nervous system, where viral replication occurs causing fatal meningoencephalitis.

Epidemiology
Rabies is a zoonosis and remains endemic in most parts of the world. Exceptions include the British Isles, most of Scandinavia and Oceania. There are many thousands of human cases per year worldwide.

Diagnostic tests

- If possible, the brain of the suspect animal is examined for the rabies antigen.

- Detection of the viral antigen in nerve endings in skin biopsy.

Disease syndromes and complications
The incubation period is usually between 20 and 90 days, but rarely can be very prolonged (up to several years). The incubation period tends to be shorter after bites on the face compared with bites on the limbs. Prodromal symptoms are common and include general malaise, fever, irritability and local symptoms (paraesthesiae, itching and pain) at the site of the healed bite wound.

- Furious rabies is the most common presentation and is caused by brainstem encephalitis. It is characterised by paroxysms of generalised arousal and terror and, in most cases, the diagnostic symptom of hydrophobia with inspiratory muscle and laryngeal spasm provoked by attempts to drink water. Within days, the patient lapses into a coma with generalised flaccid paralysis.

- Paralytic rabies is less common. It is characterised by ascending flaccid paralysis, usually starting in the bitten limb.

Therapy

Rabies encephalitis

Once the encephalitic stage is reached, rabies is almost universally fatal and intensive care is not generally recommended for confirmed cases. Only four cases of recovery have ever been documented. The prognosis is virtually hopeless.

Give sedation and analgesia, and notify public health urgently.

Bite of a suspected rapid animal

Pre-exposure immunisation does not obviate the need for postexposure prophylaxis (PEP), but shortens the course and increases its efficacy. Start PEP as soon as possible after the bite.

- Clean the wound.

- Provide passive immunisation with rabies immune globulin.

- Provide active immunisation with a course of rabies vaccine.

- PEP can be stopped if either the suspect animal remains healthy for 10 days or the animal's brain is negative for rabies antigen.

2.12.2 Dengue

Description of the organism

Dengue viruses are RNA viruses belonging to the family Flaviviridae. Dengue is transmitted from infected to susceptible humans by day-biting *Aedes aegypti* mosquitoes.

Epidemiology

Dengue is transmitted throughout the tropical and subtropical regions of the world. The most intense transmission occurs in South-east Asia, the Caribbean and Central and Southern America, with areas of infection in West Africa. *Aedes aegypti* is found throughout the world and the dengue range is gradually extending, with cases recently described in North America. There are approximately 100 million infections per year worldwide.

Diagnostic tests

- During the febrile phase: detection of viral genome by reverse transcriptase polymerase chain reaction or viral culture.

- Retrospective diagnosis: paired serology.

Disease syndromes and complications

Dengue causes more illness and death than any other arboviral infection. After an incubation period of 5–10 days, there is sudden onset of fever, headache (often with retro-orbital pain) and severe myalgia. A faint, blanching, maculopapular rash is often a clue to the diagnosis (see Section 1.3.16). Typical laboratory findings are normal white cell count, low platelets and mildly abnormal liver function.

In most cases, the illness resolves spontaneously after 5–7 days. A small proportion of cases develop bleeding and vascular leak (dengue haemorrhagic fever/dengue shock syndrome). There are four major serotypes of dengue and the severe complications associated with them often occur in patients who have previously been exposed to a different viral serotype.

Therapy

Treatment is symptomatic and supportive. Dengue haemorrhagic fever/dengue shock syndrome soon resolves if patients are supported appropriately. No special barrier precautions are needed. Viral haemorrhagic fevers are notifiable diseases.

2.12.3 Arbovirus infections

Description of the organism

More than 100 different arboviruses (arthropod-borne viruses) produce clinical and subclinical infection in humans. They are transmitted by mosquitoes, ticks, sandflies and midges. They belong to many different virus families, but this classification is not of great importance to a clinician.

Epidemiology

Most arboviruses are zoonoses and infection in humans is accidental. For a few (eg dengue, see Section 2.12.2), humans are the principal source of virus amplification and infection. Arboviruses are transmitted in most parts of the world, but the distribution is often very localised. Sudden outbreaks may occur if the range of the animal host changes, bringing the infection to a new population.

Diagnostic tests

The diagnosis is usually made by serological testing, but there is much cross-reactivity. Polymerase chain reaction-based tests are more accurate for speciation but are not readily available.

Disease syndromes

The incubation period is usually short (up to 10 days). There are four main clinical syndromes:

- acute benign fever;

- acute central nervous system disease, ranging from mild aseptic meningitis to encephalitis with coma and death;

- haemorrhagic fevers;

- polyarthritis and rash.

Therapy

- Symptomatic and supportive.

- Standard barrier precautions.

- Notify encephalitis or haemorrhagic fever to public health.

2.13 Protozoan parasites

2.13.1 Malaria

Description of the organism

Four parasite species that infect red blood cells cause human malaria. *Plasmodium falciparum* is the most important because it may cause rapidly progressive, life-threatening disease (see Section 1.3.16). The other species (*Plasmodium vivax*, *Plasmodium ovale* and *Plasmodium malariae*) do not result in serious complications in most cases. Malaria is transmitted by anopheline mosquitoes, which bite at dusk and during the night.

Epidemiology

Malaria is the most important tropical disease and cause of fever in travellers. It is distributed throughout the tropical and subtropical regions of the world.

Diagnostic tests

- Thick film (see Section 3.2) (Fig. 86): the most sensitive test, but speciation is difficult and parasitaemia cannot be assessed. It is often not available outside reference laboratories.

- Thin film (see Section 3.2) (Fig. 87): the most widely used test. Parasitaemia can be counted and species identification is easier.

- Rapid diagnostic tests: blood dipstick tests that detect malaria antigens are valuable adjuncts in the diagnosis of malaria.

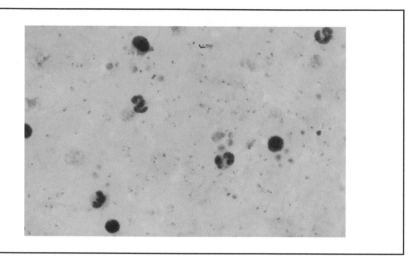

▲ **Fig. 86** Thick film in a case of *Plasmodium falciparum* malaria. The red blood cells have been lysed and abundant trophozoites can be seen.

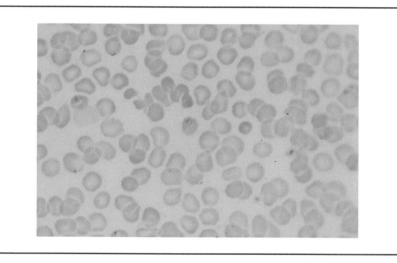

▲ **Fig. 87** Thin film from the same case as Fig. 86. *Plasmodium falciparum* trophozoites can be seen within red blood cells (5% parasitaemia).

- Serology is of no value in establishing an acute diagnosis.

Disease syndromes and complications

Incubation period

In approximately 75% of cases, *P. falciparum* malaria presents within 1 month of exposure, and 90% of cases present by 2 months. Presentation beyond 6 months is uncommon. In contrast, disease resulting from *P. vivax* or *P. ovale* can develop even years after exposure (so-called 'benign malaria').

Clinical features

No clinical features accurately predict malaria. Malaria commonly presents as fever of abrupt onset, with no localising symptoms or signs (see Section 1.3.16). However, in many cases, there are potentially confusing features such as abdominal discomfort, diarrhoea or jaundice. Typical laboratory findings in uncomplicated malaria are normal white cell count and low platelets, and there may be mild anaemia and elevation of bilirubin. The importance of *P. falciparum* lies in its capacity to cause severe disease (Table 73).

TABLE 73 COMPLICATIONS OF SEVERE *P. FALCIPARUM* MALARIA

Organ system	Complication
Neurological (cerebral malaria)	Impaired higher cerebral function Impaired consciousness Seizures
Haematological	Severe anaemia Macroscopic haemoglobinuria Disseminated intravascular coagulation
Renal	Acute renal failure
Pulmonary	Pulmonary oedema Adult respiratory distress syndrome
Cardiovascular	Shock
Metabolic	Metabolic acidosis Hypoglycaemia

Chloroquine is the drug of choice (600 mg orally immediately; 300 mg 6 hours later; followed by two 300-mg doses at 24-hour intervals) but it does not eradicate the dormant liver form of *P. vivax* and *P. ovale* that is responsible for late recurrences. To treat this exoerythrocytic form, chloroquine treatment of these species is followed by a course of primaquine. It is essential to check a patient's glucose-6-phosphate dehydrogenase (G6PD) status before prescribing primaquine and to seek advice in G6PD-deficient individuals.

 If in doubt as to the species, treat for *P. falciparum*.

Therapy

Always seek specialist advice if you are unsure or if the patient is seriously ill.

Plasmodium falciparum

The disease can progress after the start of treatment, so admission to hospital is recommended.

For practical purposes *P. falciparum* should be considered to be chloroquine resistant, so the usual treatment is quinine 600 mg po 8-hourly for 7 days, followed by three tablets of Fansidar (pyrimethamine with sulfadoxine) as a single dose or doxycycline 200 mg daily for 7 days, unless there are serious complications (see Table 73), the patient is vomiting or parasitaemia is >2% (which is a risk for development of complications). In these circumstances, intravenous quinine is used (loading dose 20 mg/kg, 1.4 g maximum) over 4 hours, followed by 10 mg/kg (700 mg maximum) over 4 hours three times daily).

Artemether-based drugs are now the treatment of choice for falciparum malaria in many parts of the world (intravenous artemether is not yet licensed in UK) and lead to faster resolution of symptoms and parasitaemia than quinine.

Hypoglycaemia and cardiac dysrhythmias are important side effects of intravenous quinine: clinical deterioration in a patient receiving intravenous quinine may be attributable to profound hypoglycaemia rather than advancing disease. Monitor blood glucose (BMstix) hourly and consider cardiac monitoring in older patients, patients with known cardiac disease or patients with a prolonged QT interval. Daily blood films (until negative) are recommended to help monitor progress. The patient can be discharged when afebrile and well with a negative blood film.

Plasmodium vivax, Plasmodium ovale and *Plasmodium malariae*

Serious complications are rare and most patients can be managed without admission provided the laboratory is certain that there is no *P. falciparum* co-infection.

2.13.2 Leishmaniasis

Description of the organism

Leishmaniasis is a zoonosis that is transmitted to humans by the bite of sandflies. The parasite is found within cells of the reticuloendothelial system.

Epidemiology

Visceral leishmaniasis is endemic in three main geographical areas: a belt that surrounds the Mediterranean basin and extends across the Middle East and Central Asia into parts of northern and eastern China; rural Sudan and Kenya; and parts of South America, particularly Brazil. Epidemic visceral leishmaniasis (kala-azar) occurs in addition in north-east India Bangladesh and the areas surrounding both of them. Most cases of cutaneous leishmaniasis (90%) are found in Central and South America (Peru and Brazil), Afghanistan, Iraq, Iran, Saudi Arabia, Algeria and Syria.

Diagnostic tests

Visceral leishmaniasis

- Parasitological diagnosis: parasites may be found in bone marrow, splenic aspirates or buffy coat.

- Serological diagnosis: detection of antileishmanial antibody.

- Skin sensitivity testing: by definition the leishmanin skin test is negative in established visceral leishmaniasis, reflecting a failure of cell-mediated immunity that enables the infection to progress. In practice this test is not commonly used now.

Cutaneous leishmaniasis

- Lesional biopsy and demonstration of parasite.

- Impression smear of biopsy, or slit skin smear or lesion border.

- Speciation can be made by polymerase chain reaction.

Disease syndromes

Visceral leishmaniasis

The incubation period is generally 2–8 months. The following are classic features.

- Fever.

- Abdominal swelling.

- Weight loss.

- Splenomegaly, which may be massive, with or without hepatomegaly. Anaemia is characteristic, often with low white cells and platelets. Liver function tests are usually near normal. There is a polyclonal increase in immunoglobulins.

- Visceral leishmaniasis is associated with advanced HIV infection and may develop many years after initial exposure.

Fever and splenomegaly are typical. In this setting, serology is often negative but parasites are abundant.

Cutaneous leishmaniasis

- After an incubation period of 1–12 weeks following the bite from an infected sandfly, an itchy papule appears at the bite site and subsequently ulcerates.

- Satellite lesions or 'sporotrichoid' spread along with regional lymphadenitis may occur.

Post kala-azar dermal leishmaniasis

- Occurs in individuals previously treated for visceral leishmaniasis.

- Most commonly reported from India.

- Causes hypopigmented non-ulcerating papules or nodules.

- May last for years.

Complications

Secondary infections, caused by suppressed immunity, are common and potentially serious, accounting for many deaths in cases of visceral leishmaniasis. Secondary bacterial superinfection of cutaneous leishmaniasis ulcers is surprisingly uncommon.

Mucocutaneous leishmaniasis (*espundia*) is due to recrudescence of previous untreated or inadequately treated cutaneous leishmaniasis infection with *Leishmania braziliensis*.

Therapy

Liposomal amphotericin is the drug of choice for visceral disease because it is the least toxic effective treatment. However, it is also very expensive. In resource-poor countries, sodium stibogluconate and aminosidine are alternatives.

Sodium stibogluconate is therapy of choice for those who have cutaneous disease acquired in Latin America to minimise the risk of subsequent mucocutaneous relapse.

2.13.3 Amoebiasis

Description of the organism

Entamoeba histolytica is an obligate parasite that resides in the large bowel. It is transmitted by ingestion of cysts in contaminated water or food. These develop into trophozoites (adult amoebae) that can invade tissues and cause disease. Only a small proportion of infections result in clinical disease.

Epidemiology

Amoebic infection occurs in all parts of the world where sanitation is poor and is much commoner in tropical countries.

Diagnostic tests

Asymptomatic intestinal amoebiasis

- Microscopy of stool for cysts.

Invasive intestinal amoebiasis

- Microscopy of fresh stool for amoebic trophozoites.

- Amoebic serology is positive in approximately 75% of cases.

Amoebic liver abscess

- Amoebic serology is positive in >95% of cases.

- Microscopy of liver aspirate: typically aspirate is thick, pinkish-brown ('anchovy sauce') and odourless (in contrast, the pus from pyogenic abscesses has an offensive smell). Microscopy shows no or few neutrophils and trophozoites may be seen in the final part of the aspirate. Bacterial culture is negative.

- Imaging: hepatic ultrasonography and CT scan (see Fig. 36b).

Disease syndromes

Disease can arise weeks, months or even years after infection.

Invasive intestinal amoebiasis

The clinical features vary from mild diarrhoea to severe dysentery. Onset is usually gradual and constitutional upset is mild. Abdominal pain is not usually severe. A relapsing course is common.

Amoebic liver abscess

Most patients do not give an antecedent history of dysentery. The dominant features are fever and sweating, weight loss and right upper quadrant pain. Hepatomegaly and localised tenderness are often found; jaundice is rare. Neutrophilia is typical; liver function is often normal. A raised right hemidiaphragm or right basal lung changes are commonly seen on the CXR. Ultrasonography or CT scanning demonstrates a filling defect in the liver, which is usually solitary.

Complications

Invasive intestinal amoebiasis

This can result in:

- fulminant colitis, especially in pregnancy or complicating steroid therapy;

- perforation of the colon;

- amoeboma, a localised inflammatory mass that may be confused with carcinoma.

Amoebic liver abscess

- Rupture into right hemithorax, pericardium (Fig. 88) or peritoneum.

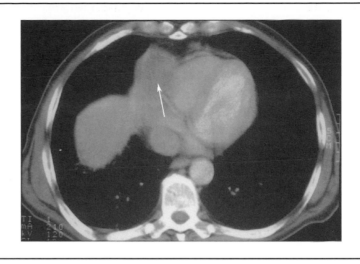

▲ **Fig. 88** CT scan showing an amoebic abscess extending up to the pericardium (arrow), placing the patient at high risk of rupture into the pericardium.

- Spread haematogenously to the lung, brain, etc. (extremely rare).

Therapy

The mainstay of treatment of invasive amoebic disease is metronidazole, which is a potent tissue amoebicide. Diloxanide furoate is used to kill amoebae in the bowel lumen.

2.13.4 Toxoplasmosis

Description of the organism

Toxoplasma gondii exists in three forms.

- Oocyst: excreted in cat faeces.

- Tachyzoite: invasive form which multiplies intracellularly.

- Cyst: the result of intracellular multiplication, containing thousands of parasites (bradyzoites).

Epidemiology

Toxoplasma gondii is ubiquitous with the domestic cat as the definitive host. The prevalence of antitoxoplasma antibodies is high in most populations (approximately 30% of UK adults).

Cysts containing viable parasites persist in the brain and striated muscle for life. Humans are usually infected by ingesting cysts in undercooked meat or from soil contaminated by cat faeces.

Diagnostic tests

- Serology: there are many different methods and so laboratory reports usually include interpretation. It is often difficult to distinguish past from acute infection.

- Culture: *T. gondii* can be isolated from bone marrow in acute disease, but this is available only in a few centres.

- Polymerase chain reaction: this can be used on amniotic fluid to assess fetal risk if the mother develops toxoplasmosis in pregnancy.

- Histology: this may be needed to diagnose focal disease, eg a brain abscess.

- Imaging: cerebral toxoplasmosis complicating AIDS is characterised by ring-enhancing brain abscesses.

Disease syndromes and complications

Infection is usually asymptomatic. The characteristic feature of clinical disease is lymphadenopathy, either localised or generalised. Headache, myalgias, low-grade fever and prolonged fatigue may occur. Acute toxoplasmosis is a cause of atypical lymphocytosis. Severe complications (neurological, ocular and myocardial involvement) are very rare in immunocompetent patients. However, note the following.

- Toxoplasmosis relapses in immunosuppressed patients, especially affecting the brain (Fig. 89), lung and eye.

- Toxoplasmosis can cause serious congenital infection in infants born to mothers who acquired an acute infection during pregnancy.

- Toxoplasmosis is the most common cause of chorioretinitis (Fig. 90), usually as a result of relapse of a congenitally acquired infection.

Therapy

Acute infection in an immunocompetent patient is not usually treated unless there are organ-specific complications or the symptoms are unusually severe or prolonged. Pyrimethamine and sulfadiazine are the main drugs used for treatment when indicated, eg in immunocompromised patients. Clindamycin can be substituted in patients with sulphonamide hypersensitivity.

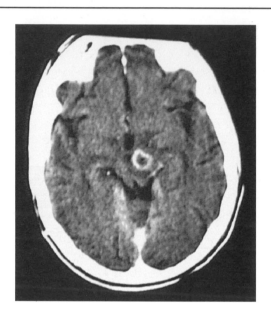

▲ **Fig. 89** *Toxoplasma* brain abscess complicating AIDS.

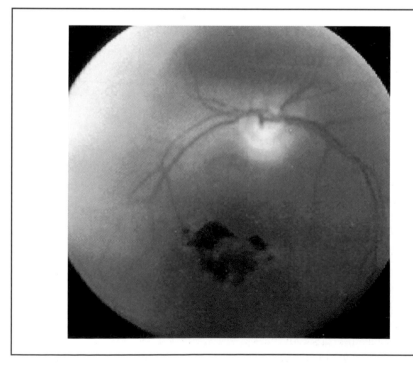

▲ **Fig. 90** Old *Toxoplasma* chorioretinitis: retinal scarring often persists for life.

2.14 Metazoan parasites

2.14.1 Schistosomiasis

Description of the pathogen

Schistosoma spp. are parasitic blood flukes. Three major species infect humans:

- *Schistosoma haematobium*;

- *Schistosoma mansoni*;

- *Schistosoma japonicum*.

Humans are infected by contact with fresh water: the parasite penetrates intact skin. Water snails act as intermediate hosts. Human

TABLE 74 DISTRIBUTION OF SCHISTOSOMIASIS	
Species	**Geographical distribution**
Schistosoma haematobium	North Africa, the Middle East, sub-Saharan Africa
Schistosoma mansoni	Sub-Saharan Africa, the Middle East, Brazil, Venezuela, parts of the Caribbean
Schistosoma japonicum	China, the Philippines, Indonesia

schistosomiasis is also known as bilharzia.

Epidemiology

It is estimated that 200 million people are infected with *Schistosoma* spp., most of these being in Africa (Table 74).

Diagnostic tests

- Identification of viable eggs: microscopy of terminal urine (*S. haematobium*) or stool (*S. mansoni* or *S. japonicum*). Eggs from all three species may be detected on rectal biopsy (see Fig. 38).

- Serology: a positive result does not distinguish current active infection from past infection.

Disease syndromes and complications

Many infected individuals have a low worm burden and are asymptomatic. Eosinophilia is typical.

Invasion

Penetration of the skin can be associated with dermatitis ('swimmer's itch'). Migration through the lungs a few days after exposure can be associated with transient fever, cough and pulmonary infiltrates.

Acute schistosomiasis (Katayama fever)

The development of adult worms and the early stages of egg deposition, days to weeks after infection, may cause a severe systemic reaction including fevers, rigors, myalgia, urticaria, lymphadenopathy and hepatosplenomegaly. High eosinophilia is typical.

Established infection

The main pathological process is granuloma formation around eggs.

- *S. haematobium*: eggs are deposited in the bladder and ureters, which may cause haematuria and other urinary symptoms.

- *S. mansoni* and *S. japonicum*: eggs are deposited in the bowel and liver, which is usually asymptomatic.

Late infection

This phase of infection causes the most clinical disease. Late complications occur as a result of fibrosis.

- *S. haematobium*: causes obstructive uropathy; chronic infection is associated with squamous cell carcinoma of the bladder.

- *S. mansoni* and *S. japonicum*: the most severe manifestation is hepatic fibrosis with portal hypertension.

Chronic intestinal disease is a cause of bloody diarrhoea. Less commonly, egg deposition occurs at other sites. Central nervous system involvement (myelopathy or focal epilepsy) and pulmonary hypertension are well recognised, but rare.

Therapy

Specialist advice is needed regarding treatment. Praziquantel is the drug of choice for all species. Steroids are also used in the treatment of Katayama fever.

2.14.2 Strongyloidiasis

Description of the organism

Strongyloides stercoralis is a worm that lives in the small bowel of humans. Humans are infected via penetration of intact skin. Infection may persist for many years as a result of a cycle of autoinfection, in which infectious larvae reinfect the same host by penetrating perianal skin or the gut wall.

Epidemiology

Strongyloides stercoralis is widely distributed in the tropical and subtropical regions of the world. It remains endemic in the southern USA, Japan and parts of southern Europe.

Diagnostic tests

- Microscopy of stool for larvae.

- Serology.

Disease syndromes and complications

Nearly all *S. stercoralis* infections are asymptomatic. Vague intestinal symptoms may occur, mimicking irritable bowel syndrome. A pathognomonic sign is larva currens, an intensely itchy, serpiginous, evanescent weal on the trunk or thighs.

Hyperinfection syndrome

Strongyloidiasis is important because overwhelming autoinfection can occur if host defences are impaired, eg by steroid or cytotoxic chemotherapy, malignancy, diabetic ketoacidosis or malnutrition. The features include diarrhoea (which may be bloody), cough, wheeze and haemoptysis, and Gram-negative septicaemia. Eosinophilia is absent. Mortality is high.

> **_Strongyloides_ hyperinfection syndrome**
>
> - Triggered by immunosuppression.
> - May occur many years after parasite exposure.
> - Eosinophilia is absent.
> - Mortality is high.

Human T-cell lymphotropic virus type 1

Strongyloidiasis is also associated with human T-cell lymphotropic virus (HTLV) type 1 infection.

Therapy

Albendazole or ivermectin is used; seek specialist advice if hyperinfection is suspected.

2.14.3 Cysticercosis

Description of the organism

The beef tapeworm, _Taenia saginata_, and the pork tapeworm, _Taenia solium_, are transmitted to humans by ingestion of undercooked meat containing the encysted larval stage (cysticercus). Adult tapeworms in the human gut, which are usually asymptomatic, release eggs. These are excreted via the faeces and develop into cysticerci if ingested by the appropriate animal host. Eggs of _T. solium_ (but not _T. saginata_) can develop into cysticerci if ingested by humans and cause the disease cysticercosis.

Epidemiology

Taenia solium is found where undercooked pork is eaten. _Taenia solium_ eggs may contaminate other foodstuffs (faecal–oral transmission) and so avoiding pork does not protect against the disease.

Diagnostic tests

Serology

This can help to establish the diagnosis but is difficult to interpret in an endemic area. Western blot is superior to enzyme-linked immunosorbent assay.

Imaging

- Plain radiography: cysticerci calcify and can be detected in plain radiographs of muscle.

- CT scan of brain: active lesions show up as hypodense areas, inside which the scolex may be seen. Old lesions calcify and are often multiple (Fig. 91).

Disease syndromes and complications

Cysticerci can invade any organ, with the major sites involved being the central nervous system, eye and soft tissues. It may be asymptomatic. Syndromes include the following.

- Neurocysticercosis: epilepsy is the most common manifestation, but there is a wide range of neurological presentations, depending on the site and number of cysts. Obstructive hydrocephalus may result from cysticerci within the ventricular system.

- Subcutaneous and muscular cysticercosis: the patient may notice subcutaneous nodules but the majority pass unnoticed.

- Ocular disease: may lead to blindness.

Therapy

Specialist advice should be sought.

- Symptomatic, eg anticonvulsant therapy and antiparasitic measures are used.

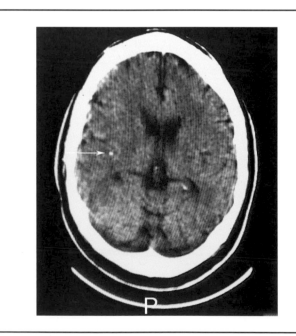

▲ **Fig. 91** CT brain scan of a patient with epilepsy, revealing a small calcified nodule (arrow) caused by past cysticercosis.

TABLE 75 FEATURES OF FILARIASIS

Pathogen	Vector	Distribution	Diagnostic tests	Disease and complications
Wuchereria bancrofti	Mosquitoes	Indian subcontinent, Central and South America, Caribbean, East Africa	Night blood for MF Filarial serology	Asymptomatic microfilaraemia (MF) Acute lymphatic filariasis Fever, lymphadenitis and lymphangitis Chronic lymphatic filariasis Lymphoedema Tropical pulmonary eosinophilia
Brugia malayi	Mosquitoes	South-east Asia		As for *W. bancrofti*
Loa loa	*Chrysops* flies	West and Central Africa	Microscopy of day blood for MF (Fig. 92)	Calabar swellings Transient subcutaneous nodules, often on the arm Irritation of eye as an adult worm traverses the sclera
Onchocerca volvulus	Blackflies	Equatorial Africa (Central and South America, Yemen)	Skin snips for MF	Chronic pruritis and excoriation Eye involvement, with gradual impairment of vision to the point of blindness

MF, microfilariae.

- Specific: praziquantel and albendazole are active against *T. solium*, but there is controversy about the merits of therapy. This is because the natural history of cysticercosis without therapy is difficult to predict, and the induction of therapy may lead to an intense inflammatory reaction and aggravate symptoms, particularly convulsions, that will require adjunctive corticosteroid use.

2.14.4 Filariasis

Description of the organism
Four filarial species commonly cause disease in humans (Table 75 and Fig. 92). Many more individuals are infected without disease. Filariasis is a cause of eosinophilia.

Therapy
Specialist advice is needed regarding treatment. Ivermectin is increasingly used.

> Diethylcarbamazine, and less commonly ivermectin, may induce an intense inflammatory reaction around microfilaria. In onchocerciasis this may damage vision.

2.14.5 Trichinosis

Description of the organism
Humans are infected by eating undercooked pork, wild boar and occasionally other meats. Adult worms in the intestine produce larvae, which disseminate in the bloodstream and penetrate and encyst in striated muscle.

Epidemiology
Infection is endemic in many parts of the world where pork is consumed. There is little infection in western Europe, although sporadic

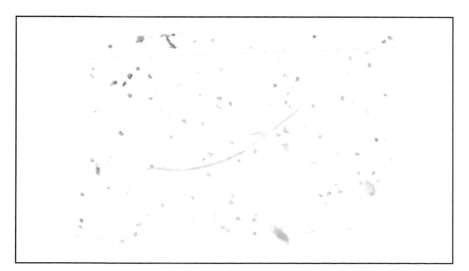

▲ **Fig. 92** Microfilaria of *Loa loa*. Microfilaria migrate through many tissues. This is from a cervical smear. (Courtesy of B. Viner.)

cases are reported in France, usually associated with wild boar hunting.

Diagnostic tests

- Serology.

- Calcified nodules may be seen on plain radiographs.

- Muscle biopsy.

Disease syndromes and complications

Light infections are usually asymptomatic. Heavy infections may manifest distinct stages.

- Invasion: abdominal pain, nausea, vomiting, diarrhoea and fever.

- Migration: myalgia, muscular tenderness and myositis, swelling of face and periorbital tissues, and fever. A high eosinophil count is typical. Complications caused by migration in the heart, lungs and central nervous system can arise.

- Encystment: gradual recovery from symptoms of migration is typical. Serological tests become positive.

Therapy

Spontaneous recovery is usual. Steroids have been used to treat severe myalgia and complications during migration. Albendazole may be used for specific treatment.

2.14.6 Toxocariasis

Description of the organism

Humans are infected by ingestion of eggs of *Toxocara canis* or *Toxocara catis* in contaminated soil. Most infections occur in children. Eggs hatch into larvae, the migration of which causes the clinical disease visceral (or ocular) larva migrans.

Epidemiology

Infections occur wherever there are significant dog and cat populations.

Diagnostic tests

Serology.

Disease syndromes and complications

Most infections are asymptomatic. There are two important clinical syndromes.

- Visceral larva migrans (VLM): myalgia, lassitude, cough, urticaria, hepatosplenomegaly and lymphadenopathy. Eosinophilia is typical.

- Ocular toxocariasis: generalised manifestations of VLM may not be present, but ocular involvement may cause visual impairment. Eosinophilia may be absent.

Therapy

Specialist advice is needed regarding treatment. Many cases recover without specific therapy. Visible larvae in the eye can be photocoagulated.

2.14.7 Hydatid disease

Description of the organism

Echinococcus spp. are small tapeworms of canines. Infected canines excrete eggs in the faeces. Eggs ingested by sheep or cattle develop into cysts. Cysts can also develop in humans (an accidental host) if eggs are ingested, most commonly by consuming contaminated vegetables or after handling dogs with contaminated hair.

Epidemiology

Echinococcus infections occur in Europe, Asia, North and East Africa, South America, Australia and Canada. Human infections occur mostly associated with sheep or cattle rearing and close proximity to dogs.

Diagnostic tests

- Imaging of the affected area: plain films (Fig. 93) and CT may strongly suggest the diagnosis.

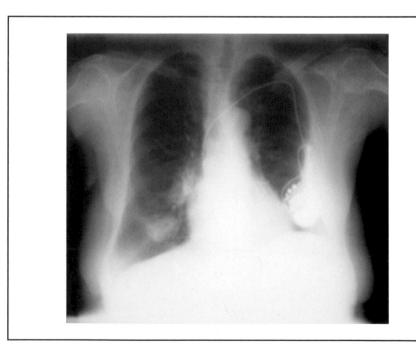

▲ **Fig. 93** CXR from a patient admitted for insertion of a permanent pacing system. An incidental lesion was noted at the right base and subsequently found to be a hydatid cyst.

- Serology: a significant number of false negatives occur, especially with solitary intact cysts at sites other than the liver.

- Direct diagnosis by microscopy if aspiration or surgery is performed.

Disease syndromes and complications

- Most infections are found incidentally on radiological examination. Cysts can affect any organ, but liver and lung are the most common sites.

- Local pressure symptoms.

- Cyst rupture may result in an allergic reaction to parasite antigens.

- Secondary bacterial infection of a cyst.

Therapy

- Specialist advice is needed regarding treatment of symptomatic disease.

- Surgical resection.

- Fine-needle aspiration and installation of a cysticidal agent.

- Medical therapy (eg albendazole) may be useful adjunctive therapy but has a low cure rate.

3.1 Getting the best from the laboratory

Although there are few practical procedures that are unique to clinical infectious diseases, the accurate diagnosis and management of infection requires the correct use and interpretation of diagnostic microbiology services. It is essential that laboratory staff are aware of the following:

- what pathogens are suspected;
- what specimens may be available;
- patient details, including recent antimicrobial therapy, travel and underlying immunocompromise.

For example, in routine practice blood cultures are discarded after 7 days' incubation and this will fail to isolate *Brucella* spp. which take 10–14 days to grow.

- Are the specimen and form correctly labelled?
- Are you sure what samples to take? If not call the laboratory.
- Where possible, try to obtain cultures before antibiotics.
- Is the specimen from the infected site?
- Does the specimen need to be transported urgently?
- Is the specimen of particularly high risk to laboratory staff?

Microbiology specimens

When trying to diagnose an infection, it is vital that the correct specimens are sent to the laboratory. Tables 76–78 detail what samples are needed and how to take them.

3.2 Specific investigations

Blood cultures

Preparation is important to reduce contamination. Proceed as follows.

1. Have the blood culture bottles ready and clean the tops liberally with alcohol.

2. The venepuncture site should be free from visible contamination or superficial infection. Liberally swab the site with alcohol or iodine and allow it to dry for 1 or 2 minutes.

3. Enter the vein using a 'no touch' technique.

4. Directly inoculate into the prepared blood culture bottles without delay. Always inoculate blood culture bottles before other samples are filled to minimise contamination.

5. Fill the bottles to their capacity (generally 10 mL/bottle) because insufficient blood volume reduces the yield.

Do not change needles between blood culture bottles. This does not reduce contamination, but does increase the risk of needlestick injury.

⚠ Always take a minimum of two sets of blood cultures (where one set = 1 aerobic + 1 anaerobic bottle). Taking only one set makes interpretation of possible contaminants very difficult.

Malaria films

Carefully examined blood films are essential in the management of malaria (see Section 1.3.16). Two types of films are used.

- Thin film: this enables the level of parasitaemia to be measured and the species identified. The film is prepared in the same way as for a regular blood film.

- Thick film: this concentrates the parasites and increases sensitivity. One or two drops of blood are allowed to dry on a glass slide and are treated with an osmotic agent to lyse the red blood cells. The slide is stained with Giemsa stain and viewed under the microscope.

Skin snips

These are used to diagnose filariasis resulting from *Onchocerca volvulus* (see Section 2.14.4). In onchocerciasis, microfilariae are found in the most superficial skin layers.

1. The skin is lifted up with a needle and a disposable blade is used to shave off a tiny skin fragment without drawing blood.

2. Typically, four to five specimens are taken from different sites.

TABLE 76 COMMON SAMPLES USED FOR THE DIAGNOSIS OF RESPIRATORY TRACT INFECTIONS

Sample	How to take	Potential pathogens
Throat swab	If exudate is visible try to swab that area. Swab gently between uvula and tonsils	β-Haemolytic streptococci Diphtheria
Sputum	Give sputum pot to the patient. Try to send purulent specimens rather than saliva. Ask physiotherapy staff to help	Bacteria and TB: microscopy and culture Not suitable for viruses or PCP
Induced sputum	3% saline is inhaled using an ultrasonic nebuliser; droplets penetrate to alveoli Use trained staff If TB is suspected, this should only be done under negative pressure isolation	Increased yield for diagnosis of TB Sensitivity of 70% for PCP
Bronchoalveolar lavage	Procedure of choice for immunocompromised host Saline aspirated through a bronchoscope wedged in terminal bronchi Samples should be sent to microbiology, virology and cytology	Bacteria/mycobacteria: microscopy and culture Viruses: IF and culture PCP: IF and cytology Fungi: cytology and culture Parasites: cytology
Gastric washings	After an overnight fast, drink 250–500 mL sterile water and then aspirate via a nasogastric tube	Detection of TB where patient is not producing sputum and BAL is not available Centrifuge, stain and culture for TB
Nasopharyngeal aspirate	Saline gargled and then spat or aspirated into sterile container	Respiratory viruses: IF and culture
Nasopharyngeal swab	Special swab is passed through nose until it reaches the pharynx	*Bordetella pertussis*
Pleural aspirate	Best transported fresh in sterile containers to both microbiology and cytology	Bacteria and mycobacteria: microscopy and culture, and PCR

BAL, bronchoalveolar lavage; IF, immunofluorescence; PCP, *Pneumocystis carinii* pneumonia; PCR, polymerase chain reaction; TB, tuberculosis.

TABLE 77 SAMPLES USED FOR THE DIAGNOSIS OF GENITOURINARY INFECTIONS

Sample	How to take	Potential pathogens
Midstream urine	Clean penis/vulval area Use sterile collecting bowl and catch midstream urine	Microscopy and culture for bacteria DNA-based tests for *Chlamydia*
Early-morning urine	All of the first voided urine collected on three mornings	TB: low yield on microscopy, but higher with culture
Terminal urine	Best in early morning and preferably the last 20–30 mL of the stream	Schistosomiasis
Genitourinary specimens	Essential to take correct samples on appropriate media	Bacteria, viruses and *Chlamydia*

3. The skin fragments are placed in a drop of water or saline and viewed under a microscope.

4. The microfilariae will emerge 30 minutes to several hours later.

Tuberculin testing

There are a number of methods described to test for skin reactivity to mycobacterial antigens. The two most widely used are the Mantoux test and the Heaf test.

Both tests aim to inoculate tuberculin purified protein derivative (PPD) into the dermis. Intradermal injection is critical, because the procedure is likely to fail if the PPD is injected subcutaneously. The forearm is the preferred site for both tests.

Mantoux test

1. 0.1 mL PPD is injected into the dermis (Fig. 94) with a fine needle.

2. The Mantoux reaction is read at 48–72 hours.

3. The reaction is measured by the area of induration rather than erythema.

PPD for use in the Mantoux test comes in strengths of 10, 100 and 1000 IU/mL.

TABLE 78 OTHER SAMPLES USED FOR THE DIAGNOSIS OF INFECTIONS

Sample	How to take	Potential pathogens
Stool	No point in sending a formed stool for analysis unless looking for parasites In dysentery, stool should be transported quickly (hot)	Culture for bacteria Microscopy for parasites Electron microscopy and ELISA for viruses ELISA for *Clostridium difficile* toxin
Blood	Inoculate into culture bottles (see below)	Aerobic/anaerobic bacteria, mycobacteria and fungi (increased with specific media)
Bone marrow	See *Haematology*, Section 3.2.	*Brucella*, *Salmonella* and mycobacteria
Serum	Timed serology	Many organisms
Wounds	If pus is present collect and send to laboratory If not, then use bacterial swabs	Bacteria and fungi
Pus	Aspirates of pus should be placed into a sterile container and transported rapidly to the laboratory	Bacteria, mycobacteria and fungi
Ascites	Transport fresh to laboratory in sterile tube Consider inoculating into blood culture bottles	Bacteria, mycobacteria and fungi readily cultured on appropriate media
Cerebrospinal fluid	Lumbar puncture (see *Acute Medicine*, Section 3.2)	Bacteria: microscopy, culture, antigen detection and PCR Mycobacteria: culture and PCR Viruses: culture and PCR Syphilis: serology Fungi: culture and antigen detection
Vesicles	If intact, aspirate fluid with insulin syringe and transport to laboratory Scrape base onto a microscope slide	Vesicle fluid can be used for electron microscopy and culture Scrapings for IF
Tissue	Separated for histology and microbiology Must not dry out, transport samples to laboratory immediately	Bacteria, mycobacteria, viruses and fungi Immunohistochemisty can be applied to tissue
Skin scrapings	Superficial scrapings with glass slide of blunt blade collected in Petri dish or envelope Nail clippings for onychomycosis	Dermatophytes and other fungi

ELISA, enzyme-linked immunosorbent assay; IF, immunofluorescence; PCR, polymerase chain reaction.

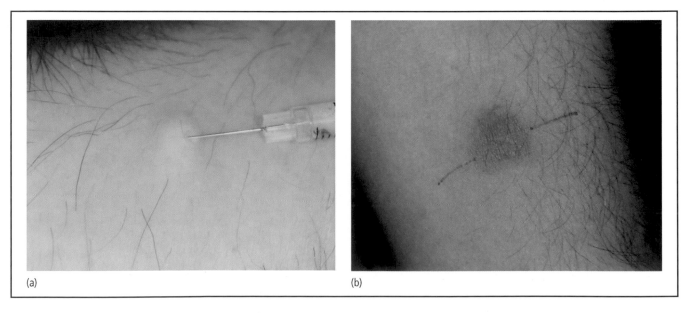

(a)　　　　　　　　　　　　　　　　(b)

▲ **Fig. 94** Mantoux test. (**a**) Injection of PPD. A 25G needle is used to enter the dermis and PPD slowly injected. If the needle is in the correct site, a 'bleb' will be raised as shown. (**b**) Positive Mantoux reaction.

- If TB is suspected, start with the 10 IU/mL strength (ie 1 IU injected); if the reaction is negative, move up to the next strength.

- When screening for exposure most people generally use the 100 IU/mL strength.

- Interpretation of the area of induration depends on whether the person has previously received BCG vaccine.

Heaf test

The Heaf test uses a spring-loaded device to fire six tiny needles 1 mm into the skin (Fig. 95). This reduces the likelihood of a false result due to operator error.

1. A drop of tuberculin 100,000 IU/mL is placed on the skin and the Heaf gun applied.

2. The gun is triggered by firm downward pressure and the six needles inoculate the PPD into the dermis.

3. The head of the gun is then discarded in a sharps bin.

4. The Heaf test is read at 5–7 days and is graded (Table 79).

> ⚠ Always check that you are using the correct strength tuberculin.
>
> - Injection of 0.1 mL of the 100,000 IU/mL solution used for Heaf testing is likely to cause a severe reaction.
> - Conversely, using the Mantoux strength solutions for the Heaf test will lead to a negative result.

Interferon-γ testing for tuberculosis

The tuberculin skin test (TST) is a relatively crude preparation of mycobacterial antigens and false-positive reactivity may occur if the recipient has previously received

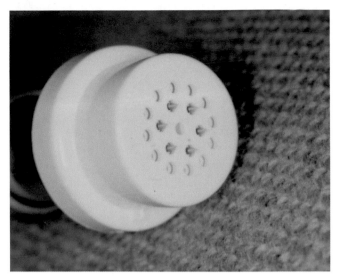

(a)

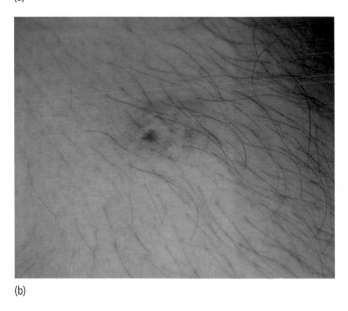

(b)

▲ **Fig. 95** (a) Heaf gun after use showing the six needles that penetrate the skin. (b) Grade 2 positive Heaf test.

TABLE 79 GRADING OF HEAF REACTION	
Grade	Reaction
0	No reaction at site
1	Discrete induration at a minimum of at least four puncture points
2	Induration of puncture sites merge to form a ring but leave centre clear
3	Confluent induration of 5–10 mm
4	Confluent induration of >10 mm

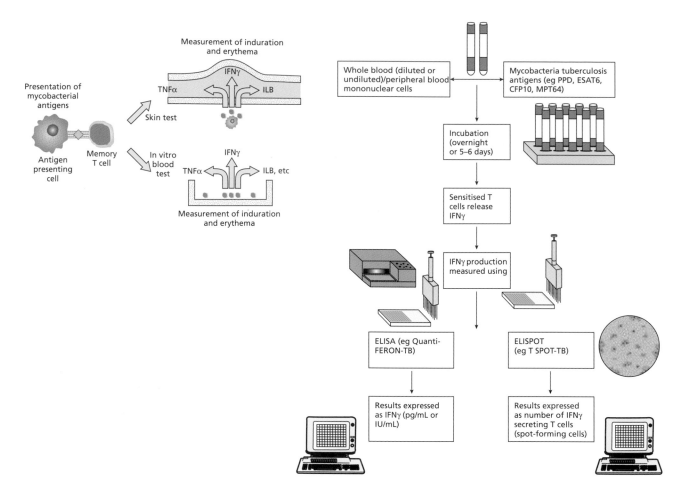

▲**Fig. 96** Summary of interferon-γ testing for TB. (Reproduced with permission from Pai M, Riley LW and Colford JM Jr. Interferon-gamma assays in the immunodiagnosis of tuberculosis: a systematic review *Lancet Infect. Dis.* 2004; 4; 761–76.)

BCG vaccine or been exposed to certain environmental mycobacteria. Conversely, the test may be unreactive in anergic patients with tuberculosis (TB) who have T-cell suppression through illness (eg HIV) or immunosuppressive therapy.

An alternative assay for the diagnosis of latent (and active) TB has recently emerged and the current commercially available tests (T spot-TB and QuantiFERON-TB Gold) measure *in vitro* interferon-γ production in response to *Mycobacterium tuberculosis*-specific antigens. The test therefore has

increased specificity compared with the TST, and also appears to have high sensitivity, including limited data on use in immunocompromised individuals.

A summary of the interferon-γ tests is shown in Fig. 96. The tests use whole blood from the patient with suspected latent or active TB, which is incubated with the purified mycobacterial antigens. Sensitised T cells release interferon-γ which is measured by a standard enzyme-linked immunosorbent assay (QuantiFERON-TB gold) or enzyme-linked immunosorbent spot assay,

which counts the number of reactive T cells (T spot-TB). The test is more expensive to perform than the TST, but uses blood and only requires one contact with the patient. QuantiFERON tests can be stored and batched for laboratory analysis.

Current guidelines for the management of TB issued by the National Institute for Health and Clinical Excellence (NICE; in 2006) recommends the use of two-step testing for latent TB with an intial skin test followed by the use of interferon-γ testing. This policy is subject to future review.

INFECTIOUS DISEASES: **SECTION 4**
SELF-ASSESSMENT

4.1 Self-assessment questions

Question 1

Clinical scenario

A 58-year-old alcoholic man presents to the Emergency Department with a cough and fever. He has a long history of smoking and is found to have a cavitating lesion on his CXR.

Question

Which of the following is *least* likely to be the cause of his pneumonia?

Answers

A Meticillin-resistant *Staphylococcus aureus* (MRSA)

B *Klebsiella pneumoniae*

C *Enterococcus faecalis*

D *Mycobacterium tuberculosis*

E Lung cancer with secondary bacterial infection

Question 2

Clinical scenario

A 19-year-old student presents with a purpuric rash and is thought to have meningococcal septicaemia.

Question

Which of the following statements regarding meningococcal septicaemia is *not* correct?

Answers

A Meningococcal infection is a notifiable disease

B Medical staff attending the patient will require chemoprophylaxis

C Ciprofloxacin can be used for chemoprophylaxis

D Many people carry meningococcal bacteria in the nasopharynx without symptoms

E Contact tracing is the responsibility of the Consultant for Communicable Disease Control (CCDC)

Question 3

Clinical scenario

A 36-year-old farmer is admitted with fever due to pneumonia. His CXR shows lobar consolidation. He is treated with amoxicillin but he remains febrile after 1 week on treatment.

Question

Which of the following diagnoses would be *least* likely to explain his persistent fever despite antibiotics

Answers

A He has an infection which is resistant to amoxicillin

B He has an atypical pneumonia which is not responding to amoxicillin

C He has developed an empyema

D He has a drug-induced fever

E He has pulmonary Lyme disease

Question 4

Clinical scenario

A 20-year-old girl is admitted with hypotension and a blanching erythema. She is thought to have a toxic shock syndrome.

Question

Which two of the following organisms are the most likely causes of her toxic shock syndrome?

Answers

A *Staphylococcus aureus*

B *Moraxella catarrhalis*

C *Streptococcus viridans*

D *Klebsiella pneumoniae*

E Group A *Streptococcus pyogenes*

F *Candida albicans*

G *Bartonella henselae*

H *Pseudomonas aeruginosa*

I *Fusobacterium necrophorum*

J *Staphylococcus epidermidis*

Question 5

Clinical scenario

A 56-year-old man presents with a 5-day history of fever and cough and has shadowing on his CXR consistent with community-acquired pneumonia.

Question

Which of the following features is *not* a recognised indicator of severe pneumonia

Answers

A Elevated urea

B Age >55 years

C Systolic BP <90 mmHg

D Confusion

E Respiratory rate >30 breaths/minute

Question 6

Clinical scenario

A 30-year-old Indian man presents with a 2-month history of back pain, fever and weight loss. He is admitted after developing increasing weakness of the legs.

Question

Which of the following statements is *not* correct?

Answers

A Brucellosis is a possible diagnosis

B He may have vertebral osteomyelitis due to *Staphylococcus aureus*

C Spinal tuberculosis is the most likely diagnosis

D Urgent radiotherapy is required

E Spinal decompression and biopsy will probably be required

Question 7

Clinical scenario

A 23-year-old intravenous drug user (IVDU) is admitted with fever and breathlessness and is noted to have a loud heart murmur on auscultation. He is thought to have infective endocarditis.

Question

Which of the following statements is correct?

Answers

A Hepatitis C infection is unlikely

B *Candida albicans* is the most frequent cause of endocarditis in IVDUs

C Earl's criteria are used for the diagnosis of endocarditis

D Urinalysis is unlikely to be helpful

E Cavitating lesions on the CXR suggest right-sided endocarditis

Question 8

Clinical scenario

A 35-year-old woman presents with a febrile illness followed by increasing breathlessness. An echocardiogram reveals an enlarged, poorly functioning heart and she is thought to have a myocarditis.

Question

Which of the following is *not* a recognised cause of myocarditis?

Answers

A Scombrotoxin poisoning

B Coxsackievirus

C Influenza virus

D Trypanosomiasis

E HIV infection

Question 9

Clinical scenario

A 42-year-old man presents with a 1-week history of fever and headache. A lumbar puncture is performed, which reveals a lymphocytic infiltrate with raised protein and low glucose.

Question

Which of the following is the *least* likely cause of his illness?

Answers

A *Listeria* meningitis

B Cryptosporidial meningitis

C Cerebral lymphoma

D *Mycobacterium tuberculosis*

E Partially treated bacterial meningitis

Question 10

Clinical scenario

A 25-year-old woman backpacker presents with fever and reduced conscious level shortly after returning from Thailand.

Question

Which of the following diagnostic possibilities is *least* likely?

Answer

A Japanese B encephalitis

B Herpes simplex encephalitis

C Tuberculosis meningitis

D Vivax malaria

E Falciparum malaria

Question 11

Clinical scenario

A 35-year-old African man presents with a 2-month history of fever and cough, and has upper lobe consolidation on his CXR. He is thought to have pulmonary tuberculosis (TB).

Question

Which two of the following tests are *least* likely to be of diagnostic value?

Answers

A Sputum microscopy and Ziehl–Neelsen staining

B Bronchoalveolar lavage

C Gastric washings

D Mantoux test

E QuantiFERON test

F HIV test

G T spot-TB test

H Nasopharyngeal aspirate

I Induced sputum

J Sputum electron microscopy

Question 12

Clinical scenario

A patient states that he has an allergy to penicillin with a previous anaphylactic reaction.

Question

Which of the following antibiotics is likely to be safest?

Answers

A Cefuroxime

B Clarithromycin

C Co-amoxiclav (Augmentin)

D Tazocin

E Ceftriaxone

Question 13

Clinical scenario

An army officer returns from Belize with an ulcerating lesion on his left forearm. Biopsy reveals the presence of amastigotes of *Leishmania braziliensis*.

Question

Which of the following statements about leishmaniasis is *not* true?

Answers

A HIV increases the risk of visceral leishmaniasis

B Cutaneous leishmaniasis is common in North Africa

C Leishmaniasis is a zoonosis transmitted by sandflies

D Amphotericin and sodium stibogluconate are both used in treatment

E Splenomegaly is not associated with cutaneous leishmaniasis

Question 14

Clinical scenario

An alcoholic homeless man presents with a 1-month history of cough, night sweats, weight loss and fever. Three sputum smears all reveal the presence of acid-fast bacilli.

Question

Regarding tuberculosis (TB) diagnosis, which of the following statements is *not* correct?

Answers

A Microscopy of a sputum smear is the most common method for TB diagnosis globally

B Sputum smear microscopy has approximately half the sensitivity of sputum culture but detects the most infectious patients

C Culture of gastric washings can be used to retrieve organisms in swallowed sputum

D Polymerase chain reaction is more sensitive than sputum culture

E CXR may be normal in pulmonary TB

Question 15

Clinical scenario

A young executive plans to visit South-east Asia for a long holiday with two friends.

Question

Which of the following issues is of *least* importance in a pre-travel consultation with a young adult embarking on a tour of Asian cities for 2 months?

Answers

A Discussion of measures to prevent malaria

B Vaccination against Japanese encephalitis

C Reproductive and sexual health

D Management of travellers' diarrhoea

E Assessing pre-existing morbidities

Question 16

Clinical scenario

At dermatological examination for a suspected basal cell carcinoma, a Nepalese lady aged 74 years is noted to have anaesthetic macules on her back.

Question

Which of the following statements about leprosy is *false*?

Answers

A It is also known as Hansen's disease

B It is caused by *Mycobacterium leprae*, which grows slowly on Lowenstein–Jensen medium

C The number of cases globally has fallen dramatically since the introduction of multidrug therapy

D Clinical expression is determined by strength of cell-mediated immunity response

E It is not highly infectious

Question 17

Clinical scenario

A patient with tuberculosis (TB) in Kabul fails to regain weight despite receiving treatment in a directly observed treatment programme.

Question

Which of the following is the *least* likely explanation?

Answers

A The patient is not taking the medication

B The drugs are not being well absorbed

C The tablets do not contain active drug

D The patient is not receiving adequate nutritional support

E The TB strain is resistant to the standard therapy that the patient is receiving

Question 18

Clinical scenario

A 35-year-old man with HIV infection complains of progressive right-sided weakness and inability to walk. While awaiting admission he suffers a generalised convulsion after which he remains unrousable. A contrast-enhanced CT scan demonstrates the characteristic ring-enhancing lesion of cerebral toxoplasmosis.

Question

Which of the following statements about toxoplasmosis is *false*?

Answers

A Infection with *Toxoplasma gondii* is rare in the immunocompetent host

B Contact with domestic cats is a risk factor for infection

C Acute infection in pregnancy is associated with fetal harm

D AIDS-associated cerebral toxoplasmosis is treated with pyrimethamine and sulfadiazine

E Toxoplasmosis is the commonest cause of choroidoretinitis

Question 19

Clinical scenario

A war veteran is found on routine screening to have the larvae of *Strongyloides stercoralis* in his stool.

Question

Which of the following statements about strongyloidiasis is *false*?

Answers

A It is associated with human T-cell lymphotropic virus (HTLV)-1 infection

B It is a common cause of diarrhoea in jungle-dwelling populations

C It is the cause of larva currens

D It is a cause of eosinophilia

E It is associated with a hyper-infection syndrome in immunosuppression

Question 20

Clinical scenario

A 64-year-old woman attends clinic with chronic swelling of the left leg which has recently become ulcerated, secondarily infected and is failing to heal.

Question

Which of these statements about filarial disease is *not* true?

Answers

A *Wuchereria bancrofti* is the principal cause of lymphatic filariasis

B Ivermectin is used in the treatment of filariases

C Infections with *Onchocerca volvulus* and *Loa loa* can both involve the eye

D Effective mosquito control significantly diminishes the incidence of onchocerciasis

E *Loa loa* infection can be diagnosed by identification of microfilaria in a smear of blood taken in the daytime, whereas *Wuchereria bancrofti* is better diagnosed by microscopic detection of circulating microfilaria in blood taken at night time

Question 21

Clinical scenario

A Turkish shepherd complains of increasing abdominal swelling and discomfort over the preceding 2 years. Abdominal ultrasound reveals multiple cysts in the liver.

Question

Select the correct pairing of clinical condition with causative organism.

Answers

A *Echinococcus granulosus* and hydatid cyst disease

B *Toxocara* spp. and cutaneous larva migrans

C *Taenia saginata* and cysticercosis

D *Schistosoma spindale* and bilharzias

E *Entamoeba coli* and amoebic liver abscess

Question 22

Clinical scenario

A 25-year-old man complains of dysuria and pain in the left leg (Fig. 97) for the last 3 days.

Question

Which two organisms are most likely as a cause?

Answers

A *Streptococcus pyogenes*

B *Neisseria meningitidis*

C *Neisseria gonorrhoeae*

D *Mycobacterium tuberculosis*

E *Chlamydia trachomatis*

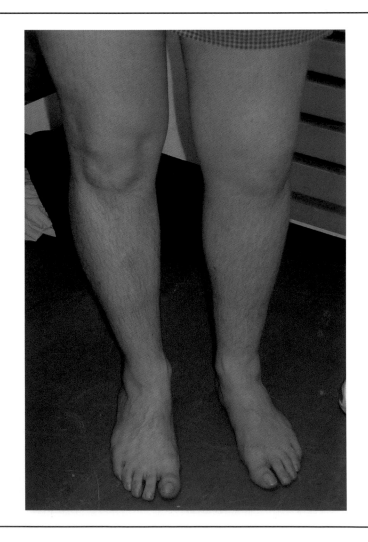

▲ **Fig. 97** Question 22.

F *Shigella sonnei*
G *Candida albicans*
H *Staphylococcus aureus*
I *Mycoplasma pneumoniae*
J *Streptococcus pneumoniae*

Question 23

Clinical scenario

Figure 98 shows a man who has had a similar rash once before. His FBC reveals lymphopenia.

Question

What condition underlies this problem?

Answers

A Diabetes mellitus
B Human T-cell lymphotropic virus-1 infection
C Systemic lupus erythematosus
D HIV
E Herpes simplex infection

Question 24

Clinical scenario

Figure 99 shows a perianal lesion that has been present for 2 weeks in an HIV-positive homosexual man.

Question

What is the most likely cause?

Answers

A Kaposi's sarcoma
B Lymphogranuloma venereum
C *Neisseria gonorrhoeae* infection
D Syphilis
E Anal carcinoma

Question 25

Clinical scenario

A 50-year-old Egyptian man presents with a 4-week history of scrotal swelling and erythema (Fig. 100). A midstream urine specimen shows pus cells but no bacterial growth after 5 days.

Question

What is the most likely cause?

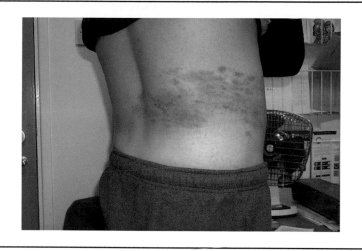

▲ **Fig. 98** Question 23.

▲ **Fig. 99** Question 24.

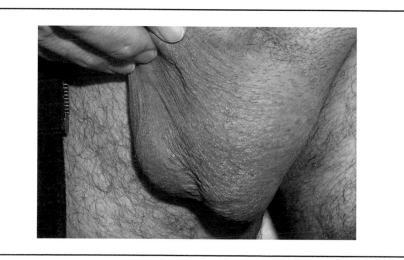

▲ **Fig. 100** Question 25.

Answers

A *Chlamydia trachomatis* infection

B *Neisseria gonorrhoeae* infection

C Tuberculosis

D Testicular carcinoma

E Mumps

Question 26

Clinical scenario

You see a newly married husband and wife for a sexual health check-up and they are having unprotected sex. Subsequently the husband is found to be HIV-positive. He tells you that you cannot tell his wife under any circumstances, even if she asks you. He also tells you that he will not reveal the diagnosis to his wife. He refuses to change his mind. She comes in several weeks later for her results and she is HIV-negative. She asks 'Is my husband OK?'

Question

You should:

Answers

A Maintain the husband's confidentiality and not tell her

B Ask her to speak to her husband

C Tell her about her husband's HIV-positive diagnosis

D Tell her that her husband was HIV-negative

E Ask her to come back later

Question 27

Clinical scenario

A 30-year-old African woman presents with cough and breathlessness for the last 5 days. She has been losing weight for the last year. Her CXR is mildly abnormal with bilateral mid-zone changes. Arterial blood gas analysis on air shows Pao_2 8 kPa.

Question

What is the appropriate treatment for the most likely diagnosis?

Answers

A Intravenous cefotaxime and erythromycin

B Intravenous co-trimoxazole 120 mg/kg daily

C Oral rifampicin/isoniazid/ pyrazinamide/ethambutol

D No treatment: await further test results

E Intravenous quinine

Question 28

Clinical scenario

An HIV-positive man is brought to the Emergency Department having had a fit. A friend says that he has complained of headaches for the last week. An emergency CT brain scan shows two 1-cm ring-enhancing lesions in the cerebral cortex. A lumbar puncture shows a cerebrospinal fluid (CSF) pressure of 35 mmH$_2$O, protein 2.5 g/L, glucose 1 mmol/L (plasma 6 mmol/L) and 100 white cells/high powered field (all lymphocytes). No organisms are seen.

Question

What is the most likely diagnosis?

Answers

A Tuberculosis

B Cryptococcal meningitis

C Cerebral toxoplasmosis

D Neurosyphilis

E Primary central nervous system lymphoma

Question 29

Clinical scenario

A 20-year-old woman presents with fever, generalised papular rash and a vulval ulcer. She recently married a man from the Caribbean after a period of separation.

Question

Which two tests are most appropriate?

Answers

A *Chlamydia* swab

B Syphilis enzyme immunoassay

C Monospot test

D Enterovirus serology

E *Chlamydia* serology

F Measles serology

G Rickettsial serology

H HIV polymerase chain reaction

I HIV antibody

J Human T-cell lymphotropic virus-1 antibody

Question 30

Clinical scenario

A 25-year-old man with a history of intravenous drug use is found on screening to have an alanine aminotransferase (ALT) of 65 U/L (normal <45).

Question

What is the most likely infectious cause of his abnormal liver function?

Answers

A Hepatitis A

B Hepatitis B

C Hepatitis C

D Hepatitis E

E Epstein–Barr virus

Question 31

Clinical scenario

A 30-year-old with closed head trauma has been stabilised on the intensive care unit. After several days he develops a swinging fever. His central venous catheter site looks inflamed and blood cultures are sent for analysis. The following day these are positive, and a Gram stain shows Gram-positive cocci in clumps.

Question

Which organism is *not* consistent with this Gram stain and clinical picture?

Answers

A Coagulase-negative staphylococci

B Meticillin-sensitive
   Staphylococcus aureus

C Meticillin-resistant
   Staphylococcus aureus

D Vancomycin-resistant
   Enterococcus

E *Staphylococcus epidermidis*

Question 32

Clinical scenario

A 40-year-old hepatitis B virus
(HBV) carrier (e antigen positive,
e antibody negative) presents with
progressive liver fibrosis and an
alanine aminotransferase (ALT)
of 30 U/L (normal <45).

Question

Which therapeutic approach
would be of most value for
long-term treatment of his
HBV?

Answers

A Adefovir therapy

B Interferon therapy

C Ribavirin therapy

D Zidovudine therapy

E No therapy

Question 33

Clinical scenario

A 38-year-old mother of two presents
with a short history of headache,
neck stiffness, photophobia and
fever. Her FBC is normal and her
cerebrospinal fluid shows 50 white
blood cells (all lymphocytes), with
normal protein and glucose.

Question

Which organism is the most likely
cause of her symptoms?

Answers

A Enterovirus

B Herpes simplex virus

C Meningococcus

D *Listeria*

E *Mycobacterium tuberculosis*

Question 34

Clinical scenario

A 24-year-old bricklayer presents
with a short history of a swollen
lymph gland in his neck. He is
otherwise well. The following
results are received from the
virology laboratory: cytomegalovirus
(CMV) IgG positive, CMV IgM
negative, Epstein–Barr virus (EBV)
nuclear antigen positive, *Toxoplasma*
IgG positive and *Toxoplasma* IgM
positive.

Question

On the basis of these results, what
would be the most appropriate drug
treatment?

Answers

A Ganciclovir

B Aciclovir

C Spiramycin

D Septrin

E No treatment

Question 35

Clinical scenario

A 25-year-old is recently
returned from Bangladesh. He
received a tattoo while he was
there and was not vaccinated
prior to departure. He presents
with jaundice and an alanine
aminotransferase of 2,000 U/L
(normal <45). His malaria screen
is negative.

Question

What test is *least* valuable in
establishing the cause of his
hepatitis?

Answers

A Hepatitis A virus IgM

B Hepatitis B virus IgM

C Hepatitis C virus RNA polymerase
   chain reaction

D Hepatitis E virus IgM

E Antibody to hepatitis B surface
   antigen

Question 36

Clinical scenario

A 50-year-old man has been
ventilated on the intensive care unit
for 12 days following a head injury.
He develops fever and worsening gas
exchange, accompanied by
shadowing on his CXR.

Question

What organism is most likely to have
caused his nosocomial infection?

Answers

A *Streptococcus pneumoniae*

B Coagulase-negative *Staphylococcus*

C *Escherichia coli*

D *Pseudomonas aeruginosa*

E *Acinetobacter*

Question 37

Clinical scenario

An 80-year-old woman is admitted
with a history of falls to a general
ward. After 3 days she develops
severe vomiting. Other patients and
members of staff are also affected.

Question

What is the most likely organism?

Answers

A *Clostridium difficile*

B Norovirus

C Rotavirus

D *Campylobacter*

E *Helicobacter*

Question 38

Clinical scenario

A 30-year-old man presents with
dual hepatitis B virus (HBV) and
HIV infection. These were acquired
some time in the past. He is HBV
surface antigen positive and e
antigen positive/e antibody negative.
He is on no therapy currently. He is
clinically stable.

Question

Which drug would be active against
both infections?

Answers

A Lamivudine

B Zidovudine

C Stavudine

D Interferon alfa

E Ribavirin

Question 39

Clinical scenario

A 60-year-old man with no previous hospital admissions presents with a sore toe. Clinically it looks to be infected, ie a localised cellulitis. A treatment course of flucloxacillin is ineffective. A swab shows that he is colonised with meticillin-resistant *Staphylococcus aureus*.

Question

Which drug could *not* be used in his treatment?

Answer

A Intravenous vancomycin

B Intravenous teicoplanin

C Oral doxycycline

D Oral rifampicin

E Oral co-amoxiclav (Augmentin)

Question 40

Clinical scenario

A 50-year-old man with a history of mitral valve disease requiring a replacement 10 years previously presents with fever. He is clinically stable. A blood culture is taken and is reported after 24 hours as showing a coagulase-negative *Staphylococcus*.

Question

Which are the two most appropriate courses of action from the list below.

Answers

A No action: likely contaminant

B Start intravenous vancomycin

C Repeat cultures

D Organise echocardiogram

E Start intravenous penicillin

F Start intravenous penicillin and gentamicin

G Start vancomycin, gentamicin and rifampicin

H Refer to surgeons urgently

I Organise typing of organism

J Start intravenous teicoplanin

Question 41

Clinical scenario

A 35-year-old male intravenous drug user presents to the Emergency Department with fever and an inflamed groin injection site.

Question

Which of the following would *not* be in keeping with a diagnosis of necrotising soft tissue infection?

Answers

A Rapid progression

B Minimal pain

C Gas in tissue planes on radiology

D Skin necrosis

E The patient being systemically unwell out of keeping with skin signs

Question 42

Clinical scenario

A 54-year-old male farmer presents with lower limb cellulitis, fever and hypotension.

Question

Which organism/risk-factor combination is *incorrect*?

Answer

A *Aeromonas hydrophila* and fresh water

B *Clostridium* and soil contamination

C Gram-negative bacilli and diabetes mellitus

D *Vibrio vulnificus* and salt water

E *Aeromonas hydrophila* and salt water

Question 43

Clinical scenario

A 65-year-old female animal-lover presents with a 4-week history of fever, weight loss and malaise. There is no recent history of travel and investigations by her GP have failed to establish a diagnosis.

Question

Which two of the following diagnoses would be *least* likely to explain her symptoms?

Answers

A Toxoplasmosis

B Crohn's disease

C Giant-cell arteritis

D Visceral *Leishmania*

E Thromboembolic disease

F Glioma

G Hepatoma

H Phenytoin use

I Lymphoma

J *Bartonella henselae*

Question 44

Clinical scenario

A 64-year-old Indian man presents with a 7-week history of fever, weight loss, worsening cough and exertional dyspnoea. He has a past history of diabetes mellitus and has had an angiogram for investigation of ischaemic heart disease recently.

Question

Which of the following would *not* be appropriate management steps at this stage?

Answers

A CXR

B Blood cultures ×3

C Empirical tuberculosis therapy

D Echocardiogram

E Urine dipstick and culture

Question 45

Clinical scenario

A 19-year-old woman has been diagnosed with chronic fatigue syndrome following exclusion of significant underlying psychiatric and organic conditions.

Question

Which of the following treatments is appropriate?

Answers

A Mineralocorticoids

B Vitamin supplementation

C Cognitive therapy

D Amitriptyline

E Fluoxetine

Question 46

Clinical scenario

A 70-year-old man is receiving intravenous antibiotics for severe sepsis. He has coexistent renal impairment.

Question

Which of the following antimicrobials does *not* require therapeutic drug level monitoring?

Answers

A Gentamicin

B Linezolid

C Amikacin

D Vancomycin

E Flucytosine

Question 47

Clinical scenario

A 23-year-old man requires urgent splenectomy following trauma sustained in a road traffic accident.

Question

Which of the following prophylactic measures does *not* have proven benefit?

Answers

A *Haemophilus influenzae* b immunisation

B Pneumococcal vaccine

C Penicillin V

D BCG

E Meningococcal vaccine

Question 48

Clinical scenario

A 35-year-old woman presents with fever and evidence of haemolysis, and with hemoglobin 9.6 g/dL (normal range 12–16). On further investigation, she is found to have cold agglutinins.

Question

Which of the following would *not* be a cause?

Answer

A Cytomegalovirus

B Lymphoma

C *Mycoplasma pneumoniae*

D Systemic lupus erythematosus

E Epstein–Barr virus

Question 49

Clinical scenario

A 22-year-old woman with cough, fever and basal lung consolidation is diagnosed with *Mycoplasma pneumoniae* infection.

Question

Which of the following is *not* a commonly recognised complication?

Answer

A Bullous myringitis

B Myocarditis

C Arthalgia

D Macular rash

E Salpingitis

Question 50

Clinical scenario

A 45-year-old man undergoing chemotherapy for malignancy develops fever and visual loss.

Question

Which of the following is *not* associated with disseminated candidiasis?

Answer

A Neutropenia

B Central venous lines

C Intravenous drug abuse

D Impaired immunoglobulin synthesis

E Parenteral feeding

4.2 Self-assessment answers

Answer to Question 1

C

Cavitating pneumonia is associated with *Staphylococcus aureus* and *Klebsiella pneumoniae* infection, particularly in alcoholic men. A history of previous hospital admissions would increase the risk of MRSA infection, although community-acquired MRSA is also being reported with increased frequency. He is also at higher risk of acquiring tuberculosis. The smoking history puts him at increased risk of lung neoplasm. *Enterococcus faecalis* does not usually cause cavitating lung lesions.

Answer to Question 2

B

Meningococcal infection is a notifiable disease and medical staff have a statutory obligation to notify the patient. Notification should take place as soon as possible by telephone to the CCDC working for the Health Protection Agency who is responsible for outbreak control and chemoprophylaxis. Rifampicin, ciprofloxacin and ceftriaxone can all be used for chemoprophylaxis. Many people are asymptomatic carriers of meningococcus: the factors that lead to invasive infection are still poorly understood. Transmission is by droplet spread and close personal contact. Medical staff attending the patient are not at risk and do not require chemoprophylaxis unless they have been involved in mouth-to-mouth resuscitation.

Answer to Question 3

E

In a relatively young man with lobar radiographic shadowing the most likely organism is *Streptococcus pneumoniae*, but atypical pneumonia, eg *Mycoplasma pneumoniae*, is also common. Penicillin-resistant pneumococci are being reported with increased frequency, particularly in patients who have recently travelled abroad, eg to southern Europe. Mycoplasma and other atypical pneumonias do not respond to amoxicillin and are usually treated with a macrolide or quinolone. Possible complications of pneumonia can include the development of an empyema or a drug-induced fever. Lyme disease may be acquired in endemic areas and causes a number of clinical manifestations (skin rash, central nervous system effects, arthritis and carditis), but it does not affect the lungs and does not present with fever and lobar consolidation.

Answer to Question 4

A and E

Toxin-producing *Staphylococcus aureus* (often associated with retained tampon use) and Group A *Streptococcus pyogenes* (usually associated with skin, soft tissue or throat infections) are the most common causes of toxic shock syndrome. *Bartonella henselae* is the cause of cat scratch fever. *Fusobacterium necrophorum* is the cause of Lemierre's disease, with initial throat infection followed by lung abscesses and septic thrombosis of the internal jugular vein.

Answer to Question 5

B

The other features form part of the CURB score (*c*onfusion, elevated *u*rea, *r*espiratory rate >30, *B*P 90 mmHg) for assessing the severity of pneumonia. Age >65 years is a risk factor (CURB 65).

Answer to Question 6

D

The subacute history and Asian origin makes tuberculosis the most likely diagnosis, but *Staphylococcus aureus* is possible and *Brucella* should be considered if he has travelled abroad prior to the onset of symptoms. He is likely to have spinal cord compression and requires urgent MRI scanning followed by decompression and biopsy. Radiotherapy is only indicated if he has an obvious metastatic tumour.

Answer to Question 7

E

Approximately 50% of IVDUs are co-infected with hepatitis C. *Candida* infections are associated with contaminated intravenous injections, but are rare. Duke's criteria are used to diagnose endocarditis. Urinalysis should be performed in suspected endocarditis and frequently reveals microscopic haematuria. Right-sided endocarditis is relatively common in IVDUs and may lead to septic emboli causing multiple cavitating lesions on the CXR.

Answer to Question 8

A

Scombrotoxin poisoning is a reaction to oily fish (eg tuna or mackerel) that has become contaminated with histamine. It gives rise to vomiting and diarrhoea but does not cause myocarditis. A large number of infective agents can cause myocarditis, including enteroviruses (echovirus, coxsackievirus and poliovirus), HIV, influenza, cytomegalovirus and Epstein–Barr virus. Trypanosomiasis is a cause of myocarditis in patients from endemic areas (Latin America).

Answer to Question 9

B

Listeria and tuberculosis are both causes of subacute lymphocytic meningitis and partially treated bacterial meningitis may present atypically with cerebrospinal fluid (CSF) abnormalities including lymphocytosis. Fungal infections, eg *Cryptococcus*, should be considered, particularly if the patient is immunocompromised. Cerebral lymphoma and other intracranial malignancies may present as subacute meningitis with abnormal CSF, when cytology is usually helpful. *Cryptosporidium* is a protozoan infection of the gastrointestinal tract that causes diarrhoea (which may be prolonged and life-threatening in patients with AIDS), but it does not cause meningitis.

Answer to Question 10

D

Japanese B encephalitis can be acquired by travellers to rural areas of South-east Asia, but is extremely rarely seen in the UK. Herpes simplex encephalitis is a devastating infection that is treatable if intravenous aciclovir is given early in the course of the disease. Tuberculosis meningitis is an important differential in someone who has travelled to an area of high prevalence. Cerebral malaria due to *Plasmodium falciparum* infection needs to be excluded urgently with a blood film. *Plasmodium vivax* infection is less serious and does not cause cerebral malaria.

Answer to Question 11

H and J

Sputum microscopy and Ziehl–Neelsen staining is the most helpful test for excluding smear-positive (highly infectious) pulmonary TB. Induced sputum may be useful (using nebulised hypertonic saline in a negative pressure isolation room) if sputum cannot be obtained; if this is unsuccessful, bronchoalveolar lavage and gastric washings are appropriate further investigations. HIV testing should be considered in all patients with suspected or confirmed TB (HIV prevalence is high in many parts of sub-Saharan Africa). Tuberculin skin testing (Heaf and Mantoux test) may be helpful, but they can be difficult to interpret and may be negative if the patient is immunocompromised and anergic. Interferon-γ tests (T spot-TB and QuantiFERON) may be more sensitive in this situation, but their use in the diagnosis of active TB has not been fully evaluated, particularly in immunocompromised patients. Nasopharyngeal aspirates are mainly used to obtain specimens for viral immunofluorescence and culture in children with upper respiratory viral infections and are unlikely to be helpful here. Electron microscopy of sputum is not indicated.

Answer to Question 12

B

Penicillin-based antibiotics such as co-amoxiclav and Tazocin (piperacillin) are contraindicated. There is 5–10% cross-reactivity with cephalosporins (cefuroxime and ceftriaxone) which should be avoided if there is a clear history of anaphylaxis. Macrolides (clarithromycin) should be safe.

Answer to Question 13

B

See Section 2.13.2. HIV-associated visceral leishmaniasis is an increasing problem and difficult to cure. Cutaneous leishmaniasis is very rare in Africa, although visceral disease is common in Sudan and Kenya. The sandfly is the vector. Massive splenomegaly is a characteristic feature of visceral leishmaniasis but is not found in cutaneous disease, which is locally limited.

Answer to Question 14

D

Diagnosing TB by sputum smear microscopy is one of the five integral elements of the World Health Organisation DOTS strategy for global TB control. This cheap and simple but relatively insensitive test detects the most infectious cases. In patients without a productive cough, and particularly in children, the retrieval of swallowed respiratory secretions from the stomach can be highly effective. TB is one disease for which polymerase chain reaction has yet to show utility beyond the identification of drug resistance on cultured strains. One in ten patients diagnosed with pulmonary TB have apparently normal CXRs in clinical studies in high-burden settings.

Answer to Question 15

B

Malaria is important throughout Asia and preventive measures should include anti-mosquito and chemoprophylactic precautions. Japanese encephalitis is estimated to affect one traveller in every million and, although widely scattered across Asia, is clearly confined to rural areas and vaccination is not routinely recommended for short-term travellers. Travellers' diarrhoea is the most frequent illness affecting travellers and discussion should cover both avoidance and early self-management. Pre-existing morbidity is most important in older travellers, but it is important that consideration is given to increased risk (for example in travellers with HIV or those who are receiving steroids or immunosuppressive therapy) and difficulties associated with specific therapies (that might require needles or refrigeration).

Answer to Question 16

B

Hansen's disease is caused by *Mycobacterium leprae*, an organism which cannot be cultured *in vitro*. It is estimated that less than 10% of those exposed to the organism develop the disease and the clinical spectrum of the disease reflects the range of cell-mediated immune responses generated. Multidrug therapy has contributed to a 90% fall in global leprosy caseload over the past 20 years.

Answer to Question 17

A

This is about treatment failure. DOTS (direct observation of treatment, short course chemotherapy) comprises five tenets: diagnosis based on sputum smear microscopy; direct observation of treatment (so A cannot be the case); political will; systematic monitoring and evaluation; and regular assured drug supply. Despite the fifth tenet of DOTS the use of fake medicines is widespread, particularly in unstable settings, and is a potentially explosive mechanism driving the emerging epidemic of TB drug resistance and multidrug resistance. Poor absorption can lead to treatment failure in patients with uncontrolled diarrhoea but is generally more important in advanced HIV co-infection. Many TB programmes augment TB therapy with nutritional support, without which weight gain is less dramatic (successful treatment often restores appetite quickly and weight gain soon follows).

Answer to Question 18

A

Serological evidence of *Toxoplasma* infection indicates that about one-third of UK adults have been infected, largely through contamination originating from cat faeces or undercooked contaminated meat. Most infections pass without any symptoms or just a mild episode of transient lymphadenitis. Congenital toxoplasmosis comprises the classic triad of chorioretinitis, intracranial calcification and hydrocephalus and is the 'T' in the neonatal TORCH screen.

Answer to Question 19

B

Gastrointestinal infection with *Strongyloides stercoralis* is associated with HTLV-1 infection, and in co-endemic areas detection of *S. stercoralis* in stool should always prompt HTLV-1 serology. Infection is usually asymptomatic, although the pathognomonic rash (larva currens) is sometimes seen. Infection is a common cause of eosinophilia, but this is notably absent in the hyper-infection syndrome seen occasionally in subjects with concurrent malignancy, steroid therapy or diabetes mellitus.

Answer to Question 20

D

Donations by Merck of free ivermectin to the global efforts to eradicate onchocerciasis and lymphatic filariasis have undoubtedly greatly advanced the successes of these two projects. While the principal morbidity of onchocerciasis is blindness ('river blindness'), *Loa loa* may simply be seen traversing the anterior chamber of the eye, causing relatively little irritation without sequelae. Onchocerciasis is transmitted by blackflies not mosquitoes.

Answer to Question 21

A

Hydatid disease is caused by *Echinococcus granulosus*, commonly transmitted by dogs. *Toxocara* causes visceral larva migrans; cutaneous larva migrans is caused by the dog hookworm. Cysticercosis is caused by *Taenia solium*, the pork tapeworm, not *Taenia saginata* (which is the relatively harmless beef tapeworm). There are many species of schistosomes, but only three with humans as their definitive host and these account for the vast majority of human schistosomiasis (bilharzia): *Schistosoma haematobium*, *Schistosoma mansoni* and *Schistosoma japonicum*. Human amoebic disease is caused by *Entamoeba histolytica*, not the harmless *Entamoeba coli*.

Answer to Question 22

C and E

The figure shows swelling of the left knee and ankle. This history suggests a sexually acquired reactive arthritis or disseminated gonococcal infection related to an acute urethritis. The absence of diarrhoea means that post-dysenteric Reiter's disease is less likely.

Answer to Question 23

D

This is typical shingles. Recurrent shingles suggests an immunocompromised state and in the presence of lymphopenia, HIV is the most likely cause. Systemic lupus erythematosus can cause lymphopenia, but would be an unusual cause of shingles unless the patient is on immunosuppressive therapy.

Answer to Question 24

D

Syphilis commonly presents with an anal ulcer (chancre) in homosexual men, and this has been linked to HIV in recent years. The onset is rather too acute for carcinoma and the appearance would not be typical of the other conditions.

Answer to Question 25

C

Sterile pyuria and the prolonged history is indicative of urogenital tuberculosis. Epididymo-orchitis due to *Chlamydia*, gonorrhoea and mumps present more acutely. Testicular carcinoma is a possibility, but less likely to cause sterile pyuria. The diagnosis can be confirmed by cultures of early-morning urine specimens and, failing that, by biopsy. Infection of other parts of the urogenital tract is possible, and there may also be concurrent pulmonary infection.

Answer to Question 26

C

You have a duty of care to the wife and know that she is in immediate danger from catching HIV. You have made all reasonable efforts to get her husband to tell her and this has failed. An individual's confidentiality is important, but there are circumstances when it can be broken, such as during a police investigation for a serious offence or, as in this case, when another person's health is seriously at risk. Under no circumstances should you lie to her: this is a serious offence which could lead to you being removed from the medical register.

Answer to Question 27

B

Significant hypoxia with only a mild radiographic abnormality is most likely to be due to *Pneumocystis carinii (jiroveci)* pneumonia. An urgent HIV test would aid the diagnosis, and bronchoscopy should be arranged as soon as possible. Hypoxia caused by bacterial pneumonia or tuberculosis would be associated with significant radiological abnormality. Malaria can cause such a clinical picture but is less likely. Withholding empirical therapy in someone so ill would not be appropriate.

Answer to Question 28

A

The combination of space-occupying lesions, high CSF protein, low CSF glucose and CSF lymphocytosis point to this case being tuberculosis meningitis with cerebral tuberculomas. The organism is not seen on microscopy in 20–50% of cases. Cryptococcal meningitis can give a similar picture, although the protein and glucose changes are not usually so marked; cerebral cryptococcomas are uncommon and the organism is normally seen on microscopy in patients as ill as this. Toxoplasmosis, syphilis and lymphoma would not cause such significant changes in the protein, glucose or white cell count.

Answer to Question 29

B and H

The major differential diagnoses are secondary syphilis and HIV seroconversion illness. In syphilis the secondary rash can appear before the genital ulcer disappears. The antibody test will be strongly positive. Genital ulcer is a common manifestation of HIV seroconversion illness along with the rash. A nucleic acid amplification technique is required for the diagnosis as the antibody test may be negative at this stage.

Answer to Question 30

C

Hepatitis C virus infection is very common in this risk group and commonly presents with the sole abnormality of a moderately raised ALT.

Answer to Question 31

D

The others are all staphylococci and can be associated with line infection, as well as contamination of blood cultures in the case of A and E (which are different names used for the same organisms). Enterococci are Gram-positive cocci, but these normally appear in chains. They can cause line infections and are an increasing problem in the intensive care unit.

Answer to Question 32

A

Adefovir would be of most value. The patient needs some kind of treatment as he has progressive disease. Interferon alfa is usually given short term and is not very effective in patients without an elevated ALT. Lamivudine would be an alternative, although resistance develops commonly.

Answer to Question 33

A

Enteroviral meningitis is the most likely. Coxsackieviruses are common causes of meningitis. Herpes simplex virus can cause this, but more commonly causes an encephalitic picture.

Answer to Question 34

E

The serology is consistent with acute toxoplasmosis, as well as past CMV and EBV. No treatment is required. Spiramycin is sometimes used in pregnancy and a range of treatments may be used for the prevention or treatment of reactivation of toxoplasmosis in the immunosuppressed.

Answer to Question 35

E

The other tests are valid as they may detect the cause of his hepatitis, which could be due to hepatitis A, B, C or E. Hepatitis B surface antibody is a screen for previous infection or vaccination status.

Answer to Question 36

D

Pseudomonas is a very common cause of ventilator-associated pneumonia. *Streptococcus pneumoniae* is common in community-acquired disease. *Acinetobacter* can be a major hazard on intensive care units.

Answer to Question 37

B

Noroviruses are very common causes of vomiting illnesses in hospitals. The other agents can all cause gastrointestinal disease, but not in this clinical context.

Answer to Question 38

A

Lamivudine is active against HIV, given in combination with other antiretrovirals. Lamivudine is also active against HBV. Other dually active reverse transcriptase inhibitors include adefovir. HBV possesses a reverse transcriptase even though it is not a classical retrovirus.

Answer to Question 39

E

Meticillin-resistant *Staphylococcus aureus* can be treated orally with rifampicin and doxycycline (often in combination). Vancomycin and teicoplanin are intravenous alternatives in more significant infections. Augmentin and flucloxacillin are not effective, and erythromycin and ciprofloxacin are also generally ineffective against typical strains.

Answer to Question 40

C and D

The organism could be a cause of infectious endocarditis on a replacement valve. However, there could be other causes of the fever and so more information is needed. A repeat culture is mandatory prior to any therapy. An echocardiogram would be valuable in defining the disease. Treatment for infection with this organism is typically 6 weeks of combination therapy, starting as in answer G, but this would be reserved for a case where the diagnosis was more clear-cut. Surgery may be necessary, but medical therapy can be tried first if the patient is clinically stable.

Answer to Question 41

B

Necrotising fasciitis usually causes severe pain and a patient who is sicker than the skin signs would suggest.

Answer to Question 42

E

Aeromonas infection is associated with contaminated fresh water.

Answer to Question 43

D and F

Visceral *Leishmania*, while a zoonosis, is not endemic in the UK. Glioma would normally present with neurological symptoms and headaches, and is not a recognised cause of prolonged fever.

Answer to Question 44

C

The patient may have developed endocarditis secondary to his recent angiography. Tuberculosis is in the differential diagnosis, but more evidence should be obtained before commencing therapy.

Answer to Question 45

C

Although antidepressants are frequently prescribed in chronic fatigue, they are of no proven benefit unless the patient has associated depression. Graded exercise and cognitive behaviour therapy have been associated with an improved outcome.

Answer to Question 46

B

Linezolid is metabolised in the liver and is safe in renal impairment. It does not require therapeutic drug level monitoring. All other agents may be toxic and require monitoring.

Answer to Question 47

D

The other measures are all recommended in patients with an absent spleen.

Answer to Question 48

D

Systemic lupus erythematosus can cause haemolysis, but not with cold agglutinins.

Answer to Question 49

E

Salpingitis is associated with *Mycoplasma hominis* and *Ureaplasma*, but not with *Mycoplasma pneumoniae*.

Answer to Question 50

D

Impaired immunoglobulin synthesis is not associated with disseminated candidasis.

DERMATOLOGY

Authors:

KE Harman, NJ Mortimer, GS Ogg and NM Stone

Editor:

KE Harman

Editor-in-Chief:

JD Firth

PACES STATIONS AND ACUTE SCENARIOS

1.1 History taking

1.1.1 Blistering disorders

TABLE 1 SKIN DISORDERS PRESENTING WITH BLISTERS OR EROSIONS

Nature of the disorder	Possible diagnoses
Immunobullous disorders	Bullous pemphigoid and pemphigoid gestationis[1] Pemphigus vulgaris[1] Dermatitis herpetiformis Mucous membrane pemphigoid
Infections	Herpes simplex[1] Varicella zoster (chickenpox)[1] Herpes zoster (shingles)[1] Bullous impetigo[1] Cellulitis (occasionally blisters, if severe)
'Reactive'	Bullous erythema multiforme[1] Toxic epidermal necrolysis Staphylococcal scalded skin syndrome[2] Bullous drug eruptions Bullous insect bites[1] Acute contact dermatitis (in florid cases)
Miscellaneous	Porphyrias (cutanea tarda is most likely) Pompholyx (dyshidrotic eczema)[1] Diabetic bullae

1. Commoner diagnoses.
2. Caused by an exfoliative toxin and not a direct effect of *Staphylococcus aureus* infection.

Introduction

It is always worth checking carefully what the patient (and even nursing or medical colleagues) means by blisters: sometimes it is quite different to what you expect! In an elderly patient with a widespread, itchy and blistering disease, bullous pemphigoid is the most likely diagnosis, but a careful history and examination will narrow down the diagnostic possibilities (Table 1). Your immediate priority is to recognise and treat diseases that may become life-threatening, in particular toxic epidermal necrolysis (TEN), pemphigus vulgaris, eczema herpeticum and varicella zoster in the immunosuppressed.

> ⚠ Widespread erosion of the skin as a result of blistering is potentially life-threatening due to the consequences of fluid, electrolyte and protein loss and, in particular, secondary infection causing septicaemia.

History of the presenting problem

The history alone may point to a particular diagnosis if key questions are asked.

- How old is the patient? This is an important consideration: this man is 75. Bullous pemphigoid typically presents in the elderly. In contrast, dermatitis herpetiformis (DH), chickenpox, pemphigoid gestationis, bullous impetigo and staphylococcal scalded skin syndrome (SSSS) usually present in children/young adults, and the latter two almost exclusively in children.

- How long has this problem been present? Infections and reactive conditions will have a short history over hours/days, whereas blisters occurring over several weeks/months, as in this case, are typical of immunobullous disorders and porphyrias.

- Does it itch? Pruritus is a very useful symptom to elicit and in this case suggests DH, pemphigoid (bullous pemphigoid and pemphigoid gestationis), contact dermatitis, chickenpox, pompholyx or insect bites.

- Is it painful? Herpes zoster, eczema herpeticum and cellulitis are painful. Tenderness or burning of the skin occurs in TEN and SSSS. The skin will also be sore if there are widespread erosions, regardless of the cause and especially if secondarily infected.

- Which drugs? A history of all medications taken in the month prior to the onset of blisters is crucial. Erythema multiforme, TEN and bullous drug eruptions may all be triggered by drugs (see Section 2.7).

- Is the patient pregnant? This is clearly not applicable here, but if a pregnant woman had similar symptoms you should consider pemphigoid gestationis, a specific dermatosis of pregnancy.

- What was the patient doing before the blisters appeared? This is particularly relevant in acute contact dermatitis. Ask about occupation and hobbies, eg a gardener with an itchy rash on his hands may be allergic to a plant. Ask about application of any creams to the affected area. In a patient with itchy blisters on the lower leg, ask about walks in long grass, which suggests bites.

- Any ulcers in the mouth? Involvement of the mucosal surfaces narrows the differential diagnosis to pemphigus vulgaris, mucous membrane pemphigoid, erythema multiforme and TEN.

> When you assess a patient with blisters or ulcers of the skin, always ask about soreness or ulceration of the mucous membranes, particularly the mouth, eyes and genitalia. Patients may be too embarrassed to tell you about genital ulcers and often fail to realise they are linked to their skin problems.

Other relevant history

Immunobullous disorders may be associated with other autoimmune diseases and DH with gluten-sensitive enteropathy. Some patients with porphyria cutanea tarda have hepatitis C or alcohol-induced liver disease. Immunosuppressed patients are more susceptible to infections, in which they are more serious. The racial background of the patient may be relevant; in the UK, bullous pemphigoid is more common in white people whereas pemphigus vulgaris is commoner in Indo-Asians.

Plan for investigation and management

Investigations

In most cases, investigations are required to confirm the diagnosis of a blistering disease. In this case, where bullous pemphigoid is the suspected diagnosis, a skin biopsy would be the key investigation. The choice of investigations will clearly be guided by the clinical findings and suspected diagnoses, but may include the following.

- Skin swabs for bacterial and viral culture for suspected infections (do not forget to use viral transport medium).

- Vesicle fluid for electron microscopy or swab base of vesicle onto glass slide for direct immunofluorescence: for urgent confirmation of suspected viral infections (speak to the laboratory).

- Blood cultures if infection is suspected.

- Blood tests: indirect immunofluorescence may be positive in immunobullous disorders (see Section 3.2); anti-tissue transglutaminase antibodies if DH suspected; herpes simplex virus and mycoplasma serology in erythema multiforme; and FBC may show eosinophilia in bullous pemphigoid or drug eruptions, and neutrophilia in cellulitis.

- Porphyrin screen: blood, urine and stool.

- Skin biopsy for histology and direct immunofluorescence (see Sections 3.1 and 3.2).

- Patch tests if allergic contact dermatitis is suspected.

> Blisters easily rupture to produce erosions, so always consider a blistering disorder if there are skin or mucous membrane erosions. Do not forget to send skin for direct immunofluorescence in these cases: histology alone is insufficient to clinch the diagnosis of an immunobullous disorder.

Management

Management of individual diseases is discussed in Section 2. Be aware that blisters rupture to produce erosions that are potentially life-threatening if they are extensive and widespread, just like burns. If there is widespread erosion of the skin then general management is as outlined for TEN and erythroderma, regardless of the diagnosis (see Sections 1.4.2 and 2.10).

Cases of TEN and SSSS will need to be admitted. Many of the other possible diagnoses could be investigated as an outpatient, but any patient with extensive blistering or erosion of the skin, regardless of cause, should be admitted. In this case of suspected bullous pemphigoid, a prompt biopsy, ideally on the day of outpatient attendance, and follow-up 1–2 weeks later with the results would be appropriate if blistering was not extensive. Treatment could be commenced pending the results if the clinician was confident of the diagnosis.

Further discussion

What are the key points that would establish whether the GP's diagnosis of pemphigus vulgaris was correct?

The history of itching and blisters in an elderly patient is typical of bullous pemphigoid, the commonest immunobullous disease in the UK. Pemphigus vulgaris does not typically itch and tends to affect younger patients. It also starts with oral ulceration in 70% of cases, so unless the patient has failed to tell his GP about his mouth ulcers, bullous pemphigoid is most likely. To be certain, a skin biopsy for histology and direct immunofluorescence will differentiate between the two (see Sections 2.4, 2.16 and 3.2).

Treatment of immunobullous disorders often involves the use of oral corticosteroids, so be prepared to discuss the potential complications of therapy and any prophylactic steps that should be taken, eg prevention of osteoporosis. Azathioprine is a commonly used adjuvant drug, so know its major side effects and be aware of the role of measuring thiopurine methyltransferase levels before starting treatment (it helps with dosing and identifies those at high risk of bone marrow suppression).

1.1.2 Chronic red facial rash

> ### Letter of referral to dermatology outpatient clinic
>
> Dear Doctor,
>
> **Re: Miss Julie McGinty, aged 25 years**
>
> Thank you for seeing this primary school teacher with a 2-month history of a red facial rash. It has not responded to multiple treatments, including antibiotics and topical steroids. I would be grateful if she could be seen soon as the rash is deteriorating, her students are making comments and she is increasingly psychologically affected by it.
>
> Yours sincerely,

Introduction

A red facial rash is a common dermatological scenario. There are many common and rare possible causes (Table 2), which can often be distinguished by a good history and examination. It is important to remember to ask exactly what has been applied to the skin, both as a cosmetic and as a medicament, as these can cause problems with both irritancy and allergy. Topical steroids can also cause their own side effects of acne, perioral dermatitis and telangiectasia (see Section 2.26). It is vital to explore the psychological impact of the rash on the patient, particularly when there is facial involvement.

History of the presenting problem

- Does the rash itch? Eczematous rashes such as atopic eczema or allergic contact dermatitis (ACD) tend to itch more than other eruptions such as acne. Fungal infections also itch.

- Did you have eczema, asthma or hay fever as a child? A flare of atopic eczema could be the diagnosis, or it could possibly be an associated irritant contact dermatitis on a background of atopy.

- What do you wash your face with/apply to the skin?

TABLE 2 DIFFERENTIAL DIAGNOSIS OF A CHRONIC RED FACIAL RASH

Frequency	Diagnosis
Common causes	Atopic eczema Contact dermatitis (allergic or irritant) Seborrhoeic dermatitis Psoriasis Acne Rosacea Perioral dermatitis (acneiform-type eruption often induced by topical steroids)
Less common causes	Systemic lupus erythematosus (SLE) Discoid lupus erythematosus (DLE) Dermatomyositis Tinea facei Sarcoidosis Photosensitive eruptions (exogenous and endogenous)

Soaps/foaming facial washes will all irritate the skin. Facial wipes/cosmetics/medications may be a potential cause of ACD. Topical steroids (and inhaled steroids) can induce acne and perioral dermatitis.

- Do you develop pus-filled spots within the rash? Acne, rosacea and perioral dermatitis may all be associated with pustules.

- Do you flush easily? This is a classical symptom of rosacea, but is not exclusive to this condition.

- Does sunlight make it worse? Cutaneous lupus and dermatomyositis are both aggravated by sunlight. Photoallergic contact dermatitis, chronic actinic dermatitis and photosensitive drug eruptions can all flare in the summer months.

- Is the rash anywhere else?

Other relevant history

- General health: SLE, dermatomyositis and sarcoidosis may all have associated systemic symptoms. Classical examples are SLE associated with joint pains, mouth ulcers, hair loss and Raynaud's phenomenon; dermatomyositis associated with proximal muscle weakness and symptoms of an underlying associated malignancy; and sarcoidosis associated with cough, shortness of breath.

- Family history: psoriasis and atopic eczema have strong familial links.

- Drugs: many common drugs may cause photosensitive eruptions, eg thiazides and tetracyclines (see Section 2.7).

- Psychological impact of the rash: the psychological impact of a visible skin condition is often

underestimated and may have a dramatic impact on a person's quality of life.

Plan for investigation and management

Investigations
Perform a full cutaneous examination, including hair and nails, to make a diagnosis and to asses the extent of the condition. Then proceed to examination of other systems depending on the diagnosis, eg musculoskeletal examination in psoriasis and full systems examination in SLE. Consider the following.

- Patch testing if ACD is suspected (see Section 3.3).

- Skin scrapings for mycological examination if tinea facei is suspected (see Section 3.4).

- Skin biopsy if SLE, DLE or sarcoid are suspected, or if the diagnosis was uncertain.

- Blood tests, eg FBC, electrolytes and renal/liver/bone function tests if systemic disorder is suspected. Other specialised tests as clinically indicated: antinuclear factor, anti-double-stranded DNA and extractable nuclear antigens for SLE and DLE; angiotensin-converting enzyme levels for sarcoid; and creatine kinase levels and tumour markers for dermatomyositis.

- CXR if sarcoid or dermatomyositis is suspected.

Management
Management should include general advice to avoid irritants on the skin such as soap, facial washes, cleansers and toners. Wash instead with a soap substitute (a bland emollient such as aqueous cream). Specific management varies between conditions (Table 3).

Follow up in outpatient clinic (time interval depending on condition), where you can review with results and start treatment and/or assess response to initial treatment regimen.

Further discussion
Patients often ask if it is safe to apply topical steroids to the face. It is important to provide reassurance that they are safe if used sensibly, with respect to the potency of steroid being applied and the length of time of application. Low-potency steroids used in the short term (several weeks), or on an intermittent basis to control disease, should cause very few problems. In the long term the continuous use of potent steroids can cause many side effects, including acne, skin thinning, telangiectasia and cataracts (see Sections 1.3.2 and 2.26).

1.1.3 Pruritus

Letter of referral to dermatology outpatient clinic

Dear Doctor,

Re: Mr Percy Potts, aged 78 years

Thank you for seeing this retired gardener who has a 2-month history of intense generalised itching that is unresponsive to topical steroids. He is otherwise in fairly good health and cares for his wife who has dementia.

Yours sincerely,

Introduction
The first point of assessment is to decide whether the itching is accompanied by a rash. The

TABLE 3 MANAGEMENT OF DISEASES THAT CAUSE FACIAL ERYTHEMA

Diagnosis	Treatment
Atopic eczema	Emollients Topical steroids (mild/moderate potency) Topical calcineurin inhibitors (tacrolimus/pimecrolimus)
Contact dermatitis	Avoid potential allergens Emollients Topical steroids (mild/moderate potency)
Seborrhoeic dermatitis	Emollients Topical steroids (mild/moderate potency) Anti-yeast treaments
Psoriasis	Emollients Topical steroids Topical vitamin D analogues
Acne	Topical benzoyl peroxide/retinoids/antibiotics Oral antibiotics (4-month courses) Oral isotretinoin Oral cyproterone acetate in females
Rosacea	Topical metronidazole Oral antibiotics (4-month courses)
Perioral dermatitis	Avoid topical steroids Oral antibiotic (usually tetracycline 4–6 weeks)
SLE	See *Rheumatology and Clinical Immunology*, Section 2.4.1
DLE	Sunblock Potent topical steroids Antimalarials
Dermatomyositis	See Section 2.5
Sarcoid	See *Respiratory Medicine*, Section 2.8.2
Tinea facei	Topical and/or oral anti-dermatophyte treatment, eg terbinafine

- Relevant temporal associations that should be explored include those related to drug ingestion, seasonal deterioration (eg ultraviolet or pollen) or foreign travel.

- Could this be scabies? Ask if there are other affected individuals in the same household or if there has been any exposure to potential sources of infestation.

- Are there any associated clinical features from the history, such as deeper swellings, that might suggest angio-oedema?

- Specifically explore whether there is a history of blister formation, which may not be present at the time of examination because of blister roof removal by scratching.

- Ask about oral symptoms that may suggest lichen planus or an immunobullous disease.

Other relevant history

A full functional enquiry should follow, with particular emphasis on features that might suggest anaemia, thyroid disease, haematological malignancy, renal or liver impairment.

Enquire about the patient's past medical history, including a history of atopic disease; drug and alcohol ingestion are also vital parts of the assessment of possible causes of generalised pruritus.

Family history is also clearly important, eg in suggesting a possible atopic diathesis or susceptibility to anaemia, haematological malignancy, thyroid disease, renal or liver disease.

differential diagnoses then fall into two largely distinct groups (Table 4), which can be further dissected on the basis of a good history and examination.

History of the presenting problem

If the pruritus is associated with a rash, then the history should start with a description of the lesions, their distribution and their timing.

> **Pruritus in the absence of a rash can indicate a serious underlying disease, including malignancy. In the history (and examination) you must search for relevant clues.**

TABLE 4 CAUSES OF PRURITUS

Pruritus without rash	Pruritus with rash
Anaemia	Eczema
Polycythaemia rubra vera	Lichen planus
Haematological malignancy	Urticaria
Thyroid disease	Scabies
Liver disease	Drug eruptions
Renal disease	Bullous pemphigoid
Drugs	Dermatitis herpetiformis
Dry skin	Pityriasis rosea
Idiopathic	Dry skin with asteototic eczema
Psychological	Sézary syndrome
	Cutaneous larva migrans
	Psoriasis (usually mild itch)

Plan for investigation and management

This will depend on whether there is a rash associated with the pruritus. Clearly, if a rash is present, then investigations will focus on relevant potential precipitants. If the rash is eczematous, then it might be reasonable to consider patch testing. If there is a history of blister formation, then an immunobullous disease such as bullous pemphigoid needs to be excluded. Scabies mites can be identified by light microscopy of the track contents. If diagnostic uncertainty remains after clinical assessment, then it may be appropriate to proceed to a skin biopsy.

If there is no rash, then appropriate investigations would include blood tests for FBC and blood film, ferritin, B_{12}, folate, C-reactive protein/erythrocyte sedimentation rate, thyroid function, and liver and renal function. If there are other clues from the clinical assessment or initial investigations, then more detailed specific investigations will be appropriate (eg full anaemia, renal or liver work-up).

A specific treatment plan may be suggested based on the clinical diagnosis and investigations. For symptomatic treatment, start with bath oils and emollients, particularly if the skin looks dry. Pruritis caused by dry skin is common, particularly in the elderly. Antihistamines can be helpful, with tricyclic antidepressants or phototherapy sometimes used if these fail.

> Pruritis is commonly caused by dry skin: recommend bath oils and emollients.

In most cases it will be appropriate to review in 3 months to assess response unless there is anything to suggest that more rapid reassessment would be warranted, eg if underlying malignancy is a possibility.

Further discussion

As well as establishing an appropriate management plan for the patient, there may be other issues to explore dependent on the likely cause. For example, if scabies is diagnosed then sources of infection (and potential for reinfection) should be addressed. If this is in the setting of a group such as a nursing home or hospital ward, then it is important to involve the local infection control team to limit disease spread: does this man's demented wife ever attend day centres or nursing homes for respite care? Institutions such as these are a common source of scabies and not all affected patients itch.

Reactions to drugs can be extremely difficult to disentangle, particularly as the timing and nature of reactions is so variable. The fact that many patients are on multiple therapies complicates matters further. If a drug reaction is diagnosed, then it may be helpful to involve the GP with staged monitored replacements of the drugs, starting with the most likely precipitants.

1.1.4 Alopecia

> #### Letter of referral to dermatology outpatient clinic
>
> Dear Doctor,
>
> **Re: Mrs Alice Cooper, aged 30 years**
>
> Thank you for seeing this 30-year-old woman with a 2-year history of progressive scalp hair loss. She has no significant past medical history.
>
> Yours sincerely,

Introduction

The first point of assessment is to decide whether her acquired hair loss is diffuse or focal/patchy, and if there are clues as to whether it might be scarring or non-scarring. By placing the nature of her hair loss into one of these categories, the differential diagnoses rapidly narrow (Table 5).

History of the presenting problem

Once it has been established that the patient has an acquired alopecia, then the history should focus on a description of the hair loss, its distribution and its temporal association with other events.

- Sudden hair loss, in which the hair may be described as coming out in handfuls, suggests an anagen or telogen effluvium (Table 6), or an extensive alopecia areata. There may be a relationship to major life events in a telogen effluvium, eg major illness, trauma or childbirth. Ask if there has been hair loss from other sites.

- Are there any symptoms to suggest the hair loss is associated with an underlying skin disease? Is there any itching or scaling of the scalp? Are there any skin problems elsewhere, or any nail or mouth involvement that might suggest lichen planus? Are there any systemic symptoms that might indicate systemic lupus erythematosus?

- If there is any possibility that the hair loss is due to cutaneous malignancy? Is there a history of significant sun exposure?

- Are there any features in the history suggestive of excess androgens, eg acne and hirsutism, or other endocrine disease, eg weight gain and cold sensitivity in hypothyroidism?

TABLE 5 CAUSES OF ALOPECIA

Distribuiton	Diagnoses
Patchy/focal with scarring	Lupus erythematosus Lichen planus Sarcoidosis Cicatricial pemphigoid Tumour (eg basal cell carcinoma) Burns Radiation Secondary to fungal kerion
Patchy/focal and non-scarring	Alopecia areata Androgenetic Traction Tinea capitis (ringworm) Syphilis
Diffuse and non-scarring	Extensive alopecia areata Anagen and telogen effluvium Iron deficiency Endocrine (eg hypothyroidism) Malnutrition Chronic disease Drugs

TABLE 6 TELOGEN AND ANAGEN EFFLUVIUM

Diagnosis	Key facts	Triggers
Telogen effluvium	15% of hairs are in the resting telogen phase: a telogen effluvium seems dramatic, but most hairs remain. It occurs 1–6 months after the trigger	Parturition or abortion Major surgery or blood loss Serious illness Fever Crash dieting Emotional stress Drugs
Anagen effluvium	85% of hairs are in the active growth anagen phase: most hair is lost in anagen effluvium, which occurs shortly after the trigger	Cytotoxic drugs Radiotherapy Poisoning (eg heavy metals)

- Does the patient tie her hair back tightly? Tension on the shafts can eventually damage the follicles. This is most commonly seen in black women who tightly braid their hair.

Other relevant history

A full functional enquiry should follow, with particular emphasis on features that might suggest anaemia or autoimmune disease. The drug history is important, with accurate start dates so that potential drug triggers can be identified or excluded. Ask about the family history, particularly in cases of androgenetic alopecia.

Plan for investigation and management

- In any patient with patchy alopecia it is important to exclude fungal infection of the scalp with Wood's light examination and microscopy and culture of skin scrapings and hairs.

- If there are features suggestive of excess androgen secretion, then appropriate endocrine investigations should be undertaken (see *Endocrinology*, Sections 2.2.3 and 2.4.6).

- Other screening blood tests may include haemoglobin, haematinics, thyroid function and an autoimmune screen including antinuclear antibodies.

- In the setting of recent severe illness or surgery, an excess ratio of telogen club follicles to anagen follicles on hair microscopy would suggest a diagnosis of telogen effluvium.

- If there is clinical evidence of scarring alopecia or if the diagnosis is unclear, then it may be appropriate to proceed to a biopsy for histology and immunofluorescence.

Further discussion

Clearly if there are other clues from the clinical assessment or initial investigations that might suggest a specific diagnosis, then more detailed relevant investigations will be appropriate (eg full anaemia or endocrine work-up).

1.1.5 Hyperpigmentation

Letter of referral to dermatology outpatient clinic

Dear Doctor,

Re: Miss Helen Potter, aged 24 years

Please could you see this young woman who has noticed increasing pigmentation on her forehead and beneath her eyes for the past 2 years. It is worse in the summer months and is increasingly a cosmetic problem to her.

Yours sincerely,

Introduction

Hyperpigmentation of the skin is a common problem of varied aetiology. It is useful to divide the causes into localised areas of hyperpigmentation, which are normally harmless (Table 7), and generalised hyperpigmentation, which may indicate an underlying systemic disease (Table 8).

Pigmentary changes are often due to an increase in melanin within the skin, but other substances such as bilirubin and drug metabolites can cause hyperpigmentation when present in excess.

History of the presenting problem

- Where is the hyperpigmentation? The distribution is vital to the diagnosis. Localisation on sun-exposed sites may indicate the common diagnosis of chloasma or a drug aetiology such as amiodarone. Acanthosis nigricans is usually confined to flexural sites (see Section 2.2). Addison's disease (see *Endocrinology*, Section 2.2.6) causes diffuse hyperpigmentation but may only have been noticed by the patient in the palmar creases or in the mouth.

- When did the hyperpigmentation occur? Most causes are acquired, but café-au-lait macules in neurofibromatosis (see Section 1.2.8) may have been present since childhood. Onset in the summer months or when pregnant is classical of chloasma.

- Is it made worse by sunlight? Freckles (ephelides) are normal on sun-exposed skin in summer months. Multiple odd freckles, a history of photosensitivity, early photo-ageing and/or skin cancers at a young age raises the possible diagnosis of xeroderma pigmentosum. Chloasma and

TABLE 7 CAUSES OF LOCALISED HYPERPIGMENTATION

Diagnosis	Clinical features
Freckles (ephelides)	Small pigmented macules (<3 mm) on sun-exposed sites. If there are many or odd freckles associated with photosensitivity and skin tumours, think of xeroderma pigmentosum
Café-au-lait macules	Consider neurofibromatosis (see Section 1.2.8)
Chloasma	Patchy symmetrical facial pigmentation on sun-exposed skin. Occurs particularly on the forehead, cheeks and upper lip, and in females
Acanthosis nigricans	Velvety thickened skin, particularly in flexures. Patient may be obese or have an underlying malignancy
Post-inflammatory hyperpigmentation	At sites of previous inflammation, eg eczema or lichen planus. Look for the remains of the preceding rash. Commoner in racially pigmented skin Fixed drug eruptions leave circular areas of pigmentation which become inflamed intermittently at the same site on re-exposure to the causative drug
Haemosiderosis	Red/brown, often speckled, pigment on lower legs in patients with venous hypertension
Drugs	For example minocycline (blue/black and symmetrical pigmentation); amiodarone and chlorpromazine (both produce blue/slate grey colour on exposed sites, eg nose)
Porphyria cutanea tarda	Diffuse 'tanned' appearance on sun-exposed sites
Pityriasis versicolor	Cause of truncal dappled hyperpigmentation and/or hypopigmentation. Fine scale
Alkaptonuria	Blue/grey pigment is generalised, but often noticed on ears and nasal tip

TABLE 8 CAUSES OF GENERALISED HYPERPIGMENTATION

Diagnosis	Clinical features
Addison's disease	Diffuse pigmentation, localised particularly in palmar creases and buccal mucosa
Ectopic ACTH/MSH	Consider small-cell lung cancer
Acromegaly, hyperthyroidism and phaeochromocytoma	Occasionally cause Addison's-type hyperpigmentation
Malabsorption, malnutrition and cachexia	Diffuse brown/grey pigmentation
Chronic renal failure	Diffuse brown/yellow pigmentation
Systemic sclerosis	Diffuse brown/grey pigmentation
Haemochromatosis (bronzed diabetes)	Grey/bronzed skin
Hyperbilirubinaemia	Yellow pigmentation, particularly sclera
Hepatic cirrhosis	Particularly primary biliary cirrhosis (brown pigmentation)
Drugs	For example busulphan, bleomycin and cyclophosphamide (brown pigmentation); mepacrine (yellow pigmentation). See Section 2.7
Carotenaemia	Generalised yellow/orange colour, particularly on the palms

ACTH, adrenocorticotrophic hormone; MSH, melanocyte-stimulating hormone.

some drug rashes are exacerbated by sunlight.

- Has the skin always looked like this, or was there a different appearance before? Many inflammatory rashes such as lichen planus or eczema may be extremely itchy and inflamed before settling and leaving post-inflammatory hyperpigmentation. Fixed drug eruptions are localised areas that become repeatedly inflamed and may blister, following ingestion of a drug, before settling to leave pigmentation in the skin.

Other relevant history

Drug history

This is vital. Drugs can cause both localised and generalised pigment changes (see Section 2.7). Many drugs, commonly NSAIDs, can cause fixed drug eruptions. Minocycline causes localised blue/black pigmentation after long-term use. Mepacrine can cause a diffuse yellow pigmentation in the skin.

General health

This is most important in cases of generalised hyperpigmentation. Is there anything to suggest endocrine problems such as Addison's disease, acromegaly, hyperthyroidism or phaeochromocytoma? Small-cell lung cancers can secrete ACTH and give similar Addison-like hyperpigmentation.

Chronic renal failure, liver failure and generalised malnutrition/malabsorptive conditions can all be associated with diffuse brown or grey pigmentation. Diabetes is associated with both acanthosis nigricans (localised) and haemochromatosis (diffuse pigmentation).

Plan for investigation and management

A full cutaneous examination is required to determine the distribution and nature of the abnormal pigmentation. Perform a full systemic examination if a systemic cause is suspected (see Section 1.2.5).

Investigations

- Blood tests: FBC, renal function, liver function, glucose, thyroid function tests and ferritin. Abnormal electrolytes (low sodium, high potassium) are expected in Addison's disease. Perform a full endocrine work-up depending on the suspected diagnosis.

- CXR: if there is diffuse hyperpigmentation to look for possible small-cell lung carcinoma.

- Skin scrapings: to look for yeast spores and hyphae if pityriasis versicolor is suspected.

Management

Management will clearly depend on the underlying diagnosis.

- Chloasma: reduce sun exposure with avoidance of the sun and the daily use of a high factor sunblock. Suggest stopping the oral contraceptive pill if this is thought to be the cause (remembering to remind the patient to use an alternative method of contraception and also of the fact that pregnancy will exacerbate chloasma!). Cosmetic camouflage can be used. Topical skin bleaches (such as hydroquinone) can help, but should be used with care due to the risk of ochronosis.

- Pityriasis versicolor: topical azoles or oral antifungal agents such as itraconazole in widespread cases.

- Post-inflammatory hyperpigmentation: there is no treatment other than reassurance that it should gradually fade with time.

- Systemic causes: treat underlying disease.

Further discussion

What is the most likely diagnosis?

In this case, with facial hyperpigmentation that gets worse in summer, chloasma is most likely. In an older patient, consider a drug such as amiodarone or chlorpromazine as the cause.

1.1.6 Hypopigmentation

Letter of referral to dermatology outpatient clinic

Dear Doctor,

Re: Mr Bikram Bhandari, age 35 years

Thank you for seeing this young Indian man who has noticed white areas of skin on the dorsum of both his hands that have been increasing in area over the past 6 months. He is anxious that it may soon spread to his face. Please see and advise.

Yours sincerely,

Introduction

Hypopigmentation is usually due to a decrease in melanin within the skin, which is either completely absent (depigmentation), as seen in vitiligo, or partially decreased (hypopigmentation), as seen in post-inflammatory hypopigmentation. The causes are best divided into

TABLE 9 CAUSES OF HYPOPIGMENTATION	
Localised	**Generalised**
Vitiligo	Albinism
Post-inflammatory hypopigmentation	Hypopituitarism
Pityriasis versicolor	Generalised vitiligo
Lichen sclerosus	
Leprosy	
Halo naevi	
'Ash-leaf' macules (tuberous sclerosis)	
Chemicals, eg hydroquinone	

those causing localised or generalised loss of pigment (Table 9).

> 🔑 As with other skin complaints, the psychological impact of conditions such as vitiligo should not be underestimated. These problems are intensified in patients with non-white skin types, where the contrast between normal pigmented skin and affected areas is exacerbated.

History of the presenting problem

- When did the pale areas appear? There are some inherited causes of hypopigmentation such as albinism (generalised) and the 'ash-leaf' and 'confetti' macules (localised) of tuberous sclerosis that are visible at birth or shortly after. Most cases of hypopigmentation are acquired. Areas of vitiligo are often first noticed in summer months when there is increased contrast between normal and abnormal skin.

- Where are the pale areas? The distribution is vital to diagnosing the cause. Vitiligo classically affects symmetrical areas of skin and may be localised or generalised. Pityriasis versicolor classically affects the trunk in small dappled patches. Halo naevi,

as the name suggests, simply affect a circular area surrounding a mole. The mole may sometimes go on to disappear completely, leaving an area of depigmented skin behind. Hypopituitarism and albinism are both causes of generalised hypopigmentation. Leprosy can cause both localised and more generalised hypopigmentation. Lichen sclerosus most commonly affects the genitalia, but extragenital involvement also occurs.

- Was there an itchy or red rash before the skin became pale? Post-inflammatory hypopigmentation is a common occurrence. The patient usually remembers a preceding rash which looked different to the pale patches left behind. Lichen sclerosus is often pruritic. Vitiligo is characteristically asymptomatic.

Other relevant history

- General health: is there any suggestion of hypopituitarism? (See *Endocrinology*, Section 2.1.8.) Is there any suggestion of autoimmune diseases such as thyroid problems or pernicious anaemia? Vitiligo has a strong autoimmune basis.

- Chemicals/drugs/topical applications: topical hydroquinone is used as a skin bleaching agent.

Occupational contact with some rubber and photographic chemicals can cause skin hypopigmentaion.

- Foreign travel: has the patient visited or lived in a country where leprosy is endemic?

- Family history: a family history of autoimmune diseases may be present in both vitiligo and lichen sclerosus.

Plan for investigation and management

Investigations

- Full cutaneous examination and relevant systems examination is needed (see Section 1.2.6). If leprosy is a possibility, palpate for enlarged nerves and test pinprick reaction to assess altered sensation in hypopigmented areas.

- Examine the skin with a Woods lamp if hypopigmentation is subtle, looking for 'ash-leaf' or 'confetti' macules. The Woods lamp is a hand-held source of ultraviolet light which fluoresces areas of epidermal hypopigmentation.

- Perform skin scrapings looking for yeast hyphae and spores if pityriasis versicolor is possible. Take a skin biopsy from an area of hypopigmentation if there is doubt about the diagnosis, to confirm lichen sclerosus or if leprosy is being considered.

- When relevant, check blood tests looking for associated autoimmune diseases in patients with vitiligo and lichen sclerosus: autoimmune profile, thyroid function tests and B$_{12}$ levels; and a full endocrine work-up if hypopituitarism is suspected (see *Endocrinology*, Section 2.1.8).

Management

- Vitiligo (see Section 2.24).

- Leprosy (see *Infectious Diseases*, Section 2.6.2).

- Post-inflammatory hypopigmentation: no treatment other than reassurance that it will improve with time.

- Pityriasis versicolor: topical azoles or oral antifungal agents such as itraconazole in widespread cases.

- Lichen sclerosus: avoidance of irritants such as soap, use of regular moisturisers and treatment with super-potent topical steroids when required. Genital lichen sclerosus is associated with a 5% lifetime risk of squamous cell carcinoma in the affected skin. There is no increased malignancy risk at extragenital sites. Patients need to be counselled about this risk and appropriate follow-up in outpatients arranged.

Further discussion

What is the diagnosis?

In this case, vitiligo is likely from the history. The symmetrical distribution on the hands is very typical (see Section 1.2.6), but post-inflammatory hypopigmentation should also be considered.

How would you manage this case?

Vitiligo does not necessarily require active treatment. Reassurance that it is not harmful, use of sunscreen to prevent burning of affected skin and tanning of normal skin, and camouflage may be sufficient, particularly in white-skinned patients. However, the psychological impact of vitiligo in brown/black-skinned patients can be devastating and active treatment is often sought. Topical corticosteroids or tacrolimus

and phototherapy are used, but no treatment is necessarily fully effective (see Section 2.24).

1.1.7 Red legs

> **Letter of referral to the dermatology outpatient clinic**
>
> Dear Doctor,
>
> **Re: Mr Reginald Perrin, aged 80 years**
>
> Please see this man with bilateral cellulitis that has failed to respond to several courses of oral antibiotics (flucloxacillin, penicillin and erythromycin). I would be most grateful if you could advise on what antibiotic should be given next. He has a history of hypertension and cardiac failure and takes nifedipine and furosemide. Please see him at the earliest opportunity as his legs are red and swollen and are causing considerable discomfort.
>
> Yours sincerely,

Introduction

This is a very common dermatology referral in routine clinical practice, and it is unlikely that the diagnosis

TABLE 10 CAUSES OF RED LEGS

Frequency	Cause
Common	Bacterial cellulitis (unilateral) Stasis/varicose eczema Deep vein thrombosis
Less common	Allergic contact dermatitis Vasculitis Erythema nodosum
Rare	Pretibial myxoedema Bacterial cellulitis (bilateral)

assumed in the letter is correct. Cellulitis is rarely bilateral and the fact that it has failed to respond to appropriate antimicrobials adds weight to the hypothesis that this is not cellulitis. The most likely diagnosis in this case is varicose or stasis eczema. A good history should explore the possible diagnoses listed in Table 10.

> 🔑 Varicose or venous eczema is eczema of the lower legs due to venous hypertension and varicose veins, but it is also very common to see eczema on the lower legs of patients with peripheral oedema in the absence of varicosities. Gravitational or stasis eczema are terms used to describe these cases, which are very common in the elderly.

History of the presenting problem

> 🔑 Does the skin itch? This is a key question. Eczema is intensely itchy and if the answer is 'yes', then the other diagnoses are unlikely.

- How long have the legs been red? A short dramatic history over several days is more likely in cellulitis, vasculitis, deep vein thrombosis (DVT) or erythema nodosum (EN). In contrast, eczema could have been present for weeks or months, gradually getting worse, although a florid acute allergic contact dermatitis (ACD) could present acutely. Pretibial myxoedema would also have been present for some time.

- Has this happened before? It is very important to know this if the diagnosis is cellulitis, because recurrent cellulitis can lead to scarring of the lymphatics and lymphoedema (see Section 1.2.7).

- Does the skin get dry and flaky? This suggests eczema.

- Is the leg painful? Another key question: cellulitis, DVT and EN are all painful. Vasculitis may be painful. Eczema is not, unless complicated by infection.

- Do you have varicose veins? Have you had any treated? Have you had a thrombosis in the leg? Any of these support a diagnosis of varicose eczema, although someone with a history of previous DVT might have developed another.

- Do your ankles swell, and are they worse at the end of the day and better in the morning? This supports a diagnosis of stasis eczema. If there is a history of lymphoedema, with fixed and long-standing swelling, cellulitis is a common complication.

- Where do you sleep? It is surprising how many elderly immobile patients sleep in their chairs, and having the legs in a dependent position day and night leads to venous hypertension and oedema. Encourage sleeping in a bed.

- Do you have a leg ulcer? A wound on the leg? Athlete's foot? These could be portals of entry for infection in cellulitis.

- Do you apply any creams to your legs? Any bought over the counter? Are you sure? ACD on the lower legs is commonly due to medicaments that may not have been prescribed. The elderly particularly use products like Germolene and Savlon, which may have been used to treat what was initially an endogenous condition like varicose eczema. ACD commonly occurs in patients with leg ulcers to which medicaments are applied with dressing changes. Patients can also develop an allergy to chemicals in rubber and as a result react to elasticated bandages, so ask about these.

- Have you been on a long flight recently, had an operation, been bed bound or immobile, or broken your leg? Have you or any family members ever had a thrombosis? You are looking for factors predisposing to DVT.

- Do you feel well in yourself or do you feel ill? Have you had a fever or are off your food? Patients with cellulitis are usually unwell with malaise or 'flu-like symptoms and fever. Patients with EN, DVT or vasculitis may have systemic symptoms too, but patients with eczema and pretibial myxoedema are usually well.

- Do not forget that one diagnosis may complicate another, eg ACD or cellulitis complicating varicose eczema and leg ulcers.

- Do you have any history of thyroid problems? Pretibial myxoedema is associated with Graves' disease.

> Bilateral cellulitis is rare and is a diagnosis to be questioned. If the skin itches, eczema is the probable diagnosis.

Other relevant history

If vasculitis or EN is suspected, enquire about factors that may be triggers or known associations, including an accurate drug history, recent infections and past medical history (see Sections 2.11 and 2.25). If there is ankle swelling, try to establish a cause, eg symptoms of cardiac failure. In this case, the patient has a history of cardiac failure but is also taking nifedipine, which will contribute to peripheral oedema.

Plan for investigation and management

Investigations

Investigations depend on your suspected diagnosis and would also be guided by findings on examination, but they might include the following.

- Bacteriology: is often negative in cellulitis, but swab any open wounds or the interdigital spaces if mucky. Take interdigital skin scrapings for mycology if scaling is present. Take blood cultures. Swab eczema if wet, weepy or crusted.

- Blood count: look for neutrophilia in cellulitis.

- Duplex Doppler venous scan to assess venous competence in varicose eczema or to look for DVT.

- Patch tests if ACD is suspected.

- Skin biopsy: may be required to confirm vasculitis or EN.

- Ankle–brachial pressure index (ABPI): compression treatment, either bandages or stockings, is an important part of managing varicose/gravitational eczema. A normal ABPI, excluding significant arterial disease, is needed to ensure that compression is safe (see Section 1.1.8).

Management

Management of individual diseases is discussed in Section 2. The management of varicose or gravitational eczema is two-fold. The eczema can be managed with emollients and topical corticosteroids, which suppress the problem but do not remove the underlying cause. Venous incompetence may be surgically correctable, but otherwise compression is the mainstay of management. This can be applied using either four-layer compression bandages, suitable for the more severe cases with leg ulcers, or compression stockings, which would be appropriate for most cases uncomplicated by ulcers. Peripheral oedema might also be managed medically with diuretics and, in this case, the nifedipine might be replaced with an alternative antihypertensive.

Review in 2 months to assess the patient's response to topical therapy and compression treatment would be appropriate.

Further discussion

So which antibiotic would you advise the GP to prescribe next?

The answer is none. It is unlikely that the patient has cellulitis, but be prepared to justify why. Most patients referred with this history have stasis or varicose eczema. However, it may be difficult to decide if the situation is complicated by ACD if topical therapies are already being applied, in which case patch tests may be needed.

1.1.8 Leg ulcers

> ### Letter of referral to dermatology outpatient clinic
>
> Dear Doctor,
>
> **Re: Mrs Sally Catlin, aged 74 years**
>
> Thank you for seeing this retired florist who has developed a nasty ulcer on her right lower leg following minor trauma. Unfortunately this hasn't responded to various creams and dressings used by the district nurses, and if anything it seems to be deteriorating. A course of antibiotics has not helped. She is otherwise well with a history of mild cardiac failure treated with diuretics. She is at the end of her tether and I would be grateful for your advice regarding investigation and management of the leg ulcer.
>
> Yours sincerely,

Introduction

An ulcer is a wound involving loss of the epidermis and partial or full thickness of the dermis. Lower leg ulceration is a common problem, with prevalence rising with age, and it can be associated with considerable morbidity. There are numerous causes, but venous disease with consequent venous hypertension and venous insufficiency accounts for almost 75% of all leg ulcers in the UK. A further 15–20% are due to arterial or mixed vascular disease, or as a consequence of diabetes mellitus (arteriopathy and neuropathy). Precise diagnosis and effective management depends on a detailed history, which should focus on the potential causes listed in Table 11, clinical examination and appropriate investigation.

History of the presenting problem

- When did the ulcer start and how has it progressed? Venous, arterial and neuropathic ulcers are commonly insidious in onset. Other causes such as infection and vasculitis often present more acutely.

TABLE 11 CAUSES OF LEG ULCERS

Frequency	Cause
Common	Venous insufficiency Arterial insufficiency Neuropathy (usually due to diabetes mellitus)
Less common	Trauma Infections Vasculitis (idiopathic, rheumatoid arthritis, lupus and antiphospholipid syndrome, Wegener's granulomatosis, polyarteritis nodosa) Neoplasia (basal cell carcinoma, squamous cell carcinoma, malignant melanoma) Lymphoedema Haematological disease Clotting disorders
Rare	Pyoderma gangrenosum Necrobiosis lipoidica Calciphylaxis (ischaemic skin necrosis, usually in patients with end-stage renal failure) Drugs, eg hydroxycarbamide

- Are there any associated symptoms? Painful ulcers may be due to many causes, but the characteristics of the pain are often helpful distinguishing factors. Aching, limb heaviness and swelling (worse at the end of the day) are characteristic of venous insufficiency. Development of pain in a previously stable ulcer may be suggestive of infection: elevation of the affected limb frequently improves these symptoms. Claudication and rest pain (in advanced disease) occur in arterial insufficiency: placing the affected leg in a dependent position improves this. Burning, paraesthesiae and numbness may be features of neuropathic ulcers, but typically these are painless. Fever and constitutional symptoms may suggest an infective cause if acute, or an autoimmune cause if chronic. Itching and scaling of the surrounding skin is typical of venous/stasis dermatitis.

- Are there any symptoms to suggest any rarer causes of ulceration, eg autoimmune or haematological disease?

- What treatments have been used? Multiple topical treatments will often have been used on chronic ulcers. Contact sensitisation is not an uncommon problem and may be suggested by the development of dermatitis/worsening of the ulcer with a particular topical product.

- Is there a previous history of ulceration? Venous ulcers are often recurrent.

Other relevant history

Ask about her past medical history to identify risk factors.

- Deep vein thrombosis, thrombophlebitis, varicose veins,

previous venous surgery and obesity may be associated with venous insufficiency.

- Diabetes mellitus, hypertension, hyperlipidaemia and smoking are risk factors for arterial disease. Patients may also have a history of ischaemic heart disease or cerebrovascular disease.

- Diabetes mellitus is the major cause of neuropathic ulceration.

- Rheumatoid arthritis and inflammatory bowel disease are both associated with pyoderma gangrenosum and vasculitis.

- Alcohol in excess is associated with neuropathy.

- Drug history: a number of drugs may be associated with peripheral neuropathy: always check in the *British National Formulary*.

Plan for investigation and management

Investigations

After explaining to the patient that under normal circumstances you would perform a complete physical examination as an adjunct to the history, consider the following investigations.

- Blood tests: FBC (anaemia, polycythaemia and infection), glucose, albumin and ferritin (nutritional deficiencies may affect wound healing), and a vasculitic screen (if the history, clinical features or biopsy suggests a vasculitic cause).

- Swabs for bacterial culture and sensitivities.

- Vascular studies: ankle–brachial pressure index (ABPI).

- Biopsy: to exclude neoplasia and vasculitis.

ABPI

Ankle systolic BP divided by the higher of the two brachial systolic BPs. The results indicate the following:

≥1	Usually normal.
0.5–0.9	Occlusive arterial disease (often claudicate).
<0.5	Severe occlusive disease (often rest pain).

⚠ Diabetics may have a factitiously high ABPI due to calcified incompressible vessels.

Management

General principles applying to the management of ulcers include the following.

- Correction of metabolic factors (eg anaemia or malnutrition) that may contribute to poor wound healing.

- Appropriate treatment of bacterial infection.

- Dressings selected according to the condition of the wound: dry wounds should be kept moist to promote healing; highly exudative wounds require absorbent dressings; and bacterial infection/colonisation may require topical antiseptics/antibiotics.

- Analgesia as required.

🔑 If venous or arterial disease is suspected, then specialist referral to a vascular surgeon for further investigation (venous colour Duplex Doppler or arteriogram) and surgical intervention should be considered.

Further management is dictated by specific causes as follows.

- Venous ulcers: leg elevation and compression (hosiery or layered bandage), provided that ABPI excludes arterial disease.

- Arterial ulcers: modification of risk factors. Stop smoking and appropriate control of hypertension, hyperlipidaemia and diabetes.

- Neuropathic ulcers: treatment of associated arterial disease (as above) and modification of risk factors (as above). May require surgical débridement of callus, infected and necrotic tissue or application of a total contact cast. Education and preventive measures, including bespoke shoes.

- Other causes: immunosuppression for vasculitis; surgical management of neoplasia; and specialist management of haematological disease and clotting disorders.

Further discussion

So what is the diagnosis and management of the retired florist?

In an elderly patient with cardiac failure and presumably peripheral oedema, varicose or stasis ulceration is most likely. It is common for an ulcer to develop in these patients following minor trauma, and unfortunately healing is unlikely whilst the leg remains swollen. Compression bandaging is often required. A complicating factor might be all the creams and dressings that have been applied in the community and which may have elicited an allergic contact dermatitis: look for eczema around the ulcer and consider the issues in Section 1.1.7 if present.

- Venous ulcers will not heal if the affected leg remains oedematous: attention must be given to treating oedema as a consequence of dependency, hypoalbuminaemia and cardiac failure.
- Legs must be elevated above the level of the hips: all too often patients sit for hours with their legs down or resting ineffectively on low foot-stools.

1.2 Clinical examination

1.2.1 Blistering disorder

Instruction

This man has a blistering disorder. Please examine his skin.

General features

Is the patient well or unwell? Is he scratching? Are there any features of dehydration or hypoalbuminaemia, which may be a consequence of fluid and protein loss if blistering is extensive? Is there an intravenous drip, which might indicate inability to drink due to severe oral ulceration?

Cutaneous examination

The key points to look for are the distribution of the blistering eruption and the morphology of lesions.

Distribution

Many blistering disorders show a predilection for certain sites (Table 12). If very localised or asymmetrical, think of an exogenous cause such as infections (Figs 1 and 2) or acute contact dermatitis (Fig. 3). Watch out for the dermatomal distribution of herpes zoster (Fig. 2) and involvement of the palms and soles in pompholyx (Fig. 4).

TABLE 12 BLISTERING DISEASES IN WHICH THE DISTRIBUTION MAY HELP MAKE A DIAGNOSIS

Site commonly affected	Diagnosis
Mucous membranes	Pemphigus vulgaris Erythema multiforme (including lips) Toxic epidermal necrolysis Mucous membrane pemphigoid
Elbows and knees	Dermatitis herpetiformis
Palms and soles	Pompholyx eczema Erythema multiforme
Lower legs	Bullous insect bites (often clustered) Diabetic bullae
Centripetal	Chickenpox Pemphigoid gestationis (often begins on the abdomen)
Photosensitive distribution	Porphyria cutanea tarda (especially backs of hands)
Dermatomal	Herpes zoster
Localised and asymmetrical	Herpes simplex (usually clustered) Bullous impetigo Cellulitis Acute contact dermatitis

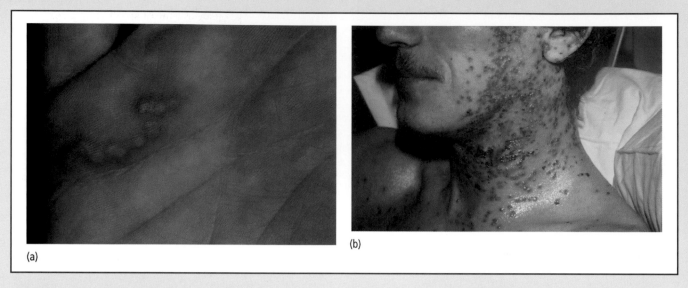

▲ **Fig. 1** (a) Herpes simplex. A localised cluster of small vesicles and pustules on an erythematous base which will become eroded and then crust over. (b) Eczema herpeticum. The herpes simplex virus spreads easily through abnormal eczematous skin and can become widespread. The clue to the diagnosis is the presence of multiple vesicles, papules and punched-out erosions which are monomorphic, ie the same size and shape. They are best seen peripherally rather than centrally, where they often become confluent. It is a painful and serious condition.

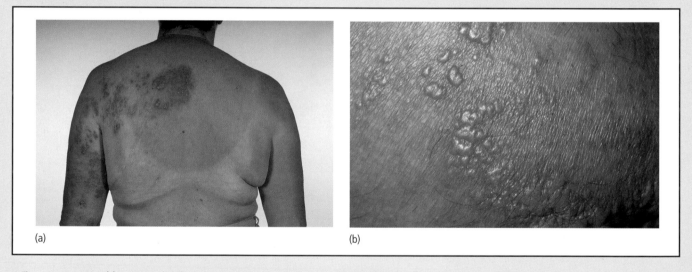

▲ **Fig. 2** Herpes zoster. (a) Pain preceded the appearance of this eruption in the left T2 dermatome. There are clusters of vesicles and pustules on a background of erythema. These will subsequently crust before healing. (b) A close-up view of herpes zoster vesicles.

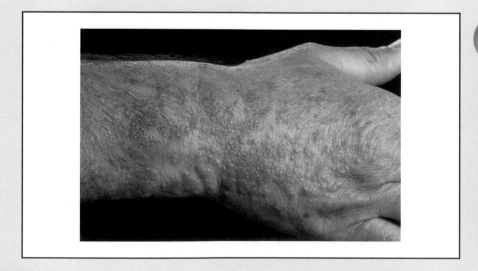

> 🔑 **Do not forget to examine the mucous membranes, particularly the mouth.**

Morphology

Close attention to the appearance of individual lesions may provide the diagnosis.

◄ **Fig. 3** Acute allergic contact dermatitis. Blisters can be seen in very acute, florid cases of allergic contact dermatitis. It is usually itchy. This patient had been gardening and was allergic to primulas. Patch tests can be used to confirm the diagnosis.

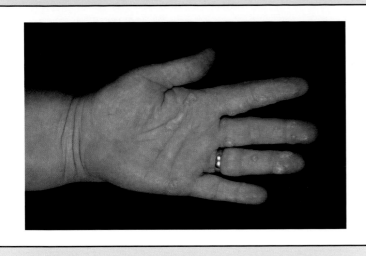

▲ **Fig. 4** Pompholyx (dyshidrotic eczema). Multiple itchy vesicles on the palms and lateral borders of the digits. The thick epidermis results in deep-seated blisters which resemble tapioca grains when the blisters are small. The soles of the feet are often involved.

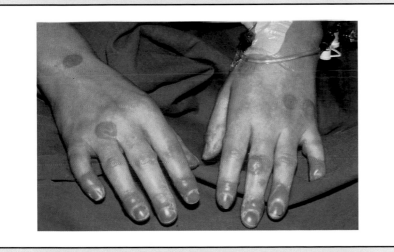

▲ **Fig. 5** Bullous erythema multiforme: blisters are seen on erythematous plaques. The eruption was most dense on the hands and feet and typical target lesions were seen elsewhere. There were oral, genital and ocular erosions. This patient had the more severe form of erythema multiforme called Stevens–Johnson syndrome (see Section 2.10). It was triggered by mycoplasma pneumonia in this case.

▲ **Fig. 6** Bullous pemphigoid. Tense blisters, some haemorrhagic, and erosions on the thigh, typical of bullous pemphigoid.

- A cluster of small vesicles or punched-out erosions is typical in herpes simplex virus infection (Fig. 1a).

- Multiple 2–3 mm monomorphic papules, vesicles and erosions on a background of eczema should make you think of eczema herpeticum (Fig. 1b).

- Target-like lesions may be seen in erythema multiforme (see Section 2.10 and Fig. 5).

- Blisters on a background of erythema and oedema are typical in herpes zoster, pemphigoid, erythema multiforme, dermatitis herpetiformis, acute contact dermatitis and insect bites (Figs 2, 3, 5–7 and 73). In contrast, underlying and surrounding inflammation and erythema is minimal in porphyria, pemphigus vulgaris (PV) and diabetic bullae (Figs 8–10).

- In toxic epidermal necrolysis (TEN) and staphylococcal scalded skin syndrome (SSSS) there is diffuse widespread erythema and the epidermis tends to shear off in sheets rather than form discrete blisters (see Figs 63 and 64).

- Are there intact blisters or have they all ruptured to produce erosions? The blisters of bullous pemphigoid are more resilient than those of PV because they are sited deeper (at the dermoepidermal junction rather than within the epidermis). As a result bullous pemphigoid blisters are often tense with fluid (Fig. 6) and may be up to several centimetres in size before bursting, whereas PV blisters are easily ruptured to leave erosions (Fig. 9).

- Are there scratch marks (linear erosions) indicating itching, which is particularly common in bullous pemphigoid and dermatitis herpetiformis?

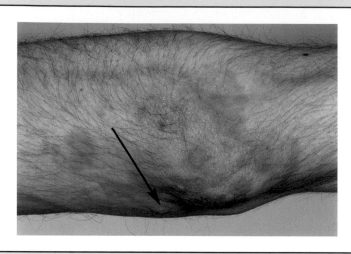

▲ **Fig. 7** Dermatitis herpetiformis. This patient with gluten-sensitive enteropathy complained of intense pruritus prior to the appearance of erythematous papules and plaques on the elbows (shown), buttocks and knees. One blister is visible (arrow).

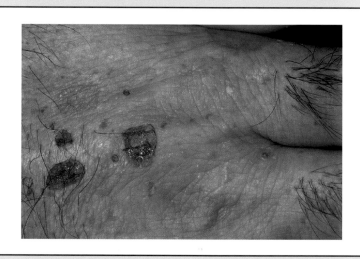

▲ **Fig. 8** Porphyria cutanea tarda. Blisters preceded these erosions seen on the dorsum of the hand of a patient who complained of skin fragility and increased hair growth (note the hypertrichosis). There is minimal inflammation of the skin and atrophic scars.

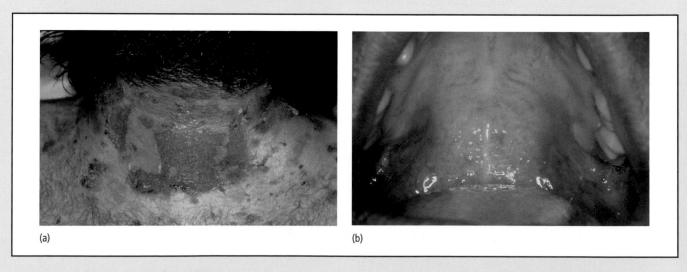

(a)

(b)

▲ **Fig. 9** Pemphigus vulgaris. (a) The fragile blisters in pemphigus rarely remain intact so erosions are more commonly seen. (b) In almost all cases, there will be erosions in the oral cavity, seen here on the soft palate.

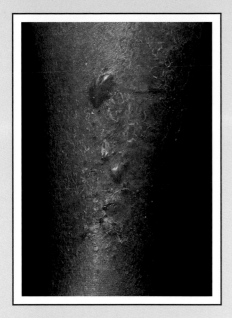

▲**Fig. 10** Diabetes. Blisters on a non-inflamed base on the lower legs of a diabetic male.

Nikolsky's sign

This is positive if a shearing force applied to apparently normal perilesional skin results in epidermal detachment. It is traditionally a sign of PV but may also be positive in TEN and SSSS.

Other features

The skin is fragile and breaks with minor trauma in porphyria cutanea tarda, when there may be scarring, hypertrichosis, hyperpigmentation and milia. Scarring is also a feature of mucous membrane pemphigoid, which can lead to blindness.

Further discussion

How would you confirm the diagnosis?

Section 1.1.1 discusses the investigations that are useful in blistering diseases. These will depend on your suspected diagnosis, but most patients with a chronic blistering disease will need a skin biopsy for routine histology and for direct immunofluorescence (see Sections 3.1 and 3.2). Be familiar

with the immunofluorescence patterns of the main autoimmune blistering diseases, bullous pemphigoid, PV and dermatitis herpetiformis (see Section 3.2).

How would you manage this patient?

Management of individual diseases is discussed in Section 2. One of the general aspects of management is wound care, in particular making sure that non-adherent dressings are used and watching out for signs of infection where the skin is eroded. Widespread erosions are potentially life-threatening, just like burns, and general management in these cases is as outlined for TEN and erythroderma, regardless of diagnosis (see Sections 1.4.2 and 2.10).

1.2.2 A chronic red facial rash

Instruction

This woman has a facial rash. Please examine her skin.

General features

As ever, take time to survey the whole patient before homing in on the face. A patient with atopic eczema might have additional involvement of the flexures and have asthma inhalers on the bedside cabinet; a patient with dermatomyositis may have involvement of the hands with additional nicotine staining providing a clue to the underlying aetiology (see Fig. 20).

When examining a patient who you are told has a localised skin problem, it is vital to examine the whole skin, including the scalp, the nails and mucous membranes. There may be hidden diagnostic clues!

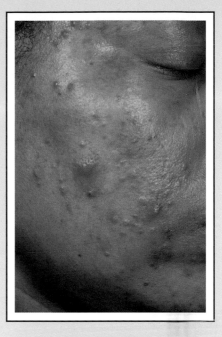

▲**Fig. 11** Acne. Comedones, the earliest feature of acne, are very prominent in this case. Erythematous papules and a pustule are also visible.

Cutaneous examination

Key points to look for include the following.

Facial skin

Look for any papules/pustules/open comedones (blackheads), which are classical signs of acne (Fig. 11). Rosacea can look similar to acne but is not associated with comedones (Fig. 12a). Severe rosacea can cause enlargement of the sebaceous glands on the nose (rhinophyma, Fig. 12b). Is there any scarring? This is important with respect to planning management in acne. Scarring also occurs with discoid lupus erythematosus (DLE) (Fig. 13) but not with systemic lupus erythematosus (SLE) (Fig. 14). Determine if the distribution is in keeping with photosensitivity playing a role, eg exacerbation of SLE, dermatomyositis or a photoallergic contact dermatitis (Figs 15 and 16). Look for sparing of photoprotected sites, eg under the chin or behind the ears (Wilkinson's triangle). What is the distribution of the rash? Is involvement localised

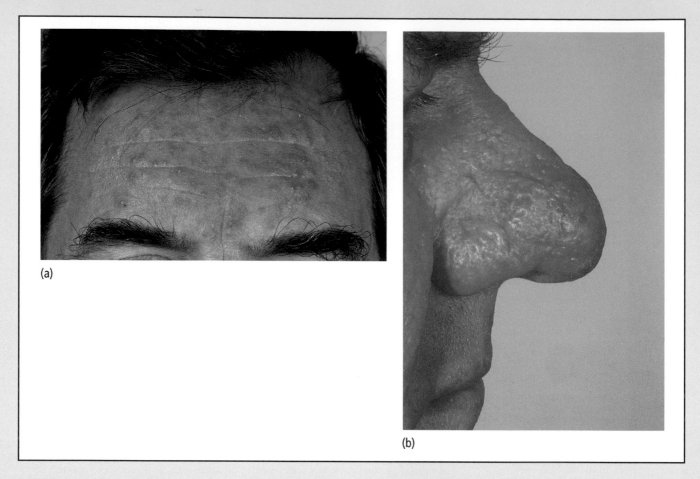

▲**Fig. 12** Rosacea. (**a**) Erythema, papules and scattered pustules typically affect the convex surfaces of the face, including the forehead as shown here. Telangiectases are also a common feature. In contrast with acne, comedones are absent. (**b**) In long-standing cases, a rhinophyma may be the end-result.

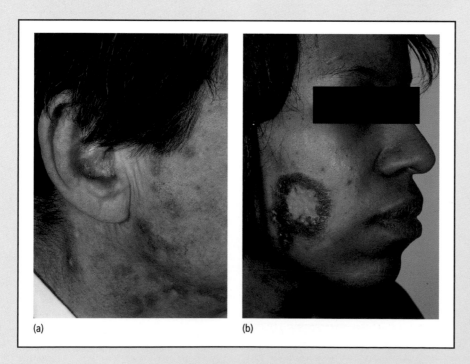

▲**Fig. 13** Discoid lupus erythematosus. (**a**) Well-defined scaly erythematous plaques. Dilated, plugged follicles may be seen on close inspection, particularly in the ears. Chronic DLE results in scarring, which is often atrophic with post-inflammatory hypopigmentation or hyperpigmentation as shown (**b**). Hyperpigmentation is commoner in racially pigmented skin.

(eg DLE, sarcoid and tinea facei) or is it more diffuse (eg eczema or SLE)? Is the rash scaly? Eczema, psoriasis, DLE and tinea will all cause scaly eruptions (Figs 17 and 18); acne, rosacea and SLE are generally not scaly.

Trunk/limbs

What is the distribution of the rash? Acne may be most severe on the chest/back; rosacea usually only affects the face. Psoriasis may look atypical on the face but have classical plaques at elbows and knees. Flexural involvement of the limbs is typical of atopic eczema. Dermatomyositis and sarcoidosis could affect other sites.

Nails

Look for any signs of psoriasis (pitting, onycholysis or subungual

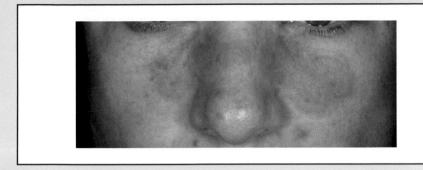

▲ **Fig. 14** Systemic lupus erythematosus. Erythematous plaques over the cheeks and bridge of the nose: a typical butterfly rash.

hyperkeratosis). Look for the presence of nail polish, a common cause of allergic contact dermatitis on the face (Fig. 19).

Hands

Search for any signs of dermatitis, eg scaling in finger webs associated with irritant contact dermatitis. Look for Gottron's papules and/or nail-fold inflammation indicating possible dermatomyositis (Fig. 20). Photosensitive eruptions classically affect exposed skin on the dorsum of the hands and the face (Fig. 15).

Scalp/hair

Is there any scarring, inflammation, scale and/or hair loss? If alopecia is present, determine if it is diffuse or localised, scarring or non-scarring (see Sections 1.1.4 and 1.2.4). Scalp scarring is identified by a change in texture of the skin and a lack of visible hair follicle openings, and in this case would most likely be due to DLE. If scale is present, determine if it is thick and silvery, as in psoriasis, or more like dandruff, as in seborrheic dermatitis. Is the patient's hair dyed? Hair dye allergy commonly presents with facial eczema.

Examination of other systems

Examination of other systems may be appropriate, eg musculoskeletal examination in dermatomyositis and joint examination in psoriasis.

Further discussion

Note the causes of a red facial rash given in Table 13. Ensure that you are familiar with the clinical features of SLE, dermatomyositis and sarcoidosis and know how you would confirm the diagnosis if one of these was suspected.

It is difficult to diagnose the cause of facial eczema/dermatitis on examination alone. In practice patients often have a mixed aetiology for facial eczema, eg a background of atopic eczema that predisposes them to irritant dermatitis caused by facial washes, and in turn possibly causes an allergic contact dermatitis to a medicament or fragrance (only discovered when patch tested).

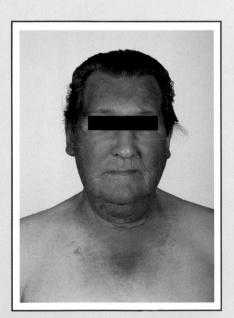

▲ **Fig. 15** Photosensitive eczema. This man complained of a scaly, itchy eruption on his face and hands. The V-shaped cut-off at the neck indicates it is photo-induced. The patient had been given a thiazide diuretic in the autumn but the rash had not appeared until spring when he began spending time outdoors gardening.

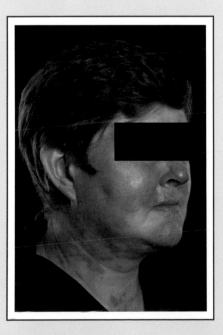

▲ **Fig. 16** Cutaneous lupus erythematosus. Scaly erythematous plaques involving almost the entire face with extension onto the neck. The 'V' of the neck was involved but there was no extension onto the torso, illustrating the photosensitivity of cutaneous lupus.

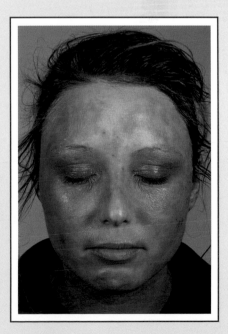

▲ **Fig. 17** Atopic eczema. Poorly defined, erythematous, scaly macules and patches. Note the additional eyelid lichenification and excoriations that are common features of atopic eczema due to rubbing and scratching. There was involvement of the limb flexures, intense itching and a history of atopy.

Station 5: Skin Examination　　**195**

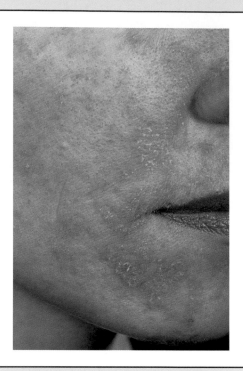

◄**Fig. 18** Seborrhoeic dermatitis. Poorly defined, erythematous, scaly macules and patches. Seborrhoeic dermatitis has a predilection for the nasolabial folds, eyebrows and scalp, allowing it to be differentiated from atopic eczema.

▼**Fig. 19** Acute allergic contact dermatitis. This non-atopic patient experienced periodic acute episodes of an intensely itchy eruption on the face (**a**) and upper chest (**b**). The prominent eyelid involvement initially prompted a diagnosis of dermatomyositis but the intermittent history was against this. The patient eventually linked episodes with the use of nail polish and in fact had a history of finger dermatitis (**c**). Patch testing confirmed allergy to toluenesulfonamide formaldehyde resin, an adhesion promoter present in nail polish. Paradoxically, allergic contact dermatitis to nail polish frequently manifests on the face and neck, due to touch, and with skilful application the fingers may be unaffected.

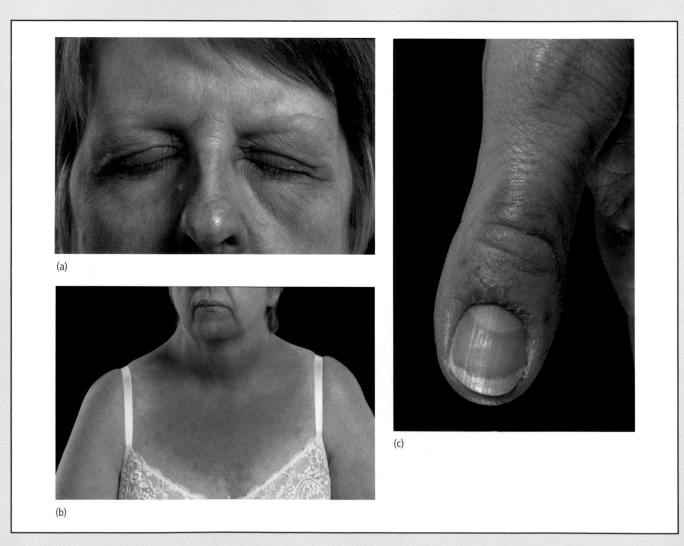

(a)

(b)

(c)

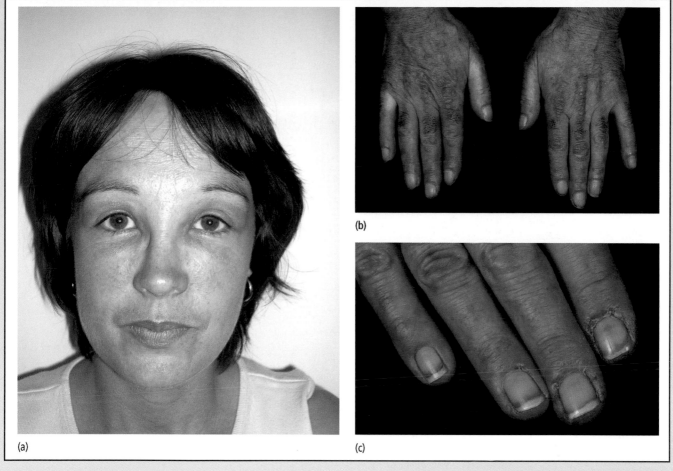

▲**Fig. 20** Dermatomyositis. (**a**) Erythema and oedema of the eyelids, typical of dermatomyositis, although this patient was initially referred with suspected contact dermatitis of the eyelids, a common mistake. Scaling and itch, features of contact dermatitis, were not present in this case. (**b**) Flat-topped purple papules and plaques running along the extensor surfaces of the fingers and onto the hands. They are referred to as Gottron's papules over the knuckles. Note the nicotine-stained fingers. This patient had an underlying bronchial carcinoma. (**c**) Ragged cuticles with erythema and telangiectases of the nail-folds are typical of dermatomyositis but can also occur in lupus and other connective tissue diseases.

TABLE 13 CAUSES OF RED FACIAL RASH: CLINICAL FINDINGS

Diagnosis	Clinical features
Atopic eczema	Erythematous scaly rash, often affecting eyelids. Generalised cutaneous involvement, particularly of flexural sites (Fig. 17)
Contact dermatitis (irritant/allergic)	Erythematous scaly rash, particularly affecting eyelids (Fig. 19). The distribution may be unusual, failing to conform to that of an endogenous eczema
Seborrhoeic dermatitis	Erythematous, 'greasy' scaly rash affecting nasolabial folds and eyebrows (Fig. 18). Other sites often involved include scalp, anterior chest and axillae
Psoriasis	Erythematous scaly localised areas on face. Frequently associated with scaly rash on the scalp (particularly at the scalp margins), nail changes and scaly plaques at extensor sites (see Figs 69, 83 and 84). Look for psoriatic arthropathy
Acne	Papules, pustules, open and closed comedones (blackheads and whiteheads). Look for associated scarring, cysts and nodules. Examine the chest and upper back (Figs 11 and 71)
Rosacea	Erythema associated with papules and pustules. No comedones. Look for rhinophyma (Fig. 12). Is often associated with flushing
Perioral dermatitis	Papules/pustules/erythema affecting a localised area around the mouth. May also affect periorbital skin
SLE	Classical malar erythema (butterfly rash, Fig. 14). Non-scarring. Other features may be present, eg Raynaud's phenomenon
DLE	Inflammatory, scarring and well-defined oval scaly plaques (Figs 13 and 16). Follicular accentuation within. May be associated with scarring alopecia. Can be mistaken for psoriasis, but there is usually limited involvement on body in cases of DLE
Dermatomyositis	Heliotrope (violet) discoloration of eyelids, periorbital oedema, nail-fold inflammation and Gottron's papules/streaking along dorsum of fingers, and ragged cuticles (Fig. 20)
Sarcoidosis	Blue/red papules and plaques infiltrating the nose (lupus pernio). Red/brown papules/plaques (Fig. 21). Systemic disease may be associated
Photosensitive eczema	Eczema as above, with a photo-induced distribution (ie dorsum of hands, 'V' of neck and the face, with sparing of covered sites) (Fig. 15)

DEL, discoid lupus erythematosus; SLE, systemic lupus erythematosus.

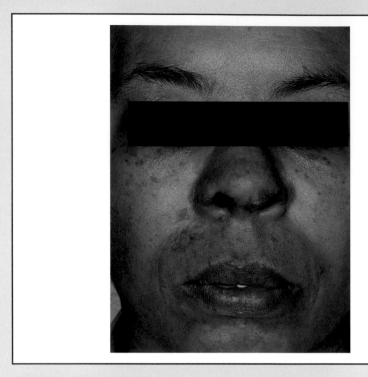

▲ **Fig. 21** Sarcoidosis. Red/brown papules and nodules around the nostrils and lips.

1.2.3 Pruritus

Instruction

This man has pruritus. Please examine his skin.

General features

Skin disease is frequently a sign of systemic disease. From the end of the bed it is worth considering a number of possible causes of pruritus (see Table 4), in order to detect any gross signs of anaemia, thyroid disease, renal or liver impairment or haematological malignancy.

Cutaneous examination

The first decision to make is whether the pruritus is associated with an underlying rash or is separate from any secondary changes, eg excoriation. If there is a rash, then the most useful starting point is often an assessment of the distribution of the lesions.

Distribution

A full cutaneous examination should be performed, but particular attention should be paid to disorders with a characteristic distribution, eg eczema (flexures), scabies (web spaces and genitals, Fig. 22), dermatitis herpetiformis (extensor surfaces, especially the elbows and knees), lichen planus (wrists and mucosae) or pityriasis rosea (trunk).

> Scratching and rubbing of normal skin can lead to secondary changes that may mislead the unwary into diagnosing a primary skin disease. Look for linear excoriations and nodules that spare areas which cannot be reached, eg the central back (Fig. 23).

Morphology of lesions

Following an assessment of the distribution of the rash, then the nature of the individual lesions should be described according to size, shape, content and colour. Many skin conditions have a characteristic morphology, but scratch marks, ulceration and secondary infection may modify the appearance. Focus on a primary or fresh lesion if possible and describe it as a macule, papule, nodule, plaque, vesicle, pustule, blister or abscess. Also describe the margins and surface characteristics, focusing on whether the lesion is round-topped, flat-topped, smooth, umbilicated, rough or scaly. In particular assess whether there is evidence of track formation (eg larva migrans or scabies, Fig. 22), blisters or vesicles (eg autoimmune bullous disorders or acute dermatitis), flat-topped violaceous papules (eg lichen planus), grouped excoriated papules (eg dermatitis herpetiformis) or weals (urticaria). Lastly, note the nature of the underlying skin, eg generalised xerosis (dryness).

> In an itchy patient, look closely for signs of scabies that may easily be missed. Are there burrows and nodules in the typical sites? (See Fig. 22.)

Further discussion

If there is no evidence of an underlying dermatosis that might explain the pruritus, then it is clearly important to be aware of other causes of generalised pruritus such as anaemia, thyroid disease, renal or liver impairment, or haematological malignancy (see Table 4), and to know what to examine for within the other relevant systems. Finally, after other options have been excluded, remember that pruritus can be associated with psychiatric disease.

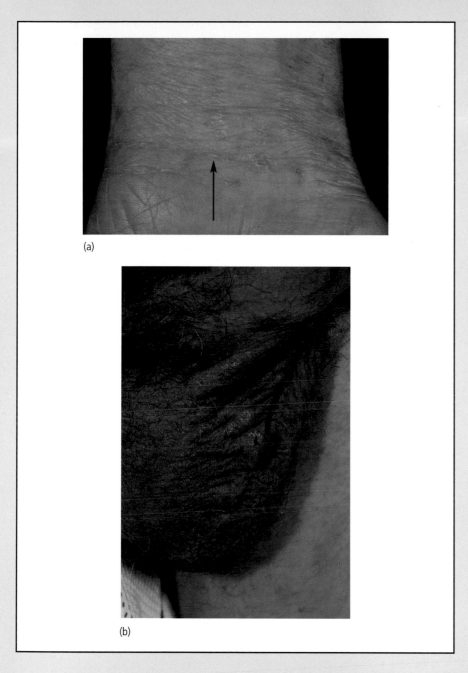

(a)

(b)

◀**Fig. 22** Scabies. Linear burrows, seen here on the flexor surface of the wrist and indicated with an arrow (**a**), and nodules on the male genitalia (**b**) are characteristic signs.

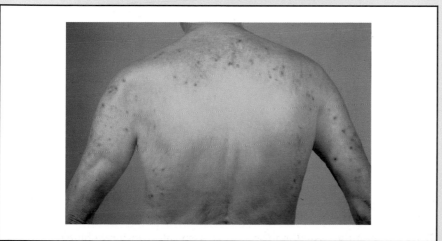

◀**Fig. 23** Skin changes secondary to scratching. There are linear scratch marks and excoriated papules, but the upper central back is spared.

Station 5: Skin Examination   **199**

1.2.4 Alopecia

Instruction

This woman has hair loss. Please examine her scalp and skin.

General features

From the end of the bed look for signs of systemic disease relevant to hair loss, eg signs of thyroid disease and virilisation. See Table 5 for causes of hair loss.

Cutaneous examination

Table 14 summarises the key clinical features when assessing a patient with hair loss. Consider the clinical findings described in Table 14 as you examine the patient.

Distribution of hair loss

The distribution of the hair loss can provide early clues to the underlying aetiology, eg preferential loss from the temples and crown might suggest a diagnosis of androgenetic alopecia. Additional patchy loss from other non-scalp sites would raise the possibility of alopecia areata. Traction alopecia can be patchy (Fig. 24), but is usually most marked along the frontotemporal hairline. Alternatively, there may be diffuse hair loss, which raises different diagnostic possibilities such as a telogen or anagen effluvium, and chronic disease or nutritional deficiencies (see Table 5).

Morphology of scalp

Is the scalp normal or is there evidence of an underlying skin disease? In alopecia areata and where there is diffuse hair loss, the scalp is normal (Fig. 25). In alopecia areata, you may see 'exclamation mark' hairs (broken hairs 3–4 mm in length, tapering and less pigmented proximally). Look for inflammation or scaling of the skin, which may indicate tinea capitis (Figs 26 and 27),

TABLE 14 CAUSES OF ALOPECIA: CLINICAL FINDINGS

Diagnosis	Clinical feature
Androgenetic alopecia	Preferential loss from temples and crown Other signs of androgen excess in women
Traction alopecia	Usually frontotemporal hairline History of braiding
Alopecia areata	Patchy hair loss Normal skin on exposed scalp 'Exclamation mark' hairs May be pitting of nails May see hair loss at other sites
Lichen planus	Patchy hair loss Inflamed or scaling skin on exposed scalp Involvement of skin apart from scalp, especially the wrists May have Wickham's striae in mouth May have abnormalities of nails
Tinea capitis	Patchy hair loss Inflamed or scaling skin on exposed scalp Usually occurs in children, especially those who are black or Indo-Asian May be cervical lymphadenopathy
Discoid lupus erythematosus	Patchy hair loss Inflamed or scaling skin on exposed scalp
Telogen effluvium	Diffuse hair loss Normal skin on any exposed scalp May be Beau's lines on nails
Anagen effluvium	Diffuse hair loss Normal skin on any exposed scalp
Chronic disease/nutritional deficiency	Diffuse hair loss Normal skin on any exposed scalp

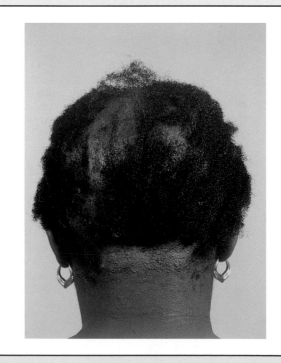

▲**Fig. 24** Traction alopecia. Patchy hair loss in a patient who had braided her hair over many years.

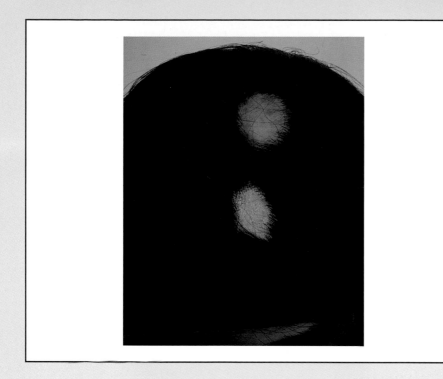

◄**Fig. 25** Alopecia areata. Round/oval, discrete patches of complete hair loss (white hairs may be preferentially spared). 'Exclamation mark' hairs are just visible at the periphery of the upper patch. The skin is entirely normal and follicles would be clearly visible on close inspection.

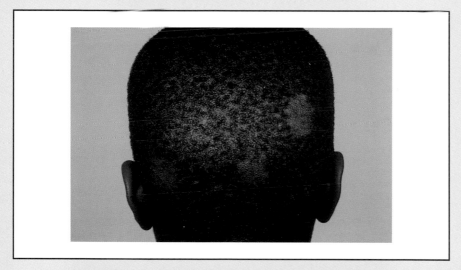

◄**Fig. 26** Tinea capitis. Discrete patches of alopecia with a scaly skin surface that could be accentuated with gentle abrasion. Tinea capitis is commonest in children, especially among black and Asian populations. Skin scrapings and plucked hairs should be sent for direct microscopy and culture.

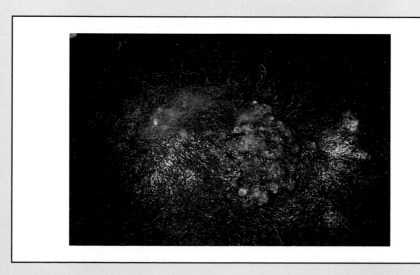

◄**Fig. 27** Fungal kerion. An inflammatory boggy mass associated with alopecia. This is due to an inflammatory response to the fungus and does not reflect secondary bacterial infection. It will respond to systemic antifungal agents alone and does not require incision and drainage.

Station 5: Skin Examination

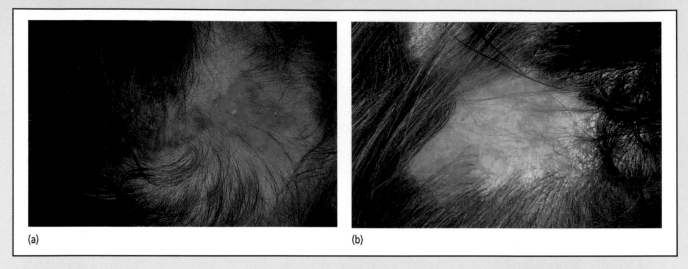

(a)　　　　　　　　　　　　　　　　　　(b)

▲**Fig. 28** Discoid lupus erythematosus. (**a**) Scaly erythematous plaques in the scalp of an adult patient who had similar lesions on the face. (**b**) Scarring alopecia following discoid lupus erythematosus. The scalp is shiny and atrophic and no follicular openings can be seen, indicating scarring in this patient who had discoid lupus. The hair will not regrow.

lupus erythematosus (Fig. 28) or lichen planus. Look for scarring: smooth, shiny skin in which the hair follicles are invisible (Fig. 28b).

Other relevant examination

Check hair-bearing sites other than the scalp, which may be affected by alopecia areata. Look at the remainder of the skin, the nails and the oral cavity, where there may be features of an inflammatory skin disease such as lichen planus or lupus erythematosus. The nails might also be pitted in alopecia areata or show Beau's lines in telogen effluvium. Are there other signs of androgen excess in females, eg acne, hirsutism and virilisation?

> ⚠ Fungal kerions are boggy inflammatory masses that most commonly occur on the scalp of black and Asian children (Fig. 27). They may be mistaken for bacterial abscesses. Samples should be taken to confirm the presence of dermatophytes and to avoid unnecessary incision and drainage.

Further discussion

How would you investigate this patient?

This will depend on your suspected diagnosis and your assessment of whether the process is diffuse or focal/patchy, and also whether there is evidence of an underlying skin disease. In some cases no investigation will be required if there is a strightforward diagnosis from the history and examination, but see Section 1.1.4 (including Table 5) for further discussion.

1.2.5 Hyperpigmentation

Instruction

This woman complains of darkening of her skin. Please examine her skin.

General features

Bearing in mind the possible causes, particularly generalised hyperpigmentation which may be associated with an underlying systemic disease (see Table 8), take time to survey the patient. Is she jaundiced or cachectic? Is there a

dialysis fistula in the forearm or a peritoneal dialysis catheter? Does she have the mask-like facies of systemic sclerosis?

Cutaneous examination

Key points to look for include the following (see Tables 7 and 8).

Facial skin

What is the distribution of the pigmentation problem? Freckles and chloasma are usually symmetrical and present at sites of maximum sun exposure, ie cheeks, chin and upper lip (Fig. 29). The pinnae and nasal tip may be discoloured in ochronosis. Are there any signs of systemic sclerosis? In porphyria cutanea tarda, there may be hypertrichosis in addition to diffuse hyperpigmentation of sun-exposed sites.

Eyes/sclera

Look for the presence of jaundice. Carotenaemia is associated with normal sclera.

Oral mucosa

Is there any pigmentation of the lips/oral mucosa? If so, consider Addison's or Peutz–Jeghers

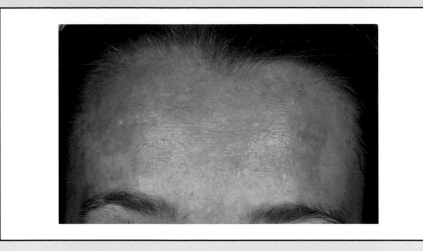

▲**Fig. 29** Melasma. Hyperpigmented patches on the forehead with a normal skin surface. There was similar pigmentation on the cheeks and upper lip, which became more prominent after sun exposure. The patient was taking an oral contraceptive pill.

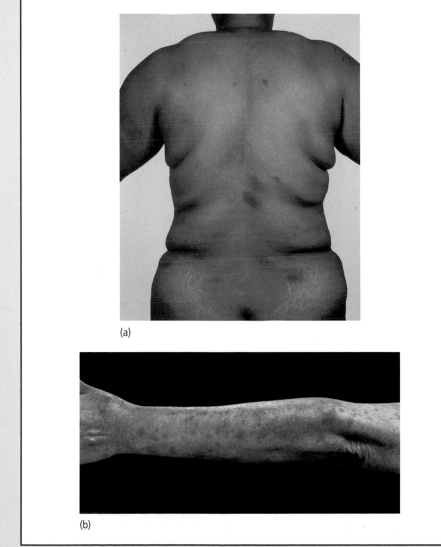

(a)

(b)

syndrome. Rare malignant forms of acanthosis nigricans can also affect the lips.

Nails

Look for signs of an inflammatory skin disease, eg psoriasis (pitting, onycholysis and subungual hyperkeratosis) or features of other skin problems, eg trachyonychia ('sand-blasted' nails) or pterygium (scarring of nail plate) in lichen planus. Any inflammatory skin condition, in particular lichen planus, could leave post-inflammatory hyperpigmentation (Fig. 30). Look for pigmentation changes of the nails, which can be caused by drugs.

Hands

Look for pigment in the palmar creases (classical sign of Addison's disease) and orange discoloration of the palms (carotenaemia). Is there freckling/discoloration of the dorsum of the hands, ie sun-exposed skin? Freckling may be severe and photo-ageing advanced in xeroderma pigmentosum. Drugs such as amiodarone and gold particularly cause discoloration at exposed sites. Haemochromatosis also causes pigmentation of exposed skin. Look for signs of systemic sclerosis, eg sclerodactyly (see Fig. 44a), digital ulcers, tight skin and telangiectases (see Fig. 44b).

Examination of trunk/limbs

What is the distribution of the pigmentation? Acanthosis nigricans

◄**Fig. 30** Two examples of post-inflammatory hyperpigmentation, which can occur after any inflammatory skin disease and particularly after lichen planus. **(a)** Several oval hyperpigmented patches. The patient complained of an intermittent red rash that always occurred at these sites. The history and physical signs are typical of a fixed drug eruption. The trigger was ibuprofen, which was taken occasionally for dysmenorrhoea. **(b)** Grey/brown macules and patches typical of the pigmentation seen after lichen planus. A careful search for one of the preceding, inflammatory lesions should be done.

Station 5: Skin Examination　　**203**

particularly affects flexural sites (Fig. 31). Addison's disease, chronic renal failure, liver disease and malnutrition may cause diffuse hyperpigmentation. Is the rash scaly? Pityriasis versicolor may cause dappled hyperpigmentation on the trunk that is scaly on close inspection (Fig. 32). Is the skin texture normal? Thickening of the skin may occur with post-inflammatory hyperpigmentation, usually secondary to rubbing of the skin, causing lichenification. Systemic sclerosis causes thickening of the dermis and change in skin texture.

Table 7 highlights the key examination features seen in diseases causing localised hyperpigmentation. Examination of other systems may be appropriate, eg abdominal examination in suspected haemochromatosis.

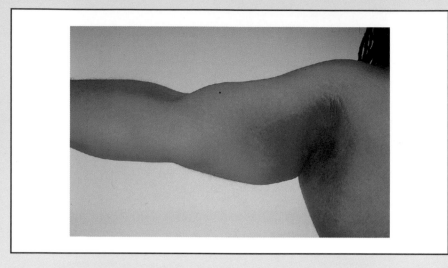

▲**Fig. 31** Acanthosis nigricans. Thickened, warty, hyperpigmented skin most commonly occurs in the flexures, including the axillae as shown.

Further discussion

Excess pigment is usually due to melanin in the skin, produced by melanocytes, as in freckles induced by sunlight. Post-inflammatory pigment is also usually melanin, released from melanocytes in the basal layer following inflammation and damage. Other substances can cause pigment changes, such as excess bilirubin causing jaundice or drug metabolites, eg minocycline.

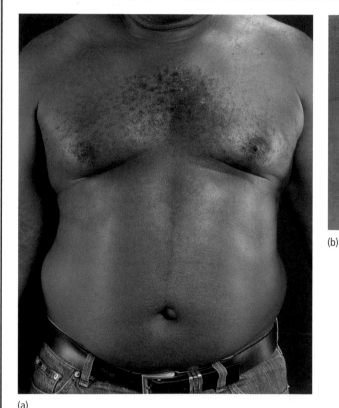

(a)

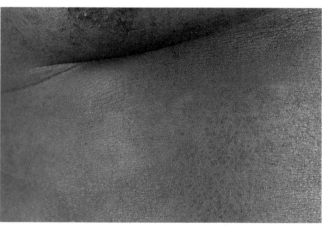

(b)

▲**Fig. 32** Pityriasis versicolor. (**a**) A hyperpigmented eruption on the torso. (**b**) On close inspection, the pigmented macules were scaly (best appreciated by gentle abrasion of the skin surface). Examination of skin scrapings by light microscopy in the clinic revealed *Malassezia* yeasts.

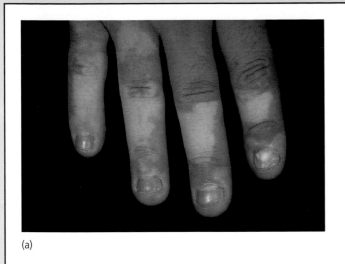

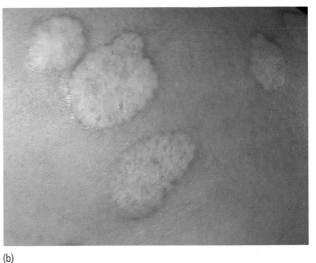

(a)

(b)

▲**Fig. 33** Vitiligo. Well-defined patches of complete depigmentation with a normal skin surface and texture (**a**). This contrasts with post-inflammatory hypopigmentation, in which pigment loss is usually partial, and with lichen sclerosus in which the skin surface is often scaly and wrinkled, and the skin feels thickened on palpation (**b**).

1.2.6 Hypopigmentation

Instruction

This woman has noticed pale patches on her skin. Please examine her skin.

Cutaneous examination

Key points to look for include the following.

- Facial skin: is there pallor of the periorbital skin? This is often seen in vitiligo.

- Nails: look for signs of inflammatory skin conditions, eg psoriasis (pitting, onycholysis and subungual hyperkeratosis), that could leave post-inflammatory hypopigmentation.

- Hands: is there pigment loss on the dorsum of the hands? Vitiligo often affects exposed sites (Fig. 33). Is the skin dry (xerosis)? Hypothyroidism is often associated with vitiligo and may present with dry skin.

- Examination of trunk/limbs.

What is the distribution of the rash?

Pityriasis versicolor may cause dappled hypopigmentation and/or hyperpigmentation on the chest and/or back (Fig. 34). Pityriasis alba is a form of post-inflammatory hyperpigmentation secondary to mild eczema and is seen on the face, usually in children. Vitiligo

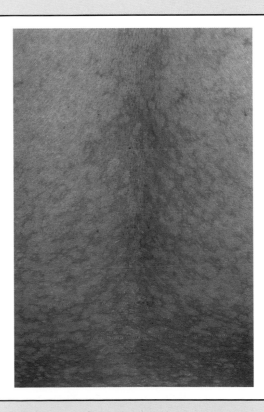

▲**Fig. 34** Pityriasis versicolor. The abnormal areas are the well-defined hypopigmented macules covered in a fine scale that can be accentuated with gentle abrasion. Skin scrapings were stained with Parker's stain, which demonstrated *Malassezia furfur*.

is often symmetrical and distal in distribution. Hypopituitarism causes generalised depigmentation.

Is the pigment completely absent or just paler than normal?

Skin pigmentation is completely absent in vitiligo, but only partially lost in other disorders such as post-inflammatory hypopigmentation.

Is the skin texture normal?

Thickening of the skin sometimes occurs with post-inflammatory hypopigmentation, usually when scratching and rubbing of the skin has caused lichenification. Lichen sclerosus may cause thickening or thinning of the skin (Fig. 33b).

Is the rash scaly?

Pityriasis versicolor is scaly, which can be exacerbated by gentle rubbing of the skin.

Are there inflamed areas?

Look for active areas of inflammation that may represent the primary lesions when hypopigmentation is post-inflammatory (Fig. 35).

Is skin sensation normal?

Leprosy may resemble vitiligo clinically, but the patches are hypoanaesthetic (test sensation to a pinprick) and often scaly.

Further discussion

The causes of hypopigmentation are shown in Table 15. Vitiligo is one of the most common causes. It has an autoimmune basis, and other autoimmune diseases that may occur in association with it include thyroid disease, pernicious anaemia, diabetes mellitus, Addison's disease, premature ovarian failure, chronic active hepatitis and primary biliary cirrhosis.

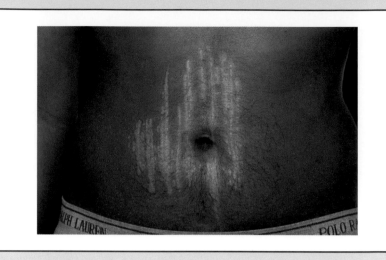

▲**Fig. 35** Post-inflammatory hypopigmentation. The patient had psoriasis. He grazed his abdomen on coral whilst diving. Psoriasis koebnerised into the grazes, leaving post-inflammatory hypopigmentation as it resolved. More typical plaques of psoriasis were visible on the limbs.

Halo naevi are a form of vitiligo where a ring of hypopigmentation appears around a pigmented mole (Fig. 36). They are common in teenagers and young adults, and are completely benign. Areas of hypopigmentation occurring around or within moles in older patients may herald the development of malignant change within the mole.

TABLE 15 CAUSES OF HYPOPIGMENTATION: CLINICAL FEATURES

Diagnosis	Clinical features
Vitiligo	Complete absence of pigment Macules, well-defined edges and no scale Often symmetrical Can be generalised
Post-inflammatory hypopigmentation	Partial pigment loss that is poorly defined Occurs at sites of previous inflammation Look for active primary lesions
Pityriasis versicolor	Dappled, scaly and well-defined macules over the chest and back
Leprosy	Partial pigment loss, hypoanaesthetic patches and may be scaly May be associated with enlarged palpable cutaneous nerves
Halo naevi	Complete loss of pigment in a well-defined area around a mole
Chemical depigmentation	Rubber chemicals via occupational exposure or iatrogenic hydroquinone can both cause 'leucoderma' (clinically identical to vitiligo)
Lichen sclerosus	White wrinkled 'cigarette paper' patches May have associated purpura Classically affects genital skin, but extragenital lichen sclerosus also occurs
Hypopituitarism	Generalised hypopigmentation due to lack of MSH

MSH, melanocyte-stimulating hormone.

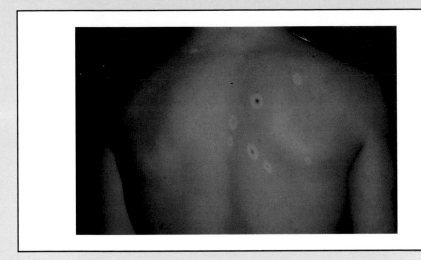

▲**Fig. 36** Halo naevi. Well-defined oval patches of completely depigmented skin that are identical to vitiligo. However, in the centre of each patch is a melanocytic naevus (benign mole) which in some cases has completely depigmented. Halo naevi are most commonly seen in teenagers and young adults, who should be reassured. The skin may re-pigment eventually.

1.2.7 Red legs

Instruction

This man has a skin disease.
Please examine his (red) legs.

General features

- You have been instructed to examine the legs, which are red, but can you see any evidence of skin disease elsewhere?

- Is the patient unwell and does he appear to be in pain or to have a fever? If yes, then cellulitis is most likely, but erythema nodosum (EN) and vasculitis are also possible.

- Thinking of rarities, is there exophthalmos or other features of Graves' disease?

Cutaneous examination

See Table 10 for a list of the most likely diagnoses, and look for the following features.

- Unilateral or bilateral? Cellulitis or deep venous thrombosis (DVT) will almost always be unilateral (Fig. 37). Vasculitis will be

bilateral. Eczema and EN could be either.

- Is there purpura and is it palpable? Palpable purpura is the hallmark of vasculitis, but be aware that extravasation of red cells can occur when the skin is inflamed, particularly on the lower legs due to gravity. In this situation there are usually tiny, non-palpable, purpuric macules, with evidence of another dermatosis, eg eczema. Severe cellulitis can also look purpuric on occasion (Fig. 38).

- Is there scaling or flaking of the skin? If yes, eczema is likely (Fig. 39).

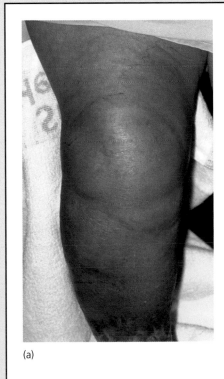

(a)

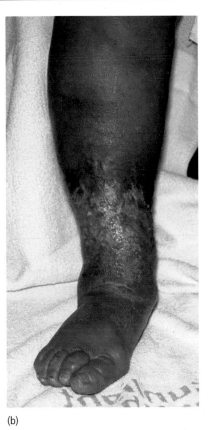

(b)

▲**Fig. 37** Cellulitis complicating varicose eczema. There is erythema of the lower leg which over 24 hours tracked up over the knee onto the thigh (**a**). The skin was hot to touch, very painful and associated with malaise and fever. The skin on the lower leg had been itchy, inflamed and red for several months (**b**) and acted as a route of infection entry resulting in cellulitis.

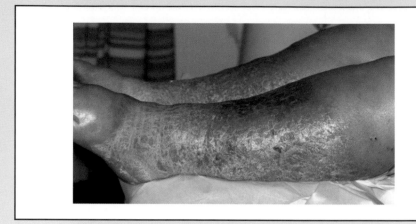

▲**Fig. 39** Gravitational eczema. Bilateral red, swollen, scaly, itchy legs are commonly seen in the elderly. In the context of venous hypertension and varicose veins, varicose or venous eczema is the diagnosis. However, leg oedema of any cause, eg due to cardiac failure, may cause eczema and in this context, if the veins are normal, the terms 'gravitational' or 'stasis' eczema are used. Treating the underlying oedema and venous hypertension, eg with compression, is just as important as treating the eczema.

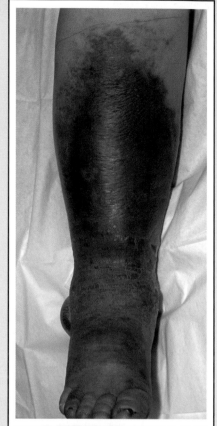

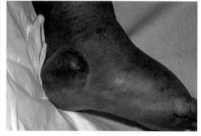

▲**Fig. 38** Cellulitis complicated by blisters and purpura. Note that the purpuric area is confluent and the other leg was unaffected, in contrast to the symmetrical multifocal purpura that would be seen in a vasculitis.

- Is the skin hot and/or tender to touch? If yes, cellulitis or EN is most likely.

- Is there a leg ulcer, a wound on the leg, eczema or evidence of athlete's foot? These all provide potential entry points for infection in cellulitis (Fig. 37). Is there oedema? Oedema of any cause, including lymphoedema, is also a risk factor for cellulitis.

- Is the erythema confluent or in several discrete patches? Cellulitis and varicose eczema will usually be confluent, whereas vasculitic lesions are discrete (purpuric macules or papules) and EN is discrete (red tender nodules, Fig. 40).

- Are there any blisters? A very acute contact dermatitis can blister. Severe cellulitis and vasculitis can occasionally blister, particularly if there is pre-existing oedema (Fig. 38).

- Is there any joint swelling? This can occur in EN, particularly the ankles.

- Are the calf muscles tender? If yes, then DVT is possible. The skin may look red or dusky due to venous congestion but would otherwise be normal.

- Are there any varicose veins or peripheral oedema, which might have triggered varicose/stasis eczema?

- Are there any other features of venous hypertension, eg hyperpigmentation (Fig. 41) and lipodermatosclerosis (Fig. 55)?

- Are there pink plaques on shin with a *peau d'orange* surface? If yes, then consider pretibial myxoedema (Fig. 42).

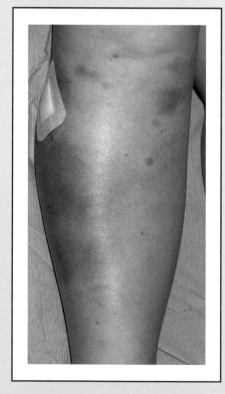

▲**Fig. 40** Erythema nodosum. Painful red nodules on the lower legs. The inflammation in erythema nodosum is deep, within fat, so the skin surface is often flat but the nodules can be palpated.

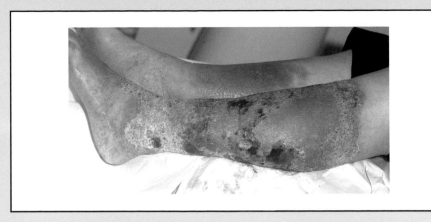

▲**Fig. 41** Varicose eczema and haemosiderin deposition. The leg in the foreground shows erythema and scaling, consistent with eczema. The other lower leg shows red/brown hyperpigmention, typical of haemosiderin deposition secondary to varicose veins, which were visible when the patient stood up.

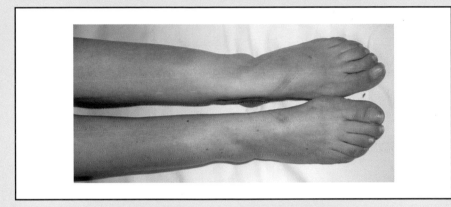

▲**Fig. 42** Pretibial myxoedema. Asymptomatic, symmetrical, oedematous, erythematous plaques on the shins in a female patient with Graves' disease. On close inspection, the skin had a *peau d'orange* surface.

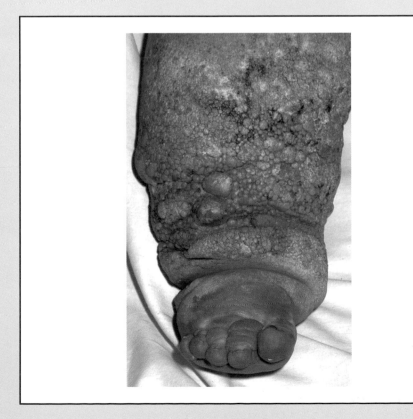

Further discussion

If the final diagnosis is eczema, how can you distinguish endogenous from allergic eczema?

Consider features in the history, eg use of creams, medicaments or elasticated bandages, which make allergic contact dermatitis a possibility. It may be difficult to distinguish between these possibilities clinically, but there may be clues such as a sharp cut-off of the rash where bandages or dressings finish. Patch tests will aid identification of the allergen so it can be avoided (see Section 3.3).

Why does cellulitis of the legs occur?

It is very important to find a reason, and failure to do so may lead to recurrent infections that damage the lymphatics and eventually lead to lymphoedema (Fig. 43). Leg ulcers and wounds will be obvious, but look between the toes for tinea pedis; if present, it needs to be treated. Leg oedema is another important risk factor that may need to be addressed.

What would you do if the patient has recurrent episodes of cellulitis?

In addition to finding and treating any portals of entry for infection, consider prophylactic antibiotics. As a guide, patients who have two or more episodes in one year should be offered either penicillin or erythromycin 250–500 mg bd (choose the lower dose in patients who weigh <75 kg).

◀**Fig. 43** Lymphoedema. A very severe example showing the secondary skin changes that occur: erythema, hyperkeratosis and scaling, papillomatosis and deep skin creases. The aetiology in this case was multifactorial but recurrent episodes of cellulitis, which damage lymphatics, was an important component.

Station 5: Skin Examination

1.2.8 Lumps and bumps

General features

Many possible conditions could be
used as the basis for a scenario such
as this, but the most likely causes
of multiple lesions are discussed
here. However, before focusing on
individual lesions, take time to
inspect the patient from the foot
of the bed. Note the distribution of
lesions and general features about
the patient that may provide clues
to the underlying diagnosis, eg
kyphoscoliosis and macrocephaly
in neurofibromatosis.

Cutaneous examination

A complete cutaneous examination,
including the palms, soles, finger
and toe nails, should be performed.
Inspect and palpate the lesions,
noting their distribution and
running through the following
list of differentials. Once you
have the diagnosis, focus your
examination to identify additional
clinical features. The following
lesions may be multiple.

Neurofibromas

Common benign tumours composed
of neuromesenchymal tissue:
skin/tan/brown coloured, soft and
rubbery papules or nodules that
may be pedunculated. They may be
solitary but multiple lesions occur
as part of neurofibromatosis (see
Table 16 for other clinical features).

Angiofibromas

Skin- to pink/red-coloured shiny
papules composed of a proliferation
of fibroblasts and an increased
number of blood vessels. Multiple
lesions on the cheeks, nose and
chin occur in 75% of patients with
tuberous sclerosis (TS). They begin
to develop within the first few years
of life. Historically these lesions
were known as adenoma sebaceum,
but they are not adenomas nor
sebaceous in origin. See Table 17
for clinical features of TS.

Xanthomas

Yellow/orange macules, papules,
plaques and nodules (composed of
lipid-laden dermal macrophages).
Cutaneous xanthomas may be
associated with hyperlipidaemia or
monoclonal gammopathy. The type
and distribution are clues to the
underlying cause (see Table 18).

Lipomas

Common, asymptomatic, benign
neoplasms of mature fat cells. They
are soft, rubbery, subcutaneous
nodules with normal overlying
skin. They occur most commonly
on the proximal limbs but can occur
at any site. Usually they are a few
centimetres in diameter but can be

TABLE 16 CLINICAL FEATURES OF NEUROFIBROMATOSIS TYPE 1 (VON RECKLINGHAUSEN'S DISEASE)

Clinical features		Frequency (%)
Cutaneous	Variable numbers of neurofibromas	90
	Café-au-lait macules (>6)	80
	Axillary and/or inguinal freckling	80
	Plexiform neurofibromas (large, drooping, 'bag-like' masses)	25
Ocular	Lisch nodules (pigmented hamartomas of the iris)	90
	Hypertelorism	25
Skeletal	Macrocephaly	50
	Kyphoscoliosis	10
Other features	Hypertension	30
	Seizures	5
	Renal artery stenosis	2
	Phaeochromocytoma	1

TABLE 17 CLINICAL FEATURES OF TS

Clinical features		Frequency (%)
Cutaneous	Hypopigmented macules	90
	Periungual fibromas (Koenen tumours)	80
	Multiple facial angiofibromas	75
	Shagreen 'leather' patch (a connective tissue naevus that is a skin-coloured plaque with an uneven surface, often on the lower back).	50
	Café-au-lait macules (usually <6)	30
Ocular	Retinal hamartomas	40
	Achromatic retinal patches	40
Dental	Enamel pits	90
	Gingival fibromas	35
Other features	Seizures	90
	Mental retardation	50

TABLE 18 CLINICAL FEATURES AND ASSOCIATIONS OF XANTHOMAS

Type	Clinical features	Distribution	Associations
Eruptive xanthomas	Multiple red/yellow papules	Extensor surfaces, buttocks and hands	Hypertriglyceridaemia Lipoprotein lipase deficiency or endogenous familial hypertriglyceridaemia Exacerbating factors include diabetes, obesity, alcohol abuse, oestrogen replacement and retinoid therapy
Tuberous xanthomas	Red/yellow papules/nodules (up to 3 cm diameter)	Extensor surface (elbows and knees)	Hypercholesterolaemia Familial hypercholesterolaemia Dysbetalipoproteinaemia (sufferers also have plane xanthomas of the palmar creases in two-thirds of cases)
Tendinous xanthomas	Smooth nodules with normal overlying skin	Achilles tendons and extensor tendons of the hand, knees and elbows	Familial hypercholesterolaemia Dysbetalipoproteinaemia Hepatic cholestasis (biliary atresia and primary biliary cirrhosis)
Plane xanthomas and xanthelasma (plane xanthomas of the eyelids)	Yellow/orange macules and plaques	Intertriginous (antecubital fossae, finger web spaces)	Familial hypercholesterolaemia (homozygous)
		Palmar creases Palms/soles initially Any site	Dysbetalipoproteinaemia Hepatic cholestasis Monoclonal gammopathy (lymphoma, multiple myeloma, chronic myelomonocytic leukaemia, Castleman's disease)

TABLE 19 CAUSES OF MULTIPLE LIPOMAS

Familial multiple lipomatosis (hereditary multiple lipomas)[1]
Dercum's disease (multiple painful lipomas, which typically affect middle-aged women)
Proteus syndrome
Madelung's disease (benign symmetric lipomatosis): mainly appear on the neck and upper torso
Gardner's syndrome (colonic polyps, epidermoid cysts and osteomas) – rare

1. Commonest.

larger. There may be one or many lesions (see Table 19 for associations).

Basal cell carcinoma and squamous cell carcinoma

Multiple basal cell carcinomas and squamous cell carcinomas may be seen in organ transplant recipients (the latter are more common in this setting) and fair-skinned individuals with a history of chronic intense sun exposure. They may also be seen in some rare genetic syndromes with either mutations in tumour-suppressor genes or deficiencies in DNA repair (see Sections 2.20 and 2.21 for clinical descriptions).

Further discussion

Neurofibromatosis type 1

A relatively common (incidence of 1 in 3,500 people) autosomal dominant disorder caused by a mutation in the gene for neurofibromin on chromosome 17. The spontaneous mutation rate is approximately 50% (Table 16).

> Café-au-lait macules are common: 10% of unaffected individuals may have between one and five of them.

Tuberous sclerosis

An autosomal dominant disorder (with spontaneous mutation rate of about 75%) caused by mutations in two tumour-suppressor genes (*TSC1* and *TSC2*). The incidence is 1 in 10,000 live births. In addition to the key clinically apparent features (Table 17), hamartomas may be found in internal organs including the brain, kidneys and heart. Wolff–Parkinson–White syndrome can also be a feature.

> Hypopigmented macules are the earliest manifestation of TS and are usually present at birth. Appearances can be very subtle (especially on pale skin) and a Wood's lamp is helpful to identify them. 'Ash-leaf' macules describe one configuration that is rounded at one end and tapered at the other. A single macule may occur in up to 5% of non-affected infants. 'Confetti' macules are multiple and small.

Xanthomas

See Table 18.

> 🔑 Patients with xanthelasma should be investigated for hyperlipidaemia, but this will only be present in 50% of cases.

Lipomas

See Table 19.

1.2.9 Telangiectases

Instruction

Please examine this woman's skin (multiple telangiectases).

General features

As ever, although you have been asked to examine the skin, take an initial general look for clues that may reveal the cause of the telangiectases, bearing in mind the possible diagnoses (Table 20). Is the patient jaundiced, suggesting liver disease, or is she pregnant? Does the patient have 'scleroderma facies'? As she moves, are there features of cerebellar ataxia?

Cutaneous examination

Key points to look for in a dermatological examination include the following.

Hands

Look for signs of SS or CREST, eg Raynaud's phenomenon, sclerodactyly, ulcers or calcinosis (Fig. 44), and for signs of dermatomyositis, eg nail-fold telangiectases or Gottron's papules (see Fig. 20). Is there palmar erythema, suggesting liver disease or pregnancy? Look for clubbing or cyanosis, which could be a sign of a pulmonary arteriovenous (AV) fistula in hereditary haemorrhagic telangiectasia (HHT).

Facial skin

Are there telangiectases on the face and, if so, are they the only abnormality, as in normal physiological telangiectases? Look for other features, such as papules and pustules in rosacea (see Fig. 12); a beaked nose and tight shiny skin in SS and CREST; freckles and

TABLE 20 CAUSES OF TELONGIECTASES AND CLINICAL FEATURES	
Diagnosis	**Clinical features**
Spider telangiectases	Blanching dilated blood vessels radiating from a central feeding vessel Common on upper body and face May be normal Multiple lesions associated with pregnancy/liver disease
Systemic sclerosis (SS) and CREST	Smooth, tight, shiny skin associated with other features of SS, eg beaked nose, microstomia, sclerodactyly and Raynaud's phenomenon
Rosacea	Telangiectatic erythema of facial skin with papules and pustules
Dermatomyositis	Telangiectases affecting nail-folds, eyelids and hands Associated with other signs, eg Gottron's papules, violaceous/swollen eyelids, proximal muscle weakness
Hereditary haemorrhagic telangiectasia (Osler–Weber–Rendu syndrome)	Autosomal dominant Numerous telangiectases at many sites, particularly the face, lips, nail-beds and mucous membranes Associated visceral arteriovenous malformations: may cause cyanosis/clubbing in lungs May be associated with hepatomegaly or anaemia due to bleeding
Ataxia telangiectasia	Autosomal recessive Telangiectases (particularly conjunctivae, ears, eyelids and cheeks), cerebellar ataxia, combined immunodeficiency and cancer susceptibility
Radiodermatitis	Telangiectases localised within pale atrophic scar tissue
Excess steroid use	Atrophy and telangiectases
Photo-ageing	Telangiectases seen mainly on face
Xeroderma pigmentosum	Premature skin ageing, multiple freckles, skin tumours/scars
Venous hypertension	Legs
Drugs	Such as calcium antagonists
Idiopathic	

CREST, *c*alcinosis, *R*aynaud's phenomenon, (*o*)*e*sophageal involvement, *s*clerodactyly, *t*elangiectasia.

photo-ageing in xeroderma pigmentosum; violaceous swollen eyelids in dermatomyositis. Look at the patient's eyes: conjunctival telangiectases occur in ataxia telangiectasia.

Mouth/mucous membranes

Is there microstomia, as in SS and CREST? Establish if telangiectases are prominent on the tongue/lips/buccal cavity (Fig. 44). The mucous membranes are almost always involved in HHT.

Examination of trunk/limbs

What is the distribution of the telangiectases? Spider telangiectases in normal people are usually confined to the upper half of the body.

Lesions in HHT may occur at any site, but preferentially also have the same distribution. In SS and CREST, telangiectases are particularly seen on the hands and face (Fig. 44).

What is the morphology of the telangiectases?

Spider telangiectases tend to be individual lesions, whereas telangiectases in HHT often form large asymmetrical sheets and may be more nodular, linear or punctate, and may pulsate. Consider the alternative diagnosis of angiokeratomas if there are small, raised, red/purple-coloured papules. In angiokeratoma corporis diffusum (Anderson–Fabry disease) multiple angiokeratomas occur, particularly

over the lower abdomen and pelvic girdle area. This condition is associated with acroparaesthesia, renal failure, ischaemic heart disease and cerebrovascular accidents.

Further discussion

What are the other clinical features of SS?

Features to look for include hypertension (may be associated with renal disease), musculoskeletal problems (arthritis/myositis), abdominal swelling/tenderness (intestinal hypomobility and bacterial overgrowth), liver disease (primary biliary cirrhosis), skin ulcers, vitiligo and respiratory problems

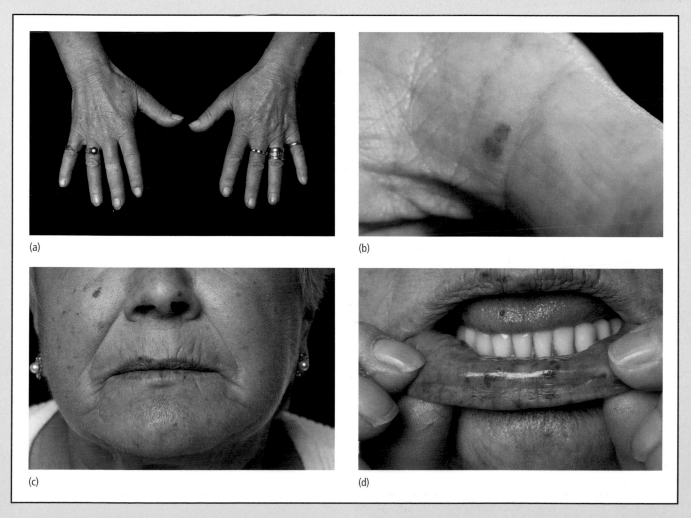

(a)

(b)

(c)

(d)

▲ **Fig. 44** CREST syndrome. The hands demonstrate sclerodactyly (**a**) and telangiectases (**b**). There were also telangiectases on the face (**c**), lips and oral mucosa (**d**).

(pulmonary fibrosis). If invited to ask any questions, enquire about swallowing problems (there are oesophageal symptoms in 45–60% of cases). CREST is a variant of SS in which there is calcinosis cutis, Raynaud's phenomenon, oesophageal dysmotility, sclerodactyly and telangiectasia.

What are the potential complications of HHT?

Recurrent epistaxis is common and may be the presenting symptom. Gastrointestinal bleeding may also occur. Any site of recurrent bleeding may lead to iron-deficiency anaemia, so be prepared to discuss the approach to this common presentation if the examiner wants to lead you away from the rarity of HHT. Pulmonary AV fistulae may cause cyanosis and dyspnoea. Liver cirrhosis due to AV fistulae has been reported.

1.2.10 Purpura

Instruction

Please examine this (elderly) man's legs (purpura).

General features

Purpura is skin discoloration due to extravasation of red blood cells into the skin. Causes to consider are listed in Table 21. When purpura is inflammatory, ie vasculitis, the patient may appear unwell. If due to simple haemorrhage, ie non-inflammatory, there may be features of liver disease (such as jaundice or abdominal distension due to ascites), the patient may be cushingoid or there may be macroglossia in amyloidosis.

Cutaneous examination

A key decision is deciding whether the purpuric lesions are inflammatory, ie vasculitic, or non-inflammatory. The morphology will help.

- Inflammatory purpura: in very early lesions look for blanching erythema due to inflammation. Subsequently lesions become purpuric and palpable (Fig. 45). Other signs of vasculitis that may be seen include splinter haemorrhages, nail-fold infarcts, haemorrhagic vesicles, pustules, subcutaneous or ulcerated nodules, ulcers and livedo reticularis.

- Non-inflammatory purpura: there is no preceding erythema and the lesions are not palpable (Fig. 46). The size of the lesions helps to determine aetiology: petechiae (ie 1–2 mm lesions) are seen in patients with platelet defects and increased vascular pressure; lesions >1 cm are seen in coagulation abnormalities and in cases with a lack of dermal support.

TABLE 21 CAUSES OF PURPURA

Category	Cause	Examples
Inflammatory	Vasculitis	Henoch–Schönlein purpura Idiopathic Connective tissue diseases Microscopic polyangiitis Wegener's granulomatosis Mixed essential cryoglobulinaemia
Non-inflammatory	Coagulation defects	Inherited, eg haemophilia Disseminated intravascular coagulation Liver disease[1] Anticoagulant therapy[1] Vitamin K deficiency
	Platelet defects	Thrombocytopenia Idiopathic Autoimmune rheumatic disorders Disseminated intravascular coagulation Hypersplenism Bone marrow damage (eg drugs or malignancy) Drugs (eg quinine, aspirin, thiazides, sulphonamides) Abnormal function Von Willebrand's disease
	Mechanical causes	Raised intravascular pressure Coughing and vomiting Venous hypertension Gravitational
	Lack of dermal support	Senile purpura[1] Corticosteroid therapy[1] Cushing's disease Scurvy Systemic amyloidosis Disorders of connective tissue (eg Ehlers–Danlos syndrome)
	Vascular occlusion	Cryoglobulinaemia and cryofibrinogenaemia (may also cause vasculitis depending on the properties of the cryoprotein) Hyperviscosity (eg Waldenström's macroglobulinaemia, paraproteinaemia) Emboli

1. Commonest causes.

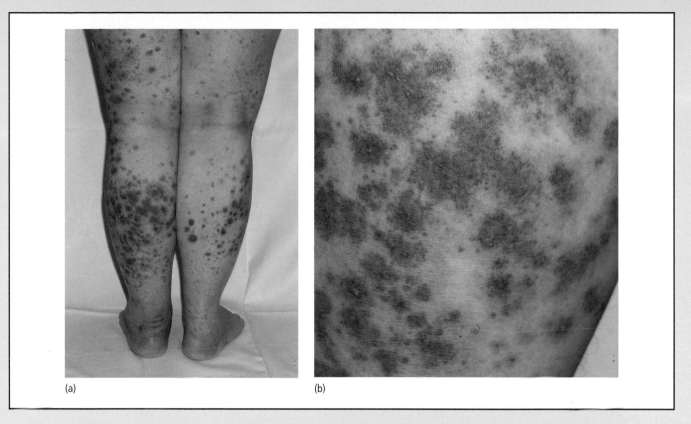

▲ **Fig. 45** Vasculitis of the skin typically affects the lower limbs (**a**). Palpable purpura is the classical sign of vasculitis and requires palpation of the skin to demonstrate failure to blanche with pressure but the appearance in (**b**) is typical.

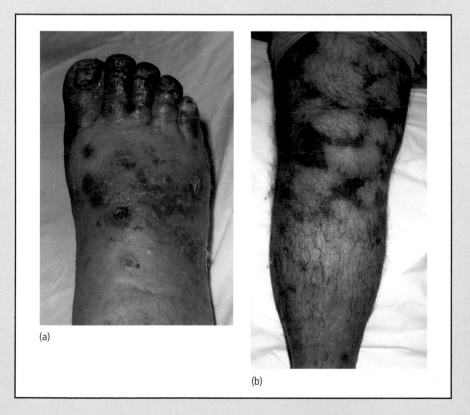

◀**Fig. 46** Cryofibrinogenaemia. This man initially presented with purpuric macules on the feet which ulcerated (**a**). During an episode of sepsis, more severe and widespread purpura was seen (**b**) followed by skin necrosis and ulceration. Skin biopsies showed occlusion of the cutaneous microvasculature with fibrin thrombi. Cryofibrinogenaemia and cryoglobulinaemia are both characterised by cryoprecipitates. Cryofibrinogen is consumed by the process of blood coagulation, so is only detectable in plasma, unlike cryoglobulins which are detectable in serum and plasma. In this patient repeat tests for cryoglobulins were negative and the diagnosis was eventually made once plasma rather than serum was sent to the laboratory.

> Palpable purpura suggests a vasculitic aetiology.

Distribution

Check the following, as the site of the purpura will indicate the cause.

- Sites of trauma, eg extensor forearms, thighs and lower legs: most likely due to coagulation and platelet defects, and a lack of dermal support.

- Eyelids: coughing, vomiting and amyloidosis.

- Ears, nose and peripheries: cryoglobulinaemia and cryofibrinogenaemia.

- Dependent sites, ie lower legs: vasculitis and venous hypertension.

Look for the following clues.

- Cutaneous atrophy: suggests steroid purpura.

- Photodamage: suggests actinic 'senile' purpura.

- Linear or geographical shapes (trauma): consider coagulation and platelet defects and lack of dermal support.

- Necrosis and ulceration: suggests vascular occlusion (Fig. 46) or severe vasculitis.

Further discussion

What is your diagnosis?

It may not be possible to arrive at a single diagnosis, but hopefully it should be possible to differentiate between the main groups of causes on the basis of the clinical findings. As always, suggest common causes before rarities: 'I am not sure, but the commonest causes of

purpura on the arms of an elderly man include senile purpura, corticosteroid use and anticoagulant therapy . . .'

How would you proceed if you thought the purpura were due to vasculitis?

Assess whether there is multisystem involvement on the basis of history, full physical examination, urine examination (dipstick for proteinuria and haematuria) and blood tests (including renal function, inflammatory markers and autoimmune/vasculitic serology, especially antineutrophil cytoplasmic antibodies and cryoglobulins). The diagnosis of vasculitis may need to be confirmed by biopsy of the skin and/or other affected organs. See Section 2.25 for further discussion.

1.2.11 Lesion on the shin

Instruction

This man has a lesion on his right shin. Please examine his skin.

General features

> Malignancy should be suspected in any patient with a history of a solitary skin lesion. The incidence of skin cancer is rising in the UK and the lower leg is the commonest site of melanoma in women.

The history given suggests a single lesion and your priority is to confirm or exclude skin cancer. Given that sun-induced skin damage is a potent risk factor for cutaneous malignancy, look at the patient's face for evidence of this, eg wrinkles, actinic keratoses, solar lentigines and solar elastosis. However, there are other diagnostic possibilities to consider (Table 22). Look for signs of Graves' ophthalmopathy or hyperthyroidism/hypothyroidism, which might indicate pretibial myxoedema (Fig. 42). Look for any clues that indicate diabetes, eg insulin pens or a glucose monitor, which may suggest necrobiosis lipoidica.

Cutaneous examination

How many skin lesions?

If there is only one, then you really must think of skin cancer.

TABLE 22 CAUSES OF A SINGLE SKIN LESION ON THE LOWER LEG

Cause	Example
Tumours	Basal cell carcinoma Bowen's disease Squamous cell carcinoma Malignant melanoma Kaposi's sarcoma
Inflammatory	Discoid eczema[1] Venous eczema
Endocrine	Necrobiosis lipoidica Pretibial myxoedema
Others	Granuloma annulare Erythema nodosum[1]

1. Usually multiple lesions.

In inflammatory diseases, there will usually be more than one single lesion and there will often be a history of itching (eczema or lichen planus) or pain (erythema nodosum). There may be more than one lesion of necrobiosis lipoidica.

Distribution

The position of the involved area can be a clue to the underlying aetiology. Involvement of the gaiter region, just above the medial malleolus, along with evidence of venous disease (eg varicosities) would suggest a diagnosis of venous eczema. Tender red subcutaneous lumps lying over the anterior shin would be in keeping with erythema nodosum (Figs 40 and 76). Necrobiosis lipoidica also tends to occur on the shin. It is vital to examine all the skin and not just the lesion in isolation: you may find other areas of involvement that implicate an inflammatory dermatosis such as discoid eczema.

Morphology of the lesion(s)

Many skin lesions have a characteristic morphology. The features of basal cell carcinoma, squamous cell carcinoma and melanoma are described in Sections 2.20, 2.21 and 2.22, respectively. Necrobiosis lipoidica presents as red/brown plaques with a waxy, shiny, yellow and telangiectatic centre that sometimes ulcerates. Pretibial myxoedema presents as erythematous plaques, often with a *peau d'orange* surface, on the shins (Fig. 42). Bowen's disease and discoid eczema are both characterised by erythematous scaly patches or plaques, but the latter is usually multiple and itchy. Kaposi's sarcomas are red/purple plaques. Erythema nodosum is described in Section 2.11.

Other relevant examination

Check for regional lymphadenopathy in the popliteal fossa and groin.

Further discussion

How would you confirm the diagnosis?

A biopsy should be performed if there is diagnostic uncertainty or if the lesion is a suspected tumour.

How would you manage a basal cell carcinoma/squamous cell carcinoma/melanoma?

See Sections 2.20, 2.21 and 2.22 for fuller discussion, but in most instances surgical excision is the primary treatment of choice. Important information to consider when reading the histology report is the histological diagnosis, the grade or stage of tumour and whether it has been completely excised.

1.2.12 Non-pigmented lesion on the face

Instruction

This woman has a lesion on the face that has been present for 6 months. Please examine her.

General features

In this scenario there are a range of differential diagnoses. Your priority in dealing with a single lesion such as this, which has been present for a relatively short period of time, is to identify or exclude skin cancer.

Thinking of lesions in terms of pigmented or non-pigmented groups helps to narrow the differential, but before homing in on the patient's face take the time to compose yourself and run through the possibilities (see Tables 23 and 24). Does the patient have fair or dark skin? Fair-skinned individuals have an increased risk of skin cancer. Is there a single obvious lesion or multiple lesions? Are there any surgical scars, possibly from excision of previous skin cancers? How old is the patient? Skin cancers are more common in the elderly.

Cutaneous examination

The skin of the face should be systematically examined in as good a light as possible. Remember to check the ears, behind the ears, the neck and the lips.

- Note the location of any lesions: is there one or are there several?

- Are there any surgical scars?

- Look for evidence of solar damage, such as wrinkles, irregular pigmentation, solar elastosis or actinic keratoses (Fig. 47).

Now focus on the particular lesion and consider the following.

- Colour: is the colour uniform or variegated?

TABLE 23 DIFFERENTIAL DIAGNOSIS OF NON-PIGMENTED LESIONS ON THE FACE

Type of lesion	Diagnoses
Dysplastic and neoplastic lesions	Actinic keratoses (Fig. 47) Squamous cell carcinoma *in situ* (Bowen's disease) Basal cell carcinoma (Fig. 48) Squamous cell carcinoma (Fig. 47) Keratoacanthoma (Fig. 49)
Benign lesions	Epidermoid cyst Pilar cyst Sebaceous hyperplasia

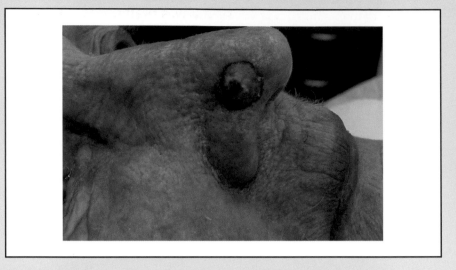

▲ **Fig. 47** A squamous cell carcinoma on the right nasal tip (the clinical extent of the tumour is marked). Note the indurated base and keratotic surface. The skin shows evidence of severe photo-ageing; wrinkles, solar elastosis (yellow waxy areas) and actinic keratoses (erythematous rough patches).

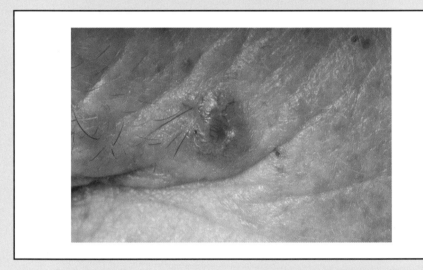

▲ **Fig. 48** A typical nodular basal cell carcinoma. Smooth, shiny, flesh-coloured papule with telangiectases.

- Size: the diameter should be measured in millimetres.

- Elevation: is it a macule, papule, plaque or nodule?

- Surface characteristics: is it smooth, rough, scaly, warty, crusted or ulcerated? Are there any other surface features, eg telangiectases?

- Palpate the lesion: is it soft or firm? Is it mobile or fixed?

Check for regional lymphadenopathy if neoplasia is suspected. When you have finished, explain to the examiner that you would ideally like to perform a complete cutaneous examination: it is common to find coincidental skin cancers in patients with solar damage.

Further discussion
See Table 23. For clinical descriptions of preneoplastic and neoplastic conditions, see Sections 2.20, 2.21 and 2.22.

Epidermoid cyst
This is the most common cutaneous cyst, often called (incorrectly) sebaceous cyst. It frequently occurs on the face and upper trunk as circumscribed nodules a few millimetres to several centimetres in diameter that may feel fluctuant on palpation. On close inspection there may be a visible central punctum, representing the follicle from which the cyst is derived and through which the contents may sometimes leak. Multiple lesions may be seen in patients with a history of acne vulgaris or Gardner's syndrome.

Pilar (trichilemmal) cyst
This is less common than epidermoid cysts, but is often impossible to distinguish from them on clinical examination. Most pilar cysts occur on the scalp. They may be single or multiple. Multiple lesions may be inherited in an autosomal dominant way.

Sebaceous hyperplasia
A common lesion caused by benign enlargement and overgrowth of the sebaceous glands. It takes the form of single or multiple yellowish papules, often with a central indentation and overlying telangiectases. It most commonly occurs on the face.

🔑 Sebaceous hyperplasia can be difficult to distinguish from basal cell carcinoma and a biopsy may be necessary.

⚠️ Uncommonly, malignant melanoma may be devoid of pigment (amelanotic) and present as an erythematous or ulcerated nodule.

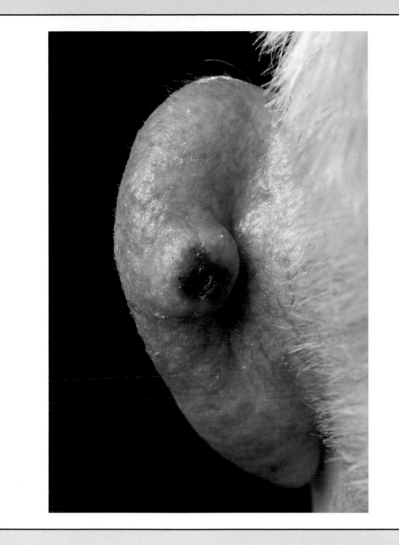

▲ **Fig. 49** Keratoacanthoma. A symmetrical dome-shaped tumour with a central keratin plug. A squamous cell carcinoma may look similar but keratoacanthomas are characterised by their rapid growth followed by spontaneous involution. In practice, most are treated as squamous cell carcinomas and excised.

1.2.13 A pigmented lesion on the face

General features and cutaneous examination

Your approach should be similar to that described in Section 1.2.12. In this case, your priority must be to identify or exclude a melanoma. The differential diagnoses to consider are listed in Table 24.

Further discussion

Solar lentigo

Found in almost all white people over 60 years of age and caused by sun damage. Well-defined yellow, light brown or tan macules without pigment variegation. Common sites include the face and backs of the hands.

Seborrhoeic keratosis

These are very common benign lesions that become more frequent

Why has this patient developed skin cancer?

Note evidence of solar damage indicating excess ultraviolet exposure, which is the most likely risk factor in the formation of a non-melanoma skin cancer. Also comment on the colour of the patient's eyes and hair; if grey, ask what the original colour was. If given the opportunity, ask about excess sun exposure, which may take the form of outdoor hobbies or work, sunbathing, sunbed use and living or working abroad. In the latter group, it is common to see skin cancer in military personnel who were posted to North Africa or the Far East during or after the Second World War.

TABLE 24 DIFFERENTIAL DIAGNOSIS OF PIGMENTED LESIONS ON THE FACE

Type of lesion	Diagnoses
Neoplastic lesions	Malignant melanoma (Fig. 50) Lentigo maligna (a subtype of malignant melanoma *in situ*) or lentigo maligna melanoma (Fig. 51) Pigmented basal cell carcinoma
Benign lesions	Solar lentigo Seborrhoeic keratosis Haemangioma: purple/black lesions (biopsy may be needed to exclude malignant melanoma) (Fig. 52) Benign naevus: symmetrical, regular border and uniform pigmentation. May be macular, papular or papillomatous. Intradermal naevi often have hairs growing from them

For discussion of the clinical features of neoplastic lesions, see Sections 2.20, 2.21 and 2.22.

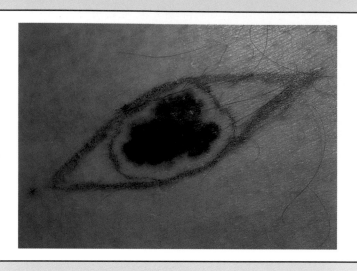

with increasing age. They are well-defined pigmented papules or plaques, often with a greasy 'stuck-on' appearance and a rough warty surface. Their colour may vary from flesh-coloured to black, but is usually a shade of brown. Lesions are often multiple.

If there is any diagnostic doubt, it is better to biopsy than miss a melanoma.

▲**Fig. 50** Malignant melanoma. Note the asymmetry, irregular border and variation in colour.

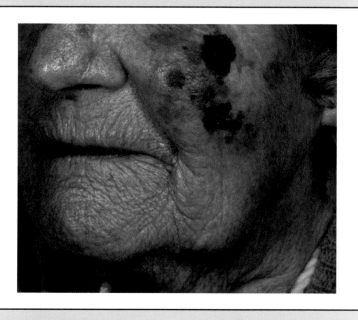

◄**Fig. 51** Lentigo maligna. An irregularly shaped pigmented lesion on the face of an elderly female with evidence of solar damage (solar elastosis and severe wrinkling). Note the variety of colours ranging from red to light brown to black. These are slow-growing tumours which typically occur on the face of the elderly. There is a long *in situ* phase during which the lentigo maligna grows radially and may become large. The development of focal nodules signifies the transition into an invasive melanoma (lentigo maligna melanoma).

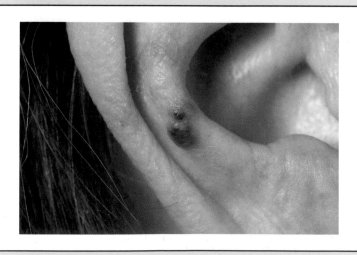

◄**Fig. 52** Haemangioma. These benign tumours may look black and menacing at first sight but on close inspection they are purple/blue in colour, may blanche with pressure and their vascularity can be seen with a dermatoscope.

1.2.14 Leg ulcers

General features

As for every clinical examination, start by assessing the patient (and her surroundings) from the foot of the bed for clues to the diagnosis. Note any dressings or bandages and then look specifically for the following.

- Are there any orthotic devices or obvious joint or foot deformities to suggest a neuropathic cause?

- Are there clues to an underlying diagnosis of diabetes, eg blood glucose monitor?

- Is there leg oedema? Bilateral oedema suggests bilateral venous disease or cardiac failure; unilateral oedema suggests venous disease.

- Are there obvious 'inverted champagne bottle legs', which are characteristic of chronic venous insufficiency?

- Is there evidence of previous surgery? Amputations or scars from possible previous bypass surgery suggest arterial disease.

- Are there obvious changes of rheumatoid arthritis in the hands that may suggest a vasculitic cause?

Cutaneous examination

Now examine the skin of the legs. Begin by focusing on the characteristics of the ulcers themselves: note their number and position(s). Table 25 is helpful in distinguishing the major causes.

Look carefully for a rolled pearlescent edge with telangiectases that may suggest an ulcerated basal cell carcinoma. Ulcerated squamous cell carcinomas often have an indurated 'heaped-up' edge. Ulcers caused by pyoderma gangrenosum typically have an undermined purple or 'gun-metal' coloured edge (Fig. 53).

Next carefully inspect the surrounding skin. Pigmentary change (haemosiderin deposition and *atrophie blanche*) is a clue to venous disease. Look for redness and scaling suggestive of venous (stasis) dermatitis (Fig. 54). Determine if surrounding skin is shiny with loss of hair and/or necrotic areas, suggestive of arterial disease. Look for changes of chronic lymphoedema, ie 'cobblestone' or warty skin change (Fig. 43). Search for purpura or livedoid changes that may suggest a vasculitic cause (see Fig. 45). Is there erythema suggestive of cellulitis (primary or secondary)?

TABLE 25 CLINICAL FINDINGS OF THE THREE MAJOR CAUSES OF LEG ULCERS

	Venous	Arterial	Neuropathic/diabetic
Location	Commonly 'gaiter area': medial lower leg overlying the course of the long saphenous vein	Bony prominences (malleoli and toes)	Pressure points (plantar surface overlying the first and fifth metatarsal heads, the great toe and the heel)
Size and shape	Typically larger, shallow (with flat or sloping edges) and an irregular border	Round and sharply marginated ('punched out')	As for arterial
Ulcer base	Often yellow sloughy exudates or red granulation tissue	Dry and necrotic with little evidence of granulation tissue. Tendons and deep tissues may be visible	May be as arterial or with exudative base if secondarily infected

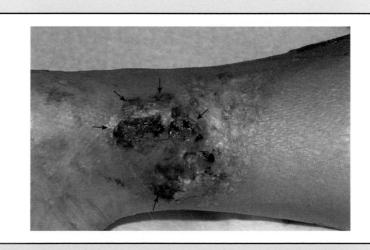

▲ **Fig. 53** Pyoderma gangrenosum. A painful ulcer, one of several, which appeared suddenly and expanded rapidly. Note the purple/grey border in areas (arrowed).

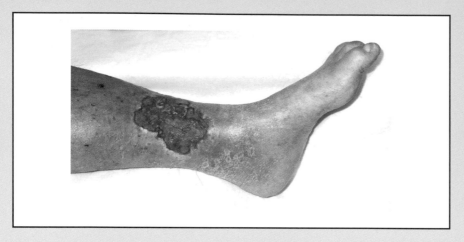

▲**Fig. 54** Venous ulcer. A superficial ulcer above the medial malleolus, the usual site. Note the surrounding erythema and scaling of the skin, consistent with venous eczema. This patient was treated with compression bandages.

> ⚠ **Acute lipodermatosclerosis** (fibrosis of subcutaneous tissue due to venous insufficiency) may present as diffuse tender erythema and warmth that may be misdiagnosed as cellulitis. There are usually other stigmata of chronic venous disease and no constitutional symptoms or fever.

Following your inspection, proceed as follows.

- Use the back of your fingers to feel the temperature of the patient's skin. Cold extremities in the presence of trophic changes suggest arterial disease. Dry skin may indicate anhidrosis due to autonomic neuropathy associated with a neuropathic cause of ulceration.

- Palpate the tissues. Firm 'woody' fibrosis suggests lipodermatosclerosis (Fig. 55). Note oedema, pitting or non-pitting.

- Consider arterial disease. Palpate the dorsalis pedis, posterior tibial, popliteal and femoral pulses on each side, noting any absence or discrepancy in volume. Check for poor capillary refill by pressing the tip of the great toe until it blanches: poor refill is defined as continued blanching for longer than 3–4 seconds. Elevate the affected limb to 60° for 1 minute: pallor of the distal extremity with reactive hyperaemia on returning the leg to the dependent position occurs in arterial insufficiency. Auscultate over the femoral arteries for bruits.

- Consider neuropathic disease and examine for peripheral neuropathy.

- Consider neoplastic disease (Fig. 56). Palpate for regional lymphadenopathy if this seems possible.

> 🔑 Some leg ulcers are the result of mixed arterial and venous disease, so stigmata of both may be present on clinical examination.

Further discussion

- See Table 11 and Section 1.1.8 for causes of leg ulcers and details of investigation and management.

- Pyoderma gangrenosum (see Section 2.18).

- Necrobiosis lipoidica: 65% of patients with this condition have diabetes (and who make up 0.03% of all diabetics). Clinically the presentation is purplish-brown plaques with yellowish atrophic centres and telangiectases, occurring generally on the shins. They may ulcerate following trauma.

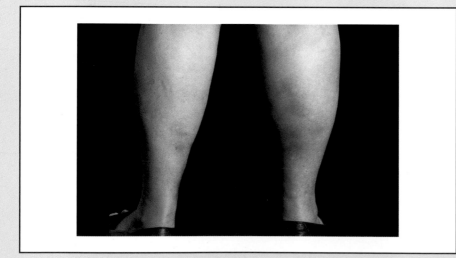

▲**Fig. 55** Lipodermatosclerosis. Erythema of the gaiter aspect of the leg. On palpation the skin is tight and 'woody'. Indentation of the contour of the lower leg is just beginning, the earliest stage in the development of 'inverted champagne bottle legs'.

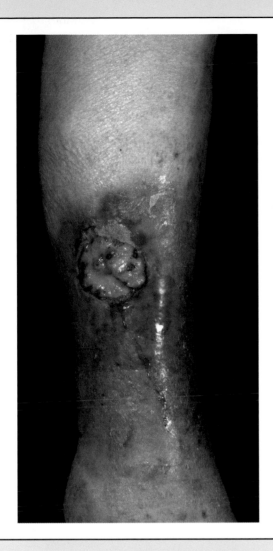

▲ **Fig. 56** Ulcerated amelanotic malignant melanoma. This case was referred as an ulcer that failed to heal, a history that should prompt suspicion. Its heaped-up base and location on the lateral aspect of the mid-lower leg, a site unusual for venous and arterial ulcers, hint at the possibility of malignancy. The clinical features in this case do not allow distinction from other tumours and the diagnosis was made histologically.

TABLE 26 NAIL CHANGES IN SKIN DISEASE

Nail abnormality	Associated diseases
Pitting (see Figs 69b and 84b)	Psoriasis (+ possible onycholysis and subungual hyperkeratosis) Alopecia areata Eczema
Trachyonychia ('sand-blasted' nails): nail surface rough and dull	Alopecia areata Lichen planus Psoriasis
Onycholysis: distal nail-bed detachment (see Fig. 84a)	Psoriasis Onychomycosis (dermatophyte nail infection) Drugs + UV light (ie photo-onycholysis). Seen with doxycycline
UV, ultraviolet.	

1.2.15 Examine these hands

Instruction

This man has a skin disease. Please examine his hands.

General features

As always, survey the patient first. There are many dermatological and systemic diseases that can cause either nail disease and/or affect the skin of the hands. There may be additional involvement elsewhere, so look for clues.

Cutaneous examination

The hands should be examined systematically. First look carefully at the nails: are there any of the abnormalities listed in Table 26?

If you suspect psoriasis then examine the rest of the skin, particularly the extensor surfaces and scalp (see Section 2.17). For lichen planus, examine the skin, especially the flexor surfaces of the wrists, and look in the mouth (see Section 2.14). If alopecia areata is suspected, check the scalp and other hair-bearing areas (see Section 2.3). For suspected onychomycosis, look for a scaly eruption on the hands and check the feet, which are often the primary source of infection (see Section 2.12).

Examine the skin on the dorsal and palmar surfaces of the hands, putting any abnormalities that you see into the following categories to enable you to generate a differential diagnosis.

Papulosquamous rash

- Psoriasis: red scaly plaques or palmar pustulosis with or without arthropathy (Fig. 57 and see Section 2.17).

- Dermatitis: atopic, irritant, allergic contact (see Sections 2.8 and 2.9).

- Lichen planus: characteristic lesions on flexor aspects of wrists; note also nail and mouth changes (see Section 2.14).

Bullae

- Erythema multiforme: examine the rest of the skin, looking for typical target lesions. Do not forget the lips and mouth (see Section 2.10 and Figs 5 and 62).

- Pompholyx (or dyshidrotic) eczema: palmar surfaces (see Fig. 4). Check the feet too.

- Porphyria cutanea tarda: dorsa of the hands. There may be erosions, skin fragility, scars and milia (see Fig. 8). Check the face for hypertrichosis and hyperpigmentation.

Nail-fold erythema

Connective tissue diseases, particularly systemic lupus erythematosus (SLE) and dermatomyositis. Look at the face for the 'butterfly' rash of SLE or scaly plaques of discoid lupus erythematosus (see Section 1.2.2), and also for other features such as livedo reticularis. In dermatomyositis there may be erythema and swelling of the eyelids, and a proximal myopathy (see Section 2.5 and Fig. 20).

Nail-fold telangiectases

- Dermatomyositis (associated nail-fold erythema and ragged cuticles).

- Scleroderma or CREST (syndrome of *c*alcinosis, *R*aynaud's phenomenon,

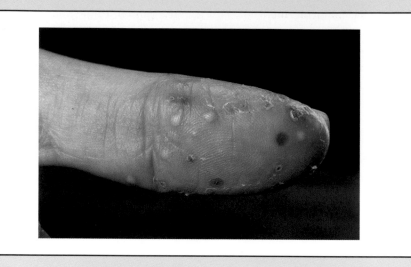

▲**Fig. 57**   Palmar plantar pustulosis. Note the background erythema and scaling of the thumb, which is studded with pustules that evolve into brown macules.

(a)

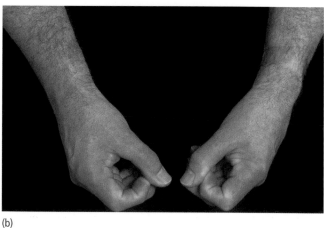

(b)

►**Fig. 58**   Diabetic cheirarthropathy. In this condition, there is thickening and stiffness of the skin with limited joint mobility so that it is impossible to oppose the palms completely, the 'prayer sign' (**a**). The patient was also unable to tightly clench his fists (**b**).

(o)esophageal involvement, sclerodactyly, telangiectasia).

- Lupus.

Sclerodactyly

- Tight, shiny, hard and waxy skin on fingers (see Fig. 44).

- Scleroderma or CREST (in which case look for the other associated signs).

- Diabetic cheirarthropathy (check for the 'prayer sign', Fig. 58).

Cutaneous calcinosis

This causes hard, chalky white deposits that may be ulcerating through the skin surface. It is also a feature of scleroderma and CREST, so look for other features such as sclerodactyly, nail-fold changes, evidence of Raynaud's phenomenon, finger pulp ulcers, telangiectases on hands and face, and scleroderma facies that would confirm this.

Periungual fibromas

These are flesh-coloured tumours arising from the periungual skin. They may be an isolated finding, but can also be a feature of tuberous sclerosis: look for facial angiofibromas, hypopigmented 'ash-leaf' or 'confetti' macules for confirmation (see Table 17 for clinical features of tuberous sclerosis).

Miscellaneous

Granuloma annulare are flesh-coloured annular plaques without surface scale. Commonly occur on the dorsal hands (Fig. 59).

Further discussion

Once you have completed your examination of the hands, offer to examine the rest of the skin to identify and demonstrate other features of the condition that you suspect.

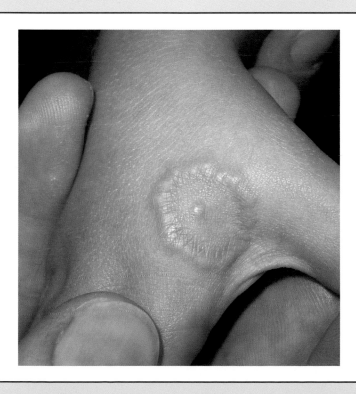

▲**Fig. 59** Granuloma annulare. A flesh-coloured annular plaque in a typical site on the dorsum of the hand.

1.3 Communication skills and ethics

1.3.1 Consenting a patient to enter a dermatological trial

Scenario

Role: you are a junior doctor working as part of a team that is recruiting patients for a clinical trial.

Mrs Sarah Hallows, aged 34 years, has long-standing severe atopic dermatitis and would be suitable for enrolment into a 6-month double-blind, randomised, placebo-controlled trial of a novel medication. The trial has been approved by the relevant ethics committee, satisfies the appropriate regulatory requirements (eg EU Clinical Trials Directive) and you are listed with other members of the dermatological team as being an approved investigator. The patient has been provided with a written information leaflet explaining that:

1. limited preliminary studies have shown that the trial drug, which is in a topical formulation, might be effective in treating her condition;

2. potential side effects include itching and burning of the skin when first applied, worsening of any pre-existing skin infections, and the fact that long-term side effects are not yet known but there is a theoretical risk of skin cancer;

3. the trial involves taking clinical photographs of her skin to document progress of the condition, and the taking and storage of blood samples for monitoring of the effects of the drug (including safety monitoring).

The information sheet also gives the telephone contact details of a research nurse involved in the project.

Your task: to discuss and obtain informed written consent for entry to the trial.

Key issues to explore

The practicalities, potential risks and benefits of the trial must be explained to the patient in terms she can understand, and she must be given the opportunity to ask any questions that she may have.

Key points to establish

Information about possible benefits and risks must be given clearly, and the following points must also be raised/addressed.

- That it is not known for certain whether the trial drug will be helpful: a clinical trial is only ethical if the outcome is uncertain.

- That the patient is under no obligation whatever to take part. If she decides not to, then she does not have to give a reason; and if she does, then she can withdraw at any time if she changes her mind.

- Her future care will not be adversely affected in any way if she decides not to participate or if she withdraws from the trial.

- That she has the opportunity to read and consider the research

information leaflet, with sufficient time to reflect on the implications of participating in the study.

- That, as in all clinical trials, her anonymity will be preserved.

- That, if she is willing to participate in the trial, you must obtain her consent in writing and give her a copy.

Appropriate responses to likely questions

Patient: there's so much to take in. I simply can't decide whether I want to take part.

Doctor: don't worry. You don't need to make a decision now. Take the information leaflet home with you and read it through again. Give yourself as much time as you need to decide. Discuss it with your family and friends if you want. Write down any questions you might have and then feel free to discuss them with me, or with the research nurse: there's a telephone number on the information sheet. Please don't feel you have to take part. If you decide not to enter the trial, it won't make any difference to your existing medical care.

Patient: does this new drug work? Will it help my eczema?

Doctor: I'm afraid we don't know. If we did know that it worked, then we wouldn't be doing a trial at all but suggesting that you used it. We only need to do trials when we're not sure whether or not a treatment works.

Patient: what's the point of me doing the trial if I don't get the real drug?

Doctor: I'm afraid that we don't know whether or not the real drug works at all: it might do, but it might not. To find out we need to test the drug against a placebo: that's a treatment that we know doesn't

have any real effect at all. You won't know, and even I won't know, if you get the real drug or not. It's the best way to decide whether a drug really works or not.

Patient: if I don't get the real drug, then I can't benefit from this trial, can I?

Doctor: yes, you're right that if you don't get the real drug then you can't directly benefit from it. But we don't know if it works at all, and unfortunately false results can be obtained if drugs are tested in other ways. However, this trial will help improve our understanding of this drug, so that you and other eczema patients in the future will hopefully benefit from this knowledge.

Patient: what happens if I'm in the trial and I get side effects? Do I ring my GP? There's no point in ringing the hospital because whenever I do that, someone just tells me to see my GP.

Doctor: no, if you had a problem that seemed to be related to the trial in any way then we wouldn't want you to ring your GP. You should contact us on the telephone number given on the information sheet: it's a direct line to the research nurse and you wouldn't be told to see your GP. It's important that we know if you, or any other patient, has any problems with the treatment so we would want you to get in touch with us if anything happened. Then we could see you if necessary and decide what needs to be done. We would also need to fully record any problems you have in your records, so that the drug can be properly assessed at the end of the trial.

Patient: what if I don't like the treatment? I don't want to be forced to continue it if I sign the form.

Doctor: you won't be forced to do anything you don't want to. If you are in the trial, you can pull out at any stage and for any reason. You don't even need to give a reason why, and it won't affect your ongoing medical care.

Patient: *I'm very worried about the chance of skin cancer.*

Doctor: because this is a very new drug, we don't know what the long-term side effects will be. However, the risk of skin cancer is a theoretical possibility based on what we know about how the drug works. There is no evidence from the trials so far that it does cause skin cancer, but we are being cautious and letting people know about this being possible. If there is a risk, it's likely to be very small indeed. But for any patient in the trial, we advise that they don't do things that increase the risk of skin cancer, like sunbathing or using sunbeds, and we suggest that they use a sunscreen in the spring and summer.

Patient: *but what if I get the placebo and my eczema gets worse? I can't stand that for 6 months.*

Doctor: if your eczema gets worse you can pull out as we've discussed already, and if that was happening we would also want to take you out of the trial so that you could go back onto your usual treatments.

Further comments
There are many excellent sources of further information on consent for research.

- General Medical Council. *Seeking Patients' Consent: the Ethical Considerations*. London: GMC, 1998. Available full text at http://www.gmc-uk.org/

- Medical Research Council. *Guidelines for Good Clinical*

Practice in Clinical Trials. London: MRC, 1998. Available full text at http://www.mrc.ac.uk/

- Medical Research Council. *Human Tissue and Biological Samples Use in Research: Operational and Ethical Guidelines*. London: MRC, 2001. Available full text at http://www.mrc.ac.uk/

There are special circumstances when patients are unable to give informed consent (eg children), and in such cases further advice from the ethics committee should be sought.

1.3.2 A steroid-phobic patient

Scenario

Role: you are a junior doctor working in a dermatology outpatient clinic.

Miss Anne Earnshaw is a 25-year-old schoolteacher with lifelong atopic eczema. She usually controls her condition with regular emollients alone. She has recently started a new job and moved house, and her eczema has become much more difficult to control in the last 2 months since these changes have occurred. Clinical examination shows active inflamed eczema affecting her trunk, limbs and face. She is otherwise well in herself. She comes to clinic requesting treatment for her eczema, but is adamant that she does not want topical steroids. She has read about a new treatment in a magazine, which is a topical form of tacrolimus that is properly reserved for cases that do not respond to first-line treatments such as emollients and topical steroids.

The information pack in the dermatology department on topical tacrolimus states that it can cause irritation and burning of the skin, and that on theoretical grounds it might increase the risk of skin malignancy.

Your task: to reassure Miss Earnshaw that a topical steroid would be an appropriate and safe part of her treatment regimen.

Key issues to explore
Why is the patient worried about using topical steroids? Has she used them in the past and had particular problems?

Key points to establish
Topical steroids do have well-recognised side effects, but are safe if used appropriately (see Section 2.26). Alternative topical treatments or oral treatments can be used, but these also have their own side effects.

Appropriate responses to likely questions

Patient: *steroids are bound to make my skin thin and fragile, aren't they?*

Doctor: it's true that strong steroids used for long periods of time, particularly at delicate sites such as the face or armpits, do cause thinning of the skin and fragility of the blood vessels in the skin. But if used sensibly, topical steroids can give very good control of eczema with a very small chance of side effects. It's all about trying to balance the risks of treatment against the benefits in a sensible manner.

Patient: *what is a safe way to use topical steroids?*

Doctor: strong steroids are used in the short term to control eczema, but they are then weaned down to milder ones, or applied less often, once the eczema is controlled. Milder steroids are used at delicate sites such as the face, and stronger steroids are used at other sites, such as the trunk, hands and limbs, if needed.

Patient: I have used topical steroids in the past, and they have worked, but my eczema has flared again immediately when I stopped taking them. Can anything be done about this?

Doctor: this is a common problem. The important thing to do is to wean off the steroids slowly once the eczema has settled. Instead of putting them on twice a day, reduce applications to once a day for a week, and then every other day, before stopping completely.

Patient: what about alternatives to topical steroids? I've read about tacrolimus in a magazine and it sounds much better.

Doctor: yes, there are new topical treatments, including tacrolimus, which do not have the same side effects as topical steroids and they can work well to settle eczema. But they have some side effects too. They can cause irritation and burning of the skin, and there is also concern about their use on sun-exposed skin as they may increase the risk of skin cancer in the long term. Because tacrolimus has not been around for very long, we can't be sure about the long-term side effects at the moment. However, topical steroids have been around for many years and we know that they are generally very safe if used properly and that's why we recommend them for problems such as yours.

1.3.3 An anxious woman with a family history of melanoma who wants all her moles removed

Scenario

Role: you are a junior doctor working in a dermatology outpatient clinic.

Mrs Julie Scott, aged 32 years and who works as a medical typist in the hospital, has been referred by her GP for assessment of her moles, some of which he thinks are abnormal. Her mother died of metastatic malignant melanoma at the age of 48 years and her maternal aunt has had two melanomas removed by a plastic surgeon in Stoke-on-Trent. She thinks her maternal grandfather had a melanoma, but he died of metastatic prostate carcinoma at the age of 76 years.

Her past medical history includes chronic fatigue syndrome and fibromyalgia. She takes amitriptyline 25 mg at night. She goes on sunny holidays two to three times a year and smokes 15 cigarettes a day. She does not drink alcohol. She 'keeps an eye on her skin' and subjectively does not feel that any of her moles have changed. Clinical examination reveals she is tanned with multiple (>100) melanocytic naevi scattered over the trunk and limbs. A number of these, particularly on the back, appear large and atypical, but none are overtly suspicious for melanoma. Complete physical examination is otherwise normal.

In view of her history she is worried that she will die of melanoma and wants all her moles to be removed. If you do not arrange this for her she is going to see a plastic surgeon privately. The dermatology consultant says that (i) it would not be appropriate to remove any of her moles; (ii) most melanomas arise in normal skin and not in moles; (iii) she should be given advice to reduce her sun exposure, which is a recognised risk factor for skin malignancy; and (iv) she should be kept under surveillance.

Your task: to explain to Mrs Scott that prophylactic excision of all her moles is not appropriate.

Key issues to explore

What is the patient's perception of her risk? Does she appreciate her other risk factor for melanoma (sun exposure) in addition to her multiple moles and family history?

Key points to establish

- That her melanoma risk is difficult to quantify, although it will be higher than someone of her age with no risk factors.

- That prophylactic excision of her moles would not prevent the development of melanoma, which is most likely to arise *de novo* in the normal skin of susceptible individuals.

- To discuss regular self-examination and educate the patient regarding changes in pigmented lesions that may suggest the early development of melanoma.

- To develop an appropriate follow-up schedule and discuss objective surveillance methods such as large-format photography.

- Modification of the risk factors for skin cancer.

Appropriate responses to likely questions

Patient: why can't you cut out all my moles?

Doctor: as you know, there are lots of them, so removing all of them would be a major undertaking. But even it we did that, I'm afraid that it wouldn't deal with the problem. Removing all your moles would not stop you developing a melanoma. Many melanomas arise in normal skin rather than in existing moles; so in addition to all the time you would need to spend having surgery, the discomfort for you and the scars, having the moles removed wouldn't necessarily reduce your risk of developing a melanoma.

Patient: you're not going to tell me I'm not at risk of melanoma, are you?

Doctor: no, I'm not going to say that. Your family history and the fact that you have a lot of moles does mean that you have a higher risk than most people. The fact that you have quite a lot of sun exposure also increases your risk of skin cancers of various sorts.

Patient: so you're just going to wait until I get a melanoma and let me die?

Doctor: no, that's not what I'm going to suggest. Unfortunately nobody can predict whether you will ever get a melanoma, but there are several things that can be done to reduce the risk. The most important risk that you can do something about is limiting your exposure to ultraviolet light; in other words cutting down on sun exposure, which we know is linked with skin cancer. We will also teach you how to regularly and systematically examine your skin, and we will

see you ourselves for follow-up appointments when we will check your skin. To help us do this we will organise some photographs of your skin that we can use as a point of reference to see if there have been any changes in your moles. By doing these things we are making sure that if you do develop a melanoma it is identified at an early stage, because if melanoma is identified at an early stage, it is treatable.

Patient: are you saying I should never go on holiday?

Doctor: no, but I am saying you need to be aware of the dangers of the sun and sunbathing. It is important that you protect your skin by limiting your sun exposure. For example, you should avoid being in direct sunshine, particularly when it's at its strongest from 11 a.m. to 3 p.m. If you are outdoors then sit in the shade, protect your skin from the sun's rays by wearing clothing and a broad-brimmed hat, and any exposed skin should be covered with a sunscreen of at least factor 15. I have an information leaflet on sun protection that I can give you.

Patient: what if I'm worried about one of my moles? It's so difficult to get an appointment: I've had to wait 10 weeks to see you.

Doctor: it's unfortunate that you've had to wait 10 weeks, but fortunately none of your moles are suspicious. However, now that you are on our books, you should telephone us so that we can bring forward your appointment if you think one of your moles has changed. I would not want you to sit at home waiting for your next appointment, which could be 6 months away.

Patient: I don't want to trust my life to a junior doctor. I want to see someone more senior.

Doctor: I would be happy to arrange for you to see my registrar or the consultant if you like.

1.3.4 Prescribing isotretinoin to a woman of reproductive age

Scenario

Role: you are a junior doctor working in a dermatology outpatient clinic.

A 20-year-old woman has been referred with acne that has failed to respond to erythromycin, oxytetracycline and minocycline. These have been prescribed at appropriate doses and each for a sufficient period of time. The patient has severe acne with nodules, cysts and scars. She is a suitable candidate for the drug isotretinoin.

Your task: to explain that isotretinoin is your recommended treatment, but that it is highly teratogenic and therefore effective contraception and monitoring on the pregnancy prevention programme (PPP) is required in women of childbearing potential. The PPP requires effective contraception (eg combined oral contraceptive pill, contraceptive injections/ implants or intrauterine devices; *not* barrier methods or the progesterone-only pill) to be instituted at least 1 month before treatment and continued during treatment and for 1 month after completion. Monitoring requires a pregnancy test when starting treatment, at monthly intervals during treatment and then a final test 5 weeks after completing treatment. Only 1 month of isotretinoin can be prescribed at a time. The manufacturers provide written information sheets and a consent form. The consultant responsible for the woman's care does not think that she should be exempted from the PPP.

Key issues to explore

- Is the patient sexually active? Do not make any assumptions, but tread delicately. You have to ask, and (in routine clinical practice) do not accept a parent's assurance: if a teenage girl attends with a parent, you might want to create the opportunity to speak to her alone. Even if a woman tells you her husband has had a vasectomy, she might be having another relationship.

- Is the patient on an effective form of contraception, or is she prepared to commence effective contraception in order to take a course of isotretinoin?

Key points to establish

- That the patient understands the risk of isotretinoin exposure during pregnancy: 'It causes severe and serious birth defects, serious malformations and the birth defects are so serious that a termination of pregnancy is usually recommended'.

- The need for effective contraception and for monitoring during treatment as well as for 1 month before and after. If she is not prepared to do this, then treatment will not be possible; if she fails to attend follow-up appointments, treatment will stop.

Appropriate responses to likely questions

Scenario 1

Woman: I'm married and I'm already on the pill. I don't mind having the pregnancy tests during treatment. It's really good that you have to be so careful. It would be terrible to become pregnant on this drug. [An unlikely response in PACES!]

Doctor: in that case, we can make plans to start treatment.

Scenario 2

Woman: I haven't got a boyfriend and I'm not on any contraception, but I don't mind going on the pill if it means I can have this treatment to make my acne better. It really bothers me and I'll never get a boyfriend with spots like this. [Another unlikely response in PACES!]

Doctor: OK. You will need to see your GP or a family planning clinic for advice on contraception because it's not my area of expertise, but let me give you these leaflets about isotretinoin and contraception for you to read. Before we can start treatment you need to have been on contraception for at least 1 month, so I'll make another appointment for you to come back in 2 months which will give you enough time.

Scenario 3

Woman: I haven't got a boyfriend and there's no chance I could be pregnant, so I don't need any pregnancy tests.

Doctor: in that case I'm sure you're not pregnant. But it is a requirement that we do pregnancy tests because we have to be absolutely sure that we do not harm any unborn babies. We have to do the test on all women patients, whether they're in a relationship or not, just to be sure.

Woman: I'll have the pregnancy tests, but I don't need any contraception.

Doctor: because isotretinoin causes such serious birth defects, it is really important that we avoid any accidental pregnancies. I'm sure you have no intention of getting pregnant, but I'm afraid that if you're not prepared to use contraception then we won't be able to give you this treatment.

Scenario 4

Woman: I'm not married and I haven't got a boyfriend, and I don't believe in sex before marriage for religious reasons. I've been told I shouldn't take the pill because I get migraines and my mother had a stroke, and I really don't want to have a coil fitted – there's just no need. But I really want to have the treatment because my acne's so bad and it's really affecting my confidence. I can see there are scars now and I don't want them to get any worse.

Doctor: I agree. I don't want to see your scars getting any worse and I think there's a very good chance that isotretinoin will help clear your acne. But this business about birth defects and contraception is really serious. It's very upsetting when patients taking this drug accidentally become pregnant, and unfortunately this does happen, which is why the rules have become so strict. We really do need to insist that all patients use contraception, although in your case it would need to be something other than the pill, which your GP or the family planning clinic could advise on.

Woman: I understand everything you're saying doctor, but because of my religious beliefs I actually find all of this quite offensive. A relationship with a man before I'm married is really out of the question. I can promise you I will not become pregnant.

Doctor: I can see that me insisting you use contraception and have pregnancy tests is very upsetting for you. I do understand your beliefs and I am not trying to offend you. But as I'm sure you realise, not all unmarried women have the same beliefs so we have to follow the guidelines.

Scenario 5

Woman: *I'm really not happy with this. There must be a way for me to sign a form and take responsibility for my actions. I just don't want to have to take a drug that I don't need to be able to a drug that I do.*

Doctor: I understand what you are saying. I cannot agree to this plan, but I can arrange for you to discuss matters with the consultant. I cannot promise, but it may be that they will allow it. If they can, then they will need to make full notes in your medical records and get you to read and sign the consent form, which indicates that you understand the risks involved and the need to avoid becoming pregnant. And you will also need to have a pregnancy test.

Further comments

The UK licence for isotretinoin was changed in December 2004 to accommodate requirements of the EU Directive and the PPP is a result of this. It is a guideline not a legal requirement, and interpretation of the phrase 'female patients at risk of pregnancy' is the issue here. There will be occasions when you judge it might be appropriate to exempt a patient from the PPP because she is not at risk of pregnancy, but you should not do this without discussion with your consultant. You must be sure that the patient clearly understands the need to avoid pregnancy and that she is reliable. You must clearly document

why she is not at risk of pregnancy and therefore exempt from the PPP. However, even if a patient is exempted, you should still obtain written consent acknowledging that she understands the risk of teratogenicity and the need to avoid pregnancy. If you do not believe the patient is reliable, do not prescribe.

1.4 Acute scenarios

1.4.1 Acute generalised rashes

Scenario

A 55-year-old man presented with a 5-day history of a non-purpuric eruption on the torso, limbs and face. Two weeks previously he had been commenced on aspirin and atorvastatin. On examination he was pyrexial (38°C) with a symmetrical eruption shown in Fig. 60.

⚠️ Several life-threatening disorders present with a rash and fever. The cutaneous findings alone may be diagnostic and enable life-saving treatment to be started without delay.

Introduction

Many disorders present acutely with a generalised rash, so diagnostic confusion is common. Table 27 lists these disorders along with key clinical features to help differentiate them. Your main priority must be to recognise and treat those that are life-threatening.

History of the presenting problem

Ask the patient about the following.

- How old are you? This man is aged 55 years. Many disorders present in certain age groups and so some diagnoses, eg Kawasaki's disease and staphylococcal scalded skin syndrome (SSSS), can be discounted here simply on the basis of age (Table 27).

- Have you been unwell recently? A prodromal illness is common in viral exanthems, and symptoms associated with a triggering infection may be present in erythema multiforme, Stevens–Johnson syndrome (SJS), toxic epidermal necrolysis (TEN), SSSS, toxic shock syndrome, scarlet fever, vasculitic rashes and acute urticaria.

- Has anyone else you know been unwell recently? Find out about any infectious contacts.

- Are you itchy? Is the skin sore? Pruritus is characteristic of urticaria and is common in chickenpox and pityriasis rosea. It may accompany drug eruptions. If the skin is tender or burning, think of TEN, SSSS and generalised pustular psoriasis.

- Do the lesions come and go? Urticarial weals last a few hours only (a characteristic feature).

- Tongue swelling, dyspnoea or wheeze? Angio-oedema or anaphylaxis may accompany urticaria.

- Where did the rash start? This information may be very helpful, eg measles and rubella typically start on the face and spread to the trunk and limbs, unlike maculopapular drug eruptions (the main differential diagnosis otherwise) (Fig. 61).

- Are you menstruating? This is relevant in toxic shock syndrome.

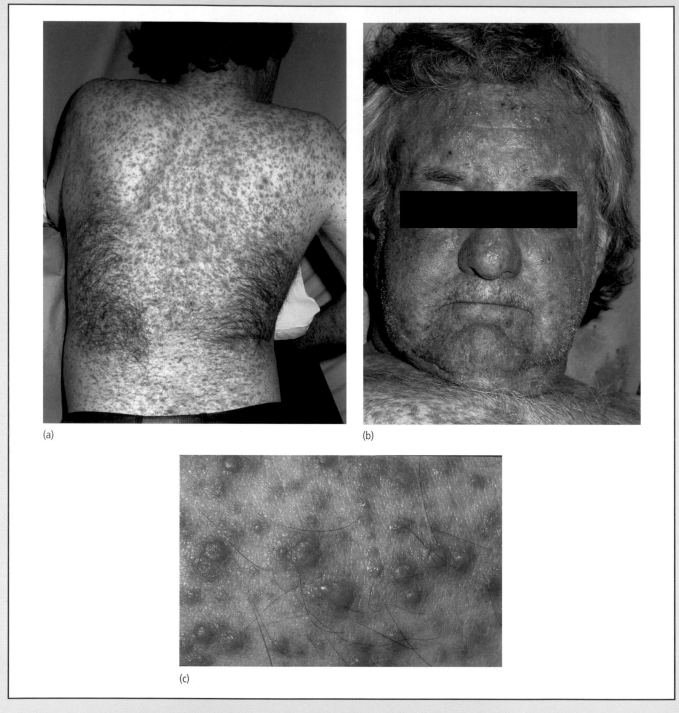

(a)

(b)

(c)

▲ **Fig. 60** A 55-year-old male with a 5-day history of a generalised eruption that was densest on the torso (**a**) and face (**b**). A close-up view is shown (**c**). He was pyrexial and had commenced aspirin and atorvastatin 2 weeks previously.

TABLE 27 Key features of disorders presenting with an acute, non-purpuric, generalised rash with or without fever

Disease	General features	Skin manifestations	Mucous membranes
Toxin-mediated disorders			
Toxic shock syndrome	Very unwell Fever, hypotension, headache, vomiting, diarrhoea, myalgia Usually in menstruating women	Generalised erythema, including palms/soles	Oral erythema ('strawberry' tongue) Red eyes
Staphylococcal scalded skin syndrome	Usually in neonates/infants Rarely in adults Unwell and fever	Generalised erythema (tender) Sloughing of epidermis Flexural accentuation Nikolsky's sign positive	–
Scarlet fever (scarletina)	Unwell High fever Tonsillitis is often the trigger	Generalised erythema, with accentuation ± petechiae in skin folds Peri-oral pallor	Red 'strawberry' tongue
Viral exanthems			
Chickenpox (varicella zoster)	Usually in children with mild prodrome. Adults more unwell Immunosuppressed patients may be very unwell Fever	Papules, vesicles and pustules, then crusts, with lesions at all stages May be haemorrhagic Often itchy Trunk > limbs	± Oral ulcers
Disseminated herpes simplex or zoster	Immunocompromised patients Very unwell Fever	Papules, vesicles, pustules, erosions and crusts May be haemorrhagic or necrotic Painful	± Oral ulcers
Measles	Prodrome (coryza, conjunctivitis, photophobia, high fever) Patient unwell Lymphadenopathy	Deep red macules/papules Onset face, then trunk/limbs	Conjunctivitis ± Koplick's spots (mouth)
Rubella	Usually in children/young adults Prodrome (mild in children) Occipital/cervical lymphadenopathy Patients are relatively well	Pale pink macules/papules Onset face, then trunk/limbs	–
Parvovirus B19	Usually in children Mild prodrome (worse in adults)	Red plaques on cheeks (slapped cheeks) Erythematous macules on limbs: lace-like pattern	–
Miscellaneous disorders			
Erythema multiforme and Stevens–Johnson syndrome	Systemically well in mild cases Unwell in more severe cases with fever	Dusky red macules ± target/iris lesions Tender May blister Densest on distal limbs, including palms/soles	Orogenital and ocular inflammation and ulceration
Toxic epidermal necrolysis	Very unwell Fever	Diffuse tender erythema ± erythroderma Epithelial detachment ± intact blisters Nikolsky's sign positive	Orogenital and ocular inflammation and ulceration
Kawasaki's disease	In infants/young children Unwell High fever Cervical lymphadenopathy Myocarditis and pericarditis	Red swollen palms/soles Erythematous macules, patches, plaques; often concentrated in napkin area	Oral erythema ('strawberry' tongue) Red lips Red eyes
Pustular psoriasis	Unwell Fever May be recent history of infection	Erythematous patches and plaques studded with numerous superficial pustules ± erythroderma	–
Urticaria	Patient usually well Pyrexial only if triggered by infection or if part of serum sickness	Weals Individual lesions last a few hours only	± Tongue swelling (angio-oedema)
Maculopapular drug eruptions	No prodrome ± fever Patient usually well	Bright red macules and papules (indistinguishable from viral exanthems) May progress to erythroderma	Often uninvolved
Drug hypersensitivity syndrome (DRESS)	Fever, eosinophilia, lymphadenopathy, facial oedema ± hepatitis, pneumonitis and myocarditis	Maculopapular or erythrodermic rash	–
Pityriasis rosea	Patient well In children/young adults Fever rare	Pink oval macules Fine scale Itchy Trunk > limbs Herald patch initially	–
Guttate psoriasis	Patient well Recent pharyngitis or upper respiratory tract infection	Scaly red papules Trunk > limbs	–
Secondary syphilis	Patient unwell Fever Lymphadenopathy Usually in adults	Scaly and coppery red macules and papules Trunk > limbs Lesions on palms/soles	Mucous patches (grey)

DRESS, drug rash with eosinophilia and systemic symptoms.

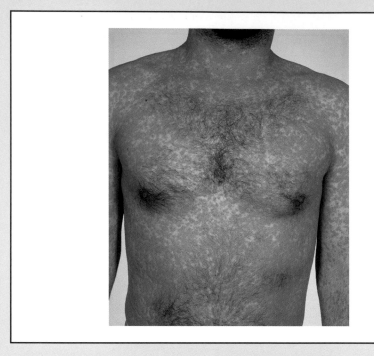

▲ Fig. 61 Maculopapular drug eruption. The acute onset of this symmetrical, non-scaly, maculopapular eruption would be consistent with either an infectious exanthem or a drug eruption. The history, distribution and general findings on examination should help differentiate. In this case, amoxicillin had been given to a patient with infectious mononucleosis.

- Have you recently done any foreign travel? Brings in a wider infectious differential: obtain specialist advice if the diagnosis is not clear.

🔑 **Drug history**

An accurate drug history is vital when assessing skin problems. Patients may fail to tell you about over-the-counter and 'alternative' therapies, so specifically ask about these in addition to prescribed drugs. Include all drugs taken in the preceding 6 weeks (see Section 2.7).

Other relevant history

Past medical history is unlikely to be relevant, except for generalised pustular or guttate psoriasis in which there may be a history of psoriasis. Immunosuppression would lower your threshold for considering disseminated herpes simplex or zoster. You could also obtain a history of drug allergy.

Examination: general features

- General impression: is the patient well, unwell or very unwell?

- Check vital signs: particularly note any fever.

- A full physical examination is required: do not forget to check for lymphadenopathy and sources of infection that may liberate toxins, eg pharyngitis, wounds and retained tampons.

- Facial oedema: commonly seen in the drug hypersensitivity syndrome, also known as DRESS syndrome (drug rash with eosinophilia and systemic symptoms).

Examination: skin

Distribution of rash

Compare the head and neck with the trunk and the limbs, and do not forget the palms, soles and flexural areas. The distribution may provide diagnostic clues, eg erythema

multiforme has a predilection for the distal limbs with lesions on the palms and soles (Fig. 62), which are spared in many other disorders. In contrast, chickenpox is usually densest on the trunk. Flexural accentuation is seen in SSSS and scarlet fever.

Morphology of lesions

Examine the individual lesions carefully. In particular, look for the following.

Blisters, erosions or positive Nikolsky sign If present, see Sections 1.1.1 and 1.2.1. In this case consider bullous erythema multiforme, SJS, TEN, SSSS, chickenpox, disseminated herpes simplex or generalised herpes zoster (see Figs 5 and 62–64).

Weals Characteristic of urticaria (Fig. 65) (see Section 2.23).

Scale If the lesions have a scaly surface, think of guttate psoriasis, pityriasis rosea and secondary syphilis (Fig. 66). Only the latter will affect the palms/soles.

Pustules Multiple tiny pustules on a background of diffuse erythema suggests a drug eruption or pustular psoriasis (Fig. 67) (see Section 1.4.2). Scanty pustules can occur in bacteraemia, particularly gonococcaemia or *Staphylococcus aureus* endocarditis.

⚠️ Do not forget the mucosal surfaces: always check the mouth, eyes and genitalia. If affected, the differential diagnosis narrows (see Table 27).

Purpura This man did not have a purpuric rash (see Fig. 45), but if confronted with an ill patient with purpura first consider life-threatening diagnoses such as:

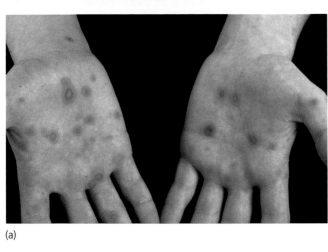

(a)

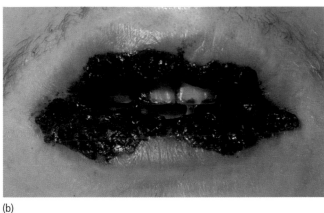

(b)

▲ **Fig. 62** Erythema multiforme. The presence of oral erosions helps to narrow the differential diagnosis when assessing patients with skin problems. In this case, typical target lesions were present on the hands (**a**) and feet; otherwise, haemorrhagic crusted erosions on the lips are characteristic (**b**).

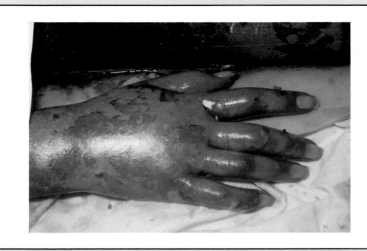

▲ **Fig. 63** Toxic epidermal necrolysis. The pigmented epidermis has sloughed off in places to reveal the raw glazed surface of the underlying dermis. Friction on 'normal' skin may slough off the epidermis (Nikolsky's sign) so skin handling should be minimised. The appearance of SSSS is similar.

- meningococcal septicaemia (see *Infectious Diseases*, Section 1.3.2);

- disseminated intravascular coagulation;

- multisystem vasculitis (see *Nephrology*, Section 1.4.3 and *Rheumatology and Clinical Immunology*, Sections 2.5.2, 2.5.3 and 2.5.4);

- haemorrhagic viral fevers.

Investigation

General blood tests

- FBC: may show eosinophilia in drug eruptions; thrombocytopenia in toxic shock syndrome and in some cases of purpura and varicella; thrombocytosis may occur in Kawasaki's disease; and neutrophilia is a feature of pustular psoriasis or underlying bacterial infection.

- Coagulation screen; if purpura is present.

- Electrolytes, renal and liver function tests: in any patient who is acutely ill.

To establish a diagnosis of infection

- Examination of blister fluid or scrapings from a blister base (Tzanck smear): these tests should be performed immediately for urgent confirmation of suspected viral infections. Light microscopy will identify virally infected cells and electron microscopy will identify virus particles. Viral antigens can be detected by direct immunofluorescence. Otherwise, send swabs for viral culture.

- Skin pustules: take swabs for bacterial culture. They will be sterile in drug eruptions and pustular psoriasis, but positive

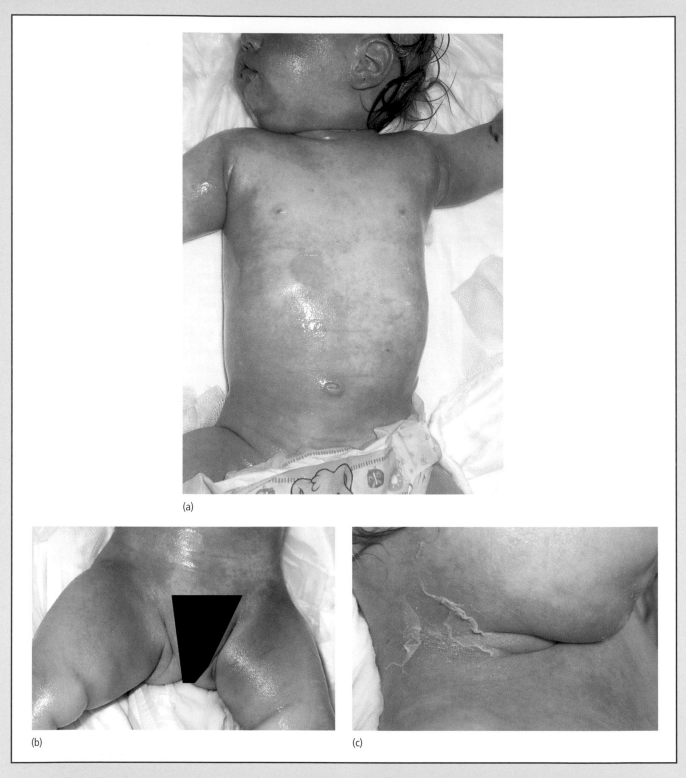

(a)

(b)　　　　　　　　　　　　　　　　　　　(c)

▲ **Fig. 64** Staphylococcal scalded skin syndrome. There is typically generalised erythema with accentuation in the flexures (**a**), such as the axillae and groin (**b**), and around the orifices. Epidermal peeling (**c**) is usually seen rather than frank blisters, and Nikolsky's sign is positive.

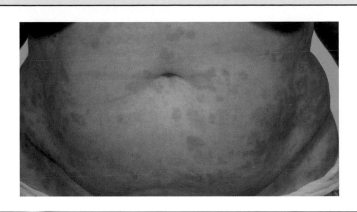

▲**Fig. 65** Urticaria. Erythematous oedematous papules and plaques which are itchy. The skin surface is normal. The key feature that distinguishes urticaria from other dermatoses is the transient nature of lesions, which last for only a few hours and leave no mark.

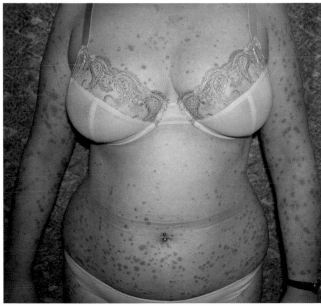

(a)

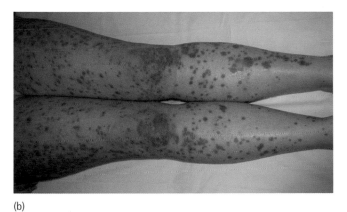

(b)

▲**Fig. 66** Guttate psoriasis. This young woman developed an acute papular eruption on her trunk (a) and limbs (b). On close inspection, the surface of these deep-red papules was scaly. In this case guttate psoriasis was triggered by a sore throat 1 week previously and the anti-streptolysin O titre was raised.

if the pustules are due to bacteraemia or there is secondary infection.

- Blood cultures.

- Swab any suspected sources of infection in toxin-mediated diseases, eg throat, umbilical stump, skin wounds, nose and vagina.

- Serological tests: mycoplasma and herpes simplex virus (HSV) serology in erythema multiforme/SJS/TEN; anti-streptolysin O titre in scarlet fever and vasculitis; acute and convalescent blood samples for serology in viral exanthems; and treponema serology if secondary syphilis is suspected.

Other tests

- CXR: look for evidence of mycoplasma pneumonia in erythema multiforme/SJS/TEN; pneumonitis in chickenpox or SJS/TEN.

- Skin biopsy: in many cases a skin biopsy will not be necessary, but proceed if the diagnosis is uncertain, particularly to distinguish SSSS and TEN.

- ECG and echocardiogram: if Kawasaki's disease is suspected.

Management

Aside from fluids and other supportive care as dictated by the patient's general condition, management will depend on the particular cause of the rash.

- Toxin-mediated disorders: treat the underlying bacterial infection. Toxic shock syndrome may lead to multiorgan failure and intensive care unit support may be needed. General management of SSSS is similar to TEN (see Section 2.10), but it is far less severe as

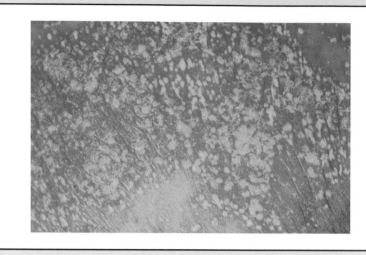

▲**Fig. 67** Pustules. Small, superficial, discrete collections of pus are sheeted across erythematous skin. The differential diagnosis is a drug eruption or pustular psoriasis.

epidermal detachment is very superficial and re-epithelialisation occurs within a few days once the underlying infection is treated.

- Erythema multiforme/SJS/TEN (see Section 2.10).

- Kawasaki's disease: aspirin and intravenous immunoglobulin reduce the long-term cardiac complications.

- Chickenpox or disseminated HSV: intravenous aciclovir.

- Urticaria: antihistamines and treat any infectious triggers (see Section 2.23).

- Drug eruptions: stop the suspected drug (see Section 2.7).

- Viral exanthems: symptomatic treatment in most cases.

- Pityriasis rosea: reassure the patient and give symptomatic treatment only, but advise that resolution takes 6–8 weeks.

- Guttate and pustular psoriasis (see Sections 1.4.2 and 2.17).

If you are unable to make a diagnosis, then consider other infectious exanthems, eg adenoviruses, enteroviruses, cytomegalovirus, Epstein–Barr virus, toxoplasmosis, leptospirosis, Legionnaire's disease, HIV seroconversion and *Listeria*, or acute rheumatic fever or connective tissue diseases such as systemic lupus erythematosus and Still's disease.

Further comments
In this case, it would be tempting to make a diagnosis of a maculopapular drug eruption given that the patient started two new drugs 9 days prior to the onset of the rash. However, this case illustrates the importance of examining the skin carefully and the clue to diagnosis is in the pictures. The clinical photographs in Fig. 60 show a symmetrical eruption densest on the trunk and face; there are multiple erythematous macules and papules, but on close inspection some were studded with small (2–4 mm) blisters and pustules. The differential diagnosis narrows the cause of the eruption to those listed in the section 'Blisters, erosions or

positive Nikolsky sign', and of those the possibilities include chickenpox, disseminated herpes zoster or HSV (the latter two usually being seen in the immunocompromised). When questioned, the patient could not recall ever having had chickenpox. He worked as a hair stylist, so there were many potential contacts and hence chickenpox was likely. Urgent direct immunofluorescence confirmed varicella-zoster virus (VZV) and excluded HSV. Liver function tests revealed an associated hepatitis. Subsequent culture of blister fluid grew VZV. The patient was well enough to be treated with oral valaciclovir as an outpatient and recovered well.

1.4.2 Erythroderma

Scenario

A 50-year-old man with a past history of psoriasis presents with a worsening rash over 2 weeks. He has recently had an upper respiratory tract infection. He is not on any regular medications. He is clearly unwell and baseline observations show he is hypotensive (BP 90/60 mmHg) and tachycardic. Examination of his skin reveals the findings shown in Fig. 68.

Introduction
Widespread confluent erythema involving more than 90% of the skin surface is termed erythroderma. There are several causes (Table 28), with psoriasis and eczema the commonest. Your first priority is to resuscitate the patient, who may be extremely unwell. The cause of erythroderma can then be established and specific treatment instituted.

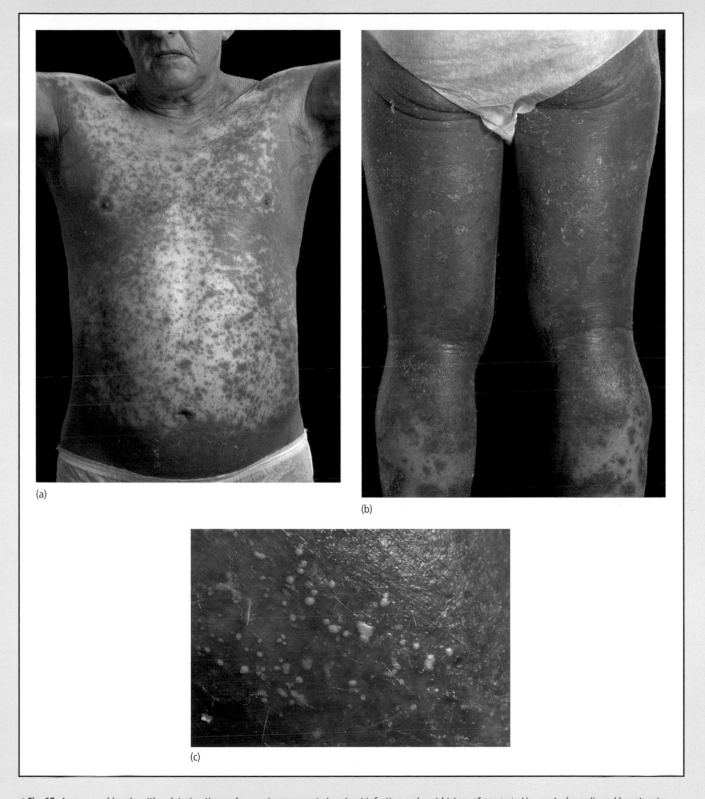

▲ **Fig. 68** A 50-year-old male with a deteriorating rash, recent upper respiratory tract infection and past history of psoriasis. He was tachycardic and hypotensive. At 36 hours after these photographs were taken, the erythema was completely confluent, leaving no normal skin. The images show his torso (**a**), legs (**b**) and a close-up (**c**).

TABLE 28 DIFFERENTIAL DIAGNOSIS OF ERYTHRODERMA[1]

Causes of erythroderma	Diagnosis
Endogenous diseases	Psoriasis (pustular and non-pustular)[2] Eczema[2] Sézary syndrome Pityriasis rubra pilaris Paraneoplastic
'Reactive' diseases	Drug eruptions[2] Allergic contact dermatitis Toxic epidermal necrolysis Infectious exanthems, eg toxic shock syndrome, staphylococcal scalded skin syndrome
Idiopathic	Approximately 30% cases[2]

1. In most cases the cause is exacerbation of a pre-existing dermatosis such as eczema or psoriasis.
2. More common causes.

⚠ Erythroderma is life-threatening because of the complications of widespread cutaneous vasodilatation, increased catabolism and the loss of normal homeostatic functions of the skin.

Complications of erythroderma

- Transepidermal fluid loss, hypovolaemia and renal failure.
- Hypoalbuminaemia.
- Excess heat convection, loss of thermoregulation and hypothermia.
- High-output cardiac failure.

History of the presenting problem

- How long has the skin been red? An acute history with no pre-existing history of skin disease is suggestive of a drug reaction, toxic epidermal necrolysis (TEN) or an infectious exanthem. Although eczema and psoriasis can sometimes progress very rapidly, there will usually be a past history. Sézary syndrome and pityriasis rubra pilaris (PRP) are slower

to evolve, and in PRP there is typically craniocaudal migration.

- Take a very careful drug history: what drugs have been taken in the last month? Ask the patient: 'Anything from "over-the-counter"? Are you absolutely sure? Not one tablet? If you think of anything, please let me know.'

- Does the skin itch or burn? Itching is severe in eczema and Sézary syndrome. Skin tenderness or burning occurs in generalised pustular psoriasis, TEN and staphylococcal scalded skin syndrome (SSSS).

- Has the patient been unwell recently? Infections may trigger exacerbations of psoriasis. There may be a prodromal illness in infectious exanthems (see Section 1.4.1).

- Check for symptoms that suggest malignancy: erythroderma can occasionally be paraneoplastic.

Other relevant history

Enquire about drug reactions and allergies. There may be a history of psoriasis or eczema.

Examination: general features

Initial assessment of the patient should include the following.

- General impression: patients with erythroderma are never well. Is this man unwell, very unwell or nearly dead? If nearly dead, immediately call for help from the intensive care unit.

- Check vital signs: temperature, pulse, respiration and BP.

- Is the patient's intravascular volume depleted? The only reliable signs in this context are a low JVP and postural hypotension. Determine JVP and BP (lying and sitting, since standing will probably not be prudent). It can be difficult to establish these in someone who is erythrodermic and unwell, but the worse the patient, the more important it is to know. If the patient is volume depleted then obtain venous access and start resuscitation immediately, while you complete the history and examination.

- A full general physical examination is required.

Examination: skin

When there is diffuse erythema, ascertaining a cause from the morphology of individual skin lesions is difficult (Fig. 69). Other clues need to be sought.

- Look for pustules: sheets of superficial pustules can occur in drug reactions and generalised acute pustular psoriasis (see Fig. 67). The distinction can be difficult, but there may be a past history of plaque psoriasis in pustular psoriasis.

- Blisters, erosions or positive Nikolsky sign: if present, think of

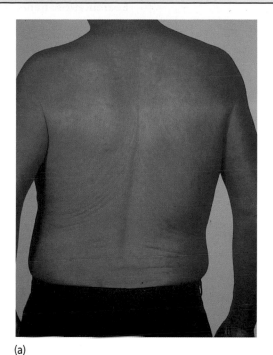

(a)

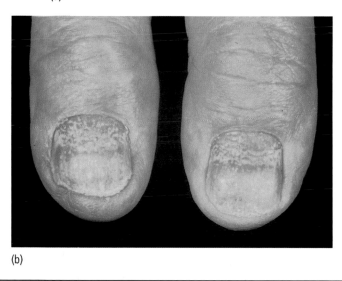

(b)

▲**Fig. 69** Erythrodermic psoriasis (a) and psoriatic nails (b). The skin was scaly on close inspection but ascertaining the cause of erythroderma is often difficult if the skin is examined in isolation. However, in this case there was a past history of plaque psoriasis and the nails were thickened and dystrophic with subungual hyperkeratosis and surface pits.

TEN or SSSS (see Sections 1.1.1 and 1.2.1) (see Figs 63 and 64).

- Scaling: common in all long-standing cases of erythroderma (Fig. 70) and may be thick in psoriasis. In very acute cases scaling may not be seen, but if present it is more suggestive of psoriasis, eczema and drug eruptions than of an infectious exanthem.

Mucous membranes

Ulceration occurs in TEN; erythema of the mouth and eyes occurs in toxic shock syndrome (TSS) (Table 27).

Lymphadenopathy

Reactive hyperplasia of regional nodes occurs in erythroderma regardless of the cause, so it is probable that small nodes will be

palpable. Large nodes suggest a diagnosis of Sézary syndrome or a drug hypersensitivity syndrome.

Palms and soles

Thickening of the skin is prominent in psoriasis, Sézary syndrome and PRP.

Alopecia

A telogen effluvium (see Section 1.1.4) may occur in erythroderma regardless of cause, but total alopecia suggests Sézary syndrome.

> Always check the nails when assessing any patient with a skin disorder. Nail abnormalities will provide diagnostic clues. In this case psoriasis would be suggested by pitting, onycholysis, ridging and thickening of the nails (see Figs 69b and 84). Nail thickening is also seen in Sézary syndrome and PRP.

Investigation

General blood tests

- FBC: may show an eosinophilia in atopic eczema or drug reactions; neutrophilia in generalised pustular psoriasis or a triggering bacterial infection; and lymphocytosis in Sézary syndrome (when Sézary cells are present on the blood film).

- Electrolytes, renal and liver function tests, coagulation screen: perform in any patient who is acutely ill.

To establish particular diagnoses

- IgE: raised in atopic eczema.

- Swabs for microscopy, culture and sensitivity: swab possible sources of *Staphylococcus aureus* infection that may have triggered TSS or SSSS, eg wounds or retained tampons.

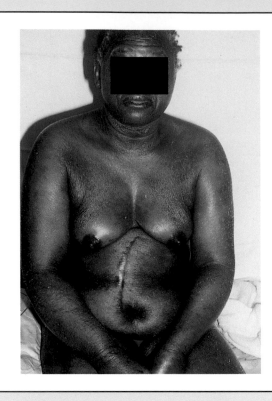

▲**Fig. 70** Erythrodermic drug eruption. The offending drug (zopiclone) was continued for several weeks and over this time the eruption became erythrodermic and scaly. It can be difficult to appreciate erythema in black skin and there is a risk of underestimating the severity of the situation. In this case the skin was hot to touch and the patient was unwell, shivering, tachycardic, hypotensive and dehydrated.

- Lymph node biopsy: if nodes are enlarged and Sézary syndrome is suspected.

- Skin biopsy.

- For further investigations relevant to TSS/SSSS/TEN, see Sections 1.4.1 and 2.10.

Other tests

- CXR and ECG: in any patient who is acutely ill.

Management

Supportive general management of the erythrodermic patient

- Fluid replacement if the patient is volume depleted: if the JVP is decreased and there is postural hypotension, give colloid or 0.9% saline rapidly until the JVP has risen

into the normal range and there is no postural drop in BP. Then give fluid at a rate equal to measured output plus a large allowance (often 2–3 L per day) for greatly increased insensible losses, adjusted in the light of clinical examination of volume status (which should be repeated at least twice daily). Particular care is required in the elderly, who may have renal and cardiac impairment.
- Keep careful fluid balance charts and weigh the patient daily (if possible).
- Monitor electrolytes and renal function daily while the patient remains acutely ill.
- Nurse the patient in a warm environment.
- Ensure the patient has bed-rest.
- Ensure adequate nutrition: oral nutritional supplements, nasogastric feeding or parenteral nutrition may be required (monitor serum albumin).
- Treat the skin with bland emollients, applied liberally and frequently.

Specific treatment

Management of individual diseases are discussed in Section 2. Erythrodermic psoriasis often requires the use of systemic treatment, particularly the acute generalised pustular form that is aggressive and life-threatening. Erythrodermic atopic eczema may settle with topical therapy alone, but it is an indicator of more severe disease that may need systemic treatment. Drug eruptions usually settle with symptomatic treatment once the drug is stopped, but systemic steroids may be required (see Section 2.7). PRP is a rare idiopathic disorder: it is difficult to treat (retinoids, ciclosporin and methotrexate have been used) but resolves spontaneously in many cases. If paraneoplastic erythroderma is suspected, treat the underlying neoplasm if possible.

Further comments

In this case, because of the patient's past history, the likeliest diagnosis is an exacerbation of his psoriasis, although one should consider all possibilities. With the finding in a hypotensive patient of sheets of tiny pustules on background erythema (see Fig. 68c), generalised pustular psoriasis is the diagnosis (see Section 2.17). Why did his psoriasis deteriorate? It is possible this was secondary to respiratory infection, but also enquire about drugs. The patient was admitted to hospital and supportive treatment commenced. He was given acitretin which brought his psoriasis under control within a few days. One month later, his skin had cleared completely.

2.1 Acne vulgaris

Aetiology/pathophysiology/pathology

Acne vulgaris is a disease of the pilosebaceous unit. It is multifactorial, involving increased sebum production (under androgen stimulation), increased keratinisation of follicles causing blocked follicle openings, proliferation of *Propionibacterium acnes* and inflammation.

Epidemiology

It is extremely common and can affect all ages, but occurs most often in teenage years. The peak age for severity is 16–17 years in females and 17–19 years in males. The face is usually affected first; the back and upper chest may be affected in 30% of patients.

Clinical presentation

Common

- Blackheads (open comedomes), whiteheads (closed comedomes) and inflamed papules, pustules and nodules in varying proportions and of varying severity affecting the face (Figs 11 and 71a), back and upper chest.

- Scarring may be evident (Fig. 71a).

- Post-inflammatory hyperpigmentation in brown and black skin.

Uncommon

- Acne fulminans: severe inflammatory/cystic acne with ulceration and associated fever, anorexia, malaise, arthralgia and leucocytosis. This usually affects males aged 14–18.

- Acne conglobata: severe nodulocystic acne, sinuses, scars and grouped comedomes without systemic symptoms. Intertriginous areas may be involved (hidradenitis suppurativa).

> Severe acne requires prompt and aggressive specialist treatment to reduce the risk of permanent scarring.

Investigation

- The diagnosis is generally made clinically.

- The sudden onset of severe acne, any unusual resistance to treatment and/or signs of hyperandrogenism should prompt investigation for an endocrine cause.

Differential diagnosis

- Bacterial folliculitis.

- Rosacea: affects adults, with erythema and pustules of the cheeks, chin, nose and forehead. There are no comedones. Flushing may be prominent (see Fig. 12).

- Perioral dermatitis: generally affects women aged 20–40 years.

Erythema, scaling, papules and pustules occur around the mouth and chin. It is often precipitated by topical corticosteroids.

- Acneiform drug eruptions.

> **Drug-induced acne**
>
> This can be caused by the following drugs.
> - Corticosteroids (oral and inhaled).
> - Androgens and anabolic steroids.
> - Phenytoin.
> - Lithium.
> - Isoniazid.
> - Quinine.
> - Disulfiram.
> - Iodides and bromides.

Treatment

This depends on the severity of the acne.

- Mild acne: topical benzoyl peroxide, salicylic acid, and retinoids with or without topical antibiotics.

- Moderate acne: systemic antibiotics (tetracyclines and erythromycin) or cyproterone acetate in females with or without topical therapy as above.

- Severe acne with scarring (or which is resistant to other treatments): oral isotretinoin (Fig. 71b).

Prognosis

- Teenage acne clears by age 25 in 90% of patients, but if untreated can be associated with significant psychosocial morbidity.

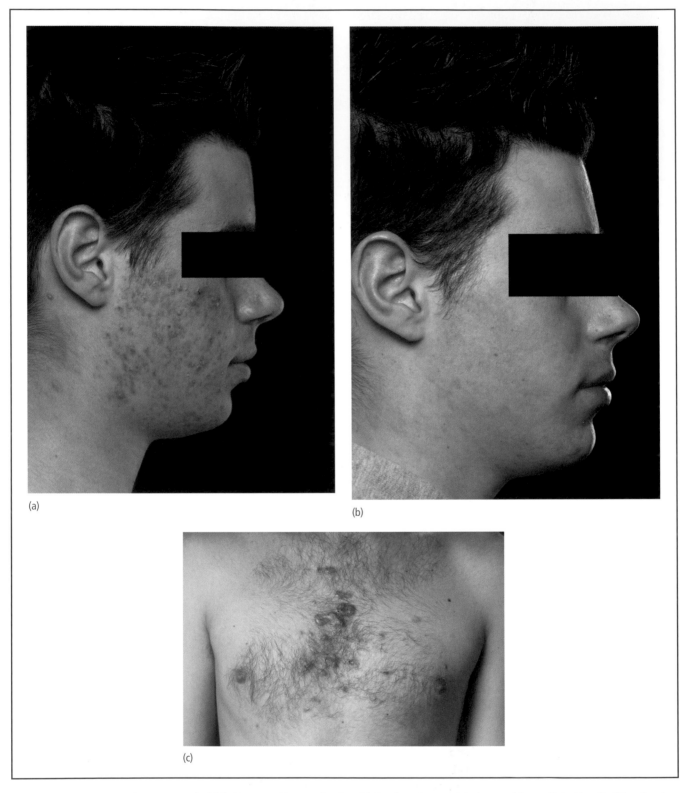

(a)

(b)

(c)

▲ **Fig. 71** Acne with scarring. This young man had failed to respond to several oral antibiotics given at appropriate doses and for a sufficient length of time. Scarring was evident in addition to comedones, papules and nodules (**a**). A course of isotretinoin cleared his acne (**b**). Sadly, in some patients the residual scarring is more severe and can be keloid (**c**).

- Severe acne with the potential for scarring requires early aggressive treatment to avoid long-term sequelae.

Disease associations

Uncommonly, acne may be associated with an underlying endocrinological disorder.

Endocrine causes of acne

- Polycystic ovary syndrome.
- Cushing's syndrome.
- Congenital adrenal hyperplasia.
- Gonadal or adrenal androgen-secreting tumours.

FURTHER READING

Hunter JAA, Savin JA and Dahl MV. *Clinical Dermatology*, 3rd edn. Oxford: Blackwell Science, 2002: 148–56.

– – – – – – – – – – – – – – – – –

Zaenglein AL and Thiboutot DM. Acne vulgaris. In: Bolognia JL, Jorizzo JL and Rapini RP, eds. *Dermatology*. Edinburgh: Mosby, 2003.

2.2 Acanthosis nigricans

Aetiology/pathophysiology/ pathology

In acanthosis nigricans (AN), epidermal proliferation is thought to occur due to stimulation of the keratinocyte insulin-like growth factor (IGF)-1 receptor.

- Benign AN can be inherited, drug induced (eg nicotinic acid or oral contraceptive pill) or associated with various insulin resistance syndromes.

- Pseudoacanthosis nigricans is associated with obesity and is more common in racially pigmented skin.

- Malignant AN is usually associated with adenocarcinomas.

Clinical presentation

Common

Pigmented, thickened and papillomatous skin with a velvety texture commonly affecting the axillae, the back of the neck and the groin (Fig. 31).

Uncommon

- Other flexural sites and the umbilicus can be affected.

- Generalised forms exist (more common in malignant AN).

- Mucous membrane involvement (in 50% of cases of malignant AN).

- Palmar involvement: 'tripe palms' (usually in cases of malignant AN).

Investigation

- Skin biopsy if there is any diagnostic uncertainty.

- Blood tests to investigate possible diabetes and insulin resistance syndromes.

- Look for underlying malignancy if suspected.

Treatment

This is none specific.

Prognosis

- Pseudoacanthosis nigricans may improve with weight reduction and drug-induced AN will improve when the drug is stopped.

- Malignant AN may improve with removal of the underlying tumour.

FURTHER READING

Judge MR, Mclean WHI and Munro CS. Disorders of keratinization. In: Burns DA, Breathnach SM, Cox NH and Griffiths CEM, eds. *Rook's Textbook of Dermatology*, 7th edn. Oxford: Blackwell Science, 2004.

2.3 Alopecia areata

Aetiology/pathophysiology/ pathology

Alopecia areata is thought to be an organ-specific autoimmune disease and shows a familial tendency. Biopsies show a perifollicular T-cell infiltrate.

Epidemiology

Alopecia areata accounts for 2% of all new dermatology outpatients each year in the UK and USA. Its overall peak onset is between the age of 20 and 50 years. Males and females are equally affected.

Clinical presentation

Common

Uninflamed, non-scaly, non-scarring oval or round patch of alopecia (Figs 25 and 72). 'Exclamation-mark' hairs at the margins are pathognomonic (these are broken hairs 3–4 mm in length that are narrower and less pigmented proximally). The scalp is the commonest site, but any hair-bearing areas can be affected.

Uncommon

- Nail pitting.

- Entire scalp or whole-body hair loss (alopecia totalis and universalis).

Investigation

Perform an autoimmune screen to exclude associated disease.

Differential diagnosis (for common presentations only)

Other causes of patchy non-scarring alopecia (see Table 5), including androgenetic alopecia, ringworm and traction alopecia – but usually the diagnosis is easily made.

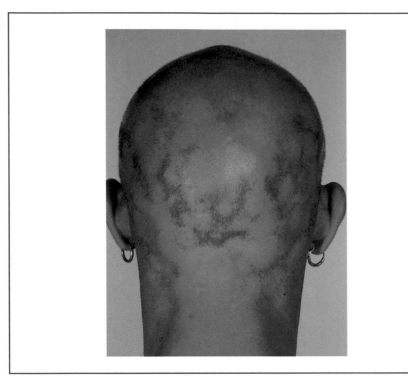

▲ **Fig. 72** Alopecia areata. Multiple oval/round patches have resulted in extensive alopecia. The skin surface appears entirely normal and hair follicles would be visible on close inspection.

dermoepidermal separation and blister formation. The target antigen in most cases is type XVII collagen (BP 180), a component of hemidesmosomes. Bullous pemphigoid is occasionally drug induced. Pemphigoid gestationis (PG) (synonym: herpes gestationis) is a rare subtype of bullous pemphigoid that occurs in pregnancy.

Epidemiology

Bullous pemphigoid can occur at any age, even childhood, but is most common in the elderly. It is the commonest immunobullous disease in Western countries. PG is associated with pregnancy, particulary the second and third trimesters.

Clinical presentation

Pruritus and a rash in a patient who is otherwise well.

Physical signs

Common

- Initially erythematous, urticaria-like plaques on which tense blisters then form (cf. pemphigus vulgaris) and which may be up to several centimetres in diameter (see Figs 6 and 73).

- Generalised distribution, but bullous pemphigoid particularly affects the flexural surfaces of limbs and PG the abdomen.

Uncommon

- Oral erosions and itchy nodules.

- Neonatal PG due to transplacental passage of pathogenic IgG.

Investigation

- Skin biopsy: will show a blister at the DEJ and direct immunofluorescence shows IgG

Treatment

Topical or intralesional steroids, contact irritants or allergens, ultraviolet light and minoxidil. Relapse is common after stopping treatment.

Prognosis

This is variable. Spontaneous regrowth of individual patches of hair may occur after a few months, but relapse is common. Poor prognostic indicators include prepubertal onset, atopy, Down's syndrome, widespread disease or scalp margin involvement.

Disease associations

Other autoimmune diseases, particularly thyroid disease, pernicious anaemia, vitiligo and systemic lupus erythematosus. Also atopy and Down's syndrome.

FURTHER READING

De Berker DAR, Messenger AG and Dawber RPR. Disorders of hair. In: Burns DA, Breathnach SM, Cox NH and Griffiths CEM, eds. *Rook's Textbook of Dermatology*, 7th edn. Oxford: Blackwell Science, 2004.

Du Vivier A. *Atlas of Clinical Dermatology*, 3rd edn. London: Churchill Livingstone, 2002: chapter 26 (Disorders affecting the hair and scalp).

2.4 Bullous pemphigoid

Aetiology/pathophysiology/pathology

Bullous pemphigoid is an autoimmune disease in which IgG binds to the dermoepidermal junction (DEJ) of skin/mucous membranes, leading to

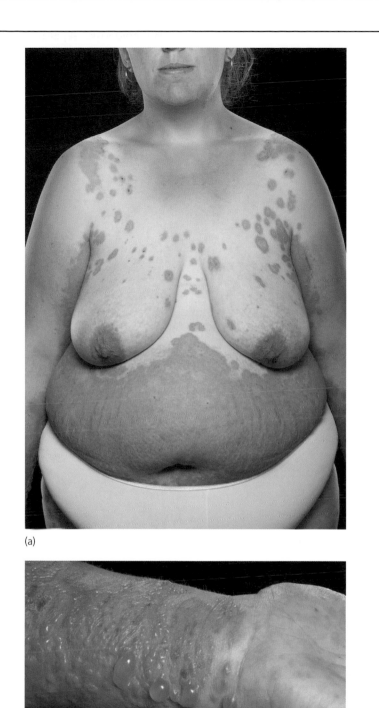

(a)

(b)

▲ **Fig. 73** Pemphigoid gestationis. A 30-year-old woman who presented in the third trimester of pregnancy with a symmetrical pruritic eruption (**a**). Tense blisters were visible on a background of erythematous oedematous plaques (**b**).

and C3 along the DEJ (see Section 3.2).

- Serum for indirect immunofluorescence: serum IgG binds to the DEJ of normal skin.

- Blood count may show an eosinophilia.

Differential diagnosis

- Bullous pemphigoid: other immunobullous diseases, urticaria, erythema multiforme and eczema.

- PG: polymorphic eruption of pregnancy and urticaria.

Treatments

- Bullous pemphigoid: topical and systemic corticosteroids with or without an adjuvant drug (commonly azathioprine).

- PG: topical corticosteroids if possible with or without systemic corticosteroids.

Complications

The commonest complications are treatment related. Infection of skin erosions may lead to septicaemia.

Prognosis

- In bullous pemphigoid there is significant treatment-related morbidity/mortality, but ultimately it may remit.

- PG resolves after delivery but may recur in subsequent pregnancies. There is a risk of premature delivery and low birth weight.

Disease associations

Other autoimmune diseases, particularly in PG. The association of bullous pemphigoid with malignancy is controversial.

FURTHER READING

Nousari HC and Anhalt GJ. Pemphigus and bullous pemphigoid. *Lancet* 1999; 354: 667–72.

Wojnarowska F, Venning VA and Burge SM. Immunobullous diseases. In: Burns DA, Breathnach SM, Cox NH and Griffiths CEM, eds. *Rook's Textbook of Dermatology*, 7th edn. Oxford: Blackwell Science, 2004.

Wolff K, Johnson RA and Suurmond D. *Fitzpatrick's Color Atlas and Synopsis of Clinical Dermatology*, 5th edn. New York: McGraw-Hill, 2005: Section 6 (Bullous disease).

2.5 Dermatomyositis

Aetiology

Dermatomyositis (DM) is an inflammatory disease of skin and striated muscle that is likely to be immunologically based.

Epidemiology

It affects all races, is twice as common in women and has a weak familial tendency. Adults aged 40–60 years are predominantly affected, and in this group there is an association with underlying carcinoma and lymphoma. Children are sometimes affected (juvenile DM).

Clinical presentation

Common

- Rash, particularly of sun-exposed sites.

- Proximal muscle weakness and pain causing difficulty climbing stairs or brushing hair.

- General malaise.

Uncommon

- Difficulties with speech and swallowing.

- Raynaud's phenomenon.

- Joint pains and swellings.

- Dyspnoea.

Physical signs

Common

- Purple/red (heliotrope) oedematous facial rash, particularly affecting the eyelids, cheeks and forehead. May be scaly. (See Fig. 20a.)

- Purple/red papules over knuckles (Gottron's papules). Streaking erythema along the dorsum of the fingers (see Fig. 20b).

- Prominent, dilated nail-fold capillaries with ragged cuticles (see Fig. 20c).

- Proximal muscle weakness.

Uncommon

- Rash that can occur on any area, particularly on the back/chest/scalp.

- Diffuse alopecia.

- Weakness, which can affect any muscle group.

- Calcification of muscles/skin (particularly in childhood cases).

- Arthritis, pulmonary fibrosis and cardiac failure.

Investigation

- Blood tests: creatine phosphokinase is often increased. In DM (cf. lupus), antinuclear antibodies/DNA binding is often negative, but Jo-1 antibodies may be detected.

- Electromyography: distinguishes neuropathic from myopathic weakness.

- Muscle biopsy: may show inflammation and oedema.

- Skin biopsy: may resemble subacute lupus.

- Tests to investigate possible underlying malignancy.

Differential diagnosis

Possibilities include systemic lupus erythematosus, polymyositis, systemic sclerosis and muscular dystrophies.

Treatment

- Treat any underlying malignancy.

- High-dose oral steroids, in a reducing regimen (remembering osteoporosis protection).

- Additional immunosuppression may be needed, eg azathioprine, methotrexate and ciclosporin.

- Physiotherapy to prevent contractures.

> Remember to think about potential side effects when using high-dose oral steroids. Consider dual-energy X-ray absorptiometry, oral bisphosphonates to prevent osteoporosis, gastric protection, monitoring of BP, and monitoring of glucose in urine.

Complications

- Respiratory failure and bulbar palsy.

- Muscle contractures and subcutaneous calcification, especially in children.

- Complications of treatment (common).

Prognosis

The overall mortality rate from DM is 25%, the majority of deaths being due to underlying malignancy.

Poor prognostic factors are old age, pulmonary involvement, skin necrosis and dysphagia. Calcinosis may be a good prognostic sign. The course of the disease is highly variable.

Disease associations

- Carcinoma and lymphoma in adults.

- Penicillamine treatment.

FURTHER READING

Goodfield MJD, Jones SK and Veale DJ. The connective tissue diseases. In: Burns DA, Breathnach SM, Cox NH and Griffiths CEM, eds. *Rook's Textbook of Dermatology*, 7th edn. Oxford: Blackwell Science, 2004.

2.6 Dermatitis herpetiformis

Aetiology/pathophysiology/pathology

Dermatitis herpetiformis is characterised by IgA deposits in the tips of dermal papillae (see Section 3.2) that are believed to be pathogenic, although the antigen is not known. Biopsies show neutrophil microabscesses in the dermal papillae or frank blister formation at the dermoepidermal junction. Dermatitis herpetiformis is associated with gluten-sensitive enteropathy and HLA-DRB1*0301, DQA1*0501/DQB1*02.

Epidemiology

Commonest in northern Europe, particularly Ireland, and rare in the black, Asian and Oriental populations. Onset can be at any age, but is typically in young and middle-aged adults (15–50 years).

Clinical presentation

Common

- Intense pruritus and burning or stinging of the skin.

- Eruption of small blisters on erythematous papules is a classical feature. More commonly, excoriated papules or urticarial wheals are seen. These typically affect the extensor surfaces, especially elbows, knees, buttocks and sacrum (see Fig. 7).

Uncommon

- Oral ulcers.

- Pruritus/burning without rash in early stages.

Investigation/staging

- Skin biopsy (histology and direct immunofluorescence).

- Serum autoantibodies: anti-tissue transglutaminase antibodies.

- Jejunal biopsy.

- Indirect immunofluorescence is always negative, in contrast to bullous pemphigoid and pemphigus vulgaris.

- Blood count may reveal changes suggesting enteropathy, eg a microcytic anaemia.

Differential diagnosis

Scabies, urticaria, bites and other immunobullous diseases.

Treatment

Sulphone drugs (usually dapsone) result in a prompt clinical response. A gluten-free diet, the long-term treatment of choice, should be commenced: response to this is slow, but it should enable sulphone drugs to be withdrawn eventually.

Prognosis

The prognosis is good if the diet is strict. Long-term dapsone may be required if a gluten-free diet is not strictly adhered to. There is a long-term risk of small bowel lymphoma, although a gluten-free diet reduces the risk.

Disease associations

Gluten-sensitive enteropathy (almost all cases, although may be asymptomatic) and other autoimmune diseases.

FURTHER READING

Wolff K, Johnson RA and Suurmond D. *Fitzpatrick's Color Atlas and Synopsis of Clinical Dermatology*, 5th edn. New York: McGraw-Hill, 2005: Section 6 (Bullous disease).

Wojnarowska F, Venning VA and Burge SM. Immunobullous diseases. In: Burns DA, Breathnach SM, Cox NH and Griffiths CEM, eds. *Rook's Textbook of Dermatology*, 7th edn. Oxford: Blackwell Science, 2004.

2.7 Drug eruptions

Aetiology/pathophysiology/pathology

Drug eruptions can mimic a wide variety of idiopathic dermatoses and many drugs can trigger each clinical pattern. They are mediated by both non-immune and immune mechanisms (types I–IV hypersensitivity), and genetic predisposition is probably important.

When assessing skin diseases, always suspect a drug trigger. In acute presentations, document the start and finish dates of all drugs taken in the preceding month. There is no test to identify the offending drug, but the most likely is chosen on the basis of timing and the track-record of the drugs consumed. Some are more likely than others.

Epidemiology

Drug eruptions are very common, occurring in around 3% of hospitalised patients. There is an increased incidence in HIV-positive individuals.

Clinical presentation

Listed below are drug eruptions with several recognised drug triggers for each. It is not an exhaustive list. Look up individual drugs up as you encounter cases in practice.

Common

- Maculopapular eruption (see Fig. 61). Onset can be up to 3 weeks after starting a drug, but is usually within 7–10 days (and 48 hours if there has been previous exposure). Causal drugs include antibiotics (especially penicillins, gentamicin and sulphonamides), gold, NSAIDs, phenytoin and carbamazepine.

- Urticaria ± angio-oedema ± anaphylaxis (see Fig. 65): onset can be up to 2 weeks in the unexposed, but can be minutes/hours if the patient is sensitised. Causal drugs include antibiotics (especially penicillins), contrast media, aspirin (NSAIDs), angiotensin-converting enzyme inhibitors, anaesthetic agents, codeine and opiates.

- Fixed drug eruption: presents with round/oval red macules/patches/plaques; these may blister and are often solitary. They resolve with hyperpigmentation (see Fig. 30a). On rechallenge, recurs at an identical site (ie fixed). Causal drugs include antibiotics (especially tetracyclines and sulphonamides), NSAIDs and barbiturates.

Less common

- Erythroderma (see Fig. 70): this may evolve from a maculopapular eruption if the drug is continued. Causal drugs include sulphonamides, penicillins, phenytoin and antimalarials.

- Erythema multiforme/Stevens–Johnson syndrome (SJS)/toxic epidermal necrolysis (TEN) (see Figs 5, 62 and 63): causal drugs include anticonvulsants, allopurinol, antibiotics (especially sulphonamides and penicillins) and NSAIDs (see Section 2.10).

- Drug hypersensitivity syndrome (DRESS syndrome: *d*rug *r*ash with *e*osinophilia and *s*ystemic *s*ymptoms): this can result in maculopapular or erythrodermic rash with fever, eosinophilia, lymphadenopathy, facial oedema with or without hepatitis, pneumonitis and myocarditis. Onset is usually 2–6 weeks after the drug has been started. Causal drugs include anticonvulsants, sulphonamides and allopurinol.

- Pigmentation: this usually has a delayed onset (months or even years). Causal drugs include amiodarone, minocycline, antimalarials, cytotoxics, chlorpromazine, oral contraceptive pill and heavy metals.

- Necrosis: 3–5 days after starting warfarin.

- Toxic pustuloderma (acute generalised exanthematous pustulosis): sheets of pustules on diffuse erythema (see Fig. 67). Causal drugs include anticonvulsants and antibiotics (especially penicillins and macrolides).

- Acne (see Figs 11 and 71): causal drugs include corticosteroids, anabolic steroids, androgens, oral contraceptive pill, lithium and isoniazid.

- Erythema nodosum (see Section 2.11 and Figs. 40 and 76): causal drugs include sulphonamides and the oral contraceptive pill.

- Lichen planus-like: causal drugs include antimalarials, beta-blockers, angiotensin-converting enzyme inhibitors, gold and diuretics.

- Photosensitivity (Fig. 15): this may not manifest until spring/summer. Causal drugs include antibiotics (especially tetracyclines), NSAIDs, amiodarone, phenothiazines and thiazides.

- Hair loss: causal drugs include cytotoxics, retinoids and anticoagulants.

- Vasculitis (see Figs 45 and 98): causal drugs include allopurinol, penicillin and sulphonamides.

- Pseudoporphyria: causal drugs include furosemide, NSAIDs, tetracyclines and sulphonylureas.

- Lupus erythematosus-like syndrome: causal drugs include procainamide, hydralazine, isoniazid, phenytoin and minocycline.

- Nail pigmentation: causal drugs include antimalarials, tetracyclines, lithium, heavy metals, cytotoxics and phenothiazines.

- Onycholysis: causal drugs include tetracyclines, cytotoxics, captopril and phenothiazines.

Investigation/staging

- FBC may show eosinophilia.

- Skin biopsy: can show variable changes depending on the type of reaction, but the presence of eosinophils suggests a drug cause.

Treatment

- Emergency: for anaphylactic reactions, give epinephrine (adrenaline), hydrocortisone and Piriton (see *Acute Medicine*, Section 1.2.33; and *Rheumatology and Clinical Immunology*, Section 1.4.2).

- Short term: stop the suspected drug and treat symptomatically. Systemic corticosteroids are used in drug hypersensitivity, particularly when there is visceral involvement, and sometimes to hasten recovery in erythroderma and SJS/TEN (see Section 2.10).

Prognosis

Generally good once the drug is stopped but SJS, TEN, anaphylaxis, erythrodermic drug reactions and drug hypersensitivity syndromes can be life-threatening. They can persist for several weeks and sometimes months.

Prevention

Avoid the drug. Document the patient's reaction to it in the medical records. Tell the patient, family and GP about this, and tell the patient to wear a Medic-Alert bracelet. It is essential to ensure that all concerned are informed: repeat exposure following a potentially life-threatening drug reaction could result in death.

FURTHER READING

Breathnach SM. Drug reactions. In: Burns DA, Breathnach SM, Cox NH and Griffiths CEM, eds. *Rook's Textbook of Dermatology*, 7th edn. Oxford: Blackwell Science, 2004.

Breathnach SM and Hintner H. *Adverse Drug Reactions and the Skin*. Oxford: Blackwell Science, 1992.

Wolff K, Johnson RA, Suurmond D. *Fitzpatrick's Color Atlas and Synopsis of Clinical Dermatology*, 5th edn. New York: McGraw-Hill, 2005: Section 20 (Adverse cutaneous drug reactions).

2.8 Atopic eczema

Aetiology/pathophysiology/pathology

An itchy, chronically relapsing, inflammatory skin disease that often occurs in association with the other atopic conditions (hay fever and asthma). Genetic and environmental factors are important (70% of cases have a family history), but inheritance is polygenic.

Much research has focused on immunological mechanisms, showing that antigen challenge preferentially activates Th2 T-helper cells, which produce interleukin (IL)-4 and IL-5. These cytokines stimulate B-cell IgE synthesis, and IgE levels are raised in 60–80% of cases. It is not clear how this leads to eczema. Recent research indicates that these immunological events may be secondary to impairment of skin barrier function, allowing increased permeation of allergens. Mutations in epidermal barrier proteins, including filaggrin, have been identified.

Epidemiology

Males and females are equally affected. Atopic eczema is common, affecting 5–15% of children by the age of 7 years and with a prevalence of 2–10% in adults. Onset is usually between 2 and 6 months of age.

Clinical presentation

Common

- Itchy macular erythema, papules and/or vesicles.

- Lichenification (skin thickening with increased markings secondary to scratching).

- Excoriations.

- Dry skin (xerosis).

- Secondary bacterial infection (impetiginised eczema).

- Follicular eczema in black people; discrete follicular papules are seen.

- Distribution varies with age: cheeks/exposed sites are usually affected in infants, and limb flexures more so in children and adults (see Figs 17 and 74).

Uncommon

- Inverse distribution of eczema, affecting extensor surfaces.

- Nail pitting.

Investigation

The diagnosis is usually clinical. Take skin swabs if secondary infection is suspected. A raised IgE and positive radioallergosorbent or prick tests support the diagnosis of atopy.

Differential diagnosis

Possibilities include seborrhoeic dermatitis, allergic contact dermatitis, scabies and psoriasis.

Treatment

- Avoid soaps and detergents and avoid wearing wool. Reduce house-dust mite exposure.

- Emollients and topical steroids.

- Treat secondary infections.

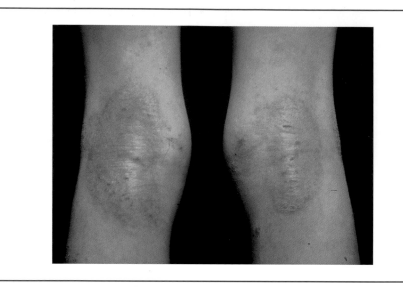

▲ **Fig. 74** Atopic eczema. There is erythema and lichenification of the skin in the popliteal fossae, a preferentially involved site. Excoriations due to scratching are also seen.

- Topical immunomodulatory drugs: tacrolimus and pimecrolimus.

- In more severe cases phototherapy, oral steroids or second-line immunosuppression with azathioprine or ciclosporin may be required.

Complications

Secondary infection with bacteria, usually *Staphylococcus aureus* or *Streptococcus*, or herpes simplex (eczema herpeticum) (see Fig. 1b and Section 1.1.1).

Prognosis

Gradual improvement through childhood, with 50% of sufferers are clear by 13 years of age.

Disease associations

Asthma, hay fever, food allergies and anaphylaxis.

FURTHER READING

Friedman PS and Holden CA. Atopic dermatitis. In: Burns DA, Breathnach SM, Cox NH and Griffiths CEM, eds. *Rook's Textbook of Dermatology*, 7th edn. Oxford: Blackwell Science, 2004.

2.9 Contact dermatitis

Aetiology/pathophysiology/pathology

Contact dermatitis (CD) is eczema of the skin induced by contact with exogenous substances. It is broadly divided into allergic and irritant reactions.

- Allergic CD (ACD) is antigen specific and occurs only in some individuals. Memory T cells develop after the initial exposure and mediate type IV (delayed) allergy on subsequent exposure. Common allergens include nickel, fragrance, plants and rubber chemicals.

- Irritants directly damage the skin. Irritant CD can develop in anyone after cumulative exposure, eg to detergents, or after a single exposure to a strong irritant, eg wet cement.

Epidemiology

Contact dermatitis is common. It accounts for approximately 30% of all reported cases of occupational disease.

Clinical presentation

Common

Allergic contact dermatitis The physical signs are those of eczema (see Section 2.8). In very acute cases there may be severe blistering (see Fig. 3). Onset later in life in a non-atopic individual and/or atypical distribution of involvement suggests CD as opposed to atopic eczema. Classical examples of ACD are hand eczema with a cut-off at the wrists in a 'glove distribution' in an individual allergic to rubber chemicals; facial eczema in a person with a nail varnish allergy (see Fig. 19); or dermatitis confined to the ear lobes and umbilicus in patients allergic to nickel in earrings and jeans studs (Fig. 75). ACD also occurs classically at sites of topical medicament exposure, eg leg ulcers or pruritus ani. Think of ACD in cases of eczema that are resistant to treatment.

Irritant contact dermatitis Hand dermatitis is most common and particularly affects the finger webs. It often occurs in individuals whose occupation involves repeated hand washing or use of detergents, eg nurses and domestic workers.

Investigation

Patch testing to confirm or exclude ACD (see Section 3.3).

Differential diagnosis

Endogenous eczema, psoriasis and fungal infections.

Treatments

Avoidance of allergens and irritants. Topical use of emollients and corticosteroids. Systemic steroids, and rarely PUVA (photochemotherapy with oral methoxy*p*soralen followed by *u*ltraviolet *A*) or oral azathioprine, are sometimes used in severe cases of CD.

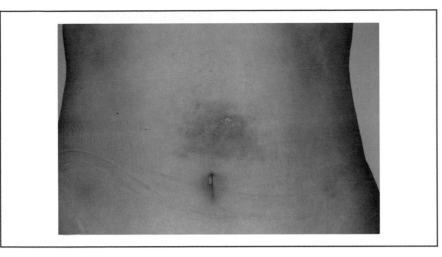

▲**Fig. 75** Allergic contact dermatitis to nickel: a characteristic site (due to contact with the stud fastener of jeans).

Prognosis

Good if the patient is able to avoid specific allergens and/or avoid exposure to irritants. Rubber and nickel are ubiquitous and are therefore difficult to avoid. Atopic patients have a worse prognosis.

Disease associations

Atopic patients are at increased risk of developing irritant CD.

FURTHER READING

Wilkinson SM and Beck MH. Contact dermatitis: allergic. In: Burns DA, Breathnach SM, Cox NH and Griffiths CEM, eds. *Rook's Textbook of Dermatology*, 7th edn. Oxford: Blackwell Science, 2004.

2.10 Erythema multiforme, Stevens–Johnson syndrome and toxic epidermal necrolysis

Aetiology/pathophysiology/ pathology

Erythema multiforme (EM), Stevens–Johnson syndrome (SJS) and toxic epidermal necrolysis (TEN) are thought to represent a spectrum of disease caused by an immunological response common to a number of stimuli, including:

- infections, particularly herpes simplex virus (HSV) and *Mycoplasma*;

- drugs, particularly anticonvulsants, allopurinol, antibiotics (especially sulphonamides and penicillins) and NSAIDs, that have usually been given 1–3 weeks prior to onset.

However, many cases (25–50%) are idiopathic. Biopsies show necrosis of keratinocytes, which may be scanty in mild cases or result in full-thickness epidermal necrosis in TEN. Recent evidence implicates activation of the FAS death receptor on keratinocytes leading to apoptosis (see *Scientific Background to Medicine 1*, Cell Biology – Cell cycle and apoptosis). There is an increased risk of this in individuals with HIV.

Clinical presentation

- Common: skin rash (often tender) with or without painful mucosal ulceration.

- Uncommon: mucosal ulceration alone; recurrent EM (often HSV triggered).

Physical signs

Erythema multiforme

- Dusky red macules, papules and plaques (target lesions are typical but not always present) (see Fig. 62).

- Typically distal limbs, including palms/soles, but the affliction may be more widespread.

- Individual lesions may blister.

- There may be mucosal ulceration.

- May or may not be signs of mycoplasma pneumonia or HSV infection.

- Patients are often relatively well.

Stevens–Johnson syndrome

- Skin lesions as in EM, but they have a tendency to be more widespread and bullous lesions are more common (see Fig. 5).

- Painful mucosal inflammation/ ulceration, including (in order of frequency) mouth and lips, eyes, genitalia and respiratory epithelium (pneumonitis). Haemorrhagic crusting of the lips is characteristic.

- Patient unwell with fever.

Toxic epidermal necrolysis

- Diffuse erythema (>10% skin surface) and tenderness, with epidermal detachment revealing raw red dermis (see Fig. 63). Erythroderma occurs in 10% of cases.

- Positive Nikolsky sign.

- Mucosal involvement as in SJS.

- Patient very unwell with a fever.

Investigations

- Skin biopsy.

- CXR: look for mycoplasma or pneumonitis.

- *Mycoplasma* and HSV serology.

- Urea and electrolytes, liver function tests and FBC (may show anaemia, leucopenia and thrombocytopenia).

Differential diagnosis

- EM: hand, foot and mouth disease; cicatricial pemphigoid; pemphigus vulgaris; cutaneous lupus.

- TEN: staphylococcal scalded skin syndrome.

Treatment

Treatment is largely supportive and good nursing care is essential. Management is as outlined for erythroderma (see Section 1.4.2), plus the following.

- Any suspected drug triggers should be stopped and triggering infections should be treated.

- If there is extensive skin involvement, nurse patients on an air-fluidised bed in an intensive care unit or burns unit.

- Skin handling should be minimal and aseptic, and strong analgesia may be needed. Topical antiseptics are often used to minimise sepsis risk.

- Fluid replacement and nutritional supplementation will be needed. Monitor fluid balance carefully.

- Involve ophthalmology colleagues if there is ocular involvement.

- Watch carefully for signs of infection.

No specific therapies are of proven benefit. Corticosteroids are controversial. The risks, especially if there are widespread erosions, may outweigh the short-term benefits.

Recent experimental and clinical data support the use of intravenous immunogobulin in TEN. Other immunosuppressants have also been used, eg ciclosporin.

Complications

Common

- Fluid and electrolyte loss. May lead to prerenal failure.

- Protein loss and hypoalbuminaemia.

- Infection ± septicaemia if there are extensive erosions.

- Inability to eat/drink.

- Scarring of mucosal surfaces (may cause blindness).

Less common

- Pneumonitis and acute respiratory distress syndrome.

- Multiorgan failure.

- Gastrointestinal bleeding.

Prognosis

The epidermis will regenerate after 3–4 weeks in TEN, but the mortality rate is 30%. Poor prognostic indicators include increasing age, increasing percentage of epidermal loss, tachycardia, hyperglycaemia, acidosis, raised urea and underlying malignancy.

Prevention

Secondary

Avoid the precipitating drug: warn the patient, family and GP of its effects and make the patient wear a Medic-Alert bracelet. Repeat exposure is likely to result in a more severe reaction, which could be fatal. For HSV-triggered recurrent EM, prophylactic aciclovir is used. Azathioprine and other immunosuppressants are sometimes used in recurrent cases.

FURTHER READING

Breathnach SM. Erythema multiforme, Stevens–Johnson syndrome and toxic epidermal necrolysis. In: Burns DA, Breathnach SM, Cox NH and Griffiths CEM, eds. *Rook's Textbook of Dermatology*, 7th edn. Oxford: Blackwell Science, 2004.

Viard I, Wehrli P, Bullani R, *et al.* Inhibition of toxic epidermal necrolysis by blockade of CD95 with human intravenous immunoglobulin. *Science* 1998; 282: 490–3.

Wolff K, Johnson RA and Suurmond D. *Fitzpatrick's Color Atlas and Synopsis of Clinical Dermatology*, 5th edn. New York: McGraw-Hill, 2005: 140–4 (Erythema multiforme syndrome), 144–7 (Stevens–Johnson syndrome and toxic epidermal necrolysis).

2.11 Erythema nodosum

Aetiology/pathophysiology/pathology

Erythema nodosum (EN) is an idiopathic disorder, but may be secondary to immune complex deposition following a number of possible precipitants (Table 29). Histology shows a septal panniculitis (inflammation of fat).

Epidemiology

The incidence of EN is 1–5 per 100,000 per year in the UK, and it accounts for 0.5% of new dermatology outpatients. The female/male ratio is 3–6:1. Peak onset is between 20 and 30 years of age.

Clinical presentation

Common

Multiple, tender, erythematous and deep nodules on the anterior shins that fade after 2–3 weeks to leave

TABLE 29 CAUSES OF ERYTHEMA NODOSUM

Type	Possible causes
Infections	*Streptococcus*
	Mycobacterium
	Chlamydia
	Epstein–Barr virus
	Yersinia
	Trichophyton spp.
	Coccidioidomycosis
Drugs	Sulphonamides
	Oral contraceptive
Others	Sarcoidosis
	Inflammatory bowel disease
	Malignancy, eg lymphoma
	Behçet's disease

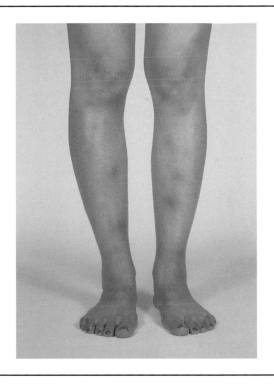

▲ **Fig. 76** Erythema nodosum. Painful, hot, red nodules which most commonly affect the lower legs. As they resolve, the colour changes simulate that of a bruise.

a bruised appearance (Fig. 76). There may be a preceding upper respiratory infection and the eruption may be accompanied by fever, malaise and arthralgia.

Uncommon
Other sites may be involved such as the arms, breasts and face.

Investigation
Perform a deep skin biopsy to confirm the diagnosis. To identify an underlying trigger, check the following: throat swab, FBC, erythrocyte sedimentation rate, anti-streptolysin O titre, serum angiotensin-converting enzyme, CXR, virological titre and *Yersinia*

titre. Consider a Mantoux test.

Differential diagnosis (if common features only are present)
Consider cellulitis, abscess or superficial phlebitis and other forms of panniculitis.

Treatment
Leg elevation and support, removal of the precipitating cause and NSAIDs. Oral steroids are rarely used and are best avoided if an infectious aetiology has not been excluded.

Prognosis
Most cases resolve in 3–6 weeks.

Disease associations
See Table 29.

FURTHER READING
Barham KL, Jorizzo JL, Grattan B and Cox NH. Vasculitis and neutrophilic vascular reactions. In: Burns DA, Breathnach SM, Cox NH and Griffiths CEM, eds. *Rook's Textbook of Dermatology*, 7th edn. Oxford: Blackwell Science, 2004.

2.12 Fungal infections of skin, hair and nails (superficial fungal infections)

Aetiology/pathophysiology/pathology
Skin, hair and nails can all be affected by fungi, ie yeasts or moulds, that adhere to and invade keratin, causing thickening of the keratin layer and varying degrees of inflammation.

- Pityriasis versicolor is caused by *Malassezia* yeasts.

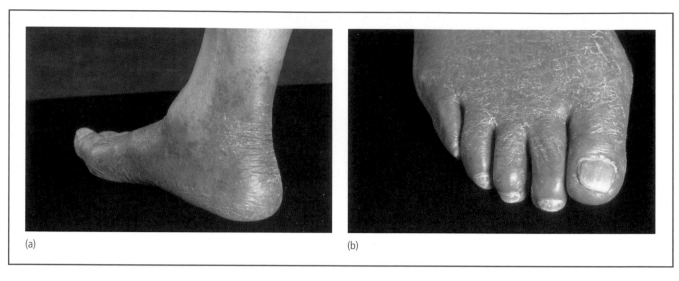

(a)

(b)

▲ **Fig. 77** Tinea pedis and onychomycosis. This non-atopic patient was referred with eczema of the feet that had failed to respond to topical corticosteroids. There was erythema and scaling of the soles extending onto the dorsum of the feet and ankles (**a**). Note the well-defined border and thickened discoloured toenails (**b**). Examination of skin scrapings in clinic revealed dermatophytes and culture grew *Trichophyton rubrum*.

- 'Ringworm' is caused by a group of moulds termed dermatophytes, of which there are three types: *Microsporum*, *Trichophyton* and *Epidermophyton*.

Clinical presentation

Common

- Tinea corporis (ringworm affecting the body): circular well-defined lesions with a raised scaly edge that enlarge peripherally with central clearing.

- Tinea capitis (ringworm of the scalp): presentation is variable. Erythema and scaling of the scalp with partial alopecia is common, often in localised patches but sometimes widespread (see Sections 1.1.4 and 1.2.4, and Fig. 26).

- Tinea pedis (ringworm of the feet, ie athlete's foot): maceration and fissuring or scaling in toe web spaces. Toe nails are also often affected in addition. Scaling may extend onto the soles and dorsum

of the feet (termed 'moccasin' pattern, see Fig. 77). Tinea pedis is a risk factor for cellulitis of the leg.

- Tinea unguium or onychomycosis (ringworm of the nails): discoloration and thickening of the nail plate with subungual hyperkeratosis (Fig. 77).

- Tinea manuum (ringworm of the hands): scaly patches with accentuation of the scaling in palmar creases. These patches are usually unilateral and often associated with tinea pedis (Fig. 78).

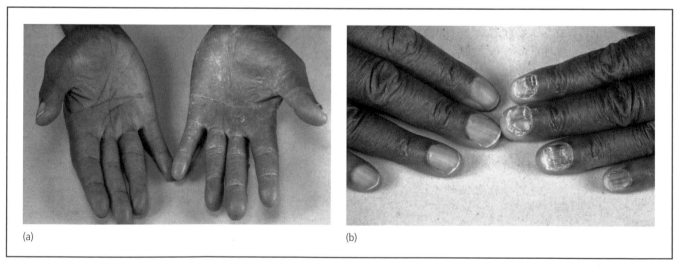

(a)

(b)

▲ **Fig. 78** Tinea manuum. Unilateral palmar scaling with accentuation in the skin creases (**a**). There was thickening and discoloration of the nails on the same hand (**b**), typical of dermatophyte infection. Examination of the feet revealed tinea pedis, the usual source of hand infection.

- Pityriasis versicolor: red/brown macules in white skin – hypopigmented or hyperpigmented in tanned/ pigmented skin. They are scaly and affect the upper torso (see Figs 32 and 34).

Uncommon

- Tinea corporis and pedis: pustules and blisters if the inflammation is severe.

- Tinea capitis: sometimes the host reaction is so great that an oozing inflammatory mass occurs (a kerion) (see Fig. 27).

Investigation

Direct microscopy and culture of skin scrapings, plucked hairs or nail clippings is required to confirm the diagnosis (see Section 3.4).

Differential diagnosis

In suspected tinea corporis, manuum and pedis, eczema, psoriasis and Bowen's disease are also possibilities.

Treatment

Dermatophytes can be treated with antifungal drugs such as itraconazole, terbinafine or griseofulvin. Localised cutaneous infections respond well to topical terbinafine. Widespread infections, tinea capitis and tinea unguium require oral therapy.

Disease associations

- Widespread dermatophyte infection can be associated with immunosuppression and injudicious use of topical corticosteroids.

- Oral candidiasis is particularly associated with HIV.

FURTHER READING

Hay RJ and Moore MK. Mycology. In: Burns DA, Breathnach SM, Cox NH and Griffiths CEM, eds. *Rook's Textbook of Dermatology*, 7th edn. Oxford: Blackwell Science, 2004.

2.13 HIV and the skin

Aetiology/pathophysiology

Skin diseases are common in HIV-infected patients. They may be caused by the primary

---

TABLE 30 SKIN CONDITIONS ASSOCIATED WITH HIV INFECTION

Cause	Skin condition
Papulosquamous diseases	Xerosis[1] (dry skin) Seborrhoeic dermatitis[1]: a reactive dermatitis of the eyebrows, glabella, scalp, sides of the nose, ears and sternal depression caused by an overgrowth of *Pityrosporum* yeasts (see Fig. 18) Psoriasis: may cause erythroderma (see Section 2.17) Morbilliform eruption, fever and lymphadenopathy (HIV seroconversion exanthem): occurs in 10–12% of patients
Infectious diseases: bacterial	Staphylococcal infections[1]: folliculitis, impetigo, ecthyma, furunculosis, cellulitis Syphilis Bacillary angiomatosis: caused by *Bartonella* spp. and characterised by purplish vascular-looking papules and nodules that may resemble Kaposi's sarcoma
Infectious diseases: fungal	Oral and cutaneous candida[1] Tinea[1] (see Section 2.12) Pityriasis versicolor[1] (see Section 2.12 and Figs 32 and 34)
Infectious diseases: viral	Herpes simplex/zoster[1] Epstein–Barr virus[1]: causes oral hairy leucoplakia Molluscum contagiosum[1]: grouped, umbilicated and dome-shaped papules Facial and perianal warts[1] Cytomegalovirus
Arthropod infestations	Scabies (see Section 2.19 and Figs 22 and 88)
Neoplasia	Basal cell carcinoma (see Section 2.20 and Fig. 48) Squamous cell carcinoma (see Section 2.21 and Fig. 47) Kaposi's sarcoma
Miscellaneous	Drug eruptions: maculopapular, erythema multiforme, Stevens–Johnson syndrome, toxic epidermal necrolysis, lipodystrophy (see Sections 2.7 and 2.10) Pruritus Diffuse alopecia Eosinophilic folliculitis: intensely pruritic papules on the forehead and trunk

1. Most common.

viral infection, consequent immunosuppression or drug treatments.

> The pattern of cutaneous findings often correlates with the CD4$^+$ cell count and viral load.

Epidemiology

Since the introduction of highly active antiretroviral therapy (HAART) in 1997, skin conditions associated with HIV (most notably Kaposi's sarcoma) have declined in frequency and severity. However, longer survival has led to the emergence of previously uncommon problems such as basal cell carcinoma.

Clinical presentation

> A vast spectrum of skin diseases may be seen in the context of HIV infection/AIDS (Table 30). Presentation may be atypical or unusually severe, and this should raise the possibility of underlying HIV infection.

Investigation

Microbiological studies, serological studies and often a skin biopsy are necessary adjuncts to clinical examination.

Differential diagnosis

- As discussed, there is a vast array of skin disorders that may be associated with HIV infection. Recognition of potentially life-threatening conditions (eg drug eruptions and disseminated viral or fungal infections) is of paramount importance.

- Markedly atypical and non-specific forms of each condition may exist and many can appear clinically very similar.

- The differential diagnosis may be narrowed by knowledge of a patient's immune status and recognition of patterns of disease correlating with this (Table 31).

Treatment

- Treatment of HIV infection with HAART often leads to improvement in associated skin disease.

- Give antibacterial, antiviral and antifungal treatment of cutaneous infections as required, guided by appropriate microbiological investigations.

- Give topical corticosteroids and topical or oral antifungal drugs (ketoconazole, itraconazole) for seborrhoeic dermatitis.

- Surgically excise basal and squamous cell carcinomas.

Prognosis

- With the advent of HAART, the prognosis of HIV infection and many dermatological conditions associated with it has improved dramatically.

- Prompt recognition and appropriate investigation and management are necessary to reduce morbidity and complications.

FURTHER READING

Chen TM and Cockerell CJ. Cutaneous manifestations of HIV infection and HIV-related disorders. In: Bolognia JL, Jorizzo JL and Rapini RP, eds. *Dermatology.* Edinburgh: Mosby, 2003.

Hunter JAA, Savin JA and Dahl MV. *Clinical Dermatology*, 3rd edn. Oxford: Blackwell Science, 2002: chapter 14 (Infections).

2.14 Lichen planus

Aetiology/pathophysiology/ pathology

The aetiology is unknown but is thought to be immunologically mediated and histology shows damage to basal epidermal cells with an associated 'band-like' dense dermal infiltrate of T cells. It can be drug-induced.

Epidemiology

Lichen planus accounts for approximately 1% of new dermatology outpatients. Females are thought to be affected more commonly than males. Peak onset is between 30 and 60 years of age.

TABLE 31 DERMATOLOGICAL DIAGNOSES CORRELATED WITH CD4$^+$ CELL COUNT			
>500 × 10^6/L	<500 × 10^6/L	<250 × 10^6/L	<50 × 10^6/L
Seborrhoeic dermatitis Psoriasis Vaginal candidiasis Kaposi's sarcoma Oral hairy leucoplakia	Psoriasis (refractory) Herpes zoster Oropharyngeal candida	Seborrhoeic dermatitis (refractory) Extensive mollusca Extensive Kaposi's sarcoma Disseminated herpes simplex Eosinophilic folliculitis Bacillary angiomatosis	Giant mollusca Disseminated cytomegalovirus

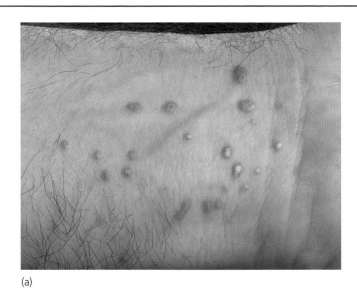

(a)

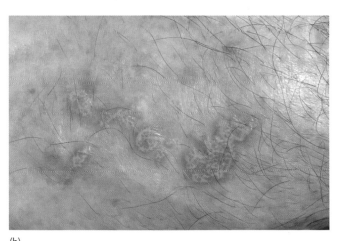

(b)

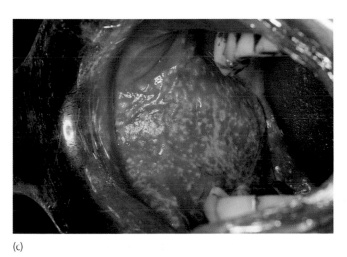

(c)

▲ **Fig. 79** Lichen planus. An itchy eruption of shiny flat-topped papules over the flexor surface of the forearm and wrist (**a**). On close inspection, Wickham's striae (fine white lines) are visible on the surface of the papules (**b**). Always check the mucosal surfaces: Wickham's striae are seen here on the buccal mucosa (**c**).

Clinical presentation

Common

Violaceous (pink/purple), itchy, flat-topped papules distributed on extremities, particularly the ventral aspect of the wrists (Fig. 79a). White streaks (Wickham's striae) may be visible on the surface of the papules (Fig. 79b). Around 50% of patients have white linear streaks in the oral cavity, particularly on the buccal mucosae (Fig. 79c). Many patients exhibit the Koebner phenomenon. Post-inflammatory hyperpigmentation is common.

Uncommon

Nails may be affected, for example by longitudinal grooves. There may also be scarring alopecia, hypertrophic lesions on anterior shins and genital involvement. Mucosal lichen planus can be erosive.

Investigation

Perform a skin biopsy.

Differential diagnosis

Possibilities include drug-induced lichenoid reactions, lichen simplex and psoriasis. Pemphigus vulgaris and mucous membrane pemphigoid can mimic erosive lichen planus of the mucosal surfaces.

Treatment

The treatment of choice is potent topical steroids. Oral steroids, ultraviolet light or systemic immunosuppressants, eg azathioprine and ciclosporin, are used rarely.

Complications

Rarely, erosive mucosal forms have been associated with the development of squamous cell carcinoma.

Prognosis

Most cases resolve within 6–9 months. A prolonged course of treatment is required if there is hypertrophic or mucosal involvement.

Disease associations

Rare associations include ulcerative colitis, primary biliary cirrhosis, hypogammaglobulinaemia and liver disease. In Mediterranean countries, lichen planus may be associated with hepatitis C.

FURTHER READING

Breathnach SM and Black MM. Lichen planus and lichenoid disorders. In: Burns DA, Breathnach SM, Cox NH and Griffiths CEM, eds. *Rook's Textbook of Dermatology*, 7th edn. Oxford: Blackwell Science, 2004.

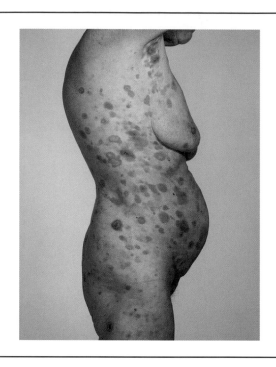

▲ **Fig. 80** Mycosis fungoides. Erythematous patches and plaques in a patient who was initially thought to have psoriasis. However, note the wide variety in colour, size and shape of individual lesions in contrast to those of psoriasis (see Fig. 83).

2.15 Lymphoma of the skin: mycosis fungoides and Sézary syndrome

Aetiology/pathophysiology/pathology

These are primary T-cell lymphomas of the skin due to clonal proliferation of skin-homing T cells (CLA+ and usually CD4+). In Sézary syndrome, there is haematogenous dissemination. Biopsies show atypical lymphocytes in the dermis that exhibit epidermotropism (cells tend to abut and invade the epidermis).

Epidemiology

Primary cutaneous lymphomas are rare, with an annual incidence of 1 per 100,000.

- Mycosis fungoides is the commonest subtype, accounting for 60% of cases of cutaneous T-cell lymphoma.

- Sézary syndrome accounts for 5% of cases.

Clinical presentation

Mycosis fungoides

This disease occurs in three stages: patch, plaque and tumour.

- In patch-stage disease, there are scaly erythematous patches that may be bizarre in shape and heterogeneous in size and colour. They show a random asymmetrical distribution but with a predilection for the pelvic girdle and breasts (Fig. 80). They may be itchy. Patches are occasionally hypopigmented.

- The appearance of erythematous polymorphic plaques heralds plaque-stage disease.

- Nodules are seen in tumour-stage disease.

All three stages may be present concurrently with or without lymphadenopathy, hepatosplenomegaly and erythroderma.

Sézary syndrome

- Pruritus ++.

- Erythroderma (scaly) (Fig. 81).

- Thickening of palms, soles and nails.

- Lymphadenopathy.

- Can occur with or without alopecia and ectropion.

Investigation/staging

- Skin biopsy.

- FBC, blood film and lymphocyte subsets: can show lymphocytosis with aberrant surface marker expression, raised CD4/CD8 ratio and Sézary cells (large atypical lymphocytes with convoluted nuclei).

- Serum lactate dehydrogenase.

- CXR.

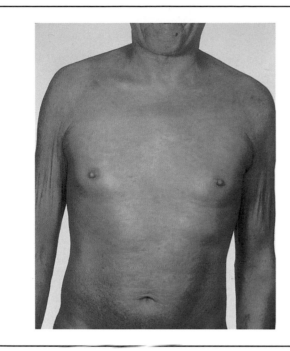

▲**Fig. 81** Sézary syndrome. A scaly erythroderma that may be indistinguishable from other causes such as psoriasis or eczema (see Section 1.4.2). However, in Sézary syndrome the lymph nodes are enlarged and Sézary cells are seen on a blood film.

- CT scan of the chest, abdomen and pelvis.

- Lymph node biopsy if there is node enlargement.

- Bone marrow examination.

- T-cell receptor gene analysis on skin, lymph node and blood to demonstrate clonality (specialist centres only).

Differential diagnosis

- Patch- and plaque-stage cutaneous T-cell lymphoma: eczema, psoriasis or tinea.

- Sézary syndrome: other causes of erythroderma, eg eczema or psoriasis (see Section 1.4.2).

Treatment

The aim is control not cure. Treatment is stage dependent, but options include topical corticosteroids, phototherapy, topical chemotherapy (eg nitrogen mustard), systemic chemotherapy, radiotherapy, immunotherapy (eg interferon), retinoids and photopheresis.

Prognosis

The natural history is variable. Patch-stage disease may persist for many years. Once there are tumours or extracutaneous disease, as in Sézary syndrome, the prognosis is poor (median survival is 1–3 years).

FURTHER READING

Whittaker SJ and MacKie RM. Cutaneous lymphomas and lymphocytic infiltrates. In: Burns DA, Breathnach SM, Cox NH and Griffiths CEM, eds. *Rook's Textbook of Dermatology*, 7th edn. Oxford: Blackwell Science, 2004.

- - - - - - - - - - - - - - - - - - -

Wolff K, Johnson RA and Suurmond D. *Fitzpatrick's Color Atlas and Synopsis of Clinical Dermatology*, 5th edn. New York: McGraw-Hill, 2005: 528–33 (Cutaneous T-cell lymphoma).

2.16 Pemphigus vulgaris

Aetiology/pathophysiology/pathology

Pemphigus vulgaris (PV) is an autoimmune disease in which IgG binds to a desmosomal component, desmoglein 3, present on the cell surface of keratinocytes. This results in dyscohesion of the keratinocytes to produce the characteristic intraepidermal blisters seen in skin biopsies. There is an association with human leucocyte antigen (HLA)-DR4 and DR14 alleles. Rare cases are drug induced.

Epidemiology

Onset can be at any age, including childhood, but is most commonly between the third and sixth decades. It occurs in all races, but there is an increased incidence in Ashkenazi Jews, Indo-Asians and eastern Europeans.

Clinical presentation

Common

- Painful oral erosions: the first feature in around 70% of cases and may be the only sign (Figs 9b and 82a,b).

- Cutaneous erosions that may be painful but do not itch, unlike in bullous pemphigoid (Figs 9a and 82c). Blisters are less commonly seen because they are fragile, but when they do occur they are usually round/oval with minimal surrounding erythema (cf. bullous pemphigoid) and are often on the upper trunk, scalp and sites of friction, eg axillae. In the scalp, crusted plaques are commoner than erosions. Nikolsky's sign is positive in uncontrolled disease.

- Anogenital or nasal erosions.

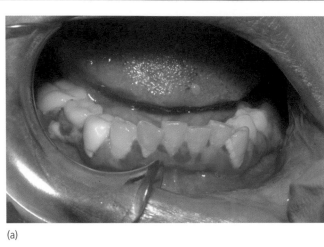

(a)

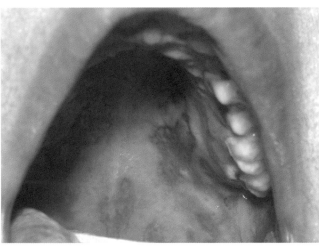

(b)

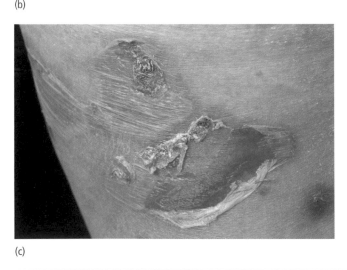

(c)

▲ **Fig. 82** Pemphigus vulgaris. In most cases PV begins in the mouth. Erosions on the gingivae (**a**), palate (**b**) and buccal mucosae are common sites. PV blisters are fragile and rupture easily (**c**). The flaccid blister roofs lie wrinkled across the blister cavity.

Uncommon

- Ocular, laryngeal and oesophageal erosions.

- Childhood PV.

- Neonatal PV: due to transplacental passage of pathogenic antibodies.

- Extensive areas of eroded skin: treatment usually prevents PV from reaching this stage nowadays.

Investigation

- Skin biopsy for histology and direct immunofluorescence: an intraepidermal blister and IgG on keratinocyte surfaces in lesional and 'normal' unaffected skin.

- Serum for indirect immunofluorescence: serum IgG binds to the keratinocyte surfaces of normal skin.

Differential diagnosis

- Pemphigus foliaceus (a rarer subtype that affects the skin only).

- Mucous membrane pemphigoid (cicatricial pemphigoid).

- Bullous pemphigoid.

Treatment

- Short-term: oral corticosteroids, usually with a steroid-sparing drug (eg azathioprine, cyclophosphamide or mycophenolate mofetil). In rapidly progressing and extensive PV, consider pulsed corticosteroids, plasmapheresis or intravenous immunoglobulin.

- Long-term: oral corticosteroids with a steroid-sparing drug (doses are slowly reduced to the minimum required).

Complications

Common

- Treatment side effects.

- Secondary infection of erosions with or without septicaemia.

- Difficulty eating and brushing teeth due to oral ulceration.

Uncommon

- Fluid, electrolyte and protein loss and septicaemia if there are extensive skin erosions.

Prognosis

PV is almost universally fatal without treatment. However, with treatment there is only a 6% mortality rate. Morbidity nowadays is mainly treatment related.

Disease associations

PV may be associated with other autoimmune diseases and is rarely paraneoplastic (lymphomas, chronic lymphatic leukaemia, thymomas, Castleman's tumours).

FURTHER READING

Nousari HC and Anhalt GJ. Pemphigus and bullous pemphigoid. *Lancet* 1999; 354: 667–72.

Wojnarowska F, Venning VA and Burge SM. Immunobullous diseases. In: Burns DA, Breathnach SM, Cox NH and Griffiths CEM, eds. *Rook's Textbook of Dermatology*, 7th edn. Oxford: Blackwell Science, 2004.

Wolff K, Johnson RA and Suurmond D. *Fitzpatrick's Color Atlas and Synopsis of Clinical Dermatology*, 5th edn. New York: McGraw-Hill, 2005: 100–5 (Pemphigus vulgaris).

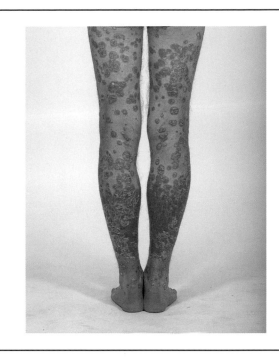

▲ **Fig. 83** Chronic plaque psoriasis. Well-defined, round/oval, deep red, scaly, erythematous plaques which are confluent on the lower legs.

2.17 Psoriasis

Aetiology/pathophysiology/pathology

Psoriasis is an inflammatory disease in which epidermal turnover is greatly increased. It is believed to be T-cell mediated, with both genetic and environmental factors playing a role. Inheritance is polygenic. Biopsies show epidermal thickening, dilation of dermal capillaries and a mixed inflammatory cell infiltrate, but CD4 lymphocytes predominate in early lesions.

Epidemiology

Psoriasis is common (prevalence 1.5–3%). It has an equal sex ratio. The onset can be at any age, but there are two peaks at 16–22 years and 57–60 years.

Clinical presentation

Common

- Well-defined, deep red, scaly plaques (Fig. 83). Removal of the scale reveals pinpoint bleeding (Auspitz sign). Plaques are usually multiple, and when symmetrical preferentially affect the extensor surface of the elbows and knees, scalp, sacrum and umbilicus.

- Nails show pitting, thickening, onycholysis (separation of nail plate from the nail-bed) and subungual hyperkeratosis (Figs 69b and 84).

Less common

- Guttate psoriasis: an acute shower of small (<1 cm) scaly plaques ('rain drops') over the trunk and limbs. Occur particularly after a streptococcal throat infection.

- Palmoplantar pustular psoriasis: chronic, erythematous, scaly plaques studded with sterile

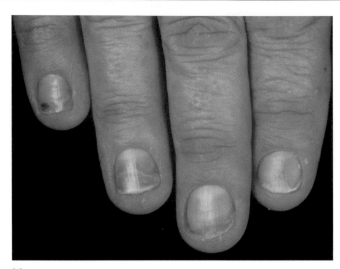

(a)

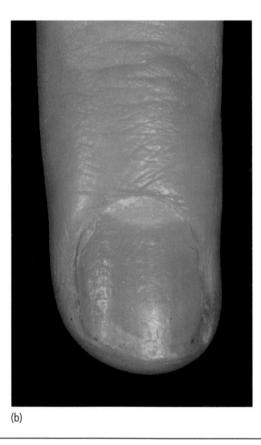

(b)

▲**Fig. 84** Psoriatic nail changes. (**a**) Onycholysis: separation of the distal nail from the nail-bed. (**b**) Pitting of the nail surface.

▲**Fig. 85** Palmoplantar pustular psoriasis. Pustules on an erythematous scaly base which evolve to leave brown macules. This variety affects the palms and soles (shown). The pustules are sterile if swabbed.

Investigation

- Perform a skin biopsy if the diagnosis is in doubt.

- Throat swab and anti-streptolysin O titre in guttate psoriasis.

Differential diagnosis

- If atypical, psoriasis may resemble eczema, discoid lupus erythematosus, mycosis fungoides or seborrhoeic dermatitis.

- Single plaques may resemble Bowen's disease or lichen simplex.

- Guttate psoriasis may resemble pityriasis rosea or secondary syphilis.

Treatment

- Topical therapies: emollients, vitamin D analogues (eg calcipotriol), steroids (particularly for palms, soles, scalp and flexures), dithranol and tar.

- Phototherapy: ultraviolet (UV)B or psoralens with UVA (PUVA).

pustules on the palms and soles (Figs 57 and 85).

Uncommon

- Erythrodermic psoriasis: generalised erythema and scaling with loss of discrete plaques (Fig. 69a).

- Generalised pustular psoriasis: widespread sheets of fiery red skin, studded with sterile pustules (see Figs 67 and 68).

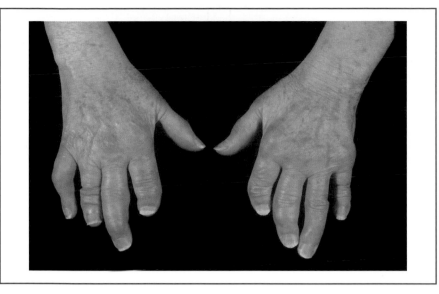

▲ **Fig. 86** Psoriatic arthritis. The arthritis mutilans variant.

- Systemic therapies: oral retinoids, methotrexate, ciclosporin, fumaric acid esters and hydroxycarbamide (hydroxyurea).

- New 'biological' therapies: currently reserved for severe cases where conventional treatments have failed (eg infliximab, etanercept, efalizumab).

Complications

- Psoriatic arthritis (Fig. 86) (see *Rheumatology and Clinical Immunology*, Section 2.3.4).

- Patients with erythrodermic, especially pustular, psoriasis are at risk of hypoalbuminaemia, hypothermia, dehydration, renal failure and septicaemia (see Section 1.4.2).

Prognosis
This is very variable, and is usually relapsing and remitting. Guttate psoriasis has a better prognosis.

FURTHER READING

Griffiths CEM, Camp RDR and Barker JNWN. Psoriasis. In: Burns DA, Breathnach SM, Cox NH and Griffiths CEM, eds. *Rook's Textbook of Dermatology*, 7th edn. Oxford: Blackwell Science, 2004.

2.18 Pyoderma gangrenosum

Aetiology/pathophysiology/pathology
Aetiology is unknown, but there are numerous disease associations (Table 32). Histology shows a mixed inflammatory infiltrate with necrosis, thrombosis and abscess formation.

Epidemiology
It is an uncommon condition, but around 50% of cases are disease associated (Table 32).

Clinical presentation

Common
Tender erythematous or haemorrhagic nodule, which usually presents on the lower leg. This enlarges and ulcerates rapidly with an irregular, bluish, raised and undermined edge (Fig. 87). It also has an erythematous margin. Ulcers may be single or multiple and may be accompanied by fever and malaise during the active phase.

Uncommon
Haemorrhagic, bullous and pustular forms are recognised. Peristomal pyoderma gangrenosum is also well recognised (Fig. 87b).

Investigation
To screen for an underlying cause, check FBC, erythrocyte sedimentation rate, immunoglobulins and protein electrophoresis, liver function and rheumatoid factor. Perform repeated microscopy and

TABLE 32 DISEASES ASSOCIATED WITH PYODERMA GANGRENOSUM

Disease category	Disease
Gastrointestinal	Ulcerative colitis Crohn's disease
Liver	Chronic active hepatitis Primary biliary cirrhosis Sclerosing cholangitis
Joints	Rheumatoid arthritis Seronegative arthropathies
Blood	Leukaemias Lymphomas Monoclonal gammopathies
Other malignancy	Carcinoma of colon, prostate and breast
Other non-malignant causes	Post-traumatic Systemic vasculitis Behçet's disease

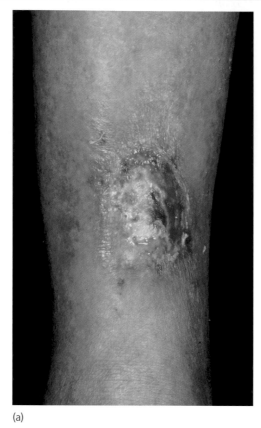

(a)

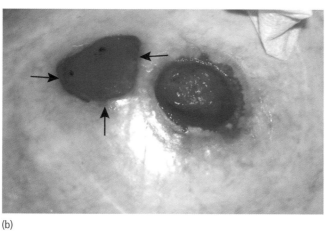

(b)

▲ **Fig. 87** Pyoderma gangrenosum. (**a**) The lower legs are the commonest site and this ulcer on the shin was very painful, evolved rapidly and the medial border was overhanging. A swab was sterile. The patient had an underlying uterine carcinoma. (**b**) Peristomal pyoderma gangrenosum is another well-recognised variant. The stoma is on the right and the ulcer on the left. Note that the border is purple/grey in areas (arrows).

culture of an ulcer swab to exclude infection. A skin biopsy may be indicated. Further tests will depend on clinical suspicion and the results of initial investigations.

Differential diagnosis (if common features only are present)
Possibilities include infection (eg *Streptococcus*, *Staphylococcus*, *Clostridium*), Behçet's disease,

vasculitis (eg Wegener's granulomatosis) and factitial.

Treatment
Treat underlying associated disease and any secondary infection. Give high-dose oral or intravenous steroids, and minocycline for subacute cases. Other systemic treatments may include sulfasalazine, dapsone, cytotoxics and immunosuppressants (eg ciclosporin, azathioprine and 'biological' agents such as infliximab).

Complications
These are usually related to an underlying disease. Septicaemia and atrophic scarring can also occur.

Prognosis
This is variable but is usually related to the underlying disease. If pyoderma gangrenosum heals it will leave an atrophic cribriform scar.

Disease associations
See Table 32.

> **FURTHER READING**
>
> Barham KL, Jorizzo JL, Grattan B and Cox NH. Vasculitis and neutrophilic vascular reactions. In: Burns DA, Breathnach SM, Cox NH and Griffiths CEM, eds. *Rook's Textbook of Dermatology*, 7th edn. Oxford: Blackwell Science, 2004.

2.19 Scabies

Aetiology/pathophysiology/pathology
Scabies is due to infestation by the mite *Sarcoptes scabiei*, which is transmitted by skin-to-skin contact. Sensitisation to *S. scabiei* takes several weeks to develop and results in the symptoms and majority of physical signs.

Scabies is a common but easily missed diagnosis that should be suspected in anyone complaining of pruritus. Search for the diagnostic burrows and scabetic nodules.

Epidemiology

Scabies can occur at any age, but occurs particularly in children, young adults (from intimate contact), institutionalised patients and healthcare workers.

Clinical presentation

Common

- Pruritus, especially at night with or without rash.

- Scabetic burrows: tan/skin-coloured linear ridges several millimetres in length. They are found especially in the finger webs, flexor surface of the wrists, lateral borders of hands/feet, penile shaft and palms/soles of infants (Figs 22a and 88).

- Scabetic nodules: red/brown-coloured and 5–20 mm in diameter. They occur particularly on the penis, scrotum, buttocks, upper thighs, waist and axillae (Fig. 22b).

- As a result of sensitisation: urticaria, eczema, maculopapular eruption, vesicles and excoriations.

Uncommon

- Crusted scabies (synonym: Norwegian scabies): a heavily crusted, localised or generalised eruption due to heavy mite infestation which occurs in the immunocompromised, mentally retarded and those with neurological disorders (Fig. 88).

Investigation/staging

Demonstrate a mite, egg or faeces. Scrape a burrow with a scalpel blade and view the material with a light microsope.

Differential diagnosis

The same symptoms could also be caused by urticaria and eczema.

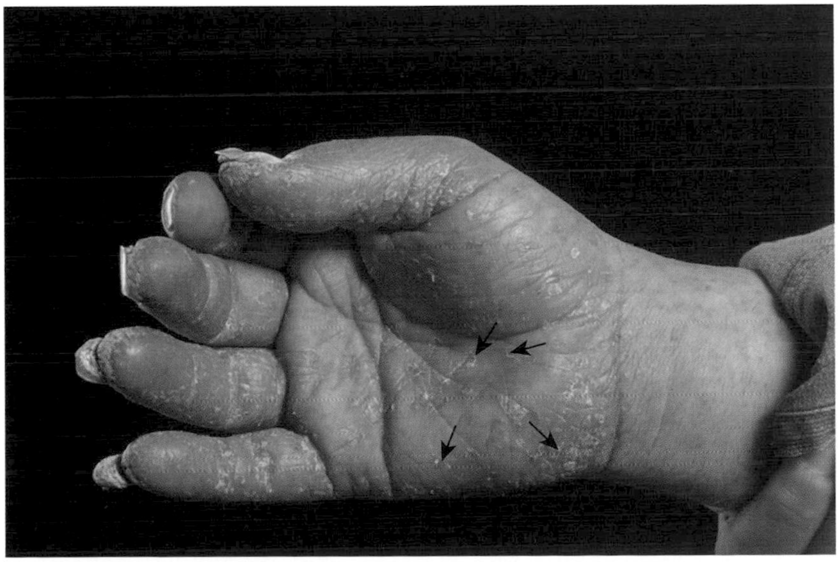

Treatments

- Permethrin, malathion or benzyl benzoate are applied topically from the neck down. In babies, the head must also be treated.

- Oral ivermectin is used for crusted scabies (unlicenced for this application).

- All household members and/or any intimate contacts of a patient should be treated simultaneously, even if asymptomatic.

- The patient's clothes/bedding should be washed (mites can survive up to 72 hours off the host, although this is probably an unimportant means of spread).

Complications

Treatment failure or reinfection is common. Secondary infection can occur and very occasionally results in septicaemia.

Prognosis

Itching may persist for several weeks following successful treatment (warn the patient) and scabetic nodules may persist for several months.

Occupational aspects

Healthcare workers are at risk.

▲ **Fig. 88** Crusted scabies. A 40-year-old male with learning difficulties referred with a hand dermatitis which had failed to improve despite topical corticosteroids. Note the hyperkeratosis and crusting of the fingertips and beneath the nails. Numerous burrows are visible on the palm (arrows).

FURTHER READING

Burns DA. Disease caused by arthropods and other noxious animals. In: Burns DA, Breathnach SM, Cox NH and Griffiths CEM, eds. *Rook's Textbook of Dermatology*, 7th edn. Oxford: Blackwell Science, 2004.

Wolff K, Johnson RA and Suurmond D. *Fitzpatrick's Color Atlas and Synopsis of Clinical Dermatology*, 5th edn. New York: McGraw-Hill, 2005: 853–61 (Scabies).

2.20 Basal cell carcinoma

Aetiology/pathophysiology

Basal cell carcinoma (BCC) is a malignant epithelial neoplasm. It tends to grow slowly and is locally invasive, but very rarely metastasises. The major risk factor is chronic intense exposure to ultraviolet (UV) radiation. UV-induced DNA damage in tumour-suppressor genes initiates tumour development.

Aetiological factors in BCC

- UV radiation.
- Ionising radiation (this has a long latency after exposure).
- Arsenic.
- Topical nitrogen mustard.
- Genetic factors, eg Gorlin's syndrome.

Epidemiology

BCC is the commonest human malignancy. The highest incidence occurs in countries with a high UV intensity and a predominantly fair-skinned population, eg Australia and New Zealand. Men are affected more frequently than women, although over the last 10 years this inequality has lessened. BCCs are no longer unusual in young adults.

Clinical presentation

Most BCCs occur on the head and neck, although up to 20% occur on the trunk and limbs.

Common

- Nodular BCC: presents as the 'classic' pearlescent papule/nodule with overlying telangiectases (Figs 48 and 89). Lesions may ulcerate and bleed with minor trauma or spontaneously. Most occur on the head and neck.

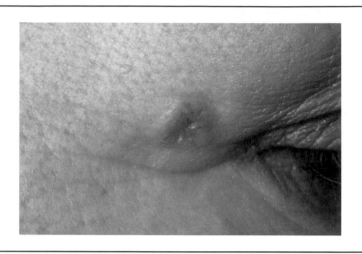

▲ **Fig. 89** Typical nodular BCC. Note the smooth shiny surface and overlying telangiectases.

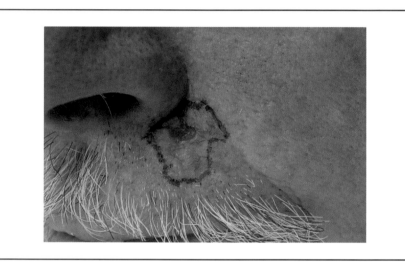

▲ **Fig. 90** Ulcerated sclerosing BCC. Note the whitish plaque and telangiectases. The clinical margins have been marked but this type of tumour often has extensive subclinical extension.

- Superficial BCC: an erythematous scaly patch or plaque, often with a narrow thread-like pearlescent border. They most commonly occur on the trunk and limbs, but may also occur on the head and neck.

Less common

- Morphoeic (sclerosing) BCC: a slowly expanding whitish/yellow plaque with a scar-like appearance (Fig. 90). Most occur on the head and neck. Presentation can be very subtle and the margins of the tumour are characteristically indistinct.

- Pigmented BCC: the pigment may be speckled or uniformly distributed throughout the lesion. Close examination may reveal the characteristic shiny 'pearly' quality and telangiectases.

Investigation

- Diagnosis can often be made on clinical grounds.

- Suspicious lesions should be biopsied to confirm the diagnosis.

- Complete cutaneous examination for other skin cancers should be performed.

- Dermoscopy can be a useful adjunct to clinical examination (see Section 2.22).

Differential diagnosis

- Nodular BCC: consider benign naevi, sebaceous hyperplasia, molluscum contagiosum and squamous cell carcinoma (SCC).

- Pigmented BCC: consider seborrhoeic keratoses and melanoma.

- Superficial BCC: consider SCC *in situ* (Bowen's disease), eczema and psoriasis.

Treatment

- The goal of treatment is complete eradication of the tumour.

- Surgical excision provides the highest cure rate, with standard histological processing or intraoperative control of tumour margins (Mohs micrographic surgery).

> Mohs micrographic surgery is a specialised technique where tissue sections from the excision margin are examined at the time of surgery to ensure histological clearance of the tumour. It is the 'gold standard' for aggressive histological growth patterns (sclerosing and infiltrating), recurrent BCCs and BCCs at sites where preservation of normal tissue is imperative (such as the nose, lips, eyelids and ears).

- Cryotherapy or curettage and electrodesication (should generally be used only for very small or superficial BCCs on the trunk and limbs).

- Radiotherapy is a useful alternative to surgery in some circumstances.

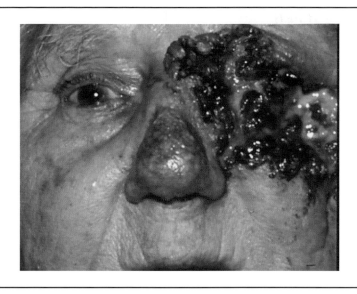

▲ **Fig. 91** This woman had neglected this basal cell carcinoma for many years. Unfortunately the outcome was fatal.

Prognosis

- With appropriate management, once a BCC has been completely eradicated it is unlikely to recur.

- While metastatic disease is extremely rare, inappropriate treatment leading to recurrence or neglect can cause significant morbidity and even mortality (Fig. 91).

- Of BCC patients, 20% will develop another unrelated BCC within 5 years.

Disease associations

- Immunosuppression (chronic lymphocytic leukaemia, transplant recipients, HIV infection) can predispose patients to the development of BCCs.

- Several rare genetic diseases involving mutations in tumour-suppressor genes may cause multiple BCCs, eg Gorlin's syndrome.

Education, prevention and early detection

- Education regarding 'sun-safe' practices and the dangers of recreational sun exposure are important preventive measures.

- Teaching patients about the importance of regular skin self-examination and to recognise the signs of skin cancer are important in early detection.

- Periodic complete skin examination by a specialist is vital for the detection of further skin cancers.

FURTHER READING

Lang PG and Maize JC. Basal cell carcinoma. In: Rigel DS, Friedman RJ, Dzubow LM, *et al. Cancer of the Skin*. Philadelphia: Elsevier Saunders, 2005.

Miller SJ and Moresi JM. Actinic keratoses, basal cell carcinoma and squamous cell carcinoma. In: Bolognia JL, Jorizzo JL and Rapini RP, eds. *Dermatology*. Edinburgh: Mosby, 2003.

2.21 Squamous cell carcinoma

Aetiology/pathophysiology

Squamous cell carcinoma (SCC) is a malignant neoplasm of keratinocytes. The major risk factor is ultraviolet (UV) radiation that causes repeated DNA mutations. However, other genetic and environmental factors may be involved in the pathogenesis.

Aetiological factors in SCC

- UV radiation.
- Smoking (lip SCC).
- Immunosuppression (haematological malignancies, organ transplant recipients and HIV).
- Cutaneous injuries (burns and frostbite).
- Chronic inflammation (eg chronic leg ulcers and osteomyelitis).
- Human papillomavirus.
- Polycyclic aromatic hydrocarbons (soot, pitch and tar, shale and mineral oil).
- Arsenic.
- Genetic syndromes with disorders of DNA repair (eg xeroderma pigmentosum).

Epidemiology

SCC is the second most common skin cancer after basal cell carcinoma (BCC). Its incidence has doubled in the last 40 years and increases significantly in individuals over the age of 40. The highest incidence occurs in countries with high UV intensity and a predominantly fair-skinned population with a tendency to sunburn (eg Australia and New Zealand). Men are two to three times more likely to develop an SCC than women. SCC is responsible for the majority of deaths due to non-melanoma skin cancer.

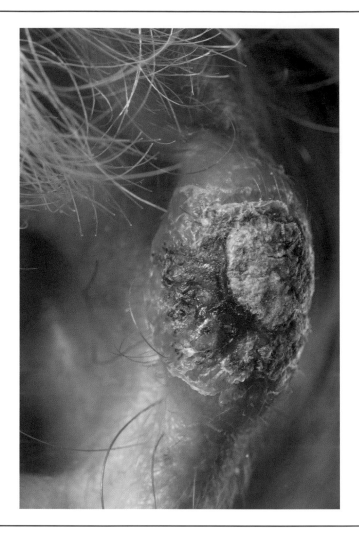

▲ **Fig. 92** Squamous cell carcinoma on the helix of the ear, a common site in men due to sun exposure.

Clinical presentation

Most SCCs (80%) develop on sun-exposed sites (head, neck and upper extremities).

Common

- Skin-coloured or erythematous firm papule/nodule, commonly with a rough, scaly, hyperkeratotic surface (Fig. 92). As the lesion becomes more advanced it may ulcerate and bleed (Fig. 93). Often the surrounding skin shows signs of sun damage, with multiple red scaly areas (actinic keratoses).

- Keratoacanthomas: these lesions develop as dome-shaped nodules with a central keratin-filled plug and grow rapidly over 4–6 weeks (see Fig. 49). They usually occur on sun-exposed skin and can reach several centimetres in diameter. They should be regarded as variants of SCC.

Uncommon

- Development within a scar or chronic ulcer.

A new nodule, area of induration or ulcer within a scar should be viewed with suspicion.

- A warty lesion on the sole of the foot, perineum or oral cavity (verrucous carcinoma).

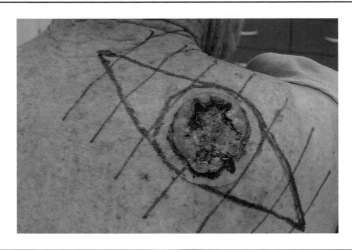

▲ **Fig. 93** Large ulcerated squamous cell carcinoma. This large lesion on the back (marked prior to surgical excision) has a poor prognosis. Note the multiple actinic keratoses and deep wrinkling of the skin around the neck, evidence of solar damage.

Investigation

- Biopsy/excision of suspicious lesions.

- Examination of regional lymph nodes for evidence of metastatic disease.

- Complete cutaneous examination for other skin cancers.

Differential diagnosis

Hypertrophic actinic keratoses/SCC *in situ*, BCC and viral warts are all possibilities that can cause similar symptoms.

Treatment

- Surgical excision is the treatment of choice (Mohs surgery for recurrent or high-risk tumours).

- Use radiotherapy if surgery is not feasible.

- Consider referral for adjuvant radiotherapy in lesions at high risk of local recurrence/metastasis.

Prognosis

- With appropriate management, the overall 5-year cure rate for primary SCC is 92% and for recurrent SCC is 77%.

- Cure rates and risk of metastasis depend on a number of variables of the tumour and the patient.

- Small (<2 cm diameter), thin (<4 mm) and well-differentiated tumours are unlikely to metastasise.

- Tumours arising in covered sites, scars or areas of chronic inflammation, on the lip and in immunosuppressed patients behave more aggressively and have an increased risk of metastasis.

- The 5-year survival rate for patients with metastatic disease is approximately 25%.

Disease associations

- Immunosuppression (in chronic lymphocytic leukaemia, organ transplant recipients and HIV infection) predisposes patients to the development of SCC. In organ transplant recipients, SCC is four times more common than BCC.

- Rare genetic diseases involving disorders of DNA repair (eg xeroderma pigmentosum).

- Chronic inflammatory conditions as noted above.

Education, prevention and early detection

- Education regarding 'sun-safe' practices and the dangers of recreational sun exposure are important preventive measures.

- Teaching patients the importance of regular skin self-examination and to recognise the signs of skin cancer are important in early detection.

- Periodic complete skin examination by a specialist for those at risk of recurrence or metastasis and for the detection of new unrelated skin cancers is vital for those who recover from SCC.

FURTHER READING

Miller SJ and Moresi JM. Actinic keratoses, basal cell carcinoma and squamous cell carcinoma. In: Bolognia JL, Jorizzo JL and Rapini RP, eds. *Dermatology*. Edinburgh: Mosby, 2003.

- - - - - - - - - - - - - - - - - - -

Nguyen TH and Joon J. Squamous cell carcinoma. In: Rigel DS, Friedman RJ, Dzubow LM, *et al. Cancer of the Skin.* Philadelphia: Elsevier Saunders, 2005.

2.22 Malignant melanoma

Aetiology/pathophysiology

Malignant melanoma is a tumour arising from melanocytes. It is the leading cause of death from skin disease and accounts for 80% of deaths due to skin cancer. Ultraviolet (UV) radiation and a genetic predisposition (10–15% of melanomas are familial) are the most important aetiological factors. Risk factors are listed below.

> **Risk factors for the development of melanoma**
>
> - Red/blonde hair, fair skin and freckling.
> - Multiple melanocytic naevi (>100).
> - Atypical (dysplastic) naevi (may be clinically indistinguishable from melanoma).
> - History of multiple episodes of sunburn in childhood and adolescence.
> - Personal or family history of melanoma.

> **ABCD system**
>
> When a malignant melanoma is a possibility, check the following:
> Asymmetry.
> Border irregularity.
> Colour variegation (tans, browns and black; uncommonly white, red and grey).
> Diameter (>6 mm).

> A change in an existing mole (colour, size, shape, elevation or bleeding) or a new mole should arouse suspicion.

Common

- Superficial spreading melanoma: a macular pigmented lesion with most of the above features (Figs 50 and 94).

- Lentigo maligna: a type of melanoma confined to the dermoepidermal junction (melanoma *in situ*). The classical site is on the cheek in an elderly patient with sun-damaged skin. It presents as a flat, irregularly shaped and pigmented macule that can grow to several centimetres (Fig. 51). There is often a long *in situ* growth phase before invasion (lentigo malignant melanoma).

Epidemiology

- Incidence of melanoma is rising and has increased three-fold since the early 1980s.

- Highest incidence occurs in countries with a high UV intensity and a predominantly fair-skinned population with a tendency to sunburn (eg Australia and New Zealand).

- Lifetime risk in the UK is approximately 1 in 100, in the USA 1 in 65 and in some parts of New Zealand as high as 1 in 15.

Clinical presentation

Melanoma can present in a variety of ways. This variation is generally due to the stage of disease at presentation. Most early melanomas present as pigmented macules. These usually increase in diameter before they become elevated. The ABCD system is a useful check-list when considering pigmented lesions and can be used to identify the vast majority of early melanomas.

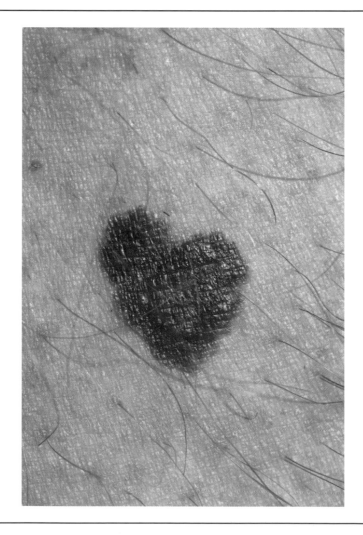

▲ **Fig. 94** Malignant melanoma. Note the irregularity of shape and colour. Fortunately this tumour was still *in situ* when excised and the prognosis excellent.

Less common

- Nodular melanoma with or without ulceration (Figs 56 and 95): these lesions are usually more advanced and have a worse prognosis than the superficial spreading variety. The presence of ulceration is a poor prognostic factor.

- Acral lentiginous melanoma: these lesions arise on the palms or soles. They are rare in white people, but in some racial groups (Chinese and Japanese) are the most common subtype.

- Amelanotic melanoma: this presents as a skin-coloured, pink or red macule, papule or nodule. Nodules often have a friable weeping or bleeding surface. Close examination may sometimes reveal areas of pigment.

- Subungual melanoma (Fig. 96): a pigmented streak (possibly with colour variation) in a finger or toenail. Look carefully for associated pigmentation of the proximal nail-fold (Hutchinson's sign).

- Metastatic melanoma: there is evidence of regional lymph node or distant metastases.

Investigation

- All patients should have a total cutaneous examination (including the scalp, palms and soles, and digital web spaces).

- If there is any suggestion that a lesion could be a malignant melanoma, it should be excised urgently and sent for histopathological examination.

- Skin cancer specialists use dermoscopy as an adjunct to clinical examination in the evaluation of pigmented lesions.

- Sentinel lymph node biopsy: this involves identification of the primary draining lymph node and removing it for histological analysis. If positive, the lymph node basin is then dissected. Currently there is no evidence that this improves overall survival but it acts as a prognostic guide.

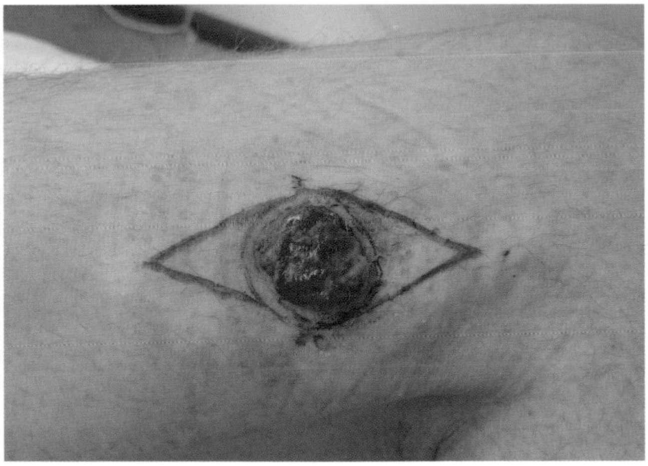

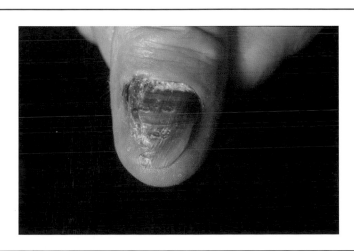

▲ **Fig. 95** Large ulcerated nodular malignant melanoma on the thigh (initial margin of excision is marked). Unfortunately this man has neglected this lesion for too long. Note that pigmentation is seen at the edge of the tumour, which strongly suggests a diagnosis of melanoma.

▲ **Fig. 96** Subungual melanoma. Note the pigmentation of the nail-bed and proximal nail-fold (Hutchinson's sign) where the nail has been removed at one edge.

> Dermoscopy (dermatoscopy and epiluminescence microscopy) involves the use of a hand-held tool (dermatoscope) to magnify the skin and enable visualisation of structures that cannot be seen with the naked eye. In skilled hands this enhances clinical diagnosis of skin lesions, but training and experience is required for it to be effective.

> ⚠ Malignant melanoma kills but caught early it is potentially curable with surgical excision. If you cannot be 100% sure that a lesion is benign, you should refer the patient urgently for a specialist opinion. Some melanomas cannot be diagnosed on clinical grounds alone and a high index of suspicion is necessary to avoid missing potentially lethal skin cancers.

TABLE 33 RECOMMENDED SURGICAL EXCISION MARGINS FOR MALIGNANT MELANOMA ACCORDING TO BRESLOW THICKNESS

Breslow thickness (mm)	Margin
In situ	5 mm
<1	1 cm
>1	2 cm

Differential diagnosis

A number of benign lesions need to be distinguished from melanoma (for helpful discriminating factors see Section 1.2.13):

- benign naevi;

- lentigos;

- seborrhoeic keratoses;

- haemangiomas;

- pigmented basal cell carcinoma.

Treatment

- Perform a surgical excision initially with a 2-mm margin of clearance. Subsequent wider excision depends on the Breslow thickness (Table 33).

- There is no evidence that elective or therapeutic (where there are clinically evident nodes) lymph node dissection confers any overall survival advantage.

- Radiotherapy, chemotherapy and immunotherapy can be used for advanced metastatic disease. This is generally palliative or as part of a clinical trial.

Prognosis

- The depth of invasion is measured predominantly by the Breslow thickness (vertical tumour depth measured in millimetres from the granular cell layer of the epidermis). This is the most important predictor of survival in malignant melanoma (Table 34).

- Patients whose melanomas are diagnosed and excised at the earliest stages of disease have close to a 100% chance of survival. Unfortunately, patients presenting with advanced disease have a very poor prognosis.

All clinicians need to be able to recognise the signs of melanoma to enable the earliest possible intervention.

Disease associations

- Immunosuppression: in organ transplant recipients, chronic haematological malignancies and HIV.

- Xeroderma pigmentosum: a rare inherited condition with deficiency in DNA repair mechanisms.

Education, prevention and early detection

- Education regarding 'sun-safe' practices and the dangers of recreational sun exposure are important preventive measures.

- Teaching patients the importance of regular skin self-examination and to recognise the signs of melanoma are important factors in the early detection of melanoma.

- Periodic complete skin examination by a specialist for those at risk of recurrence or metastatic disease and for the detection of new unrelated skin cancers is vital for patients who survive a malignant melanoma.

FURTHER READING

Nestle FO and Kerl H. Melanoma. In: Bolognia JL, Jorizzo JL and Rapini RP, eds. *Dermatology*. Edinburgh: Mosby, 2003.

Rigel DS, Friedman RJ, Dzubow LM, *et al. Cancer of the Skin*. Philadelphia: Elsevier Saunders, 2005: 175–201.

2.23 Urticaria and angio-oedema

Aetiology/pathophysiology/pathology

Urticarial weals or hives are secondary to vasodilatation and leakage of capillary fluid into the interstitium. Angio-oedema occurs when this process involves the deeper tissues. Cases can be

TABLE 34 THE 5-YEAR SURVIVAL RATE FOLLOWING A DIAGNOSIS OF MALIGNANT MELANOMA ACCORDING TO TUMOUR THICKNESS

Breslow thickness (mm)	5-year survival (%)
<0.75	95
0.76–1.5	85
1.51–4.0	65
>4.0	45

TABLE 35 CLASSIFICATION OF URTICARIA

Classification	Cause
Ordinary urticaria: acute	Drugs, eg penicillins Foods, eg fish, nuts and eggs Bee/wasp stings Infections
Ordinary urticaria: chronic (if >6 weeks duration)	Idiopathic (most cases) Drugs Infections Systemic lupus erythematosus Autoimmune thyroid disease Rarely lymphoproliferative disease
Immune complex urticaria	Serum sickness Urticarial vasculitis
Physical	Dermographism Delayed pressure urticaria Vibratory Heat and solar exposure Cold Water
Cholinergic	Exercise and heat

classified according to aetiology and duration (Table 35). In most of them the final common pathway is mast cell degranulation releasing inflammatory mediators including histamine.

Epidemiology

These are common conditions. The lifetime risk is 15% and the prevalence 0.1% in the UK. They can occur at any age.

Clinical presentation

Common

Itchy erythematous macules develop into weals (Fig. 65) and can occur anywhere. Weals generally last a few hours before fading to leave normal skin. In up to 50% there is associated angio-oedema with facial and mucosal swelling.

Uncommon

Consider urticarial vasculitis if individual weals last longer than 24 hours or are associated with purpura.

Investigation

None is required for most acute cases with no angio-oedema. Consider a radioallergosorbent test to specific allergens if there is a suggestion that there is an allergic trigger. Perform a skin biopsy and vasculitis screen (eg antinuclear antibody and complement) if urticarial vasculitis is suspected. In chronic urticaria, thyroid antibodies, FBC, erythrocyte sedimentation rate, autoantibodies, immunoglobulins and protein electrophoresis can be used to exclude underlying disease. C4 complement levels, if normal, help to exclude C1 esterase inhibitor deficiency.

Differential diagnosis (common only)

Erythema multiforme and early-stage bullous pemphigoid are possibilities. However, lesions in both of these last more than 24 hours.

Treatment

Avoid precipitating cause, eg allergens or drugs such as aspirin, opiates or angiotensin-converting enzyme inhibitors. Give non-sedating or sedating H_1 receptor antihistamines, and add H_2 receptor antihistamines if required. Rarely give oral steroids. Use epinephrine (adrenaline) for cases of life-threatening anaphylaxis (see *Acute Medicine*, Section 1.2.33; and *Rheumatology and Clinical Immunology*, Section 1.4.2). Hereditary angio-oedema is treated with danazol prophylactically, and whole plasma or C1 esterase inhibitor concentrate during acute episodes.

Complications

Very rarely these cases develop severe angio-oedema with respiratory compromise.

Prognosis

Half of individuals with urticaria clear within 6 months. Approximately 25% will persist for many years.

Disease associations

Hereditary or acquired C1 esterase inhibitor deficiency, and also systemic vasculitis.

FURTHER READING

Grattan CEH and Kobza Black A. Urticaria and mastocytosis. In: Burns DA, Breathnach SM, Cox NH and Griffiths CEM, eds. *Rook's Textbook of Dermatology*, 7th edn. Oxford: Blackwell Science, 2004.

2.24 Vitiligo

Aetiology/pathophysiology/pathology

Vitiligo is believed to be an organ-specific autoimmune disease. It causes loss of melanocytes within lesions and an infiltrate of T cells at the lesion margins.

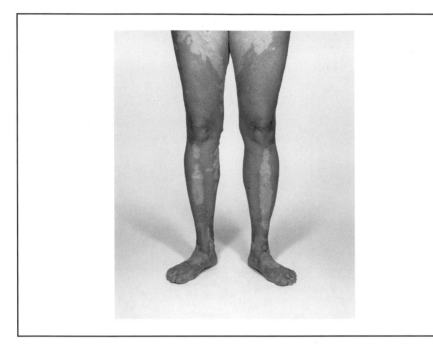

▲ **Fig. 97** Vitiligo. Note the remarkable symmetry that is often a feature of this condition.

FURTHER READING

Bleehen SS and Anstey AV. Disorders of skin colour. In: Burns DA, Breathnach SM, Cox NH and Griffiths CEM, eds. *Rook's Textbook of Dermatology*, 7th edn. Oxford: Blackwell Science, 2004.

2.25 Cutaneous vasculitis

Aetiology/pathophysiology/pathology

Cutaneous vasculitis has numerous triggers, including:

- infections;

- drugs;

- malignancy;

- some autoimmune conditions.

The underlying pathogenesis is thought to be vessel-wall damage triggered by immune complex deposition. Other contributing factors include stasis due to gravity or pressure, previous damage to vessel walls, blood viscosity and cold.

Biopsies show destruction and fibrinoid change of the vessel walls. The inflammatory infiltrate is predominantly composed of neutrophils, which fragment to form 'nuclear dust'.

Epidemiology

It is very common: people of any age can be affected, and the ratio between men and women is equal.

Clinical presentation

Common

- Palpable, purpuric (do not blanch on pressure) papules and plaques (Figs 45 and 98). These are commonly on the lower legs and arms.

- Fever, arthralgia and malaise.

Epidemiology

Vitiligo is common, affecting all races (0.5–1% prevalence worldwide). Between 30 and 40% of sufferers have a positive family history. In 50% of cases the onset is before 20 years of age.

Clinical presentation

Common

Depigmented (and sometimes hypopigmented) macules develop symmetrically (Figs 33 and 97), with a predilection for sun-exposed sites and sites of trauma (Koebner phenomenon). Vitiligo can cause hair depigmentation.

Uncommon

Vitiligo is rapidly progressive and inflammatory in 1% of cases. This is a rare restricted and segmental form which is not associated with autoimmune disease.

Investigation

Usually none is required, although some exclude associated autoimmune disease.

Differential diagnosis (common only)

Post-inflammatory hypopigmentation and pityriasis versicolor are both possibilities.

Treatment

Frequently unsatisfactory and may just provide camouflage. If the situation is severe, consider ultraviolet light and potent topical steroids. Provide photoprotection of vitiligo lesions, which burn easily.

Complications

Sunburn and cutaneous malignancy can occur in sun-exposed sites due to loss of protective melanocytes.

Prognosis

Vitiligo is slowly progressive in most cases, and 10–20% of patients show spontaneous repigmentation.

Disease associations

Autoimmune disease is the main association, particularly thyroid disease, pernicious anaemia, diabetes mellitus and alopecia areata.

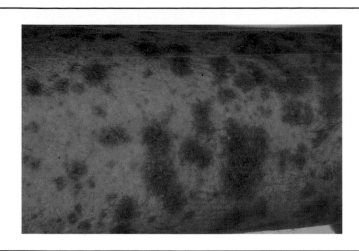

▲ **Fig. 98** Cutaneous vasculitis triggered by a streptococcal infection. This purpuric eruption was present on the lower legs of a man who was systemically well. There was no evidence of multisystem involvement. A throat swab grew group A *Streptococcus* and the anti-streptolysin O titre was elevated.

Uncommon

- Splinter haemorrhages and nail-fold infarcts.

- Nodules, haemorrhagic blisters and skin necrosis.

- Renal, pulmonary, gastrointestinal and central nervous system involvement.

Investigation

Perform skin biopsy to confirm vasculitis. Direct immunofluorescence will show perivascular IgA in the Henoch–Schönlein purpura subtype.

Screening for visceral involvement

Check renal function, liver function, BP, urine dipstick for blood and microscopy for casts, and CXR.

Investigating the cause

- FBC (white count high if infection).

- Anti-streptolysin O titre.

- Blood cultures.

- Throat swab.

- Hepatitis serology.

- Antinuclear antibody, double-stranded DNA (to investigate

possible lupus) and rheumatoid factor.

- Antineutrophil cytoplasmic antibody.

- Syphilis serology.

- Complement: is usually high; C4 is low in cryoglobulinaemia.

- Cryoglobulins.

- Immunoglobulins and protein electrophoresis.

Differential diagnosis

Meningococcaemia, subacute bacterial endocarditis, disseminated intravascular coagulation, viral haemorrhagic fevers and other vasculitides (eg polyarteritis nodosa, Wegener's granulomatosis) are all possibilities. In the context of thrombocytopenia, many inflammatory rashes may be purpuric.

Treatment

- Rest and elevation of the lower legs if affected.

- Treatment of any triggering infection or associated disease.

- Oral prednisolone if severe acute vasculitis or systemic involvement. Adjuvant drugs (eg

immunosuppressants, dapsone) may be required for chronic or recurrent disease.

Disease associations

These include viral and bacterial infections (eg group A *Streptococcus* and hepatitis B and C), drugs (see Section 2.7), connective tissue diseases (eg lupus erythematosus, rheumatoid arthritis, Sjögren's syndrome), malignancies, cryoglobulinaemia, cryofibrinogenaemia and paraproteinaemia.

Prognosis

Cutaneous vasculitis usually affects the small vessels and in most cases is a benign self-limiting disease. In 80% of cases, the skin only is affected; 60% of cases are idiopathic and 10% are chronic. Multisystem disease may be life-threatening.

FURTHER READING

Barham KL, Jorizzo JL, Grattan B and Cox NH. Vasculitis and neutrophilic vascular reactions. In: Burns DA, Breathnach SM, Cox NH and Griffiths CEM, eds. *Rook's Textbook of Dermatology*, 7th edn. Oxford: Blackwell Science, 2004.

2.26 Topical therapy: corticosteroids and immunosuppressants

Principle

The skin lends itself to local delivery of therapy, which enables maximal concentration at the site of disease while minimising systemic toxicity. Many medicaments are available in topical forms, eg corticosteroids, antibiotics, antihistamines, antifungals, retinoids, tar and dithranol. However, not all drugs can be applied topically because of poor epidermal penetration. The following section deals mainly with corticosteroids, which are used very commonly in dermatological practice. However, the recently introduced topical immunomodulators (tacrolimus, pimecrolimus and imiquimod) represent an important step forward in the treament of skin disease and are also discussed.

Topical corticosteroids

Indications
Topical corticosteroids can be used in cases of eczema (all types), lichen planus, discoid lupus erythematosus, alopecia areata, lichen sclerosis, lichen simplex, keloid scars, vitiligo, psoriasis (particularly palmoplantar and flexural varieties) and sarcoidosis.

Contraindications
- Excersise caution when treating widespread plaque psoriasis.

- Infections, acne and rosacea are all contraindications for topical corticosteroid use.

Practical details
- Many topical steroids are available mainly in cream and ointment formulations.

- Classified according to potency: very potent, potent, moderate and mild (see *British National Formulary*).

- Initiate treatment with a steroid of adequate strength (disease dependent) for initial control, then reduce the potency/frequency to the minimum for satisfactory disease control.

- Use only mild steroids on the face (very susceptible to side effects).

- Palms/soles need potent steroids as the skin is thick.

- Milder steroids should be used in children compared with adults.

- Ointments are greasy, so are good if the patient's skin is very dry.

- Creams are water based. They achieve better penetration than ointments if the skin is weepy. They are also more cosmetically acceptable as they are less greasy than ointments. However, they do contain preservatives, with the risk of contact dermatitis.

Complications

- Local: facial acne and steroid rosacea, perioral dermatitis, atrophy and fragility, easy bruising, telangiectases, striae, infections (eg tinea incognito), contact dermatitis (especially with creams) and hypopigmentation.

- Systemic: inhibition of pituitary–adrenal axis and other systemic effects due to absorption (if potent steroids are applied over large areas). As a guide, no more than 50 g of a very potent or 100 g of a potent product should be used per week. Withdrawal of systemic or extensive topical steroids may precipitate erythrodermic or pustular psoriasis.

Topical immunomodulators

Pimecrolimus and tacrolimus
Both are calcineurin inhibitors and thus their mechanism of action is similar to ciclosporin. Both are only licensed for treating atopic eczema but have been used successfully for a number of other immunologically mediated skin diseases. Tacrolimus is as effective as potent topical corticosteroids and pimecrolimus is equivalent to mild corticosteroids. Their main advantage is that they do not cause skin atrophy so are useful for treating sensitive sites, eg the face. Their main side effect is burning/tingling of the skin for 15–20 minutes after application. There may be an increased risk of skin cancers in the long term and therefore ultraviolet exposure must be minimised in users of these products. They are considerably more expensive than topical corticosteroids.

Imiquimod
This activates Toll-like receptor 7, leading to liberation of inflammatory cytokines. It has antiviral and antitumour activity. It is licensed for treatment of external genital and perianal warts and for superficial basal cell carcinomas, but has also been successfully used off licence to treat a variety of other conditions, eg Bowen's disease, extramammary Paget's disease and recalcitrant cutaneous warts. The application site may become very inflamed and even ulcerate.

> **FURTHER READING**
>
> Berth-Jones J. Topical therapy. In: Burns DA, Breathnach SM, Cox NH and Griffiths CEM, eds. *Rook's Textbook of Dermatology*, 7th edn. Oxford: Blackwell Science, 2004.

2.27 Phototherapy

Principle
Phototherapy is the use of artificial ultraviolet (UV) radiation to treat skin diseases. Both UVB and psoralens with UVA (PUVA) are used for this purpose. Psoralens are photosensitising drugs that enhance the effect of UVA. They are most commonly given orally but can be applied topically. Narrow-band UVB (TL01) covers a tighter

wavelength range than conventional UVB and is more effective.

Indications

Clearance of dermatoses responsive to UV therapy (eg psoriasis, mycosis fungoides and atopic eczema) or, less commonly, prevention of some photodermatoses (eg polymorphic light eruption).

Contraindications

- Patients with a past history of excessive phototherapy and/or cutaneous malignancies.

- Light-aggravated disease, eg systemic lupus erythematosus and porphyria.

- Use of PUVA in patients with renal or liver disease.

Practical details

Before procedure

- Choose the most appropriate phototherapy (narrow- or broad-band UVB, or topical or oral PUVA). This will depend on the patient, the disease and local facilities.

- Discuss possible complications/side effects with the patient.

- For oral PUVA, weigh the patient to calculate the psoralen dose.

- Assess the patient's sensitivity to phototherapy by phototesting to establish the starting UV dose.

The procedure

- For oral PUVA, patients must wear UVA protective glasses as soon as psoralens are swallowed and for the remaining daylight hours.

- Patients stand/lie inside the cabinets in which bulbs emit UV of specific wavelengths.

- The eyes, face and male genitalia are shielded.

- UVB is typically given three times a week and PUVA twice a week. Treatment times and UV doses are usually increased at each visit. The length of course varies depending on the patient's response to treatment.

Complications

- Major: increased risk of cutaneous malignancies with long-term use (particularly with PUVA).

- Minor: burning, nausea with oral psoralens, photo-ageing, PUVA freckling and PUVA itch/cutaneous pain.

FURTHER READING

Griffiths CEM, Camp RDR and Barker JNWN. Psoriasis. In: Burns DA, Breathnach SM, Cox NH and Griffiths CEM, eds. *Rook's Textbook of Dermatology*, 7th edn. Oxford: Blackwell Science, 2004.

2.28 Retinoids

Principle

The term 'retinoids' covers both synthetic and natural forms of vitamin A. Their mode of action is unknown but they have effects on cell proliferation and differentiation. Specific receptors belong to the family of steroid/thyroid/vitamin D receptors.

Indications

- Severe recalcitrant acne.

- Psoriasis.

- Other disorders of keratinisation, eg keratoderma and Darier's disease.

Contraindications

- Absolute: pregnancy, renal disease, liver disease, breast-feeding, dry eyes syndrome.

- Relative: concurrent tetracyclines or vitamin A supplements, hyperlipidaemia, diabetes, children and depression.

Practical details

Before treatment

Check fasting lipids and liver function tests. If the patient is at risk of becoming pregnant, initiate the pregnancy prevention plan by excluding pregnancy (by laboratory test) and ensuring the patient takes effective contraception (of at least one form and preferably of two concurrent forms) for at least 1 month prior to starting treatment. Provide patients with written information about the risks and benefits of retinoids as well as contraception. Written consent is essential, with full explanation of risks and benefits, including the importance of contraception and the consequences of becoming pregnant.

The treatment

Isotretinoin is used for at least 16 weeks for acne. Dose schedules have been debated, but some use 0.5 mg/kg daily for the first few weeks and then increase to 1 mg/kg daily depending on the patient's response. In females on the pregnancy prevention programme, advice is currently to prescribe 1 month of treatment at a time with monthly pregnancy tests.

Acitretin is used for psoriasis and disorders of keratinisation. Treatment tends to be prolonged, with a dose in the range 10–50 mg/day.

For both isotretinoin and acitretin, fasting lipids and liver function tests are performed 1 month after starting treatment and then at intervals of 3 months.

After treatment

For isotretinoin, female patients should take a pregnancy test 5 weeks after stopping treatment. Pregnancy should be avoided for 2 years (acitretin) or 1 month (isotretinoin) after stopping treatment. Patients should also avoid giving blood for 1 year (acitretin) or 1 month (isotretinoin) after stopping treatment.

Outcome

Treatment with isotretinoin for 16 weeks produces dramatic sustained improvement in acne scores for the majority of patients. In those with psoriasis or chronic disorders of keratinisation, the effects usually produce disease suppression rather than cure.

Complications

There are several potential complications but the most important are teratogenicity, depression, derangement of plasma lipids and liver function tests, and initial worsening of acne. If pregnancy occurs or is suspected in any female patient during treatment or in the 5 weeks after therapy, then the patient should stop isotretinoin treatment immediately and should receive advice from a physician specialised or experienced in birth defects. The patient should inform the primary prescriber of isotretinoin and her GP. The supplier and the Medicines and Healthcare Products Regulatory Agency should be informed if pregnancy is confirmed.

Important information for patients

The side effects should be explained. Common side effects are rough dry mucous membranes, dry eyes, myalgia and arthralgia. Less common but important side effects include teratogenicity, worsening of acne, benign intracranial hypertension, diffuse thinning of hair, photosensitivity, diffuse interstitial skeletal hyperostosis, depression, and disturbances of lipids and liver function tests. Strong emphasis should be placed on the risk of teratogenicity and females should sign a consent form indicating that they understand the risks and the importance of effective contraception for 1 month prior to treatment, during treatment and for 2 years (acitretin) or 1 month (isotretinoin) after stopping treatment.

FURTHER READING

See Section 1.3.4.

Hunter JAA, Savin JA and Dahl MV. *Clinical Dermatology*, 3rd edn. Oxford: Blackwell Science, 2002.

3.1 Skin biopsy

Principle

To obtain a sample of skin for histological, immunohistochemical or microbiological analysis.

Indications

- Aid to diagnosis.
- Excision of a cutaneous neoplasm.
- Tumour grading and staging.

Contraindications

Relative contraindications include coagulation abnormality, local anaesthetic hypersensitivity, sites of poor healing, eg lower leg, high risk of keloid formation, eg upper trunk, and black skin. Specifically, confirm that there is no history of hypersensitivity reaction to local anaesthetic or latex, bleeding diathesis, poor healing, keloid formation or anticoagulant medication.

Important information for patients (consent)

Consent should be obtained from all patients and they should be given advice on the risk of scar formation (including keloid), infection and bleeding, other disease-specific risks and the benefits of the procedure.

Practical details

Before procedure

Equipment Prepare a sterile biopsy pack to include local anaesthetic, scalpel/disposable punch biopsy, skin hook, needle holder, suture material and dressing.

- The choice of suture material depends on the site and size of the biopsy. In general, for a diagnostic biopsy of 0.5–1 cm a non-absorbable suture can be used: 5/0 for face and 4/0 elsewhere.

- Prepare a specimen tube for receipt of the sample. The choice of transport medium depends on the analysis; 10% formalin is most commonly used for samples requiring histological analysis, but must be avoided for those undergoing immunofluorescence and microbiological analyses. Contact your laboratory for the preferred local transport media.

Anaesthetic The most commonly used local anaesthetic is 0.5–2% lidocaine with or without epinephrine (adrenaline). Epinephrine is avoided for the extremities, eg digits, where intense vasoconstriction can result in tissue necrosis.

Plan the procedure If possible, choose a covered site with a low risk of keloid formation and away from vital structures (eg temporal artery). Know your anatomy! It can be helpful to include both normal and abnormal skin within the biopsy to enable histological comparison. Before anaesthetising, mark the site using a surgical marker and, if possible, run the incision along natural skin tension lines.

The procedure

1. Protective glasses and sterile gloves should be worn.

2. After preparing a sterile field, local anaesthetic is infiltrated into the subcutis.

3. An elliptical scalpel biopsy provides more information than a 3–4 mm punch biopsy and is the preferred method when possible.

4. After lifting the tissue specimen with the skin hook (as opposed to forceps which can cause tissue traumatisation), the sample is separated from underlying tissue and placed in an appropriately labelled container.

5. Sutures are usually placed to achieve haemostasis and good wound margin apposition.

6. A sterile dressing is applied and sharps disposed of in an appropriate receptacle.

After procedure

- Give the patient written information about wound care.

- Sutures are routinely removed in 5 days from the face; 7 days from the trunk and arms; and 10 days from the back and legs.

- The specimen is transported and stored according to the recommendations of the local pathology or microbiology department. It is important to give as much information as possible to the pathologist as clinical–pathological correlation is often crucial.

Complications

Rarely there can be severe hypersensitivity reaction, eg to local anaesthetic or latex. More common possibilities include bleeding, local infection, keloid scar formation, and damage to underlying structures.

FURTHER READING

Cerio R and Calonje E. Histopathology of the skin: general principles. In: Burns DA, Breathnach SM, Cox NH and Griffiths CEM, eds. *Rook's Textbook of Dermatology*, 7th edn. Oxford: Blackwell Science, 2004.

3.2 Direct and indirect immunofluorescence

Principle

Direct immunofluorescence (DIF) detects antibodies and complement deposited in the skin *in vivo* and indirect immunofluorescence (IIF) detects serum antibodies that react with normal skin *in vitro*.

Indications

- DIF: diagnosis of diseases associated with immunoreactant deposition (Table 36).

- IIF: a less sensitive alternative to DIF in some diseases, but allows measurement of antibody titre which can be helpful for disease monitoring.

Practical details

Before investigation

- DIF: take a skin biopsy (see Section 3.1). Transport the sample according to local guidelines (usually in Michel's medium or saline, or snap frozen in liquid nitrogen). A punch biopsy will usually be sufficient. Lesional (affected) skin should be sampled in some diseases but normal unaffected skin is better in immunobullous diseases because false negatives can be obtained if blistered (lesional) skin is sampled.

- IIF: take serum.

The investigation

- DIF: five sections of the patient's skin are incubated with fluorescein-labelled antibodies to IgG, IgA, IgM, C3 and fibrinogen. After washing, antibodies bound to sections are viewed with a fluorescence microscope.

- IIF: patient's serum at several different dilutions is incubated with sections of normal skin. After washing, steps are identical to DIF (anti-IgG or IgA only, according to the suspected disease). The result is expressed as the highest serum dilution at which antibodies are detected, eg 1 in 100.

After investigation

The results are interpreted along with the clinical and pathological findings (Table 36). However, DIF is the gold standard investigation in immunobullous disorders (Fig. 99).

FURTHER READING

Bhogal BS and Black MM. Diagnosis, diagnostic and research techniques. In: Wojnarowska F and Briggaman RA, eds. *Management of Blistering Diseases*. London: Chapman & Hall Medical, 1990.

3.3 Patch tests

Principle

To identify substances that provoke type IV (delayed) hypersensitivity and which may be the cause of an allergic contact dermatitis. Patients are tested against a standard battery of the most frequently encountered allergens. Additional series are available if relevant to the individual patient, eg for hairdressing chemicals, plants and plastics.

TABLE 36 DISEASES IN WHICH DIRECT OR INDIRECT IMMUNOFLUORESCENCE MAY BE HELPFUL

Disease	DIF findings	IIF findings
Pemphigus	Intercellular IgG + C3	± Intercellular IgG
Pemphigoid (all forms)	IgG + C3 along DEJ	± IgG along DEJ
Dermatitis herpetiformis	IgA + C3 in dermal papillae	Negative
SLE	IgG, IgM, IgA + C3 along DEJ	± ANA
DLE	IgG, IgM, IgA + C3 along DEJ	Negative
Lichen planus	Fibrinogen along DEJ	Negative
Porphyria cutanea tarda	± Perivascular IgG	Negative
Vasculitis	Perivascular C3 and fibrin (IgA in HSP)	Negative
Amyloid	Clumps of immunoglobulin in papillary dermis	Negative

ANA, antinuclear antibodies; DEJ, dermoepidermal junction; DLE, discoid lupus erythematosus; HSP, Henoch–Schönlein purpura; SLE, systemic lupus erythematosus.

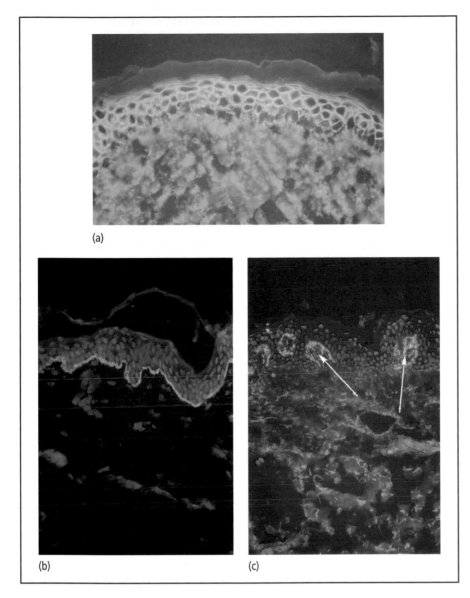

(a)

(b)   (c)

▲ **Fig. 99** Direct immunofluorescence. Antibodies in the skin fluoresce green. Cell nuclei have been counterstained red, allowing easy identification of the epidermis. (**a**) Pemphigus vulgaris: IgG antibodies bind to the cell surface of keratinocytes and show up as fine green lines around cells in the epidermis. The overall appearance resembles a chicken-wire fence. (**b**) Bullous pemphigoid: a green line runs beneath the epidermis due to binding of IgG at the dermoepidermal junction. (**c**) Dermatitis herpetiformis: granular deposits of IgA are present within the dermal papillae (arrow). (Courtesy of Professor M. Black, St Thomas' Hospital.)

Indications

Any patient suspected of having an allergic contact dermatitis (see Section 2.9).

Contraindications

Testing is unreliable if the patch test site (usually upper back) is not clear of eczema, if the patient is taking oral immunosuppressants or if the skin is suntanned.

Practical details

Before procedure

- Take a full history and examine the patient to elicit possible allergens. Ask specifically about allergens encountered at work and via hobbies.

- Minor complications are explained (see below) and the patient is asked to avoid disturbing the patches.

The procedure

- Allergens are usually purchased from manufacturers at specific concentrations in a base. Small quantities are placed in chambers (usually small, aluminium 'finn' chambers) and secured to the upper back with hypoallergenic tape. The application sites are marked on the back and recorded in the notes.

- Patch tests are commonly 'read' after 2 days, when the patches are removed, and again after 4 days. Allergic reactions, which are erythematous, palpable and sometimes vesicular, are graded and recorded (Fig. 100).

After the procedure

The patch test results are interpreted with respect to the history and examination. The relevance of the results are discussed and advice and leaflets on which substances to avoid are given to the patient.

Complications

- Major: small risk of sensitising the patient to a new allergen.

- Minor: itching or post-inflammatory hyperpigmentation/ hypopigmentation at the site of a positive reaction. Aggravation of eczema at distant sites due to percutaneous absorption of an antigen.

FURTHER READING

Wilkinson SM and Beck MH. Contact dermatitis: allergic. In: Burns DA, Breathnach SM, Cox NH and Griffiths CEM, eds. *Rook's Textbook of Dermatology*, 7th edn. Oxford: Blackwell Science, 2004.

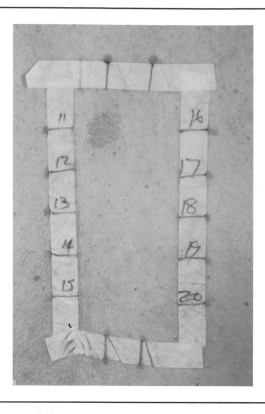

▲ **Fig. 100** Patch tests. A car mechanic presented with hand eczema. There is a positive reaction to patch 11 which is a chemical present in black rubber such as car tyres.

sugar paper, which is then folded to hold the specimen (black cardboard wallets for this purpose are available in some institutions).

- Nail clippings and hairs (plucked) can be collected as above or in plain specimen pots.

- Skin scrapings may be placed on a glass slide with one or two drops of potassium hydroxide solution and covered with a glass cover slip. This allows direct microscopic examination. However, experience is required to identify fungal hyphae/spores, so this is usually only performed by dermatologists or laboratory staff.

After the investigation

Specimens should be carefully labelled and sent to the laboratory. Culture for fungi may take up to 6 weeks.

3.4 Obtaining specimens for mycological analysis

Principle

To obtain an adequate sample for mycological analysis (microscopy and culture).

Indications

Confirmation of the diagnosis of superficial fungal and yeast infections of the skin, hair or nails.

Practical details

Before investigation

A thorough cutaneous examination (including hair and nails) is important in order to detect involved sites and exclude dermatoses that may simulate fungal infections, eg nail changes in psoriasis.

The investigation

- In the case of skin lesions the scaly edge should be scraped with a blade (number 10 blade is ideal) and scales collected on black

- Dermatophytes exist in the superficial surface layer of the skin (stratum corneum) so only superficial scale is required. Care must be taken when using a sharp blade not to traumatise the skin.
- When taking nail clippings specialised nail clippers are required. It is crucial to include subungual debris to avoid false negatives.
- Laboratories vary widely in their ability to detect fungal elements with microscopy. If samples are negative, consider sending a repeat specimen and/or reconsider the diagnosis. Always send the laboratory as much material as possible to reduce the risk of false negatives.

DERMATOLOGY: SECTION 4
SELF-ASSESSMENT

4.1 Self-assessment questions

Question 1

Clinical scenario

A 35-year-old Indo-Asian man is referred with a 2-week history of blisters and erosions on the upper torso. He also complains of oral ulceration for 3 months.

Question

What is the most likely diagnosis?

Answers

A Dermatitis herpetiformis
B Erythema multiforme
C Pemphigus vulgaris
D Mucous membrane pemphigoid
E Porphyria cutanea tarda

Question 2

Clinical scenario

An 18-year-old woman presents with a 4-day history of cough, difficulty eating and a rash. She has oral ulceration with crusting of the lips, and lesions on her hands and feet.

Question

What is the most likely diagnosis?

Answers

A Secondary syphilis
B Toxic epidermal necrolysis
C Pompholyx
D Erythema multiforme
E Pemphigus vulgaris

Question 3

Clinical scenario

A 50-year-old man presents with blisters on the backs of his hands.

He has a history of alcohol excess and smokes, but is not on any medication. He is tanned, has one intact blister and has several scars on the back of his hands.

Question

Which two investigations will establish the diagnosis?

Answers

A CXR
B Red cell porphyrin levels
C Liver function tests
D Examination of urine under Wood's light
E Skin biopsy for histology
F Skin biopsy for direct immunofluorescence
G Abdominal ultrasound scan
H Hepatitis C serology
I Urinary porphyrin levels
J HIV test

Question 4

Clinical scenario

A 70-year-old woman has a long-standing ulcer on the gaiter aspect of her left leg, just above the medial malleolus. Over 3 weeks she has developed an itchy, flaky and erythematous eruption involving the left lower leg.

Question

What is the most likely diagnosis?

Answers

A Varicose eczema
B Allergic contact dermatitis
C Cellulitis
D Pretibial myxoedema
E Vasculitis

Question 5

Clinical scenario

A 70-year-old woman has a long-standing ulcer on the gaiter aspect of her left leg, just above the medial malleolus. Over 3 days she has developed pain, erythema and swelling of the left lower leg. She feels unwell and has a fever.

Question

What is the most likely diagnosis?

Answers

A Varicose eczema
B Allergic contact dermatitis
C Cellulitis
D Pretibial myxoedema
E Vasculitis

Question 6

Clinical scenario

A 24-year-old woman presents with painful red nodules on the lower legs.

Question

Which of the following would be the two *least* useful investigations?

Answers

A CXR
B IgE levels
C Serum angiotensin-converting enzyme
D Thyroid function tests
E Pathergy test
F Erythrocyte sedimentation rate
G Anti-streptolysin O titre
H Mantoux test
I Throat swab
J Colonoscopy

Question 7

Clinical scenario

A 40-year-old man with a 20-year history of stable chronic plaque psoriasis presents with erythroderma which has developed over 1 week. He is shivering, tachycardic and hypotensive. On examination he is red all over, but there are also sheets of tiny pustules.

Question

What is the most likely diagnosis?

Answers

A Erythrodermic psoriasis
B Sézary syndrome
C Gonococcal septicaemia
D Erythrodermic eczema
E Acute generalised pustular psoriasis

Question 8

Clinical scenario

A 30-year-old woman is erythrodermic on admission to hospital. She is clearly unwell. She has oral ulceration, and in some areas of her skin the epidermis is peeling off. She has a history of atopic eczema and epilepsy, and 2 weeks ago started carbamazepine.

Question

What is the most likely diagnosis?

Answers

A Anticonvulsant hypersensitivity syndrome (DRESS syndrome)
B Stevens–Johnson syndrome
C Erythrodermic eczema
D Toxic shock syndrome
E Toxic epidermal necrolysis

Question 9

Clinical scenario

A 70-year-old man is erythrodermic.

Question

What two complications is he *least* likely to encounter?

Answers

A Cardiac failure
B Hypothermia
C Pressure sores
D Paralytic ileus
E Prerenal failure
F Peripheral oedema
G Hypovolaemia
H Hypoalbuminaemia
I Deep vein thrombosis
J Cerebrovascular accident

Question 10

Clinical scenario

A 16-year-old girl has a 2-day history of a rash. She is taking amoxicillin prescribed for a sore throat. She has bright red cheeks, a macular eruption on the arms and legs and complains of headache.

Question

What is the most likely diagnosis?

Answers

A HIV seroconversion
B Rubella
C Parvovirus B19 infection
D Drug eruption in a patient with Epstein–Barr virus infection
E Measles

Question 11

Clinical scenario

An 18-year-old woman presents with a 2-week history of a pruritic eruption consisting of multiple scaly, 1–2 cm pink patches, which are mainly on the torso. One week prior to the onset, she had noticed a single patch on the abdomen diagnosed as ringworm by her GP.

Question

What is the most likely diagnosis?

Answers

A Guttate psoriasis
B Secondary syphilis
C Rubella
D Pityriasis rosea
E Eczema

Question 12

Clinical scenario

A 30-year-old woman presents in the third trimester of pregnancy with a 3-week history of intense itching and blisters on the abdomen. A skin biopsy is taken for histology and direct immunofluorescence.

Question

Which of the following is the most likely abnormality to be revealed?

Answers

A Intercellular IgA antibodies in the epidermis
B Intercellular IgG antibodies in the epidermis
C IgA in the dermal papillae
D IgG along the dermoepidermal junction
E An intraepidermal blister

Question 13

Clinical scenario

A 25-year-old man with irritable bowel syndrome presents with intense itching on the elbows and knees. On examination there are excoriated papules.

Question

Which two abnormalities are investigations most likely to find?

Answers

A Hypothyroidism
B Pernicious anaemia
C Gluten-sensitive enteropathy
D Oral ulceration
E IgG in the dermal papillae
F Intraepidermal blisters in a skin biopsy
G Macrocytic anaemia
H IgA in the dermal papillae
I Microcytic anaemia
J IgG along the dermoepidermal junction

Question 14

Clinical scenario

A keen gardener presents with a scaly erythematous eruption on his face, neck and hands (Fig. 101). He is otherwise well but takes doxycycline for rosacea.

Question

What is the most likely diagnosis?

Answers

A Chronic actinic dermatitis

B Lupus erythematosus-like drug eruption

C Photosensitive drug eruption

D Lichen planus

E Drug hypersensitivity syndrome

Question 15

Clinical scenario

A 20-year-old man presents with lesions on the hands and feet and oral ulceration (Fig. 102).

Question

What is the most likely trigger or disease association?

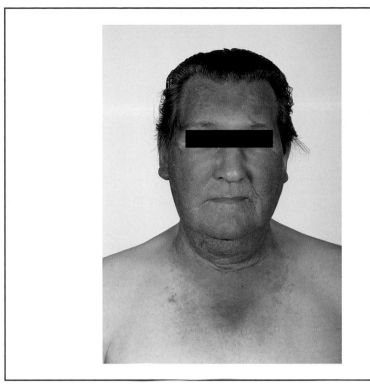

▲ **Fig. 101** Question 14.

Answers

A Coxsackie virus infection

B Crohn's disease

C *Mycoplasma* infection

D Human papillomavirus infection

E Behçet's disease

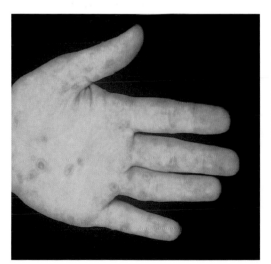

(a)

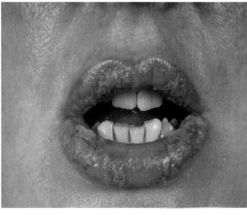

(b)

▲ **Fig. 102** Question 15.

Question 16

Clinical scenario

A 50-year-old man gives a 10-year history of scaly erythematous patches on the buttocks and upper thighs. You suspect a diagnosis of mycosis fungoides.

Question

Which is the *least* useful investigation?

Answers

A Skin biopsy

B Sézary cell count

C T-cell receptor gene analysis on the skin biopsy

D CD4 and CD8 immunohistochemical stains on the skin biopsy

E FBC

Question 17

Clinical scenario

A 40-year-old woman presents with a 4-month history of painful oral ulceration. Two weeks ago she developed cutaneous erosions on the upper back and chest.

Question

What abnormality is most likely to be revealed by direct immunofluorescence?

Answers

A Intercellular IgG in the epidermis

B IgG along the dermoepidermal junction

C IgG in the dermal papillae

D Intercellular IgA in the epidermis

E IgA in the dermal papillae

Question 18

Clinical scenario

A care-home worker with no history of skin disease develops intense itching of the skin.

Question

Which site would be *least* likely to reveal diagnostic clues?

Answers

A On the male genitalia

B Wrists

C Instep of the foot

D Finger-web spaces

E Scalp

Question 19

Clinical scenario

A teenager with eczema is worried about using topical corticosteroids.

Question

Which two of the following are *not* side effects associated with injudicious use of topical corticosteroids?

Answers

A Cutaneous atrophy

B Purpura

C Increased risk of skin cancer

D Photosensitivity

E Hypopigmentation

F Striae

G Inhibition of the pituitary–adrenal axis

H Acne

I Perioral dermatitis

J Telangiectases

Question 20

Clinical scenario

A 16-year-old girl is referred to clinic for management of her acne. She has been taking minocycline 100 mg od for the last 6 months. On examination she has active nodular inflammatory acne affecting her cheeks, chin and forehead. There is some early atrophic scarring on her cheeks.

Question

What is the most appropriate therapeutic intervention?

Answers

A Add topical benzoyl peroxide

B Increase minocycline to 100 mg bd

C Oral isotretinoin

D Change to doxycycline 100 mg od

E Add the oral contraceptive pill

Question 21

Clinical scenario

A 79-year-old man is referred to clinic with a recurrent basal cell carcinoma beneath the left eye which had been incompletely excised several years previously (Fig. 103). He takes warfarin for an aortic valve replacement and medication for hypertension, but otherwise his general health is good.

Question

How would he be best managed?

Answers

A Cryotherapy

B Refer for Mohs micrographic surgery

C Observation and then regular follow-up

D Wide local excision

E Referral for radiotherapy

Question 22

Clinical scenario

A 76-year-old woman is referred by her GP with a worsening ulcer on the left medial lower leg. On examination she has changes of venous insufficiency and oedema, and a shallow sloughy ulcer overlying the medial malleolus. Her arterial pulses are all palpable.

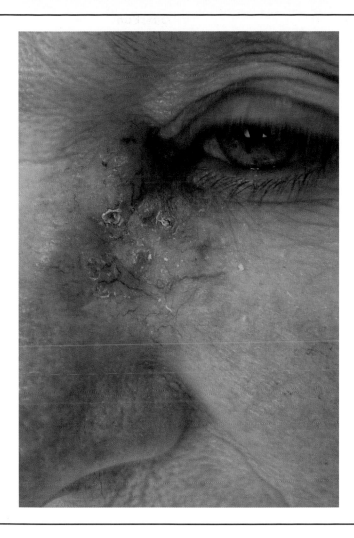

▲**Fig. 103** Question 21.

Question

What is the most appropriate therapeutic intervention?

Answers

A A high-protein diet
B Systemic immunosuppression
C Intravenous antibiotics
D Antiseptic dressings
E Elevation and compression bandaging

Question 23

Clinical scenario

A 38-year-old HIV-positive man is referred because of a mildly pruritic rash on his face and chest. His CD4$^+$ cell count is >500×10^6/L.

Question

What is the most likely diagnosis?

Answers

A Seborrhoeic dermatitis
B Psoriasis

C Eosinophilic folliculitis
D Molluscum contagiosum
E Bacillary angiomatosis

Question 24

Clinical scenario

A 52-year-old woman is referred to the Dermatology Clinic with several months' history of generalised pruritus. On examination, apart from non-specific excoriations, she is noted to have yellowish plaques on her upper eyelids and a smooth skin-coloured nodule overlying her left Achilles tendon.

Question

What is the most likely diagnosis?

Answers

A Familial hypercholesterolaemia
B Primary biliary cirrhosis
C Dysbetalipoproteinaemia
D Diabetes mellitus
E Lipoprotein lipase deficiency

Question 25

Clinical scenario

A 40-year-old woman presents with a recurrence of a facial rash that has previously been diagnosed as rosacea.

Question

Which of the following clinical features would *not* be in keeping with this diagnosis?

Answers

A Telangiectasia
B Pustules
C Easy flushing
D Comedones
E Rhinophyma

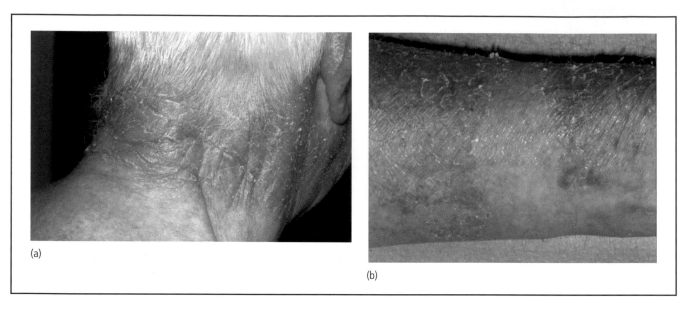

(a)

(b)

▲**Fig. 104** Question 26.

Question 26

Clinical scenario

A 60-year-old man presents with a 1-month history of a rash (Fig. 104). He believes that it has been caused by exposure to sunlight while gardening. He is taking many new medications and you wonder whether he has developed a photosensitive drug eruption.

Question

Which of the following drugs do you think may have caused this rash?

Answers

A Codeine

B Beta-blocker

C Thiazide diuretic

D Angiotensin-converting enzyme inhibitor

E Warfarin

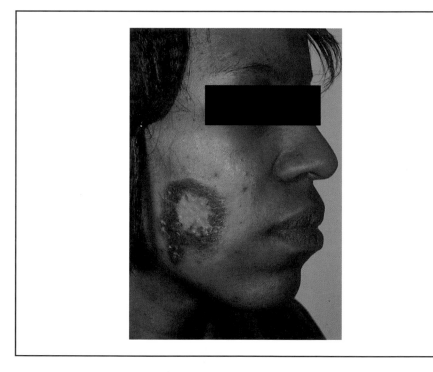

▲**Fig. 105** Question 27.

Question 27

Clinical scenario

This 30-year-old woman presents with a scarring hypopigmented area on the right cheek, surrounded by hyperpigmentation (Fig. 105). Close inspection reveals follicular plugging. It is asymptomatic and has been slowly enlarging over 6 months.

Question

What is the most likely diagnosis?

Answers

A Discoid lupus erythematosus

B Systemic lupus erythematosus

C Tinea incognito

D Contact dermatitis

E Sarcoidosis

Question 28

Clinical scenario

A 20-year-old woman presents to her GP with white patches on the dorsum of the hands. Clinical examination reveals complete loss of pigment but otherwise normal skin, in keeping with a diagnosis of vitiligo. She asks if this is a worrying problem and whether it is associated with any other diseases.

Question

Which of the following is *not* likely to be associated with vitiligo?

Answers

A Premature ovarian failure
B Hyperthyroidism
C Lichen sclerosus
D Addison's disease
E Iron-deficiency anaemia

Question 29

Clinical scenario

A previously well 18-year-old young man presents with a 1-week history of multiple erythematous scaly plaques over his trunk. This eruption followed a severe throat infection that was treated with penicillin.

Question

What is the most likely diagnosis?

Answers

A Erythema multiforme
B Erythema nodosum
C Guttate psoriasis
D Pustular psoriasis
E Lichen planus

Question 30

Clinical scenario

A 35-year-old woman presents with painful, hot, red lumps on her lower legs. You suspect a diagnosis of erythema nodosum.

Question

Which of the following is *not* a recognised trigger of erythema nodosum?

Answers

A Streptococcal infection
B Staphylococcal infection
C Epstein–Barr virus
D Oral contraceptive pill
E Malignancy

Question 31

Question

Subjects with alopecia areata show which of the following features.

Answers

A Preferential loss of pigmented hairs
B Predominant neutrophilic infiltrate around hair follicles in the catagen phase of the hair cycle
C Clear association with traumatic events
D Frequent demonstration of associated fungal hyphae on light microscopy of hair bulb
E Bamboo-cane appearance to hair shaft on light microscopy

Question 32

Clinical scenario

A 43-year-old man presents with intensely itchy papules on ventral aspects of his wrists bilaterally.

Question

A differential diagnosis would be *unlikely* to include:

Answers

A Lichen planus
B Scabies
C Dermatitis
D Urticaria
E Psoriasis

Question 33

Clinical scenario

A 78-year-old man presents with symptoms suggestive of a colonic carcinoma.

Question

Which of acanthosis nigricans, dermatomyositis, superficial thrombophlebitis, pyoderma gangrenosum and pruritus can be associated with internal malignancy?

Answers

A All.
B None.
C Acanthosis nigricans, dermatomyositis and pruritus.
D Acanthosis nigricans, dermatomyositis, superficial thrombophlebitis and pruritus.
E Acanthosis nigricans, dermatomyositis, pyoderma gangrenosum and pruritus.

Question 34

Clinical scenario

A 30-year-old woman presents with an intermittent pruritic eruption which has been occurring for several months. Lesions last a few hours only and disappear leaving no mark, suggesting a diagnosis of urticaria. She is atopic and had a nut allergy as a child.

Question

Which of the following are true?

Answers

A Chronic urticaria is strongly associated with atopy
B Respiratory compromise in patients with anaphylaxis may be more severe if there is a history of asthma
C Acute urticaria typically responds to topical steroids
D A cause can be identified in most patients with chronic urticaria
E Infant nut allergy persists into adult life in most patients

Question 35

Clinical scenario

A 40-year-old woman with a history of hypothyroidism presents with a

2-month history of depigmented patches on her hands.

Question

Which of the following are true?

Answers

A Vitiligo can cause depigmentation of hairs

B Melanocytes within affected areas are still present but do not produce melanin

C Re-pigmentation occurs principally from the margins of affected skin

D Vitiligo occurring in patients with malignant melanoma carries a poor prognosis for the melanoma

E Vitiligo can cause leuconychia

Question 36

Clinical scenario

A 40-year-old builder with a background of mild atopic dermatitis presents with a 2-month history of deterioration affecting his hands.

Question

Which of the following are true?

Answers

A Individuals with atopic dermatitis are less susceptible to cutaneous infections

B If scabies is suspected, then it is usually not necessary to ask about close contacts

C Prick tests would be a useful investigation

D Pompholyx is rarely itchy

E Patch testing may identify contact allergens

Question 37

Clinical scenario

A 40-year-old man presents with symptoms and signs suggestive of scarring alopecia secondary to lichen planus.

Question

Which of the following is true?

Answers

A The scalp is a common site of involvement for lichen planus

B Lichen planus is strongly associated with malignancy and a careful search should be initiated

C Hair regrowth at scarred sites does eventually always occur but only very slowly

D Topical steroids are completely ineffective for treating lichen planus

E It can be difficult to distinguish scarring alopecia due to lichen planus and lupus erythematosus

Question 38

Clinical scenario

A 70-year-old woman with eczema complains of 'bruising'. Examination reveals purpura on the forearms only.

Question

Which is the most likely diagnosis?

Answers

A Warfarin treatment

B Thrombocytopenia

C Senile purpura

D Cutaneous vasculitis

E Systemic amyloidosis

Question 39

Clinical scenario

A 30-year-old woman presents with painful lesions on the lower legs.

Question

Which is the most likely diagnosis?

Answers

A Necrobiosis lipoidica

B Pretibial myxoedema

C Erythema nodosum

D Varicose eczema

E Thrombophlebitis

Question 40

Clinical scenario

A 30-year-old black woman with epilepsy presents with a short history of fever, facial oedema, lymphadenopathy and a widespread rash.

Question

Which of the following abnormalities is most likely to be revealed by blood tests?

Answers

A Neutropenia

B Eosinophilia

C Raised bilirubin

D Neutrophilia

E Thrombocytopenia

4.2 Self-assessment answers

Answer to Question 1

C

Dermatitis herpetiformis and porphyria cutanea tarda do not cause oral ulceration. The history is too long for erythema multiforme, which also preferentially affects the hands/feet/distal limbs. The history is classical of pemphigus vulgaris, which is commoner in Indo-Asians than white people. Mucous membrane pemphigoid tends to affect older patients and cutaneous involvement is less common than in pemphigus vulgaris.[2]

Answer to Question 2

D

The history is too short for pemphigus vulgaris. Pompholyx affects the hands and feet but not the mouth. Toxic epidermal necrolysis tends to be widespread. Secondary syphilis and erythema multiforme both affect the hands and feet, but only the latter gives crusted lips (a typical sign) and oral ulceration severe enough to make eating difficult. The cough suggests *Mycoplasma* pneumonia may be the trigger.

Answer to Question 3

D and I

The history is very suggestive of porphyria cutanea tarda (PCT) in which abnormal porphyrin levels can be detected in urine but not in red cells, causing urine to fluoresce red/pink under Wood's light. Liver disease often accompanies PCT but is not diagnostic. A skin biopsy may show changes compatible with, but would not be diagnostic of, PCT.

Answer to Question 4

A

The site of the ulcer is typical of a varicose ulcer. An itchy, flaky, erythematous eruption would be compatible with eczema but none of the options C–E. Therefore varicose eczema is most likely, but an allergic contact dermatitis is possible and could be secondary to dressings or medicaments applied to the ulcer.

Answer to Question 5

C

The history is very suggestive of cellulitis: having a pre-existing leg ulcer is a recognised risk factor.

Answer to Question 6

B and D

The history suggests erythema nodosum and many of the tests listed would help check for recognised triggers of this, including sarcoidosis

(A, C, F, G, I), tuberculosis (A, F, H), Behçets disease (E) and inflammatory bowel disease (J). Thyroid disease is not a recognised risk factor and IgE levels would not be helpful.

Answer to Question 7

E

He is red all over, ie erythrodermic, so C can be discounted. Furthermore, gonococcal septicaemia causes scanty pustules. A, B, D and E all cause erythroderma, but the pustules point to acute generalised pustular psoriasis. This diagnosis is also compatible with the systemic symptoms and signs.

Answer to Question 8

E

The oral ulceration and skin peeling discount A, C and D. The extent of the skin disease (erythrodermic) indicates toxic epidermal necrolysis rather than Stevens–Johnson syndrome, but both can be triggered by carbamazepine, as can DRESS syndrome.

Answer to Question 9

D and J

There is considerable morbidity attached to being erythrodermic, particularly in the elderly. Cardiac failure, hypothermia, hypovolaemia and hypoalbuminaemia, and consequently prerenal failure and peripheral oedema, are well-recognised complications. Pressure sores and deep vein thrombosis could arise from immobility. D and J are possible but less likely.

Answer to Question 10

C

The bright red cheeks suggests 'slapped cheek syndrome', ie parvovirus B19 infection, and the

other signs and symptoms are compatible with that diagnosis.

Answer to Question 11

D

Diagnoses to consider with acute scaly exanthems are guttate psoriasis, syphilis and pityriasis rosea. The patch appearing 1 week before is typical of the 'herald patch' of pityriasis rosea.

Answer to Question 12

D

The history is suggestive of pemphigoid gestationis. A, B and E would be seen in pemphigus, and C in dermatitis herpetiformis.

Answer to Question 13

C and H

An intensely itchy eruption on the elbows and knees suggests dermatitis herpetiformis, so perhaps the patient's irritable bowel is actually coeliac disease. A, B, G and I are possible findings in dermatitis herpetiformis. D, E, F and J would not be found.

Answer to Question 14

C

Figure 101 shows an eruption in a photosensitive distribution, making A and C possibilities, but perhaps B also. Doxycycline is a well-recognised cause of photosensitive drug eruptions. Chronic actinic dermatitis is endogenous.

Answer to Question 15

C

Figure 102 shows crusted lips and classical target lesions on the palms, which are typical of erythema multiforme. *Mycoplasma* infection is a well-recognised trigger.

Answer to Question 16

B

A and C–E are all useful investigations. Sézary cells, which are seen on a blood film, would not be expected in localised mycosis fungoides, but are seen in Sézary syndrome, in which there is very extensive skin involvement (erythroderma).

Answer to Question 17

A

The history is typical of pemphigus vulgaris in which oral lesions often precede those on the skin by several months.

Answer to Question 18

E

The first diagnosis to exclude in any care worker who starts itching is scabies. A–D are all common sites to find scabetic burrows. In adults, the head is not affected.

Answer to Question 19

C and D

See Section 2.26 for further discussion. Topical corticosteroids are not associated with skin cancer, unlike the newer topical immunomodulators such as tacrolimus in which there may be an increased risk.

Answer to Question 20

C

This girl's acne is moderate to severe and has not responded to an appropriate course of a tetracycline. Aggressive treatment is required to suppress her acne and prevent further scarring. Isotretinoin is indicated in this case.

Answer to Question 21

B

A recurrent poorly defined tumour at a high-risk site is a clear indication for Mohs micrographic surgery (see Section 2.20), which has the best chance of rendering the patient tumour free. Because basal cell carcinomas grow slowly and rarely metastasise, they are sometimes not given the 'respect' afforded to other skin cancers. However, disease recurrence can cause considerable morbidity and may even lead to the loss of an ear, eye or nose. If a Mohs service is not available, then a plastic or dermatological surgeon should undertake excision with a wide margin.

Answer to Question 22

E

This is the mainstay of management for venous ulceration. Venous ulcers will never heal if the leg remains oedematous and dependent.

Answer to Question 23

A

Seborrhoeic dermatitis is one of the commonest skin diseases associated with HIV infection. The distribution is typical of this, but not for psoriasis. The other conditions listed tend to occur with lower CD4+ cell counts.

Answer to Question 24

B

Hepatic cholestasis may be associated with tendinous and plane xanthomas (including xanthelasma) and would also explain her pruritus.

Answer to Question 25

D

Comedones are a feature of acne.

Answer to Question 26

C

The commonest drugs that cause a photosensitive rash are antibiotics (especially tetracyclines), NSAIDs, amiodarone, phenothiazines and thiazides.

Answer to Question 27

A

Discoid lupus erythematosus and sarcoid can both cause scarring skin lesions, but the location here would be typical of lupus.

Answer to Question 28

E

All of the other conditions can have an autoimmune basis and are associated with vitiligo.

Answer to Question 29

C

If an acute generalised rash is scaly, consider guttate psoriasis, pityriasis rosea and secondary syphilis. Guttate psoriasis is often triggered by infection.

Answer to Question 30

B

Erythema nodosum can be triggered by a wide range of infections including bacterial (*Streptococcus*, *Mycobacterium*, *Yersinia*, *Chlamydia*), viral (Epstein–Barr virus) and fungal (*Trichophyton* spp., coccidioidomycosis), and by drugs (sulphonamides, oral contraceptive pill) and other conditions (sarcoidosis, Crohn's disease, ulcerative colitis, Behçet's disease, malignancy).

Answer to Question 31

A

The infiltrate is predominantly lymphocytic. The hair shaft is normal under light microscopy, and if fungal hyphae are observed then consider alternative diagnoses.

Answer to Question 32

E

Although psoriasis can be itchy, this is rarely a major feature and when present is not usually intense. Itchy lesions on the wrist are common in lichen planus, scabies and atopic dermatitis. Urticaria is itchy and can occur anywhere.

Answer to Question 33

A

Internal malignancy is well documented as occurring in association with all the diseases mentioned. Indeed, new-onset dermatomyositis in males over 40 years of age is associated with neoplasia in up to 66% of cases. The commonest primary sites are the lungs, breasts, female genital tract and gastrointestinal tract.

Answer to Question 34

B

Most individuals with chronic long-term urticaria do not have an exogenous trigger. IgE-mediated urticarial reactions to foods usually follow a clear pattern and can be investigated by skin-prick tests or serum IgE quantification.

Answer to Question 35

A

Melanocytes are thought to be destroyed by a T-cell and/or autoantibody-mediated mechanism. Re-pigmentation may occur from the margins but also commonly arises from the follicular epithelium within the area of the lesion, giving rise to a speckled appearance. Vitiligo in patients with melanoma is thought to carry a better prognosis.

Answer to Question 36

E

Individuals with atopic dermatitis are susceptible to several infections but in particular *Staphylococcus aureus* and herpes simplex virus. New-onset dermatitis or a changing pattern may be worth investigating for potential contact allergy by patch testing. Prick tests may detect type I allergy, which is not relevant here.

Answer to Question 37

E

Scalp involvement is certainly well documented but typical sites include ventral aspects of the wrists and lower legs, and oral mucosa. Significant scarring will result in complete permanent absence of hair. Scalp lupus and lichen planus can be very hard to distinguish clinically and histologically.

Answer to Question 38

C

All can cause purpura. Localisation on the forearms is typical of senile purpura and reflects solar damage to the connective tissue such that the skin often appears atrophic. Corticosteroid use may exacerbate senile purpura.

Answer to Question 39

C

All preferentially occur on the lower legs. Only C and E would typically be painful and C is much more likely to give multiple lesions in a young woman.

Answer to Question 40

B

The history is suggestive of a drug hypersensitivity reaction, also known as DRESS syndrome (drug rash with eosinophilia and systemic symptoms). Features include a maculopapular or erythrodermic rash with fever, eosinophilia, lymphadenopathy, facial oedema with or without hepatitis, pneumonitis and myocarditis. Anticonvulsants are common culprits and the onset is typically 2–6 weeks after the drug is started, sometimes longer.

THE MEDICAL MASTERCLASS SERIES

Acute Medicine

ACUTE MEDICINE

Infectious Diseases and Dermatology

INFECTIOUS DISEASES

Haematology and Oncology

HAEMATOLOGY

ONCOLOGY

Cardiology and Respiratory Medicine

CARDIOLOGY

RESPIRATORY MEDICINE

Gastroenterology and Hepatology

GASTROENTEROLOGY AND HEPATOLOGY

PACES Stations and Acute Scenarios 3

Neurology, Ophthalmology and Psychiatry

NEUROLOGY

Nephrology

NEPHROLOGY

Rheumatology and Clinical Immunology

RHEUMATOLOGY AND CLINICAL IMMUNOLOGY

PACES Stations and Acute Scenarios 3

INDEX

Note: page numbers in *italics* refer to figures, those in **bold** refer to tables.